Assessing
health needs
of people from minority
ethnic groups

Edited by

Salman Rawaf
*Director of Clinical Standards,
Merton Sutton and Wandsworth Health Authority;
Senior Lecturer, St George's Hospital Medical School, London*

and

Veena Bahl
*Adviser in Ethnic Minority Health,
Department of Health, London*

ROYAL COLLEGE
OF PHYSICIANS

FACULTY OF PUBLIC
HEALTH MEDICINE

Acknowledgements

The Editors, the RCP and the Faculty of Public Health Medicine are grateful to the Department of Health for a contribution to the running costs of the preparatory workshop and to the production of this book. Administrative assistance and secretarial support to the workshop were provided by Omwony Owjok, Janet Anderson, Margaret Reverend, Margaret Simmons, Diane Baker, Wendy Meynell and John Amosu. We are grateful to Omwony Owjok for the preparation of the background papers for the workshop, to Carol Baxter, Pat East, Joseph Ryan and Helen Fraser for their editorial support, to Mariam Al-Khudhairy for her computer and technical inputs, and to Diana Beaven, Amanda May and the publications department at the RCP for their excellent production of the book. Special thanks to all members of Merton Sutton and Wandsworth Health Authority's department of public health for support and various contributions. Last but not least, a word of thanks to all colleagues for their effort and energy in reviewing and commenting on all the chapters.

SR
VB

Royal College of Physicians of London
11 St Andrews Place, London NW1 4LE

Registered Charity No. 210508

Faculty of Public Health Medicine
4 St Andrews Place, London NW1 4LB

Registered Charity No. 263894

Copyright © 1998 Royal College of Physicians of London
ISBN 1 86016 0581

Typeset by Dan-Set Graphics, Telford, Shropshire
Printed in Great Britain by Sarum Print Limited, Salisbury, Wiltshire

A Catalogue record of this book is available from The British Library

Dedication

This book is dedicated to the memory of the late
Dr Anthony Hopkins whose inspiration and
support gave rise to this book and to its
predecessor on the health of people from
ethnic minority groups in the UK.

Foreword

The recent White Paper which sets the future agenda for the health service, *The new NHS: modern, dependable,* and the Green Paper that followed, *Our healthier nation: a contract for health,* together provide a new impetus for addressing minority ethnic health. They acknowledge explicitly that in the UK today the likelihood of people living long and healthy lives depends largely on how well off they are, where they live and their ethnic background. Both documents provide ample opportunities for addressing inequalities and improving health, and stress that services should be based on local needs and priorities. Health needs assessment, is therefore, a prerequisite for any 'health improvement programme'. Directors of public health, supported by their health authority teams and working in collaboration with primary care groups, hospital clinicians, local authorities and local communities, have a leading role in profiling, assessing and prioritising the specific health and social needs within their region.

The publication of this book – on the 50th Anniversary of the National Health Service and at the start of an ambitious programme to reshape the service – is therefore timely and most welcome. It will be helpful both to commissioners and providers of health care who work with educators, social services, businesses and local communities and who now have the responsibility to improve the health of their populations, particularly those who are disadvantaged and many of whom come from minority ethnic groups.

This much needed book, published by the Royal College of Physicians and the Faculty of Public Health Medicine in collaboration with the Department of Health provides an excellent source of reference and guidance for public health physicians, primary care teams and all those with a special interest in improving the health of minority ethnic groups.

We believe that the book sets a cornerstone in the complex process of assessing population needs and improving health. It re-affirms the high priority given to addressing minority ethnic health by planners, commissioners and providers of services.

June 1998

Tessa Jowell, MP
Minister for Public Health
Department of Health

KGMM Alberti
President
Royal College of Physicians of London

June Crown
President
Faculty of Public Health Medicine

Contributors

Tanzeem Ahmed *Director, Confederation of Indian Organisations UK, London*

Elizabeth N Anionwu *Dean of Nursing at Thames Valley University, Wolfson School of Health and Sciences, Ealing, London*

Veena Bahl *Adviser in Ethnic Minority Health, Department of Health, Wellington House, London*

Carol Baxter *Senior Lecturer, University of Central Lancashire, Preston*

Raj Bhopal *Professor of Epidemiology and Public Health, Department of Epidemiology and Public Health, School of Health Sciences, The Medical School, University of Newcastle, Newcastle upon Tyne*

Raman Bedi *Professor, National Centre for Transcultural Oral Health, Eastman Dental Institute, University of London*

Jean Chapple *Consultant in Public Health Medicine, Kensington and Chelsea and Westminster Health Authority, and Honorary Senior Lecturer, Department of Epidemiology and Public Health, Imperial College School of Medicine at St Mary's, London*

Martin J Commander *Senior Research Fellow, Department of Psychiatry, University of Birmingham, Northern Birmingham Mental Health NHS Trust, Birmingham*

Edward Coyle *Consultant in Public Health, South Glamorgan Health Authority, Cardiff*

Jenny Douglas *Lecturer in Health Education, School of Education, University of Birmingham*

Gilroy Ferguson *Clinical Consultant, Personal Performance Consultants UK Ltd., Manchester, and former Chair, Manchester Action Committee on Health Care for Ethnic Minorities, Manchester*

Hamid Ghodse *Professor and Director, Centre for Addiction Studies, St George's Hospital Medical School, London*

Valena Gilffilian *Health Promotion Programme Manager, Specialist Health Promotion Service, Springfield Hospital, London*

Ian Harvey *Senior Lecturer and Consultant in Public Health, Centre of Applied Public Health Medicine, University of Wales College of Medicine, Cardiff*

Tanya Hoare *Senior Lecturer, Department of Health Care Studies, Elizabeth Gaskell Campus, Manchester Metropolitan University, and former Research Officer, Centre for Cancer Epidemiology, Christie Hospital NHS Trust, Manchester*

Anthony Hopkins *late Director, Research Unit, Royal College of Physicians, London*

Ghada Karmi *Visiting Professor, Faculty of Environment and Social Studies, University of North London*

Elizabeth EM Kernohan *Director of Clinical Epidemiology Research Unit, University of Bradford, Bradford, and Deputy Director of Public Health, Bradford Health Authority*

Ali Kubba *Consultant Community Gynaecologist, Lambeth Health Care NHS Trust and UMDS Department of Obstetrics and Gynaecology, London*

Zarrina Kurtz *Consultant in Public Health Medicine, South Thames (West) Regional Health Authority, London*

Pui-Ling Li *Chairman, London Chinese Health Resource Centre, London*

Steve Maingot *Information Manager, Ealing Hospital NHS Trust, Middlesex*

Richard Mugisha *ex-Caseworker, Uganda Community Relief Association, London*

Alan McNaught *Regional Health Sector Development Adviser, Glendon Hospital, Plymouth, Montserrat, West Indies*

Sarah Nansukusa *Co-ordinator, Uganda Community Relief Association, London*

Ahilya Noone *Consultant Epidemiologist, Scottish Centre for Infection and Environmental Health, Glasgow*

Felicity Owen *Health Promotion Manager, Merton Sutton and Wandsworth Health Authority, Surrey*

Omwony Owjok *Ethnic Minority Link Worker, Department of Public Health, Merton Sutton and Wandsworth Health Authority, Wilson Hospital, Mitcham, Surrey*

Adenekan Oyefeso *Senior Lecturer, Department of Addictive Behaviour, St George's Hospital Medical School, London*

Salman Rawaf *Director of Clinical Standards, Merton Sutton and Wandsworth Health Authority, Mitcham, Surrey, and Senior Lecturer, St George's Hospital Medical School, University of London*

Samad Samadian *Consultant Physician and Honorary Senior Lecturer (Care of the Elderly), St Helier Hospital, Carshalton, Surrey/St George's Hospital Medical School, London*

SP Sashidharan *Professor of Community Psychiatry, University of Birmingham, Northern Birmingham Mental Health Trust, Birmingham*

Leena Shah *Research Officer, Centre for Applied Public Health Medicine, University of Wales College of Medicine, Cardiff*

Salma Uddin *General Practitioner, Wallington, Surrey*

Sheila Webb *Consultant in Public Health Medicine, Bradford Health Authority, Bradford*

Editors' introduction

Health needs assessment is a continuous process of profiling and determining priorities for any given population or subgroup in a defined area or locality. The process becomes a fruitless exercise when health authorities and providers of health care are not at a stage where their dialogue with the communities are long-standing and where there is no mutual trust between these communities and the NHS. Preventable diseases and avoidable mortality burden a high proportion of people from minority ethnic groups. There are excellent opportunities to improve their health. However, without a proper and comprehensive health (and social) needs assessment, these areas of potential and needed improvements cannot be identified, prioritised and acted upon properly. Health authorities, working in collaboration with providers of health care, service users and communities, have a leading role in developing the framework for and conducting the health needs assessment exercises at district-wide, borough and locality levels.[1-3]

The 1991 census was the first to include ethnic origin. More than 3 million people (about 6%) were then classified as non-white.[4] Today, in a multicultural Britain, the total number in minority ethnic groups is much higher and it has been projected that by the year 2011 a third of Londoners, for example, will come from a minority ethnic background, excluding the Irish.[5] Already in many cities minority ethnic groups constitute the bulk of the population and tend to cluster in particular areas of the city. Minority ethnic groups are not homogeneous; it is well recognised that these are diverse and particular religious and cultural groups that may be further defined in relation to social class and geographical location. Some of these groups are trapped in a cycle of disadvantage and inequality, as the gap between the rich and the poor, which is associated with a similar gap in health, has also widened since the early 1980s.[2] *Our healthier nation* recognises that today people's chance of a long and healthy life is fundamentally influenced by how well off they are, where they live and their ethnic background.[2] Proportionately more people from ethnic minorities are socially excluded owing to illness, disability, poverty and racism. Social exclusion can be a cause as well an effect of ill health.

The twenty-five chapters of the book provide theoretical and practical frameworks to assess health (and social) needs. They also provide a knowledge base for the understanding of various aspects of health, service delivery and approaches to dealing with minority ethnic health. We hope that the book will be a source of reference for those planning, delivering and looking at new strategies for improving the health of minority groups.

Assessing the health (and social) needs of minority ethnic communities requires the use of a range of methodologies and the development of alliances across a wide sprectrum of organisations from community and voluntary organisations to academic institutions and commercial design and market research organisations. Local health studies should employ a range of methodologies to ensure that quantitative and qualitative information is gathered, and minority ethnic communities should be involved throughout the needs assessment process. The authors of the 25 chapters decant the theories and practical experience involved in assessing the health needs of people from minority ethnic groups. After the setting of national perspectives, Chapters 2–5 address the theoretical framework for both quantitative and qualitative approaches to health needs assessment, setting priorities based on such assessment and monitoring the health status and progress of any programme. Promoting healthy living and encouraging health choices are an essential component of health promotion to avoid and reduce risk factors. Chapters 6 and 7 focus on the theoretical and practical aspects of assessing health promotion needs. Chapters 8–19 outline the framework and the practical aspects of assessing health needs for the main disease problems, care groups and services of significance to minority ethnic groups. Refugees within and between countries are increasing in number in almost every part of the world. Europe has taken a fair share of the burden in recent years. These groups have their own unique health and social problems which often arise in very traumatic circumstances. Chapter 20 addresses the special and challenging problems of refugees and asylum seekers. Health needs assessment cannot be complete and of value without involving the communities concerned and taking account of their perceptions and expectations of the issues in question and the proposed solutions. Chapters 21–24 highlight the experience of the main minority ethnic groups (Asians, Africans, Chinese refugees) with the health service and their involvement in health needs assessment processes. Last but not least, Chapter 25 is an overview, linking the needs assessment process with 'health improvement programmes'.

The health gaps faced by people from minority ethnic groups are not simply a national problem. They are international issues which many countries have to tackle with commitment, individually and in collaboration.[6] Although this book has been written from the UK perspective, using examples and experiences from the National Health Service, most if not all the chapters and conclusions could be of great use to many countries in the world. We hope that public health physicians and practitioners, clinicians, health service managers, planners and policy makers, other health professionals and organised groups of society will be able to use the book and build on their experiences to address the health issues of concern to their minority ethnic communities. Our joint aims are to improve the health of our total population through addressing the roots of ill health, whether social and economic deprivation, social exclusion or lack of effective health care programmes, and ensuring that the mainstream service are responsive to the population needs irrespective of colour, origin, religion, gender or age. We were very much inspired by the tremendous success of the earlier book published by the Royal College of Physicians of London on access to health care for people from black and ethnic minorities.[7]

Today more than half of the minority ethnic population in the UK were born here. Awareness of cultural diversity is essential not only in addressing specific health problems and unequalities but also more importantly in creating harmonious coexistence in a truly multicultural and multiethnic society. Health and population are both dynamic issues. Keeping a book of this nature up to date until the moment of final production is a challenge which we accepted working closely with dedicated and distinguished experts in their field. We hope that our endeavour will contribute to the improvement of the population including those from minority ethnic groups.

Salman Rawaf
Veena Bahl

References

1 Secretary of State for Health. *The new NHS: modern, dependable.* London: Stationery Office, 1997.
2 Secretary of State for Health. *Our healthier nation: a contract for health.* London: Stationery Office, 1998.
3 Department of Health. *The Chief Medical Officer's project to strengthen the public health function in England.* London: Department of Health, 1998.
4 Balarajan R. *Ethnic diversity in England and Wales.* An analysis by health

authorities based on the 1991 census. London: NIESH, 1997.
5   Turnberg L. *Health services in London: a strategic review.* Report of an
independent advisory panel. London: Department of Health, 1997.
6   Thurm K. A speech by the US Deputy Secretary for Health and
Human Resources at the UK/US international conference *Health
gain for black and minority ethnic communities,* London, September 1997.
7   Hopkins A, Bahl V, eds. *Access to health care for people from black and
ethnic minorities.* London: RCP Publications, 1993.

Contents

Part 2 CONSUMER EXPERIENCES

Part 1

HEALTH NEEDS ASSESSMENT

1 | Ethnic minority groups: national perspective

Veena Bahl
Adviser to the Department of Health

The aim of this chapter is to highlight developments in the Department of Health in relation to ethnic minority health and how they impact on mainstreaming ethnic minority health in the National Health Service (NHS). The developments also demonstrate how health needs assessment plays a major role in commissioning services.

Like most health care systems in the world the British NHS is facing the challenges of demographic changes, new diseases, technological advances, and increased consumer sophistication and expectation.[1] These mean ever increasing demands on health services, rising costs and considerable organisational changes to meet these demands and challenges. Health authorities, therefore, have to develop their integrated strategies for improving the health of their local population, a task that will be manageable only if they focus efforts by undertaking realistic needs assessments.

The White Paper *The new NHS* highlights new roles and responsibilities for health authorities, trusts and primary care groups.[2] *Our healthier nation*, the Green Paper, highlights action by the government as a whole in partnership with local organisations to improve people's living conditions and health.[3] It puts forward specific targets for tackling some of the major killer diseases and proposals for local action.

The government's public health agenda is set to tackle root causes of illness and reduce inequalities in health.[4-6] The key determinants of health – income, employment, housing, social exclusion, pollution, minority status and gender – are important issues when tackling the health of minority ethnic groups. The inequalities among the 3 million people (6% of the total population; Fig 1) in minority ethnic groups are very marked. Some examples are the high proportion of manual classes in Bangladeshis and Pakistanis in comparison with the white population. Unemployment is highest in

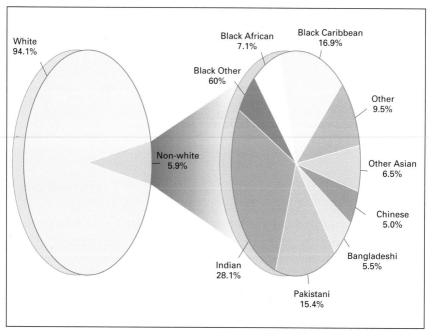

Fig 1. *Ethnic composition of the population of England and Wales.*[9]

Bangladeshi men, with 1 in 3 out of work. About a quarter of black Africans and Caribbeans are unemployed (Fig 2). Unemployment in young adults of all minority ethnic groups exceeds that in whites. In particular, unemployment among young men from the black Caribbean and African communities is more than double the rate in young white men. There are marked ethnic differences in housing tenure. Over a third of black and Bangladeshi households reside in accommodation rented from the local authority (Fig 3).

Differences in housing conditions show dramatic variations between ethnic groups. Whilst 2% of white households are over-crowded, 47% of Bangladeshi and 29% of Pakistani households are overcrowded (Fig 4). Minority ethnic groups often concentrate in the inner city and are clustered in particular areas. In some inner city areas minority ethnic groups constitute the majority of the population. For example, over 40% of the district population in Newham are from such groups.

It is important to understand the diversity among minority ethnic groups. They are not homogeneous groups. Each group has its distinct characteristics and health status. Almost all ethnic minority populations have a younger age structure than the white population. However, the Pakistani and Bangladeshi populations

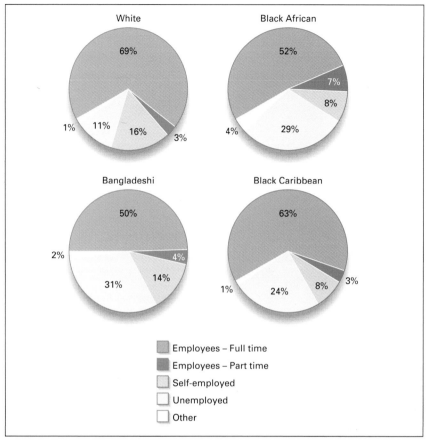

Fig 2. *Economic status in each ethnic group in England and Wales: economically active males.*[9]

have a much younger age profile than other minority ethnic groups (Fig 5).

The differing health status and disease patterns among minority ethnic groups are very marked in some areas. For example:

- death rates from coronary heart disease among Asians aged under 65 years are more than 50% higher than the England and Wales average (see Chapter 17);
- the death rate for stroke among those aged under 65 years born in the Caribbean is nearly twice as great as the England and Wales average;
- perinatal mortality among Pakistani born mothers is nearly twice the United Kingdom national average (see Chapter 14);
- sickle cell disease occurs most commonly in the African and African-Caribbean populations (see Chapter 12);

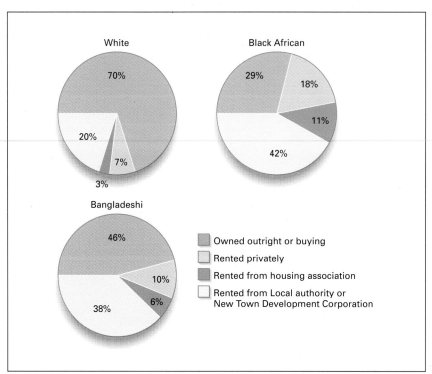

Fig 3. *Housing tenure in each ethnic group in England and Wales.*[9]

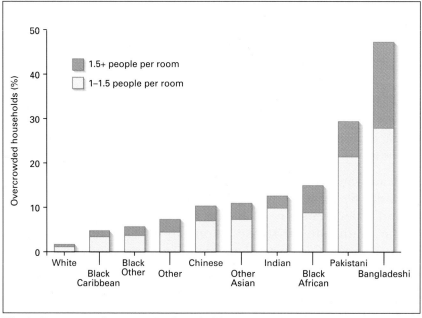

Fig 4. *Percentage of overcrowded households in each ethnic group in England and Wales.*[9]

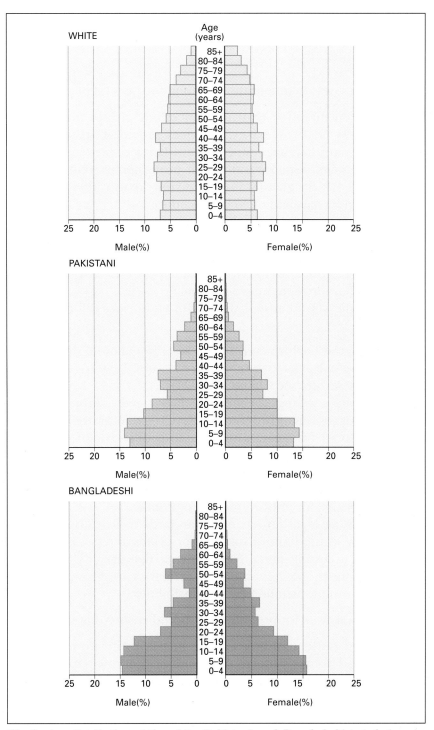

Fig 5. *Age distribution of the white, Pakistani and Bangladeshi populations in England and Wales.*[9]

- diagnoses of schizophrenia may be 3–6 times higher among African-Caribbean groups than in the indigenous population (see Chapter 19);
- rates of uptake of cervical screening among Bangladeshi women are less than half those among the general population.

It is well documented that minority ethnic groups find it difficult to access health services.[7] Services provided are often not appropriate and language and cultural barriers prevent a useful dialogue between patients and health professionals, often leading to minority ethnic groups not receiving health advice or not having an understanding of NHS procedures.

With this background, health needs assessment must be comprehensive and take into account the determinants of health. *The new NHS* White Paper ascribes clear roles to health authorities, primary care groups, NHS trusts, local authorities and the public in the health improvement programme.[2]

Some of the key areas that the health authorities will undertake are:

- Assessing the health needs of the local population, drawing on the knowledge of other organisations, in particular the voluntary sector (see Chapters 21–24).
- Drawing up a strategy for meeting those needs, in the form of a health improvement programme developed in partnership with all the local interests and ensuring delivery of the NHS contribution to it.
- Deciding on the range and location of health care services for the health authority residents, which should flow from and be part of the health improvement programme.
- Determining local targets and standards to drive quality and efficiency in the light of national priorities and guidance, and ensuring accessible and effective service delivery.
- Supporting the development of primary care groups so that they can rapidly assume new responsibilities.

Health improvement programmes should ensure that there is:

- increased understanding among health professionals of the health and disease patterns of the minority ethnic population;
- provision of appropriate information on health and health services for minority ethnic groups to increase their understanding of the health and disease patterns within their communities; they need to understand the action required to prevent morbidity and mortality;

- use of ethnic minority media locally and nationally to promulgate health messages; the emergence of ethnic TV and radio stations directed to specific communities has proved an excellent way for communicating with these communities;
- development of alliances with local authorities, the voluntary sector and public agencies; key players will be individuals and organisations working closely with minority ethnic groups.

The health needs assessment process should ensure that ethnic minority health is part of the mainstream agenda of the health authorities, primary care groups and NHS trusts. Pilot work and project funding, unless in new areas of development, should be mainstreamed. It is important for health authorities, trusts and primary care groups to demonstrate to these groups that mainstreaming ethnic minority health is a key agenda for authorities.

Some key components of health needs assessment are: involving stakeholders; improving available information; developing dialogue and consulting communities; targeting and setting quality standards; commissioning services; supporting providers to achieve change.

Involving the stakeholders

The NHS White Paper and the Green Paper both point to new stakeholders in developing local and national health programmes. Patients, health professionals, local authority personnel, people within community organisations, primary care groups, community health councils and media are stakeholders. The NHS White Paper puts emphasis on developing primary care groups to take a crucial role in commissioning services. Primary care personnel should be encouraged to debate on issues of access, equity and patient empowerment and this should be part of their ongoing training.[8] Not all the stakeholders will be aware of the health agenda and workings of the NHS. The health authorities need to ensure that all stakeholders are well versed in these issues if they are to make informed decisions on the health agenda of their local populations. The stakeholders should bring their experience relevant to key determinants of health to the local discussions of the health agenda. Often local authority personnel have greater experience of housing, unemployment and child care issues which impact on health. These experiences where possible should become part of local health improvement programmes.

Improving available information

Needs assessment is useful only if it is continually updated to take account of changes in the structure and composition of local populations and changing needs. The information on minority ethnic health has improved in the past few years. However, as the diversity within these groups is recognised, more relevant data are needed to influence the health improvement programmes. The Department of Health is aware of the need to develop data on minority ethnic health and has taken a number of steps to bridge this gap. The following are some examples.

Census data

The Department of Health commissioned the National Institute for Ethnic Studies in Health and Social Policy to analyse data from the 1991 census carried out by the Office for National Statistics. This was the first census to provide information about ethnic groups. The report of the study provides a useful basis on which health authorities can assess the health needs of their local populations.[9]

Contract minimum data set (CMDS)

It is important that health authorities, trusts and primary care groups recognise the need for adequate ethnic monitoring. Minority ethnic data set is an essential tool in understanding the use of health services by these groups. It is important that health authorities, trusts and primary care groups ensure that these data are collected and used locally. The health authorities and trusts should also collect data on their local groups that may not be traditionally recognised, eg Irish, Somalis.

CMDS is the set of data items defined as a national standard by which providers account to commissioners for how their performance has measured up against the agreed contract/service agreement specifications. From April 1995, ethnic group classification was introduced into the CMDS for inpatients and day cases. Substantial evidence of increased morbidity and low uptake of services among ethnic minorities has been a major factor driving the need to collect such data which are essential for the development of effective commissioning and health care provision. Work on ethnic monitoring in primary care is being developed. This will ensure that the needs of patients are better understood, and some of the complex workloads are identified, eg the relationship between linkworkers and the primary care team.

A report commissioned by the Department of Health offers managers and health professionals advice on using the data and describes how specific needs assessment activities could be supported by the new data.[10] Some examples are:

- linking patterns of morbidity with specific minority ethnic groups, eg linking tongue or mouth cancers with groups who chew tobacco products;
- comparing national epidemiological profiles of ethnic minorities with the local profile, eg whether the incidence of coronary heart disease among young people born in the Indian subcontinent is above or below the expected two- to three-fold excess over the white population;
- comparing local profiles with epidemiological data from countries of origin of specific groups, eg noting that diagnostic rates for schizophrenia in African-Caribbeans are higher in England than they are in Jamaica;
- identifying unusual profiles, eg the incidence of cervical cancer in some groups of Asian women;
- looking for patterns of inherited conditions, eg congenital malformations in Pakistani babies.

The report also highlights good practice in the use of data by commissioners and providers of health care.

Epidemiological information

As part of the Health of the Nation strategy,[11] the Department of Health funded the publication *Ethnicity and health*[12] which provides epidemiological information about ethnic minorities in the following areas: coronary heart disease; mental illness; cancer; HIV/AIDS and sexual health; accidents; infant health; haemoglobinopathies. The publication is aimed at commissioners of health care and sets out the known and substantial differences in health between different minority ethnic groups and the population as a whole.

Ethnic minority database

The Department of Health has funded SHARE (Services in Health and Race Exchange), a database at the King's Fund Centre designed to collate information on ethnic minority health. It also gives information on initiatives undertaken in the statutory and voluntary sector. The database is used extensively by health and social welfare agencies.

National Institute for Ethnic Studies in Health

The Department of Health has also funded the National Institute for Ethnic Studies in Health and Social Policy (NIESH) to run a database on epidemiological information specific to the needs of minority ethnic groups. Such a tool will be of great help to health authorities, trusts, local authorities, the voluntary sector and other bodies in assessing the health needs of their total or targeted population.

Surveys

Reports on surveys sponsored by the Department of Health include the following:

- Policy Studies Institute: a survey, which includes a large sample of members of ethnic minorities, aiming to identify lifestyles and access to health services.[13]
- Office for National Statistics: a survey to identify feeding patterns of infants in Asian communities.
- Royal College of General Practitioners and Office for National Statistics: a study of morbidity statistics within general practice.[14] The report presents statistics on the reasons why people consult general practice as perceived by GPs and practice nurses, and provides a comparison of incidence and prevalence between different groups in the community.
- Health Education Authority: a health and lifestyle survey of ethnic minority groups, covering smoking, alcohol, exercise and the use of health services.[15] This should help commissioners and providers of health promotion to complement local strategies and target their resources.

Developing dialogue and consulting communities

Commissioning decisions should reflect, as far as is practicable, what people need. In developing service specifications and in monitoring service delivery, commissioners must assess the local community and take account of local people's views.[16]

Diversity within minority ethnic groups should be recognised. Within particular cultures there will be differences of outlook between different generations; it is important to remember this when opening a dialogue with the local community. Some health authorities, such as Ealing, Parkside and Manchester, have developed extensive programmes of community consultation. There are also many examples of good practice in patient consultation among commissioning practices. Understanding of diversity within these groups needs to be increased.

The ethnic minority voluntary sector has not been sufficiently developed in the past to address health matters; the main concerns have been with issues such as housing, employment and education. Many voluntary organisations are not conversant with how systems in the NHS work and are particularly unfamiliar with the significance of the recent changes in organisational structure. Not knowing which levers to press, they are often ineffective in bringing concerns about ethnic minority health to the attention of commissioners of health care.

Another study funded by the Department of Health found that much of the ethnic minority voluntary sector was unable to participate effectively in national and local strategies for improving ethnic minority health because they were unfamiliar with the Health of the Nation initiatives. The report recommended that health agencies undertake development work with this section of the voluntary sector in order to enable them to take a more active role in the formation of local health strategies and contributing to the development of commissioning strategies that ensure the delivery of effective health services to ethnic minorities.[17]

A report by the Confederation of Indian Organisations showed that health authorities were not always aware of the existence of the relevant voluntary organisations.[18] Even organisations that initiated contact were not involved in subsequent consultations. It is also important for the authorities to recognise the importance and benefits of encouraging service provision by voluntary organisations. A report[19] by the King's Fund states that these organisations are important because:

- they are language and culture specific, user friendly and accessible;
- they are an integral part of a community's networks;
- they are aware of many of the difficulties encountered by individuals within their communities;
- they have the potential for influencing, positively or negatively, the perceptions of a community about the work of the health agencies;
- this approach promotes partnership in achieving change.

Training must be provided for the voluntary organisations to raise their awareness of health issues and to enable them to understand the mechanisms of the NHS so that they can operate effectively within its structure. The voluntary organisations need to give an informed opinion and also need to be given up-to-date information on health services. Voluntary organisations often find it difficult to make the first contact with the authorities in an environment that is very official and formal. Public health physicians and service managers should meet the ethnic minority groups on their own ground and engage them in dialogue to find out their needs. This will go a long way towards empowering communities and creating a good understanding between them and the health services. It is essential that the dialogue should be ongoing so that changes in circumstances are registered. Structures will have to be put in place to ensure that this happens.

Targets and setting quality standards

The rights and standards for patients set out in the Patient's Charter[20] are a central part of the government's programme to improve the delivery of services to the public. Within the charter the following areas have particular significance for ethnic minority patients:[21]

- the right to be given detailed information on local health services and the options available;
- the right to privacy, dignity and respect for religious and cultural beliefs.

Ethnic minority groups have highlighted their concerns about provision of culturally sensitive services and the issues relating to the Patient's Charter standards. Some examples are:

- provision of information that takes into account lifestyles and culture, and is available in different languages;
- improving access to health services by provision of linkworkers and advocates;
- providing appropriate diets to meet religious and cultural needs;
- meeting religious needs of ethnic minority communities.

The Department of Health has introduced a number of initiatives in this area:

- since 1989, £5m has been made available by the Department of Health to health authorities, trusts and voluntary organisations to develop resources and projects to improve information and access to health services for ethnic minorities;
- funding demonstration projects to have a better understanding of the role and employment patterns of linkworkers and

advocates, and evaluation of the work done by linkworkers in maternity care;[22]

- a directory funded by the Department of Health, cataloguing a number of initiatives,[23] addresses the Health of the Nation key areas, the rights and standards outlined in the Patient's Charter, and covers leaflets as well as larger initiatives such as research projects; also the directory is designed to help welfare and health agencies learn about existing initiatives and available resources, and to identify any gaps;

- the NHS Executive has issued guidance on how to meet the spiritual needs of patients and how to work with local communities to achieve this.

Using the commissioning process

The NHS White Paper reflects the changes in the commissioning process.[2] Primary care groups, community care and health authorities are key commissioners. Service commissioning needs to be informed by local stakeholders and to reflect the views of the local public and users of services. The commissioners need to develop mechanisms to reach the local groups that are hard to reach through the available channels, eg Somalis and Turkish groups. Commissioners need to listen to the views of local staff who serve the minority ethnic groups, such as linkworkers, community nurses and other professional staff. Commissioners also need to develop mechanisms by which they evaluate the use of services by minority ethnic groups. The services provided should be comprehensive in coverage and cooperative in approach to ensure that all the local health services (primary and secondary care) are embedding good practice. This will lead to ethnic minority families getting appropriate care from all parts of the health service.

Training is an important and integral part of commissioning. Trained health professionals are able to deliver more appropriate services and help towards achieving the mainstreaming goal of the commissioners in minority ethnic health.

A report[24] by the Office for Public Management highlighted that health authorities were at different stages of developing work on commissioning. Lessons can be learnt from this. These findings are:

- There was considerable interest and a considerable amount of work in ethnic minority health being undertaken by purchasers in a number of authorities.

- However, among purchasers there was little organisational focus in this area, irrespective of the level of minority ethnic population density. Minority ethnic health did not feature in commissioners' mission statements or in their stated priorities, and health gain targets in this area had not yet been developed.
- Public health specialists were generally aware of issues in ethnic minority health. For example, national profiles of minority ethnic morbidity and mortality were relatively well known. However, the specific health needs of local minority ethnic populations were poorly understood. Public health specialists need to influence the commissioning process as they take responsibility for the health needs assessment of the population.
- Some senior commissioning managers argued that the paucity of information about local minority ethnic populations was the major obstacle to developing minority ethnic health policy and service developments. Others thought that such information would make little difference, that national information could reasonably indicate local needs, and that the missing element was the intention to change. There were strong differences about the balance between information and action.
- Information about interventions was rare. Where it existed, it was limited in scale and range.
- Any developments undertaken by commissioners were of a diagnostic nature. Action was generally intentional and under formulation. This may have reflected relative immaturity in the development of purchaser organisations at the time of the fieldwork.
- Senior commissioning managers perceived little pressure from regional offices to address the issue; almost all mentioned that minority ethnic sensitive purchasing did not feature in their corporate contracts.
- Most chief officers ascribed their limited focus and action on minority ethnic health to the major organisational changes which were preoccupying commissioners. This period was seen as one of unprecedented change for them.
- Senior commissioning managers were committed in principle only.

The report concluded that the development of effective commissioning activities for ethnic minority health needed a multifocal strategy. This would aim to bring pressure to bear at several points in commissioner organisations. The principal elements of such a strategy were:

- to encourage commissioners to develop strategies for improving the health of ethnic minorities;
- to involve the communities in needs assessment and service planning;
- to develop alliances with agencies such as local authorities and universities to improve ethnic minority health.

It is also important that health authorities make their commissioning intentions public, disseminate the information to ethnic minority groups, and develop mechanisms for the wider ethnic minority communities.

A survey[19] of purchasers by the King's Fund acknowledged that significant progress had been made in redressing inequalities. However, it pointed out the need for prolonged, concerted action to embed ethnic minority health issues in the thinking of commissioners and providers. The central requirement outlined in the annual priority and planning guidelines undoubtedly pushed ethnicity up the management agenda. A number of initiatives were being developed to research health needs and to forge links with minority ethnic communities in order to establish standards. Nevertheless, the report revealed that there was limited use of targets and measures of success in relation to ethnic minorities in primary care service specification. There was little evidence of an integrated approach in community care plans or in the planning of local authority services. There was a tendency to rhetoric which was not backed up by action plans. What was needed was more communication, cooperation and coherence between commissioners and providers.

Commissioners can use the commissioning process to specify how providers should deliver culturally competent services. Service specifications and quality standards must clearly state the objectives to be achieved and should be formally recorded either in service agreements or schedules attached to such agreements.

The service agreements/contracts should be explicit about what is expected in terms of the quality, quantity and cost of services. Ethnic minority health should be an integral part of the commissioning process. *Facing up to difference*[19] highlights that achieving equality of opportunity for staff, and securing services that meet the needs and wishes of ethnic minority populations, should be a core element of commissioning.

Supporting providers to achieve change

Providers need support in fulfilling their work programmes set by the commissioner. They need to understand their local communities. They need to know if the services they provide are meeting the needs of the community. Commissioners must know the needs of the community and communicate those needs to providers to enable them to develop services and bring about desired changes. Training for both providers and purchasers on multicultural and multiracial issues is crucial.

Also important is the monitoring of quality standards. The consumer plays an important role in this. As well as direct communication from users, feedback can be gathered through the complaints and suggestions received by providers and community health councils. The views of professionals also play a key role.

It is important that the health needs assessment process takes into account the need to embed good practice into the mainstream work of the NHS. There are already a number of examples of good practice but they need to be incorporated into the health profession practice. The minority ethnic communities need to see the process of mainstreaming ethnic minority health to demonstrate to them that the health service has taken into account their culture and lifestyles in delivering services.

Conclusions

Ethnic minority health should be part and parcel of the mainstream service delivery. Commissioner development is an ideal mechanism for achieving this. Commissioners and providers can draw upon a number of Department of Health initiatives. Health service professionals and managers must:

- involve the stakeholders;
- improve information on ethnic minority health;
- consult the community in depth and more widely;
- set local targets and quality standards for ethnic minority health;
- build ethnic minority health into the mainstream of the organisational process of commissioning and providers' work programmes to take account of the needs of ethnic minority populations;
- learn lessons from regular reviews of progress.

References

1 Smith R. The future of healthcare systems: information technology and consumerism will transform healthcare worldwide. *British Medical Journal* 1997; **314**: 1495–6.

2   Secretary of State for Health. *The new NHS: modern, dependable.* London: Stationery Office, 1997.

3   Secretary of State for Health. *Our healthier nation: a contract for health. Consultation document.* London: Stationery Office, 1998.

4   Chief Medical Officer. *Chief Medical Officer's project to strengthen the public health function in England.* London: Department of Health, 1998.

5   Jowell T. *Health gain for black and minority ethnic communities.* Speech by the Minister for Public Health at a US/UK international conference, London, September 1997.

6   Gabbay J. Our healthier nation: can be achieved if the demands allow it. *British Medical Journal* 1998; **316**: 487–8.

7   Hopkins A, Bahl V. *Access to health care for people from black and ethnic minorities.* London: Royal College of Physicians, 1993.

8   National Health Service Executive. *Primary care: the future.* London: NHSE, 1996.

9   Balarajan R. *Ethnic diversity in England and Wales.* London: NIESH, 1997.

10 Office for Public Management. *Playing the numbers game ... to achieve equality in purchasing and provision.* London: OPM, 1997.

11 Department of Health. *The health of the nation: a strategy for health in England.* London: HMSO, 1992.

12 Balarajan R. *Ethnicity and health: a guide for the NHS.* London: Department of Health, 1993.

13 Nazroo JY. *The health of Britain's ethnic minorities.* Fourth national survey of ethnic minorities. London: Policy Studies Institute, 1997.

14 Office of Population Censuses and Surveys. *Morbidity statistics in general practice: fourth national survey 1991–1992.* London: HMSO, 1995.

15 Health Education Authority. *Health and lifestyles: black and minority ethnic groups in England.* London: HEA, 1994.

16 National Health Service Executive. *The views of local people in purchasing for health.* London: Department of Health, 1992.

17 Singh J. *Developing the role of the black and minority ethnic voluntary sector in a changing NHS.* London: Department of Health, 1998.

18 Confederation of Indian Organisations. *Building on strengths: inquiry into health activity in the Asian voluntary sector.* London: CIO, 1993.

19 Chandra J. *Facing up to difference: a toolkit for creating culturally competent health services for black and minority ethnic communities.* London: King's Fund, 1996.

20 Department of Health. *The patient's charter.* London: HMSO, 1991.

21 Baxter C, Baylav A, Fuller J, *et al. The case for the provision of bilingual services within the NHS.* London: Department of Health, 1996.

22 The Maternity Alliance. *Consumer empowerment: a qualitative study of linkworker and advocacy services for non-English speaking users of maternity services.* London: Maternity Alliance, 1996.

23 Department of Health. *Directory of ethnic minority initiatives.* London: Department of Health, 1996.

24 Office for Public Management. *Responding to diversity: a study of commissioning issues and good practice in purchasing minority ethnic health.* London: OPM, 1996.

2 | Theoretical framework

Salman Rawaf
*Director of Clinical Standards, Merton Sutton and Wandsworth
Health Authority, and Honorary Senior Lecturer,
St George's Hospital Medical School, London*

Assessment of the health and social needs of any population (or group within it) is an essential and integral part of delivering high-quality health care to that population or targeted group (Fig 1). The 1990 and 1997 health service reforms in the UK put major emphasis on the process of health needs assessment to use finite resources more effectively, and direct efforts towards proven interventions.[1–3]

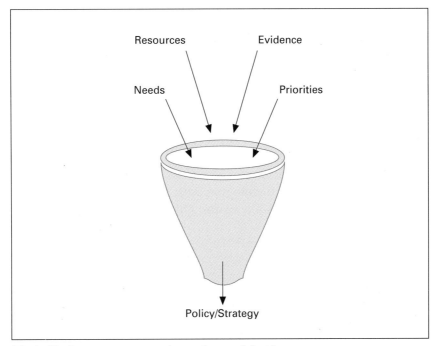

Fig 1. *Needs assessment as an integral part of the plan.*

What is health needs assessment?

Assessing the health and social needs of the population is a complex, long-term and continuous process. There has been much debate as to what 'health and social needs' are, how best to assess them, and how to influence health (and social) care delivery. This has led to many theoretical models addressing numerous conceptual and methodological issues, but problems are often encountered in their practical applications. Medicine is not a linear science. There is a wide range of definitions of health and illness, lack of data, and wide variation of needs from one community to another over time.[4-6] Needs have also been categorised into normative (based on previous provision of services), felt (what people feel), expressed (demand for services) or comparative (in comparison with other groups or populations) needs.[7]

Neither 'needs' nor 'health' is easy to define. Definitions of the latter have ranged from the simple absence of disease to the multiple comprehensive notions of well-being expressed by different cultures. It is essential to distinguish between 'health needs' and 'health care needs'. The former is a broad term, while the latter is more specific. Health needs are related to the overall aim of a healthier population, and are influenced by many factors such as socioeconomic status, housing, environment, cultural and social background, religious beliefs and customs. Health care needs, however, relate to the identified health-related problems, which can benefit from preventive treatment and care measures.

With this definition in mind, need is influenced by the professional perceptions of benefits and scientific evidence on the effectiveness of the intervention(s) available at the time of problem identification. Furthermore, another set of influences on need and the ways people express it are the social values that people build through their perceptions of health and illness, and experiences with and expectations of the health services. The population's needs are therefore changing with time, and subject to wide interpretation in different places and cultures.

Needs, demands and wants

Needs are what people can benefit from; demands are services they ask for that may or may not be needed and supplied. Demands are influenced by many factors, such as level of education, social class, information about service availability, health professionals' experience with the health service, cultures and beliefs, and finance. Wants are what people desire, whether or not they are translated into demands.

Stevens and Gabbay identified possible overlapping fields in matching needs and demands with supply of health care, such as: needed but neither supplied nor demanded (eg rehabilitation services); supplied but neither needed nor demanded (eg Caesarean sections in women with a history of previous section); demanded and supplied but not needed (eg prescription of antibiotics for uncomplicated viral upper respiratory tract infections); needed, demanded and supplied (the ideal and the most efficient scenario) (Fig 2).[5] Using this model, it is essential in any health needs assessment process for a given condition to analyse the relationship between need, demand and supply and draw a conclusion on how best the community can be served. This will help in priority setting and targeting resources to those most in need, using the most effective interventions (see Chapter 4).

Reasons for needs assessment

The purpose of any health (and social) needs assessment is to determine the range of services required to meet the identified needs of diverse populations exposed to or suffering from a condition, but it is also used for a variety of reasons, depending on who is assessing the needs,[8] such as:

- to improve service planning (commissioning) and resource allocation;

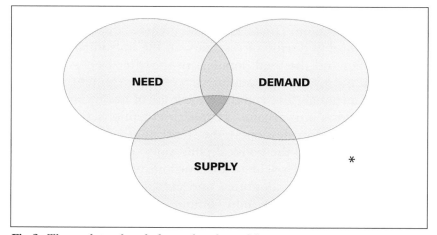

Fig 2. *The overlaps of need, demand and supply.*[5]
* Potential service is not needed, demanded or supplied.

- to identify health matters where further improvements might be made;
- to identify the most effective intervention(s) for a condition;
- to achieve social change through social marketing (for successful marketing people are grouped according to the similarity of their needs);[9]
- to monitor changes in relation to factors that influence and determine health;
- to justify funding;
- to generate information for advocacy;
- to respond to central directives;
- to justify decisions already made;
- to advance research and development;
- to confirm or enhance information;
- to display technical competence;
- to form part of service evaluation.

Whatever the reason, the process is about collecting relevant data on an individual's or the population's needs for current or future use of services, information or products. However, no needs assessment is able to quantify precisely the services required to meet these needs. The needs identified should be seen as the most probable for quantifying services that will benefit individuals and communities.

Approaches to needs assessment

The process of health needs assessment is more than the collection of routine data to measure the extent of a disease or disability in any given community (Table 1). It also includes the assessment of the impact of that disease or disability on the individuals affected, their families and the total population; the effectiveness of interventions at the levels of prevention, screening, treatment, rehabilitation and terminal care; and the availability of health (and social) services. It takes into account people's perceptions and expectations, the views of professionals, the social values about the condition in question, and the political philosophy and care underlying service provision.[6,8] To achieve this, various approaches to needs assessment have been identified and embarked upon at central and district levels.[1,10,11] The most common approaches are the epidemiological, the comparative and the corporate. In practice, a combination of these three and other approaches is used at local level.

Table 1. Health needs assessment

- Population profile
    - population structure
    - environment (general, work, housing etc)
    - lifestyles
    - culture and religions
- Measurements of disease and disability
- Service utilisation
- Effectiveness of intervention
    - promotion
    - prevention
    - screening
    - treatment
    - rehabilitation
- 'Measurement' of perceptions and expectations
    - population
    - professionals
- Social values
- Political philosophy

The *epidemiological* approach is based on the interaction between the agent, the host and the environment. It combines the measures of incidence and prevalence of the condition, and the efficacy and effectiveness of intervention and health care. The expected disease burden can be calculated by applying known published incidence and prevalence data to the local population, complemented with data from local studies.

The *comparative* approach to needs assessment uses process and outcome indicators to compare the services received by populations in different localities, to identify any differences in service utilisation. Such comparisons must take into account the local variation in risk exposure, level of morbidity and mortality, and availability of services. Comparisons are a powerful tool for investigating health service delivery, especially in the context of UK capitation-based funding.

The *corporate* approach to needs assessment is based on the process of professional, public, and other interested parties' consultations. Although such an approach may provide valuable qualitative data on population needs, it does not always give us the appropriate indication of the extent of the problem (see Chapters 3 and 6).

Other approaches to needs assessment are attempted for specific health and social problems, for example: the various qualitative methods for assessing health care needs which rely on conceptual analysis and presentation;[12] the variety of tools for health status measures;[13] capture-recapture techniques which allow accurate counts of populations difficult to reach;[14] and the 'living epidemiology' and other approaches of health needs assessment at general practice level[15,16] (see Chapter 11).

Sources of information

Whatever the approach, health needs assessment requires accurate and reliable information. Such information could be obtained from a variety of sources.

Routine or 'secondary' data sources

Utilising existing data is the most common method of assessing health needs. This includes demographic data, health and social population surveys, mortality data, service utilisation data (hospital, community services), waiting lists and times, morbidity data from registers, and prescribing data from general practice. Although mortality data are more accurate and reliable, their usefulness in health needs assessment is limited. Morbidity data are either inaccurate or incomplete. Hospital data give more accurate diagnoses but at the severe end of the spectrum of the disease or health problem. Currently, general practice morbidity data, however, are unreliable, inaccurate in diagnosis and not available for meaningful use for health needs assessment.

Survey or 'primary' data sources

Both quantitative and qualitative data could be collected through a specially conducted survey to identify the extent of the problem, as well as the ways to respond to it. Data collected through these methods, complemented with routinely collected data, will provide more accurate and reliable health needs assessment of the condition in question. Several methods are commonly used[17] (see Chapters 3 and 6):

- Interviews (direct and indirect)
- Focus groups
- Content analysis
- Key informant
- Consensus methods
- Case study evaluation

- Participatory rapid appraisal
- Community development approaches.

Effectiveness of interventions data

It is estimated that only 20% of health service activity has ever been formally evaluated.[18] Many health interventions are undertaken even though the expected outcome has not been made explicit or quantified. Despite the huge volume of scientific and medical research around the world, the connection between science and health care has until recently rarely been made. While the primary objective of medical research has been to understand the mechanisms of disease and produce new treatment, there was little or no concern about the effectiveness of new treatments, interventions or their implications.[19] With limited resources available to health care, investment should be in treatments and interventions that are effective and achieve the desired health gain for the population they serve. Therefore, commissioning policies of health authorities and general practitioners (GPs) should be based on scientific evidence of effectiveness, and contracts/service agreements should encourage providers of health care to use such evidence in their normal clinical practices.[20,21]

Other sources of data

In assessing health care needs all possible sources of data should be explored: social (eg housing, employment data), social trends, Home Office (migration, refugees, crime, drug notifications), education, transport, agriculture, environment, social security and consumerism data.

Current problems with needs assessment

Despite extensive work both at central and local levels, methods of needs assessment have to be developed further to achieve meaningful changes in service delivery. Current methods are merely ways to *count* and *describe* needs, but very few assess such needs (in terms of weight, value, evaluation, or priority rank). They are heavy on database and data driven analysis but thin on interactive social processes where a range of acceptable values is expressed to define needs.

The quasi-market philosophy of the 1990 NHS reforms encourages purchasing of service based on assessed needs. However, the nature of the current market (where demand far outstrips supply) leaves many health care purchasers (health authorities, commissioning GPs) with limited choices. Providers, many of whom exert a monopoly, find little convincing reason to change current practices. Even in a free market such as the USA, the impact of formal needs assessment on some service delivery can be illusive[22] when it is based on purely numerical terms. This numerical counting, to be a meaningful process for needs assessment measurements, has to be expanded to help in deciding against competing priorities, within an acceptable social value framework. In real terms need will depend on benefits as well as costs. Therefore, both cost and cost-effectiveness have to be taken into account when needs are assessed.[11] Such an approach entails investing in interventions that yield the maximum health gain per unit of expenditure.[23] It also requires good data and analysis to assist the decision-making process. However, there is a danger of decisions being made on the basis of cost alone. This is true at a time when the crude cost containment is seen as the panacea for the resource challenges confronting the NHS. Indeed, some health economists, during the first year of the 1990 reforms, dismissed the need for health needs assessment for priority setting and advocated the purely economic approach which is based on getting the greatest benefit for each pound spent.[24] Furthermore, the extension of general practice fundholding, in terms of both number and types of fundholding, will reduce the role of health authorities as commissioners of health care.[25] With the reduction in commissioning power, it is assumed that the health authorities will be able to place greater emphasis on health strategies that require a sound and dynamic system of population health needs assessment.[26] However, such a shift in commissioning power is a move away from a population based commissioning which takes into account the major influences on health.[27] New methods should be developed to address the population's health needs through general practice commissioning without losing equity and accessibility to health care. The 1997 White Paper *The new NHS* replaces the internal market with a system of 'integrated care' based on partnership (between HAs, primary care groups, and trusts) and performance.[2]

The universe of disease or condition

Every individual, whether healthy, at risk or ill, has a health need, which could be addressed directly or indirectly by the individual, carers and community or health services. For successful health

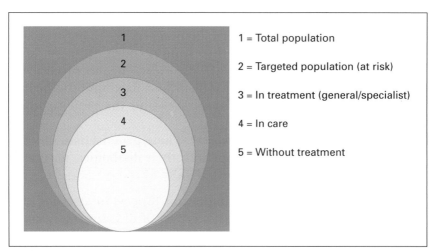

Fig 3. *The population's segmentation.*

needs assessment, people are grouped according to the similarity of their needs (Fig 3).

In general terms, the population could be segmented into five major categories.

- *The 'healthy' people.* They need to keep well through avoiding health risks and maintaining their good health and sense of well-being. The level of health promotion interventions, including primary prevention of exposure to risks and diseases, could be assessed.
- *Those at 'higher risk' of developing illness.* They need to reduce their exposure to risk in order to prevent illness. Assessing the levels of risk factors in these groups and the interventions needed to modify or remove these risk factors is required: screening, early diagnostic services, and health promotion for recognition of the risk and modification or minimisation of exposure to such risk(s).
- *Ill individuals.* They need an accurate, timely, rapid and effective diagnosis and treatment to cure the disease, prevent or reduce complications, and prevent premature death. Such a group needs accessible and effective health services at primary, secondary and tertiary level, to provide prompt diagnosis and treatment. Also, they need health promotion interventions about the condition in question and how to deal with the immediate and long-term issues that may be associated with the problem.

- *Those with 'residual' health problems or complications following treatment.* Such a group needs rehabilitation services to improve the quality of life, prevent further long-term disabilities, and improve social performance. It also needs health promotion activities to understand the problem and maximise the health benefit available from health services and the patients' own initiatives.
- *Those with a permanent health problem.* These patients have specific health and social needs to cope with their disabilities, maximise their quality of life, and live with dignity.

Population segmentation is an important process in assessing the needs for a disease (eg diabetes), a group of diseases (eg respiratory diseases), or services (eg maternity services). Specific and appropriate interventions and services will therefore be made available for each group (Fig 4). Furthermore, population segmentation will be very useful in targeting certain groups at a 'higher' exposure to risk factors of disease, and in marketing certain services to those who will benefit most.[8,28,29]

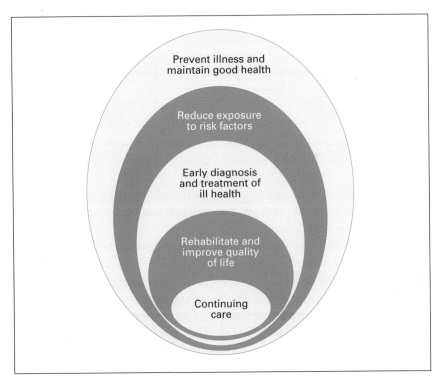

Fig 4. *The universe of health care.*

Ethnicity and health

Human health is among the most complex of all dynamic systems. Health at any given time integrates the long-term influences arising from being born into, and growing up in, a particular historical context along with the contemporary influences of the social and physical environment. This means that accumulated effects and current influences constantly interact in all people, healthy as well as ill.

Ethnic groups are not homogeneous. They differ in their genetic susceptibility, culture, and exposure to risk factors, perceptions of health and illness, and expectations of health and social services (Table 2). Ethnic differences in health and disease patterns are well documented.[30] However, data on the incidence of various diseases among ethnic groups are limited, simply because until recently ethnicity was not routinely recorded in hospital admissions, outpatients, community services and cancer registration.

Table 2. The ethnic difference

- Different disease patterns (incidence and prevalence)
- Different cultures
- Different perceptions and expectations (health and illness)
- Services not sensitive to needs
- Racism and discrimination
- Inequalities
- Lack of peoples' involvement in planning and organisation of their health services

Needs assessment setting

The health (and social) needs assessment of a total population or a group of people can be based on a nationwide, country, county, borough, district, locality or practice population. It is normally related to a disease/condition/procedure (diabetes, hip replacement), a group of diseases (gastrointestinal disorders, substance misuse), care group (children, elderly), population subgroups (Asians, refugees), services (genitourinary, family planning), or any combination of the above (asthma in children, suicide in the elderly). The usual boundaries for the population's needs assessment are the district health authority boundaries as a well defined geographical area. However, locality and practice based needs assessments are increasingly becoming a reality, despite major shortcomings with data reliability and usefulness of the information for health care planning.[31-34] The less well defined boundaries of the practice registered population, and the right of GPs to remove patients from their practice lists, make it difficult to obtain a reliable needs assessment for population-wide interventions. The proposed primary care groups (PCGs) may be able to overcome this problem by functioning as a 'mini district' in collaboration with the health authorities.[2]

Involving the stakeholders

Health needs assessment is not simply a scientific and technical process. It is a social process of involving many local stakeholders and trying to reconcile different views.[35] Local resident people, GPs and primary care teams, hospital and community consultants, nurses and other professionals, community health councils, voluntary organisations, community leaders, social service departments and local education authorities are the main stakeholders who should be involved in the process. The aim is that commissioned services should match the health needs, local circumstances and expectations of the resident population in a culturally sensitive way.

References

1 National Health Service Management Executive. *Assessing health care needs.* London: Department of Health, 1991.
2 Secretary of State for Health. *The new NHS: modern, dependable.* London: Department of Health, 1997.
3 Ham C, Hunter DJ, Robinson R. Evidence based policy making. *British Medical Journal* 1995; **310**: 71–2.
4 Buchan H, Grey M, Hill A, Coulter A. Right place, right time. *Health Service Journal* 1990; **101**: 400–1.
5 Stevens A, Gabbay J. Needs assessment, needs assessment. *Health Trends* 1990; **23**: 20–3.
6 Rawaf S. Purchasing for the health of black and ethnic minority people: some practical considerations. In: Hopkins A, Bahl V, eds. *Access to health care for people from black and ethnic minorities.* London: Royal College of Physicians, 1993.
7 Bradshaw J. A taxonomy of social need. In: McLachlan G, ed. *Problems and progress in medical care.* Oxford: Oxford University Press, 1972.
8 Rawaf S. Assessing the health needs for cancer services for people from ethnic groups. *British Journal of Cancer* 1996; **74** (Suppl XXIX): 35–7.

9 Rawaf S, Clancy C, Fraser H, Owen F. Social marketing: a public health perspective. In: *Drugs and alcohol: Malta – a microcosm of the Mediterranean region.* Malta: Sedqa, 1997.

10 Crown J. Needs assessment. *British Journal of Hospital Medicine* 1991; **46**: 307–8.

11 Stevens A, Raftery J. *Health care needs assessment: the epidemiologically based needs assessment reviews.* Oxford: Radcliffe Medical Press, 1994 (Two volumes).

12 Fitzpatrick R, Boulton M. Qualitative methods for assessing health care. *Quality in Health Care* 1994; **3**: 107–13.

13 Donovan JI, Frankel SJ, Eyles JD. Assessing the needs for health status measures. *Journal of Epidemiology and Community Health* 1993; **47**; 158–62.

14 LaPorte RE. Assessing the human condition: capture-recapture techniques. *British Medical Journal* 1994; **308**: 5–6.

15 Shanks J, Kheraj S, Fish S. Better ways of assessing health needs in primary care. *British Medical Journal* 1995; **310**: 480–1.

16 Gillam SJ. Assessing the health care needs of populations: the general practitioner's contribution. *British Journal of General Practice* 1992; **42**: 404–5.

17 Soriano FI. *Conducting needs assessments: a multidisciplinary approach.* California: Sage, 1995.

18 Dunning M, Needham G. *But will it work, doctor?* Report of a conference about involving users of health services in outcome research. Oxford: Consumer Health Information Consortium, 1994.

19 Smith R. The scientific basis of health services. *British Medical Journal* 1995; **311**: 961–2.

20 Secretary of State for Health. *The National Health Service: a service with ambitions.* London: HMSO, 1996 (Cm 3425).

21 Gray JAM. *Evidence-based healthcare: how to make health policy and management decisions.* Edinburgh: Churchill Livingstone, 1997.

22 Kimmel WA. *Needs assessment: a critical perspective.* Washington: Office of Program Systems, 1983.

23 Drummond MF, Maynard A. *Purchasing and providing cost-effective health care.* Edinburgh: Churchill Livingstone, 1993.

24 Donaldson C, Mooney G. Needs assessment, priority setting, and contracts for health care: an economic view. *British Medical Journal* 1991; **303**: 1529–30.

25 NHS Executive. *Developing NHS purchasing and GP fundholding* (EL(94)79) London: NHSE, 1994.

26 Ham C. The future of purchasing. *British Medical Journal* 1994; **309**: 1032–3.

27 Fulop NJ. The future of purchasing health authorities will have little power to implement strategies. *British Medical Journal* 1995; **310**: 59–60.

28 Kotler P, Roberto EL. *Social marketing: strategies for changing public behaviour.* New York: Free Press, 1989.

29 Secretary of State for Health. *The health of the nation.* London: HMSO, 1991.

30 Balarajan R, Raleigh VS. *Ethnicity and health: a guide for the NHS.* London: Department of Health, 1993.

31 Scobie S, Basnett I, McCartney P. Can general practice data be used for needs assessment and health care planning in an inner-London district? *Journal of Public Health Medicine* 1995; **17**: 475–83.

32 Hopton JL, Dlugolecka M. Need and demand for primary health care: a comparative survey approach. *British Medical Journal* 1995; **310**: 1369–73.

33 Murray SA, Graham LJC. Practice based health needs assessment: use of four methods in a small neighbourhood. *British Medical Journal* 1995; **310**: 1443–8.

34 Murray SA, Tapson J, Turnbull L, *et al.* Listening to local voices: adapting rapid appraisal to assess health and social needs in general practice. *British Medical Journal* 1994; **308**: 698–700.

35 Department of Health. *Variations in health: what can the Department of Health and the NHS do?* London: Department of Health, 1995.

3 | Qualitative before quantitative

Leena Shah
Research Officer, University of Wales College of Medicine, Cardiff

Ian Harvey
Senior Lecturer/Consultant, University of Wales College of Medicine, Cardiff

Edward Coyle
Consultant in Public Health Medicine, South Glamorgan Health Authority, Cardiff

This chapter describes the use of a specific needs assessment methodology in South Glamorgan in relation to the local minority ethnic groups. The rationale for the two-phase strategy (quantitative preceded by qualitative approaches, both comparing key variables between the minority ethnic and the white majority populations) is laid out. The findings of Phase I (qualitative) are presented here and their linkage with Phase II, which has not yet been completed, is discussed. Recommendations for purchasers and providers are also made. For the purpose of this chapter, 'health' is used in the wider sense implying that social factors are central to health.[1] 'Need' has several domains, two of which are normative need (professionally defined) and felt need (population defined)[2] (see Chapter 2).

Towards an information strategy

The NHS and Community Care Act 1990 was implemented in April 1991. It established, for the first time, a distinct purchaser function with an explicit responsibility to purchase health gain for its resident population following assessment of health needs.[3] To this end purchasers will select, from their providers, the most effective interventions at low cost.

Health needs assessments should be undertaken within a prioritised framework. In Wales, the 'strategic intent and direction' method introduced by the NHS directorate[4] has guided purchasing authorities to develop their 'local strategies for health'.[5] This strategic framework prioritises areas for change within the purchasers' agenda, and these areas need rigorous investigation prior to recommending further investment or disinvestment. It is axiomatic that strategic change must be guided by a good intelligence base using the best available data.

To fulfil the role effectively, commissioners need information. Health authorities work in an environment where high information content and intensity is essential. South Glamorgan Health Authority's ethnic minorities needs assessment programme is part of a broader information strategy. The specific aim of targeting minority ethnic groups is to develop a comprehensive intelligence base so that effective strategic planning can be carried out.

Why minority ethnic groups?

A number of reasons exist for specifically focusing on minority ethnic communities.

Strengthening the local strategies for health

In line with the NHS changes, *Strategic intent and direction for the NHS in Wales*[4] has guided purchasing authorities to develop 'local strategies for health' which review health needs based around ten health gain areas.[5] This approach moves away from more established client group approaches to planning. Since the South Glamorgan Health Authority area is the only one that has a significant proportion of people from minority ethnic groups, it could be included, where suitable, within the 'local strategies for health'.

Demography

The minority ethnic population in South Glamorgan, unlike that of other Welsh health authorities, is large enough to be of significance to policy makers.[6] South Glamorgan County Council was one of the few to undertake an intercensal survey (10% of households), in 1986, which incorporated a question on ethnic group.[7] This section of the population was estimated to comprise 5.5% of the total county population. Initial data from the 1991 census, which was available after Phase I was completed, enumerated the local minority ethnic population at 18,707 (4.8% of the total county population of 392,779). This covers a diverse range of proportions when broken down into localities.[8] Figure 1 shows the size of ethnic groups in accordance with preliminary 1991 census data. South Glamorgan has the largest minority ethnic population of any county in Wales and therefore its health agencies have taken the lead.

Lack of information

A central concern for health care purchasers was the absence of the most basic information regarding each of the main minority ethnic groups. A literature review showed that, though there was a body of knowledge regarding ethnic minorities, little was in a form that would guide health and social care purchasers.[9–13] For example, there was limited knowledge of health status, health beliefs, why people seek health care, deterrents to using a particular service, images and perception of the NHS and social care systems, what services were thought to be required, what could be done to encourage the dissemination and uptake of existing and new types of services, and whether the needs of this section of the population differed from those of the indigenous population.

In addition, the minority ethnic population of South Glamorgan is diverse. Whilst some communities have been established for several generations, there are also newcomers such as refugees. This has compounded the problems for local purchasers, since there is no single group on which services should be targeted. Moreover, the available information, anecdotal and otherwise, on assessments undertaken and services provided, at the time of planning the project, showed that the services were underutilised by the communities concerned.[14,15]

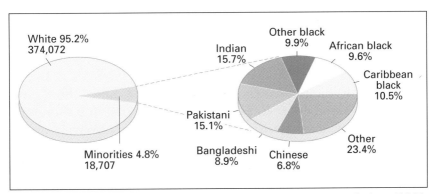

Fig 1. The size of South Glamorgan's minority ethnic population (1991 census).[8]

To redress this perceived problem, many service providers initiated the funding of additional or 'special' services through short-term monies, often without carrying out prior assessments. Hence, the pattern showed some developments of specific services[16] but that, on the whole, service responses were lacking in coordination and strategic direction. Such patterns of service development are common throughout many UK district health authorities, and initiatives in South Glamorgan in the past 14 years are not atypical.[9,16–18]

Local health needs assessment

Investigation strategy

It can be argued that studies of health needs are difficult owing to the complexity of ideas and beliefs underlying a view of health.[19] Lay concepts of health have only recently been seen as offering a valuable contribution to research and development in health services. Studies of health and social care needs are particularly important when addressing minority ethnic communities where cultural norms surrounding health and illness may differ from those of the ethnic majority population. These norms will also be influenced by patterns of migration, age and the socioeconomic structure of each population.

We took the view that a combination of qualitative and quantitative approaches would help to address these complexities. The qualitative phase would develop the hypotheses and the quantitative phase would test the hypotheses. The specific reasons for developing the project as a two-pronged approach are outlined below, together with definition of the techniques used for data collection and data analysis in Phase I. The specific approach is shown in Fig 2.

Qualitative before quantitative

By definition, qualitative research is the what, how, where and when of a phenomenon, its essence and ambience.[20] It is therefore about meaning, characteristics and descriptions. Conversely, quantitative research refers to counts and numbers. Historically, social science appears to have more respect for quantitative than for qualitative research, with numbers perhaps implying precision. A common criticism of qualitative research is that it is non-scientific. The criticism suggests an absence of validity. Nevertheless, our

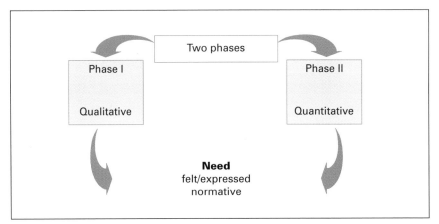

Fig 2. The investigation strategy.

investigative project specifically selected a qualitative methodology to collect data from both the target population and various professionals.

Although qualitative research has been criticised as being devoid of validity owing to the absence of quantification, it is now being explicitly recognised in health service research and development strategies. Aside from providing insights into the complexities of the real world, it is seen to be non-directive and develops investigations without preconceived ideas,[20] whereas in quantitative methodology prior assumptions of the investigators can influence the research and its findings:[21]

> One of the hazards of designing very structured data collection instruments such as questionnaires and pro-formas is that the designers have perspectives, experiences and knowledge of the subject of inquiry which are different from the likely respondents. This is particularly the case in health care, where surveys and studies are often designed by health professionals. Unless this design is also based on an understanding of the respondents' experiences, knowledge and perceptions, the information gathered is likely to be of limited value, if not misleading.

The above considerations were the deciding factor for us in electing to take a qualitative approach in the first instance. However, despite their strengths, there are limitations to qualitative approaches. A comparison of the two types of methodology is shown in Table 1 against the criteria of people-centredness and representativeness or generalisability.[21] In view of the complementary nature of the two approaches, we decided to employ both, starting with the qualitative.

Table 1. Qualitative and quantitative methods compared[21]

Method	People-centredness	Generalisability/Representativeness
Qualitative	High	Low
Quantitative	Low	High

Some initiatives have been systematically developed involving pilot studies, evaluation and formal bidding for revenue funds to develop services within the allocated provision. Local investigations have also been undertaken in South Glamorgan, such as a symposium on the health needs of ethnic groups[9] and a survey of ethnic minorities and health services.[17] Other initiatives bore no relation to an overall strategy, moving from 'soft money' funding to inexplicit developments. Whilst many of these initiatives provided a specialised service, little was known about their effectiveness.

This needs assessment project was therefore undertaken with a view to developing a good intelligence base for purchasing. It was decided to develop a programme that comprehensively examined the health and social care needs of minority ethnic communities – a programme that would ultimately help in the planning of health and social care provision that was both efficient and user-orientated. Thus, the investigation aimed to examine issues of the point of equity of access and provision to all local citizens, and also to consider an efficient allocation of resources. It was also decided to compare ethnic minority with ethnic majority needs and relate them to existing service provision.

Qualitative methods

The scope of qualitative methods has been reviewed for use in assessments of health needs by Welsh health authorities.[21] The Welsh Office funded Community Consultation and User Feedback Unit identified the following methods as being both appropriate and acceptable to the local community:[21] in-depth interviews, observation studies, discussion groups, annual rounds of public meetings, panels, patient groups and fieldwork intelligence for users and the public. Given the priorities of the work, the nature of the task and constraints of time, the project purchased consultancy from an anthropologist and the method chosen for Phase I was ethnographic assessment using focus groups. These focus groups were sometimes divided by culture, gender, age and specific client groups, depending on the topic area being explored. The data (verbatim transcripts) were analysed by carrying out a content analysis. A discussion of the methods (ethnographic assessment, content analysis) is developed below.

Ethnographic assessment

Ethnographic assessment has been used by sociologists and anthropologists for a long time, though there is no agreement on its conceptual meaning or application.[20] Essentially, ethnography is seen as the description of a culture so that an understanding of another way of life is shown. The central aspect is to place researchers in the midst of their study targets. In this way various phenomena are examined from the participant's points of view and these observations are then represented as accounts.

We undertook a micro ethnographic assessment as opposed to a macro one (the latter often referred to as 'general'). The basic difference is that macro ethnography attempts to describe the entire way of life of a group whereas micro ethnography concentrates on penetrations at specific points in the larger setting, group or institution. Typically, these specific points are collected because they represent salient elements in the lives of participants in some manner and also in the life of the larger institution. The other fundamental difference is that micro ethnography focuses more directly upon the face-to-face interaction of members of the group or institution under examination, so outcomes and implications can be directly considered.

In undertaking a micro ethnographic assessment, we used focus groups to collect data. Focus groups are a specific technique within the broader category of group interviews. Krueger[22] defines focus groups as 'a carefully planned discussion designed to obtain perception on a defined area of interest in a permissive, non-threatening environment ... the discussion is conducted by a skilled interviewer ... and is relaxed, comfortable and often enjoyable for participants as they share ideas and perceptions'.

Focus groups were first used in the 1930s when there was increasing doubt about traditional models of information gathering. Such models were criticised for the excessive influence of interviewing techniques and the predetermining of agendas. Social scientists saw non-directive interviewing as an improved source of information. This approach is aimed at creating a permissive environment where different perceptions and points of view can be sustained without pressuring the participants to vote or plan. This technique has been popular in private sector market research throughout the world for some time and has grown in popularity in all spheres, including politics, the media and the film industry. More recently, public sector organisations have begun to discover the potential of this technique. In Britain, the public sector's interest in obtaining consumer views has increased the use of qualitative research and, indeed, focus group techniques.

Content analysis

In such qualitative research approaches, content analysis is a well defined technique used for analysing data. Broadly defined, content analysis is 'a technique for making inferences by systematic and objective identifying of special characteristics of messages'[23] – where the process seeks connections among identified and categorised elements, the main objective being 'the discovery of regularities'.[24] Its aim is to classify the many words of a text into fewer content categories.[25]

Content analysis can be carried out on at least three levels: the analysis of words, phrases and themes, the latter being the chosen level of analysis in this study. This approach adopts a careful and systematic analysis of the discussions, which then provides insights and clues about the discussions.[26]

Unlike quantitative data analysis, qualitative data analysis can make only limited use of computer programmes, so it is often carried out manually. The raw data (that is the taped focus group discussions and interviews) were first transcribed verbatim. For people who did not speak English, the tapes were first translated into English. Using the typed transcripts, criteria and themes were developed in a process of open coding, where the analyst examined the data, line by line, to identify themes. When carrying out the open coding, the analyst adhered to Berg's point[20] that the criteria for selecting categories must be sufficiently exhaustive to account for each different message in the contents of the discussions; they must also be rigidly and consistently applied, so that other researchers or readers who may look at the same message obtain the same results. Once the open coding procedure was completed, the frequency of occurrences in each category was counted and important propositions and conclusion were drawn.

A total of fourteen focus group sessions were undertaken, with members from the seven largest minority ethnic communities.

There were two focus groups per community, one each for men and women, this being the expressed needs of the target groups. In order to address normative needs, which are professionally defined, a series of open interviews were undertaken with selected professionals who were likely to come in contact with ethnic minority clients and their families. As already established, content analysis of themes was carried out thereafter. Ten themes were developed from analysis of the focus group transcripts in a way that covered every issue raised, with the exception of 'dross', a technical term used by Burnard.[26] Similarly, seven themes were developed from the interviews with health and social care professionals and nine categories from the GP interviews. A follow-on study of local GPs' perceptions of the health and social care needs of minority ethnic elders confirmed many of the findings from our interviews with GPs.[27]

Findings from the qualitative phase

Unlike quantitative results, qualitative information is contextual. Short reports, of necessity, remove the information from context and can lead to misinterpretations. However, the constraints of this book do not allow for the presentation of the complete findings. What follows is a summary of the main findings according to the themes identified. It is essential that these findings be not taken out of context, so readers are advised to refer to the main published document[6] for further details. Table 2 lists the main themes found, and the themes by subgroups are shown in Table 3.

Table 2. The themes in Phase I[6]

By communities	By health professionals	By GPs
Communication	Communication	Illness presentation
Cultural issues	Service provision	Self treatment
Dependency	Professional role	Patient expectation
Compliance	Specific issues	Compliance
Alternative medicine	Compliance	Special clinics
Ties with home countries	Awareness	Assumptions
Attitudes to health care	Expectation	Perceived needs
Service provision		Health issues
Other services		
Issues related to age		

Table 3. A comparison of the themes[6]

	Afr	Ban	Chi	Guj	Pak	Sik	Som
Female respondents							
Communication	–	*	*	*	*	*	*
Cultural	–	+	+	+	+	+	+
Dependency	–	*	*	*	*	*	*
Compliance	+	+	+	+	–	–	+
Alternative medicine	–	–	+	–	–	–	–
Ties with home	–	+	+	+	+	+	*
Attitudes	*	–	+	+	–	–	–
Services	*	+	+	+	–	+	+
Age	+	+	+	+	–	–	–
Male respondents							
Communication	–	*	*	*	*	+	*
Cultural	–	+	+	*	+	*	+
Dependency	–	+	+	+	+	–	+
Compliance	–	+	+	+	+	+	–
Alternative medicine	–	–	+	+	–	–	–
Ties with home	–	*	+	+	+	+	*
Attitudes	*	+	*	*	+	*	+
Services	*	+	+	*	+	*	*
Age	+	+	+	+	+	+	+

– No interest shown in the issue during the discussion.
+ Issue considered to be fairly important, though may have been discussed as a result of prompting from mediator.
* Issue considered to be very important and was often stressed, repeated and critically assessed. (Afr, African Caribbean; Ban, Bangladeshi; Chi, Chinese; Guj, Gujarati; Pak, Pakistani; Sik, Sikh; Som, Somali.)

Communication

The single most important factor to emerge among participants whose first language was not English was the linguistic barrier when interacting with health and social care professionals. They commented mainly on their constant need to be accompanied by family members or voluntary workers and the dependency that this engendered. Difficulty of understanding official letters and forms was frequently mentioned, and participants called for more translated leaflets giving basic information regarding availability and type of service.

Dependency

The theme of dependency was an important observation which has crucial implications for service provision. The following example will help to elaborate. We interviewed two health professionals separately, both with the same duties. One said that she targeted women with her advice, whereas the other said that she tried to talk to both the women and their husbands. Not surprisingly, when asked about problems of compliance, the latter found no problems. The former, however, reported that her advice was often not followed by the women.

Culturally, this highlighted the differences between individualism and collectivism. These features characterise Western and Eastern cultures respectively. In the former there is a greater tendency towards individualism, whilst Eastern cultures can often appear to be collective and family orientated. The above example demonstrates the need for professionals to adopt a collective approach when dealing with many ethnic minority groups. In particular, our survey showed that the women respondents of Asian, Somali and Chinese origin were more likely to be dependent on the men and other family members for decision making. This may well be not only a reflection of the senior role that men often play within families but also because they are more likely, as a result of employment, to speak English and therefore be conversant with the wider community.

Compliance

A number of issues raised came within the theme of compliance. Compliance, or action in accordance with request, covers issues such as the following of medical advice, including the voluntary uptake of screening tests and dealing with appointment systems. Failure to follow medical advice transcends culture. However, particular to the context of this work, it would be reasonable to assume non-compliance would be aggravated by poor communication between the patient and the health professional. In relation to screening tests it was found that, even though they may have had such tests, very few Asian, Somali and Chinese women reported that they knew about smears or mammography. It also became apparent that there was a high uptake rate when the women were given adequate explanation about the importance of such tests and what to expect.

The other interesting issue was that of appointment systems. Some respondents strongly disliked appointment systems, especially in GP surgeries. The professionals also raised appointment keeping as an important issue in relation to their ethnic minority clients. Our conclusion was that education needed to be targeted so that appointment systems could be understood. The concept of one slot per person and the importance of punctuality in particular need to be explained. The problem of appointment systems is not confined to ethnic minority groups but it is fair to assume that language and communication barriers lead to increased frustration for all concerned.

Service provision

All group discussions revealed that the respondents were not aware of how local health and social care systems operated, the services that were available and what their rights were. Consequently, they relied on informal support networks within the community and voluntary sector. The need for an interpreting service, more translated leaflets and an appropriate catering policy in hospitals was also expressed. In relation to dental care and the services of opticians, the participants appeared to make only reactive rather than preventive use.

Attitudes to and expectations of health and social care

There was a mixture of attitudes, some negative and some positive. Conflicting views such as 'standards are better here' or 'the doctor service is not good here because they don't examine us as much' were frequently expressed. The findings suggested that some of the respondents had expectations that fell outside the usual role of the service, perhaps because they were used to family doctors providing drugs and a wider consultation than basic examination, prescriptions or referrals.

Views of health and social care professionals

Many of the issues raised by the community groups were mirrored by the professionals, in particular verbal and written communication, which could cause tremendous frustration for both client and staff groups. The need for a more accessible interpreting service was emphasised, as were many other issues, such as the provision of more cultural information on ethnic minorities and more leaflets in various minority languages, and the need for services generally to be delivered from a multiracial and more flexible perspective rather than in the current Britocentric/Eurocentric manner. A specific problem in relation to the specialist health and social care staff employed to target this section of the population was that their roles were not understood by the clients. This, together with the fact that there were not enough specialist workers, led the clients to seek help from sources such as welfare workers, so these professionals were becoming overstretched in work.

The next steps

The main function of the initial inquiry was to develop an intelligence base by aiming to:

- carry out an ethnographic assessment to identify key health and social care issues of concern to the ethnic minority populations (service users and non-users) in South Glamorgan and compare them with the ethnic majority;
- assess current perceptions of services;
- identify key service providers and assess their perceptions on the issues of concern pertaining to needs assessment of the ethnic minority groups;
- establish a strategy of planning and development for the short term and develop plans for the long term;
- develop hypotheses for the questionnaire that is to be used for Phase II (the quantitative phase) of the study.

To this end, the study has enabled a strategy and recommendations to be proposed to provider units. Table 4 lists the recommendations for action.

Clearly, ethnic minority health care *must* be brought on to the mainstream agenda of South Glamorgan Health Authority. The recent reforms have provided an excellent opportunity for this:[28]

> There are already signs that the recent NHS reforms are demonstrating the need for significant change to the strategy of the Authority to meet the health needs of the residents of South Glamorgan. Wales is acknowledged nationally and internationally to be in the forefront of strategic intent to improve the health status of its people.

Therefore, local ethnic minority health care needs must be incorporated in the new strategic vision of the South Glamorgan Health Authority. The authority must ensure that ethnic minority health care needs are reflected in the purchasing plan. The provision of information and good community consultation must be made; to this end information bases on the ethnic make-up of the area will

Table 4. The recommended strategy

Short-term recommendations
Communications plan
Staff training programme
Centralised translations of material
Food and health policy
Phase II – the quantitative survey
Monitoring/evaluation

Medium-term recommendations
Comprehensive interpreting service
Health forum – user and non-user/staff/agency participation
Service specifications in contracts
Equal opportunity programme/ethnic monitoring
Local information base
Monitoring/evaluation

Long-term recommendations
Empowerment programme – health promotion/education
Monitoring/evaluation

---

need to be established.[29] Information must also be improved for health service planners and professionals.

Assessment of services will need to be made in order to develop an effective ethnic minority dimension: efficiency (value for money); effectiveness (for individual patients and for the population as a whole); access to services (in terms of location and time); relevance to need (for the whole community and appropriate care for the individual); social acceptability (including responsive to user view); and equity (equal treatment for equal needs). Patient's Charter issues must also reflect quality service provisions to meet the needs of all local groups.

The recommended strategy

The recommendations in Table 4, which concern South Glamorgan Health Authority as a purchaser of services, an employer and a provider of services, have been developed at business and operational levels only, omitting the authority's corporate aspects such as the political market, budget sources and priority setting. Ultimately the aim is to create an equity of service access and to provide a needs based and culturally sensitive service, thereby improving the health status of minority groups.

Communications programme

It is crucial that a communications plan be established to communicate the outcomes of this survey as well as to promote the understanding of the Patient's Charter. The health authority is already implementing the Patient's Charter by developing: a health charter for people of South Glamorgan with the Family Health Services Authority; a consumer helpline; unit patients' charters; and a consumer guide to health and social services (with County Council social services, voluntary organisations and community health councils). It is recommended, therefore, that the ethnic minority dimension be incorporated in this and, thereafter, promotional programmes be undertaken. The promotional/communications plan should be ongoing.

Staff training programme

This programme should aim to train staff in cultural issues, racism and health and ethnicity matters. Equipped with such knowledge, practitioners can provide a culturally sensitive service.

Centralisation of ethnic minority related health promotion material

All materials, such as leaflets and other resources, relating to health promotion and the ethnic minorities should be made available from a central source in South Glamorgan. It seems logical to delegate this to the health authority's health promotion centre which already undertakes this role. In view of the dearth of appropriate leaflets/resource in this field, it is recommended that the health authority, at national level, ask Health Promotion Authority Wales to produce and distribute such adequate material. This task is both costly and large, but also greatly needed.

Completion of Phase II

Undertaken by the Centre for Applied Public Health Medicine, University of Wales College of Medicine.

Food and health policy for multicultural groups

It is advised that this policy be re-examined and reactivated. Particularly, this recommendation is aimed at secondary care (providers) and dietary provision for multicultural patients.

Comprehensive interpreting unit (communication) programme

Our survey has shown that there is a major problem in communication. The few specialist staff are not only underfunded but overloaded with work. Therefore, it is recommended that a comprehensive interpreting/linkworker unit be set up, with laid down policy for access. If 'tokenism' is to be avoided, such initiatives should be well researched (based on existing *good* practices elsewhere in Britain) and properly funded. It is to be considered a business move and should be aimed to improve the service delivery as well as equip employees. Also, the aim should be to avoid resource wastage which is costing the authority more than it should in 'person hours' and administrative inadequacies. Ultimately, this service should be operated as a business, generating income by providing a service to health service provider units and other health and social care organisations.

Participation mechanisms programme

A black health forum should be established that allows the health authority to set up directly a dialogue with its customers and members of staff. The involvement of the local community health council should be considered as well as other ethnic minority organisations in the field (such as the black mental health group AWETU). Also, a black workers' group should be set up comprising all those from ethnic minority backgrounds who are employed by the organisation, with a consultation process between this group and the planning departments.

Service specifications in contracts

To be completed after the Phase II survey.

Equal opportunity programme/ethnic monitoring

Undoubtedly, racial discrimination is a most difficult problem for health workers and the National Health Service (NHS) to accept and confront. To many people it seems a great contradiction that a caring service tolerates discrimination and inhuman treatment of the vulnerable and those in need. The long chain of inquiries and scandals in mental health and learning disability hospitals should warn us that this situation is not impossible. It is commonly acknowledged that racial discrimination is widespread in Britain; it would be bizarre if it were suggested that the NHS was somehow untouched by it. The difficulty appears to be that of motivating NHS workers, managers and authorities to give racial equality high priority.[13]

There needs to be an *active* equal opportunities policy, which covers the *twin* areas of recruitment and service access/delivery. Such a policy should incorporate views of good equal opportunities policy nationally. It is reiterated that such a policy should be active, concentrate on both employment and service, and be ongoing.

It is suggested that equality targets be set up to be achieved over a five-year period. The targets should employ and promote workers of ethnic minority origin in such a way that they proportionately represent their respective population ratios county-wide and at all occupational levels of the organisation.

Data on ethnicity in employment and service provision must be comprehensively collected and monitored. This is to be in addition to the Department of Health's recommendations for the health service to collect ethnicity data on inpatients and day cases from April 1995. Systems need to be established.

Local information base

Calman in *On the state of the public health 1991* reported the following:[30]

> In order to provide health care that reflects the needs of the local population, a health authority's first requirement is accurate information about the ethnic mix of the population, their cultural habits and their health status .... there are deficiencies in the available data on the demography and patterns of disease in black and ethnic minority populations.

It is the recommendation of this report that the health authority build up information bases on local ethnic minority needs for policy planners and professionals. Improvements in NHS data collection will help; for example, the planning of ethnicity data on day cases and inpatients (to be collected by health authorities as part of the contract minimum data set from April 1995) will provide a monitor on the use of such services by these groups. Also, organisations such as the King's Fund Centre's Services in Health and Race Exchange (SHARE), which aims to gather and disseminate information, will help to improve services. However, this health authority will need to collect its own data and develop an information system. To this end, adequate ongoing research and development activities will have to be developed. A good start can be made after the Phase II survey has been completed.

Health education and health promotion programme

Much of the above should be ongoing and systemised. In addition to that, however, an educational strategy needs to be developed. Such a strategy should aim to empower users and non-users so that people increase control over and thereby improve their health. Although this has to be immediate, it is also a long-term strategy which has to be ongoing. Again, this must be considered a business move, with all the elements of cost effectiveness but providing what the client perceives to be of value.

This strategy is not resource neutral, but considerable enhancements in service can be achieved through the application of good practice following systematic management audit. The report and its recommendations are being used as the basis for a constructive dialogue with provider units. It is intended that the recommendations be incorporated within the service specifications of contracts in coming years. It is also hoped that the GP fundholders can assess the feasibility of addressing some of the issues relevant to primary care. With regard to primary care, as highlighted in the initial report, GPs need more support for particular problems

Conclusion

Greater use of qualitative methods has been recently recommended to purchasing authorities in the assessment of the health needs of ethnic minorities.[31] This chapter demonstrates the value of using the qualitative method of focus groups to identify key themes and issues specific to different ethnic groups and those common across groups in regard to health and health service usage. These findings are useful to purchasing authorities as they can be rapidly integrated into the service specifications which underpin contracts. Also, providers can use the findings in assessing their general policies in regard to ethnic minorities which can lead to changes in their training and communications strategies. At a more strategic level, the study's findings can be used by all purchasing authorities with ethnic minority populations in Wales in updating their 'local strategies for health'. This will contribute to the wider health strategy in Wales, as articulated by the 'strategic intent and direction', which aims to take the people of Wales into the 21st century with a level of health on course to compare with the best in Europe.[4]

The report in this chapter is interim and the utility of the overall approach in linking the qualitative findings to a quantitative comparison between the ethnic minority and majority populations has yet to be undertaken. Several of the identified issues are suitable for further assessment in the second phase quantitative survey alongside the more standard variables pertaining to health status and service usage. It is hoped that the quantitative survey will include assessment of issues relevant to the concerns of the communities themselves.

Ad hoc cross-sectional quantitative surveys are expensive, particularly where obtaining a representative sample from the main ethnic groups will require an extensive initial census. Preceding the quantitative survey by a qualitative phase has ensured that it will be more focused on issues where further investigation is required and that relate to the concerns of communities. This is particularly important where there are several distinct ethnic groups.

There has been concern that new health service research initiatives to underpin the purchasing process will exclude qualitative methods.[32] It is hoped that this report will encourage the overall approach to be utilised more widely by purchasing authorities, and that a qualitative phase in formal assessments of health needs will become more widely established.

Acknowledgements

Many contributions have been made in order to complete the study. Specific thanks are given to: Dr Charles Davison, Medical Anthropologist, Department of Public Health, University of Glasgow; Dr Philip Burnard, Director of Postgraduate Nursing Studies, University of Wales College of Medicine; South Glamorgan Adult Education Centre; Barnardo's Multicultural Resource and Information Centre; and organisations in the Project Steering Group (South Glamorgan Race Equality Council; the Welsh Office; South Glamorgan Social Services; South Glamorgan Health Authority Health Promotion Centre).

References

1   World Health Organisation Regional Office for Europe. *Targets for health for all: targets in support of the European strategy for health for all.* Copenhagen: WHO Regional Office for Europe, 1985.
2   Bradshaw J. The concept of social need. *New Society* 1972; **30:** 640–3.
3   Department of Health. *The National Health Service and Community Care Act 1990.* London: HMSO, 1990.

4 Welsh Health Planning Forum. *Strategic intent and direction for the NHS in Wales.* Cardiff: Welsh Office NHS Directorate, 1989.

5 Welsh Health Planning Forum. *Local strategies for health: a new approach to strategic planning.* Cardiff: Welsh Office NHS Directorate, 1989.

6 Shah L, Harvey I, Coyle E. *The health and social care needs of ethnic minorities in South Glamorgan: phase 1 – a qualitative study.* Cardiff: University of Wales College of Medicine and South Glamorgan Health Authority, 1993.

7 South Glamorgan County Council. *South Glamorgan 1986 social survey of 1 in 10 households.* Cardiff: South Glamorgan County Council, 1986.

8 Office of Population Censuses and Surveys. *1991 census local base statistics.* London: HMSO, 1992.

9 South Glamorgan Health Authority Health Education Centre. *The health needs of ethnic groups.* Report of a symposium held on 11 September 1980. Cardiff: South Glamorgan Health Authority, 1981.

10 Glendenning F, ed. *The elders in ethnic minorities.* In association with the Department of Adult Education of the University of Keele and the Commission for Racial Equality. Stoke-on-Trent: Beth Johnson Foundation Publication, 1979.

11 Johnson MRD. Health and social services: making space for ethnic minority need. *New Community* 1991; **17**: 624–32.

12 Ahmad WIU, Kernohan EEM, Baker MR. Health of British Asians: a research review. *Community Medicine* 1989; **11**: 49–56.

13 McNaught A. *Race and health policy.* London: Croom Helm, 1988.

14 Shah L, Williams P. *The housing needs of Asian elderly in Cardiff: a research report.* Cardiff: Centre for Housing Management and Development, City and Regional Planning, University of Wales College of Cardiff, 1992.

15 Karseras P. *A profile of South Glamorgan's ethnic minority communities.* Cardiff: Minority Cultures Resource and Information Centre, Butetown Health Centre, South Glamorgan Health Authority, 1991.

16 South Glamorgan Health Authority and Family Health Services Authority. *Collaboration in practice.* Cardiff: South Glamorgan Health Authority and Family Health Services Authority, 1993.

17 Jones J. *Ethnic minorities and health service in South Glamorgan: a small survey of the views of ethnic minority groups in South Glamorgan.* Cardiff: South Glamorgan Race Equality, 1983.

18 Smaje C. *Health, race and ethnicity: making sense of the evidence.* London: King's Fund Institute, 1995.

19 Coyle E. *The health and social care needs of ethnic minorities in South Glamorgan: a project protocol.* Cardiff: South Glamorgan Health Authority, 1991.

20 Berg BL. *Qualitative research methods for the social sciences.* Massachusetts: Allyn and Bacon Publications, 1989.

21 Morgan J, Everett T, Hawley A. *Local strategies for health: developing public involvement – guidance notes.* Cardiff: Welsh Health Common Services Authority (Community Consultation and User Feedback Unit), 1992.

22 Krueger RA. *Focus groups: a practical guide for applied research.* Newbury Park: Sage Publications, 1988.

23   Holsti OR. *Content analysis for the social sciences and humanities*. Reading: Addison-Wesley, 1969.
24   Tesch R. *Qualitative research: analysis types and software tools*. New York: Falmer Press, 1990.
25   Weber RP. *Basic content analysis*. Beverly Hills: Sage Publications, 1985.
26   Burnard P. *Perceptions of AIDS counselling: a view from health professionals and AIDS counsellors*. Aldershot: Avebury, 1992.
27   Shah L. A survey of general practitioner opinion on minority ethnic elderly contact. In: *Towards a good old age? The G.O.A.L. project*. Cardiff: South Glamorgan Social Services/South Glamorgan Race Equality Council, 1993.
28   Harrhy GL. *Revised organisation and management arrangements*. Cardiff: South Glamorgan Health Authority, 1992.
29   Bahl V. *Purchasing and contracts*. SHARE Newsletter, King's Fund Centre, Issue 4, December 1992.
30   Calman KC. *On the state of the public health 1991*. London: HMSO 1992.
31   White M, Bhopal R. Health promotion for ethnic minorities. *Health For All By the Year 2000 News* (Faculty of Public Health Medicine of the Royal College of Physicians) 1993; **22**: 2–3.
32   Pope C, Mays N. Opening the black box: an encounter in the corridors of health services research. *British Medical Journal* 1993; **306**: 315–8.

4 | Setting priorities for health care

Raj Bhopal
Professor of Epidemiology and Public Health,
University of Newcastle upon Tyne

Priority setting is an all-important ongoing activity which, in the context of British health care in particular, needs more debate, analysis and research. In a static or shrinking economy the need for a rational and just means of priority setting becomes glaringly obvious. However, priority setting is complex and ill understood and has yet to find its rightful place at the top of the agenda for purchasers and providers.

Epidemiological concepts and data underpin priority setting, but decisions on consumption of resources are always heavily influenced by political matters (Fig 1, Table 1). For example, the high priority given to heart disease, diabetes, childhood leukaemia, child abuse and Legionnaires' disease can be understood in the context of the characteristics in the table. The relatively low priority for mental retardation, sexually transmitted diseases, suicide and senile dementia can also be understood. The Health of the Nation strategy illustrates well the balance, at national level, between epidemiological and political considerations.[1]

Within the Healthier Nation programme there is emphasis on the health and health care of minority ethnic groups.[1,2] Scarce resources of time, energy and new funds need to be applied to maximise the benefits to the health of minority ethnic groups. What principles should guide us here? This chapter presents an overview of past decision making processes, and presents a new approach for the future.

Analysing approaches to priority setting

Past approaches to priority setting can be examined in four ways: analysing the nature and emphasis of past initiatives;[3,4] analysing the nature and emphasis of current initiatives (unpublished materials collected by the public health network, the Health

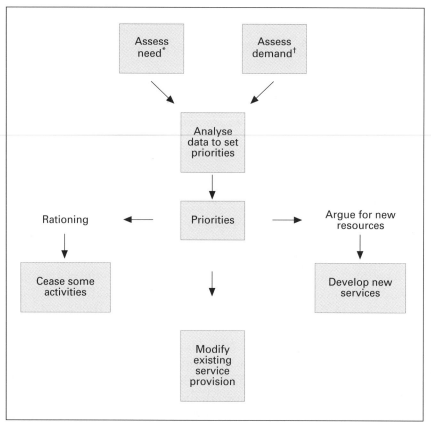

Fig 1. *The place of priority setting in relation to need for, demand for and provision of services.* *Using demographic, lifestyle, sociological and epidemiological data; †Using the views and patterns of past behaviour of professionals, pressure groups, patients and the public

Education Authority, and Dr Omwony Ojwok and Dr Salman Rawaf of Merton and Sutton Health Authority for the 'health needs' seminar); reading extensive scientific and other literature;[5-14] and assessing the opinions of decision makers. However both current and planned future activities and present opinions reflect only past approaches. For the purpose of illustration, I shall focus henceforth on British residents whose ancestry lies in the Indian subcontinent (referred to, for brevity, as Asians).

First conclusion of analysis: lack of agreement

The most striking observation arising from the above analysis is that there is no agreed sense of priority,[5-14] and (partly from

Table 1. Some characteristics of problems given high priority*

- *Epidemiological and clinical factors*
  The problem is: common;

  severe in its effects;

  long-lasting;

  communicable;

  externally, or iatrogenically, acquired;

  one of the young;

  treatable.

- *Social, economic and political factors*
  The problem is: of high public and political interest;

  economically important;

  lobbied for by pressure groups;

  free of stigma;

  socially acceptable;

  of interest to health professionals.

---

*Problems that do not have these characteristics, or have opposite characteristics, are given low priority.

unpublished observations) that past approaches have been tactical rather than strategic.[3,4] The tactics have been based on grasping opportunities, usually arising from distinct 'minority ethnic group problems' to be solved. For instance, national attention was aroused by the problem of so-called 'Asian' rickets[15] and much attention was devoted to this problem in the 1970s. Another problem which gained national attention concerned the use of surma, an eye cosmetic, and traditional remedies containing lead.[16] These 'problems' drew attention to the cultures of minority ethnic groups as a prime consideration in driving new initiatives for their care. The mother and baby campaign remains the biggest single national initiative in ethnic minority health to date; its emphasis was also around culture and communication as key issues.[17] The scientific literature in the 1970s mirrored the issues to which the service was devoting attention, with emphasis on a number of diseases and health problems, particularly nutrition and infectious diseases. Tuberculosis, for example, received focused attention and publicity.[18] What little evidence there is on professional opinion indicates that there is no clear, agreed view on priorities. However, professional views seem to have been deeply influenced by the focus of the literature.[4,19–21]

Second conclusion of analysis: mismatch between needs and provision of services

At the time that attention was focused on such matters as rickets and surma (1960s and 1970s), 45.3% of deaths of British residents born in the Indian subcontinent were due to ischaemic heart disease and cerebrovascular disease. The figures are shown in Table 2. The corresponding percentage of deaths from ischaemic heart disease and cerebrovascular disease for women (data not shown in table) were 22% and 16.1%, respectively. These two diseases were dominating causes of death. Yet, until the 1980s this fact went largely unnoticed. The key publication on immigrant mortality placed heavy emphasis on relative mortality experience, and the tables gave rankings based on standardised mortality ratios.[22] My coworkers and I have discussed elsewhere the importance of examining death data using numbers of deaths.[4,19,23]

Table 2. Deaths and standardised mortality ratios (SMR) for male immigrants* from the Indian subcontinent aged 20 and over; total deaths 4,352

Cause	SMR	No. of deaths	% of total
By rank order of SMR			
Homicide	341	21	0.5
Liver and intrahepatic bile duct neoplasm	338	19	0.4
Tuberculosis	315	64	1.5
Diabetes mellitus	188	55	1.3
Neoplasm of buccal cavity and pharynx	178	28	0.6
Total		187	4.3
By rank order of number of deaths			
Ischaemic heart disease	115	1,533	35.2
Cerebrovascular disease	108	438	10.1
Bronchitis, emphysema and asthma	77	223	5.1
Neoplasm of the trachea, bronchus and lung	53	218	5.0
Other non-viral pneumonia	100	214	4.9
Total		2,626	60.3

Standardised mortality ratios, compared with the male population of England and Wales, which was by definition 100.
*In these data the immigrants have not been categorised by ethnic group. (Source of original data for the construction of this table: reference 16, Table A14.3.)

While some health education material had been specifically adapted for minority ethnic groups, up to 1987 no item listed in the catalogues of the Health Education Authority concerned heart disease. In 1987 information was available for ethnic minorities on a wide range of other matters, including lice and colostomy.[4,24] The emphasis, however, was on birth control, infant care and feeding. In the 1990 catalogue, four of 179 items concerned heart disease. The underlying basis for this gap between need and provision is discussed elsewhere,[4,19,23] and the implications of the mismatch between need and provision for future strategy are of great importance. To address this mismatch the Health Education Authority, for example, has set up a central database of nationally available resources, which relate to the health of minority ethnic groups.[25]

The message of the above analysis is that for the future a strategic approach, based on agreed principles, is essential. The strategic approach should meet key needs, based on an analysis of the circumstances and health status of ethnic minority groups, and not merely focus on matters where the differences between the ethnic minority and majority groups are stark. In short, absolute and not relative needs should dominate our strategy. Table 2 shows the key causes of death in immigrants from the Indian subcontinent, first ranked on the standardised mortality ratio, a measure of relative excess or deficit of deaths, and then the actual number of deaths. The patterns are quite different. The former pattern guides research effort, the latter is the focus of service planning.[19,23]

Third conclusion of analysis: high priority issues are focused in quality of health care

In setting priorities, the perceptions, opinions and attitudes of decision makers are important, though they are hard to gauge objectively. On the basis of my experience in committees and other groups asked to assess priority needs, one issue has stood out – the enhancement of the quality of communication. Here, communication refers to more than the exchange of words; it encompasses mutual respect, understanding of life circumstances and culture, clearer use of language, and empowerment of individuals to say what they want and ask questions without fear or inhibition. Little research has been reported on interpreters, linkworkers and patients' advocates,[17,26,27] but many health authorities have either implemented relevant schemes or aired the issues. Alas, even this basic requirement of good communication with ethnic minority patients, fundamental to quality health care, is not an ingrained and routine part of the National Health Service.

Similarly, other basic issues such as correct recording of names, appropriate food in hospital, and the opportunity for examination by a doctor of the same gender, have yet to be attended to in most parts of the health service,[28] despite a long period of education and exhortation.[29]

The problems I have identified are: failure to agree priorities; too heavy a focus on so-called specific 'ethnic' issues at the expense of larger problems shared by the whole population; and non-implementation of basic services which, on informed opinion and research, are high priorities. A strategic rather than tactical approach is needed, and guiding principles, some of which are offered below, are required.

Towards a set of principles

A hierarchy of health and health care needs, and a set of standards based on equity, is outlined as the principles underlying a strategy development.

Clinical care for ethnic minority groups of a quality equal to national standards

- Equal access to advice and facilities
- Equal respect from carers
- Equally clear and effective communication
- Equally suitable accommodation, facilities and services such as food
- Equally effective clinical diagnosis, therapy and advice

Preventive care/health promotion of a quality equal to national standards

- Equal access to an appropriate range of information/advice
- Equally effective communication
- Equally acceptable and relevant information
- Focus on common and preventable diseases/health problems
- Focus on matters perceived as important by ethnic minority groups
- Equal efforts to involve the community

The principles encapsulated in the above hierarchy are:

- National standards of quality of health care to be applied to ethnic minority groups

- Emphasis on basic needs, irrespective of similarities or differences between ethnic minority and majority populations
- Emphasis on quality of service rather than specific conditions

Further principles that in my view ought to guide the strategy are:

- Focus on a few priorities rather than a large number.
- Be guided by priorities identified by, and for, the general population, eg those in *Our healthier nation*,[1] for the similarities in the life problems and health patterns of ethnic minorities exceed the dissimilarities.[4,30]

Implementing priority actions

Finally, how do we implement a programme of work associated with given priorities? The key principles are clear policy[31] and integration.[32] Action is required at national, regional, district, provider and community level. The policies, strategies and action plans at each level need to be harmonious. This cannot happen without priority setting.

References

1   Secretary of State for Health. *Our healthier nation. Consultation paper.* London: Stationery Office, 1998.
2   Balarajan R, Raleigh VS. *Ethnicity and health: a guide for the NHS.* London: Department of Health, 1993.
3   Donaldson LJ, Odell A. Planning and providing services for the Asian population: a survey of district health authorities. *Journal of the Royal Society of Health* 1984; **104**: 199–202.
4   Bhopal RS, Donaldson LJ. Health education for ethnic minorities: current provision and future directions. *Health Education Journal* 1988; **47**: 137–40.
5   Donovan JH. Ethnicity and health: a research review. *Social Science and Medicine.* 1984; **19**: 663–70.
6   Ahmad WIU. Policies, pills and political will: a critique of policies to improve the health status of ethnic minorities. *Lancet* 1989; **i**: 148–9.
7   Department of Health. *On the state of the public health.* Annual report of the Chief Medical Officer for 1991. London: HMSO, 1992.
8   Cruikshank JK, Beevers DG. *Ethnic factors in health and disease.* London: Wright, 1989.
9   Bhopal RS. Needs of black and ethnic minorities. *British Medical Journal* 1992; **305**: 1156.
10 Ahmad WIU, ed. *'Race' and health in contemporary Britain.* Buckingham: Open University Press, 1993.
11 Karmi G, McKeigue P. *The ethnic health bibliography.* London: North East and North West Thames RHA, 1993.
12 Smaje C. *Health, 'race' and ethnicity.* London: King's Fund Institute, 1995.

13 Health Education Authority. *Health and lifestyle: black and minority ethnic groups in England.* London: HEA, 1994.

14 British Medical Association. *Multicultural health care.* London: BMA, 1995.

15 Ford JA, Colhoun EM, McIntosh WB, Dunnigan MG. Rickets and osteomalacia in the Glasgow Pakistani community, 1961–1971. *British Medical Journal* 1972; **2**: 677–80.

16 Aslam M. *The practice of Asian medicine in the United Kingdom.* PhD thesis, University of Nottingham, 1979.

17 Rocheron Y, Dickinson R. The Asian mother and baby campaign: a way forward in health promotion for Asian women? *Health Education Journal* 1990; **49**: 128–33.

18 Medical Research Council. National survey of tuberculosis notification in England and Wales, 1978–1979. *British Medical Journal* 1980; **281**: 895.

19 Bhopal RS. Health care for Asians: conflict in need, demand and provision: a prerequisite for health. In: *Equity.* Proceedings of the 1987 summer scientific conference of the Faculty of Community Medicine. London: Faculty of Community Medicine and the World Health Organisation, 1988: 52–5.

20 Bhopal RS, White M. Health promotion for ethnic minorities: past, present and future. In: Ahmad WIU, ed. *'Race' and health in contemporary Britain.* Buckingham: Open University Press, 1993.

21 Bhopal R. Is research into ethnicity and health racist, unsound, or important science? *British Medical Journal* 1997; **314**: 1751–5.

22 Marmot MG, Adelstein AM, Bulusu L. *Immigrant mortality in England and Wales 1970–78.* Studies on medical and populations subjects, No. 47. London: HMSO, 1984.

23 Senior P, Bhopal RS. Ethnicity as a variable in epidemiological research. *British Medical Journal* 1994; **309**: 327–30.

24 Bhopal RS. Health education and ethnic minorities. *British Medical Journal* 1991; **302**: 1338.

25 Health Education Authority. *Health-related resources for black and minority ethnic groups.* London: HEA, 1994.

26 Hopkins A, Bahl V, eds. *Access to health care for people from black and ethnic minorities.* London: Royal College of Physicians, 1993.

27 Parsons L, Day S. Improving obstetric outcomes in ethnic minorities: an evaluation of health advocacy in Hackney. *Journal of Public Health Medicine* 1992; **14**: 183–91.

28 Madhok R, Bhopal RS, Ramaiah RS. Quality of hospital service: an 'Asian' perspective. *Journal of Public Health Medicine* 1992; **14**: 271–9.

29 Henley A. *Asian patients in hospital and at home.* London: King Edward's Hospital Fund for London, 1979.

30 Williams R, Bhopal R, Hunt K. Health of a Punjabi ethnic minority in Glasgow: a comparison with the general population. *Journal of Epidemiology and Community Health* 1993; **47**: 96–102.

31 Bhopal RS, Parsons L. A draft policy for adoption by health authorities, purchasers and providers of health care. In: Hopkins A, Bahl V, eds. *Access to health care for people from black and ethnic minorities.* London: Royal College of Physicians, 1993.

32 Kelly MP, Charlton BG, Hanlon P. The four levels of health promotion: an integrated approach. *Public Health* 1993; **107**: 319–26.

5 | Monitoring health status

Alan McNaught
Regional Health Sector Development Advisor, Eastern Caribbean

Steve Maingot
Information Manager, Ealing, Hammersmith and Hounslow Health Authority, London

Monitoring the health and illness, service utilisation and communities' expectations and experiences is a fundamental step in any process of health needs assessment of the population and evaluation of the effectiveness of the service provision (see Chapter 2). Furthermore, targeting the resources towards those in most need requires a proper system of monitoring. In a multiethnic society, people from different cultures have different disease patterns, different perceptions of health and illness, and different expectations and experiences of the health services. The recognition of such differences and how the health service is responding requires appropriate data on all ethnic groups within any given community. Ethnic monitoring, therefore, became the focus for many researchers and policy makers.[1,2]

The Department of Health booklet *Ethnicity and health* has highlighted the inequalities in health care provision to various ethnic minority groups in Britain.[1] The sad aspect of this, however, has been the amount of time it has taken health policy makers, in a multiracial society, to realise that there is a need for a focus on grounded knowledge and its dissemination in any strategy to improve the health and health care experience of a section of British society that remains disadvantaged in some areas, according to all known indicators.[3–6] The lack of appropriate epidemiological data on health and disease burden in these groups and, until recently, routine data on service utilisation meant less focused and targeted policies to address these inequalities. In 1984 and 1988, we noted that routine National Health Service (NHS) data did not record ethnicity, and were not related to the use of health services. The one exception was mortality statistics, collected by the

Registrar General.[7,8] Much the same point was made in one of the opening sections of the Department of Health report.[1]

Whilst how much and what we know are important, it is even more critical to place this knowledge in context. It is equally critical to express clearly the reasons why monitoring the health care needs and status of ethnic minorities is essential.

Social context of monitoring

It is well documented that, in most areas of social policy, the knowledge of policy makers and the contents of formal information systems tend to lag behind the experience of people in the community, especially those experiencing a particular phenomenon. This is very pronounced in the field of race relations and more so in the area of ethnic minority health care.

The confidence of ethnic minority people in the NHS is still not high despite many efforts at all levels. This results from the culmination of widespread experience of racial discrimination at the hands of individual health workers and a perception that the NHS as a social system does not take ethnic minority health seriously. This has been reinforced during the past decade by the popular association of Africa and, by extension, black people as being the source of the AIDS epidemic.[9,10]

If the NHS is to pay more than lip service to its responsibilities under the Race Relations Act, monitoring is only a start to a substantial programme of action to improve the quality and relevance of services to ethnic minority groups in general practitioner (GP) surgeries, community clinics and hospitals.

Organisational context

Delivering effective health care that is tailored to the needs of the various communities is a complex process. Commissioners and providers of health care have to be sensitive to cultural diversity in the area they serve. The Department of Health document referred to previously was aimed at purchasers.[1] There is also a need to focus on the many racial equality issues that providers must take rather more seriously than they do at the moment, and their responsibility for delivering health care and as major local employers.

We know from a considerable body of research that organisational action in support of racial equality has to go beyond 'working for equal opportunities' and providing 'ethnically sensitive services'.[4] Slogans like these are an inadequate way of promoting change in a complex and conservative organisation like the NHS.

In the late 1980s, one of us (AM) undertook two studies to identify how health authorities attempted to improve services to ethnic minorities and their performance as equal opportunities employers.[8] Both studies showed failure of endeavour to improve services and performance. The following are the main reasons for these failures:

- Ethnic minority issues tended to be used primarily as an attempt to secure more resources without any modification to service style or scope.
- The initiatives and services that were developed to meet the needs of ethnic minorities were often poorly resourced and marginal.
- There was a general unwillingness to consult with or draw ethnic minority communities into these initiatives, reflecting a paternalistic approach to this section of the population.
- Targets and outcome measures were unclear and inadequately identified.
- Little or no attempt was made to draw on existing knowledge and research, to generalise or disseminate what were perceived as good standards and practice.
- There was often confusion and conflict among key policy makers.
- Ethnic minority advisers were employed without a clear brief and were allowed to function with inadequate support.
- Equal opportunities employment procedures were restricted to low status staff groups.

For both commissioners and providers, these detailed observations can provide the basis of a checklist to test the strength of their equal opportunities initiatives. Policies to provide health care services to those entitled to receive them on a 'colour blind' basis take no account of the particular needs of different cultural and ethnic groups, and may result in inappropriate and thus ineffective provision of health care.[11]

Ethnic monitoring

Ethnic monitoring is an essential process to improve the quality and sensitivity of the health service to meet the different needs of a multiethnic society. There are eight areas of monitoring:

1 *Population monitoring.* The 1991 census provided, for the first

time, an opportunity to identify the structure of various ethnic groups in any given geographical area.[12] Such a self-classification of ethnicity has been criticised, and further work is needed to refine the Office of Population Censuses and Surveys classification of ethnic groups. Mapping ethnic density by electoral wards will be a useful tool to focus the attention of policy makers and service providers to meet the needs of the population they serve. Furthermore, with population mobility, migration and asylum seeking, such monitoring will be essential to plan services for these groups.

2 *Monitoring variations in health.* Significant variations in health have been documented in Britain in relation to geographical area, ethnicity, social class, occupation and gender.[13] Monitoring these variations will enable health authorities, GP commissioners and providers of health care to develop plans that identify and tackle these variations and to evaluate interventions.[14]

3 *Monitoring the health status of the different ethnic minority groups.* Chapter 2 provides a clear framework of the approaches and methods of collecting appropriate quantitative and qualitative data to assess the population health status (see also Chapters 3 and 11). Understanding the health status of these groups will facilitate the decision-making processes in prioritising resources, targeting health service provision, promoting equity and avoiding prejudice.

4 *Monitoring service utilisation.* Routine data collection on health promotion, primary care, outpatient and inpatient care and support services should include ethnic coding. The experience of the introduction of ethnic codes to all hospital admissions, which was introduced into the NHS in 1995,[15] should be generalised to all other service provision.

5 *Monitoring the effectiveness of interventions.* With the expanding demands on a health service with finite resources, the new culture of the NHS will be driven by evidence-based medicine[16] and knowledge-based decision making.[16] Systematic reviews show some consistency between scientific findings and can help to facilitate a rational decision-making process among policy makers.[16-18] The application of these findings to different ethnic groups is important, as certain conditions or diseases are exclusive to or more prominent in some racial groups.

6 *Monitoring people's experiences and satisfactions with the services provided.* Measurement of patients' views is an essential component of monitoring and evaluating the performance of the health service and the quality of care delivered. Although many standard

methods have been developed to measure consumers' views and patients' satisfaction,[19] special consideration should be taken when dealing with ethnic minority groups. Some of these groups are less vocal than others. Limitations are imposed on many others because of their residence status (eg refugees), cultural code of practice, or previous experiences. Furthermore, the instruments (eg questionnaires) used should be sensitive enough to detect the true level of satisfaction and views about services.[20]

7 *Monitoring employment and equal opportunities policies.* The discrimination in service provision to a multicultural society and in employment in the NHS is well documented.[4,21] A programme of action to address the barriers that face ethnic minority staff, and have sometimes prevented the health service from providing the best possible care for all its patients, was launched by the Department of Health in December 1993;[22] its outcome has yet to be seen.

8 *Monitoring the outcome.* Outcomes could be population health outcomes, individual intervention outcomes, or organisational performance outcomes.[23–25] Results of outcome measures at all these levels should be published regularly in simple formats and made widely available to patients and communities.

Monitoring also requires evaluating the effect of service interventions, assessing the adequacy of contracts or service agreements for ethnic minority health, social acceptability and epidemiological analysis of ethnic monitoring data. Ethnic monitoring should be part of the mainstream gathering and analysis procedures, not an add-on operating in isolation. Systems set up in isolation tend to be marginalised, wither and die.[11]

Many initiatives were undertaken by the Department of Health to ensure that the health needs of ethnic minority groups are recognised and met, for example, the establishment of the ethnic health unit, and the funding and commissioning of health authorities, trusts, voluntary organisations and charities to undertake various projects looking at different aspects of ethnic minority health.[26] The Department of Health is working with commissioners, co-ordinating initiatives and disseminating examples of good practice in the field, and has identified the implementation of ethnic monitoring of inpatients as a key priority.

With the exception of hospital admissions, information about ethnicity is not uniformly collected at present. It has not been a compulsory variable, so the information differs in completeness and content. Some effort has been made in the area of maternal and child health information to collect ethnicity of mothers and children. Since April 1995 the inpatient minimum data set includes ethnicity variables.[15]

From monitoring to action

Monitoring of the health status of ethnic minority people is a crucial first step in delivering on any commitment to racial equality in health care. To assist policy makers and managers effectively, the form of monitoring adopted has to be multilayered and action orientated. The focus should include:

- routine and one-off epidemiological surveys and studies;
- data on service uptake;
- information on employment profiles within the NHS;
- dissemination of research and related studies.

The process should not stop at this. The data collected should be used to inform a clear strategy and targets to improve the health and related welfare of this section of the population. Health care commissioners (health authorities and commissioning 'primary care groups') should take responsibility for ethnic monitoring, and ensure through the contracting/commissioning processes that providers are collecting the minimum monitoring data and implementing equal opportunity policies. They should also ensure that these monitoring processes are communicated on a regular basis to patients and the communities at large.

Improving services for people from ethnic minority communities

Some health authorities are setting up task groups to develop a local focus on Department of Health, national and regional ethnicity health programmes. This should involve the review of needs, with an appropriate programme and action plan with targets across the geographical areas they serve, and accountability at board level This should be supported with an effective system of monitoring and review.

Policy implications

Dr Femi Nzegwu in her treatise *Black people and health care in contemporary Britain* indicated that there was a significantly high level of dissatisfaction with the delivery of health care.[20] How can health authorities become more responsive to the needs of ethnic minorities without being able to identify unmet needs and monitor needs that are met? There is a need to stimulate vigorous activity at local level, by local groups, as part of involving local people in the commissioning of health care.[27,28]

There is a need for committed and resourced support to community groups who often have clear ideas about the needs of their populations. These groups will form the linchpin in any efforts to integrate the needs of ethnic minorities into mainstream health care delivery.

To support the monitoring process, it is necessary to have well funded research led by researchers and other professionals from the ethnic minority communities on lifestyle and utilisation patterns and, most important, specific health needs within these population groups. The new framework for assessing performance, proposed in the NHS Executive's consultation document, will shift the focus to provide a comprehensive view of performance.[29] Assessments that include health improvements, access to services, effective delivery of appropriate health care, efficiency, patient and carer experience, and health outcomes will no doubt strengthen the monitoring of population health, including that of ethnic minorities.

Acknowledgements

We are grateful to Dr Salman Rawaf for his suggestions and contributions to this chapter.

References

1   Balarajan R, Raleigh V. *Ethnicity and health: a guide for the NHS.* London: Department of Health, 1993.

2   Ohiri S. The politics of racism, statistics, and equal opportunity: towards a black perspective. In: Bhat A, Carhill R, Ohiri S, eds. *Britain's black population,* 2nd edn. Aldershot: Arena, 1988.

3   Ahmed WIU, ed. *Race and health in contemporary Britain.* Buckingham: Open University Press, 1993.

4   Cox J, Bostock S, eds. *Racial discrimination in the health service.* Staffs: Penrhos, 1989.

5   Balarajan R, Raleigh VS, Yuen P. Hospital care among ethnic minorities in Britain. *Health Trends* 1991; **23**: 90–3.

6   Balarajan R. Ethnicity and variations in the nation's health. *Health Trends* 1995; **27**:114–9.

7   McNaught A. *Race and health care in the United Kingdom.* London: Health Education Council, 1985.

8   McNaught A. *Race and health policy.* Beckenham: Croom Helm, 1988.

9 Sabatier R. *Blaming others: prejudice, race and worldwide AIDS*. London: Panos, 1988.

10 Panos Institute. *The third epidemic: repercussions of the fear of AIDS*. London: Panos, 1990.

11 Jones A. The ethnic monitoring process. In: Karmi G, ed. *Ethnic monitoring in health service provision*. London: North East and West Thames Regional Health Authorities, 1991.

12 National Institute for Ethnic Studies in Health and Social Policy. *Ethnic diversity in England and Wales: an analysis by health authorities based on the 1991 census*. London: NIESH, 1997.

13 Department of Health. *Variation in health: what can the Department of Health and the NHS do?* Report by the variation subgroup of the Chief Medical Officer's Health of the Nation working group. London: Department of Health, 1995.

14 Department of Health. *On the state of the public health*. Annual report of the Chief Medical Officer for 1995. London: HMSO, 1996.

15 NHS Executive. *Collection of ethnic group data for admitted patients*. Leeds: Department of Health, 1994 (circular EL(94)77).

16 Secretary of State for Health. *The National Health Service: a service with ambitions*. London: HMSO, 1996 (cm 3425).

17 Gray JAM. *Evidence-based healthcare: how to make health policy and management decisions*. Edinburgh: Churchill Livingstone, 1997.

18 Mulrow CD. Rationale for systematic reviews. In: Chalmers I, Altman DG, eds. *Systematic reviews*. London: BMJ Publishing Group, 1995.

19 Fitzpatrick R, Hopkins A, eds. *Measurement of patients' satisfaction with their care*. London: Royal College of Physicians, 1993.

20 Nzegwu F. *Black people and health care in contemporary Britain*. Reading: International Institute for Black Research, 1993.

21 London Association of Community Relation Councils. *In a critical condition: a survey of equal opportunities in employment in London's health authorities*. London: LACRC, 1985.

22 National Health Service Management Executive. *Ethnic minority staff in the NHS: a programme of action*. Leeds: NHSE, 1993.

23 Rawaf S. Personal communications, 1996.

24 McColl AJ, Gulliford MC. *Population health outcome indicators for the NHS*. London: Faculty of Public Health Medicine, 1993.

25 Thornicroft G, Tansella M. *Mental health outcome measures*. Berlin: Springer-Verlag, 1996.

26 Department of Health. *Directory of ethnic minority initiatives*. London: Department of Health, 1996.

27 Safder M. *User-sensitive purchasing*. London: King's Fund, 1993.

28 National Health Service Management Executive. *Purchasing for health: a framework for action*. London: Department of Health, 1993.

29 NHS Executive. *The new NHS – modern and dependable: a national framework for assessing performance*. Consultation document. London: DoH, 1998 (EL(98)4).

6 | Lifestyle and health choices

Salman Rawaf
*Director of Clinical Standards, Merton Sutton and Wandsworth
Health Authority, Surrey*

Felicity Owen
*Health Promotion Manager, Merton Sutton and Wandsworth
Health Authority, Surrey*

Velena Gilffilian
*Health Promotion Programme Manager, Merton Sutton and
Wandsworth Health Authority, Surrey*

The term 'lifestyle' is widely used in the health vocabulary but it has been misunderstood[1] and not defined in a simple way. To many people lifestyle is seen as the individually determined behaviours that shape the health of an individual. The outcomes of these behaviours could either positively or negatively contribute to an individual's health.

Lifestyle is determined through the influence of primary and secondary socialisation of the individual and, indeed, for some individuals and groups through 'tertiary socialisation', ie settling in another environment through migration. According to Nutbeam, lifestyle is taken to mean 'a general way of living based on the interplay between living conditions in the wide sense, and individual patterns of behaviour as determined by socio-cultural factors and personal characteristics'.[2] Thus, lifestyle could be seen as the product of the interaction of genetic, social, economic, political and environmental factors, personal choices and influences, and is amenable to alteration, modification and change over time.

Health is not just an individual responsibility. Our health is, to a large extent, governed by the physical, social, cultural and economic environments in which we live. To encourage individuals to make healthier choices, while ignoring the social and environmental circumstances that conspire to make them ill, is a fundamentally defective strategy and unethical.[3,4]

This chapter outlines the different lifestyles in different communities and cultures, the impacts of these lifestyles on health, what encourages healthy choices, the individual versus community approaches to healthy choices, and the methods of assessment and monitoring of the population's lifestyles. Studying and understanding individuals' lifestyles in various communities and groups has a dual purpose: to enhance and promote positive health, and to prevent ill health through alteration and adoption of healthy but attractive and acceptable choices.

Different lifestyles in different cultures

A person's lifestyle will be determined not only by personal factors such as race and ethnicity but also by cultural background. These interactions, together with the environment, which includes social, political and economic differences, will all combine to influence health. Culture is therefore one of the major determinants of lifestyle. Helman defined culture as a set of guidelines, explicit and implicit, that individuals inherit as members of a particular society, which tells them how to view the world, how to experience it emotionally, and how to behave in relation to other people, supernatural forces or gods, and the natural environment.[5] He sees culture as also providing individuals with a way of transmitting these guidelines of values and attitudes to the next generation, by using symbols, language, art and ritual. Helman's definition is an expansion of that of Kessing.[6] Linking these definitions to the experiences of many minority ethnic groups, in particular the first and some of the second generations, through what we described earlier as 'tertiary socialisation' and the continuous process of change and adaptation, the sets of cultural guidelines are clearly seen as dynamic and amenable to change. Moreover, within the same culture many subcultures exist with different beliefs and behaviours that are in line with the social and material background of that society. People from the same ethnic groups think and behave in different ways according to, for example, their education, wealth, employment, religion, health and social status.

Factors influencing lifestyle

Beliefs and values

For many people from the same culture, shared beliefs and values are important components of the cultural guidelines that govern their attitudes and behaviours. The added support that can be provided by individuals who share similar beliefs, views and circumstances may be one of the reasons why people from minority ethnic communities may be found in identified clusters.

People's behaviours during health and illness are based on their beliefs and values. These are subjected to the influences of culture (original, modified or adopted); health information from education, relatives, friends and the media; personal and family past experiences with illness; experiences with the health services; and socioeconomic status. Health, illness and death are important concepts in every culture and may have different interpretations in different cultures. Even within the same culture, people's conceptions about each of these may be divergent. For example, adult and young people who were born and educated in Britain may have different beliefs and interpretation of values from those of an older generation who migrated to this country.[7] Furthermore, professionals from the same culture who speak the same language may have different interpretations of their clients' beliefs and values, as the subculture of these professionals may be profoundly different from that of the main culture. Therefore, in researching various cultures, including the lifestyles adopted and the relation of such lifestyles to health and illness, one should avoid the problem of 'ethnocentricity', ie the interpretation of one culture using the norms of another. The use of the ethnographic assessment,[8,9] ie when the assessor or the researcher suspends his or her own belief system and observes/investigates with full neutrality, will minimise bias and elicit valid information (see Chapter 3).

Social class

A person's lifestyle is firmly linked to his or her social class status. Whitehead, in her report *The health divide,* outlines the major health experiences and differences throughout England according to social class.[10] Stillbirths and perinatal deaths, used as indicators of health, were much more numerous in social classes IV and V than in any of the other classes. This was also mirrored for men and women of working age who fell into the same class structure. For those of retirement age the author reported that mortality gradients were 50% higher in class V than in class I. People who owned their own homes had lower standard mortality ratios than those in council/rented accommodation who tended to be at the lower end of the social class scale. She suggests that inequalities in health and regional differences identified in the Black report[11] continued into the 1980s, and makes reference to the increasing high mortality rates in the north and north-west compared with the relatively lower rates in the south and south-east. Such systematic variations in mortality and morbidity rates between different groups of the population have continued in the late 1990s. There were marked differences by occupational class, sex, region and ethnicity in life expectancy, healthy life expectancy, and incidence of and survival from a range of diseases.[12] Similar findings were reported by the British Medical Association.[13]

Many minority ethnic groups are in the major cities of the United Kingdom. Data from the 1991 census confirm this. The top cities for minority ethnic concentration, excluding inner and outer London, are major industrialised cities. Their concentration is undoubtedly due to the labour shortages in the 1950s and 1960s. High numbers in Greater London are there for similar reasons: the prospect of work, feelings of safety, being with family and friends, and knowing that cultural habits and lifestyle will be identified. London is also the point of entry for many minority groups. The Jarman underprivilege scores have highlighted many inner city areas as deprived. Ethnicity is part of this categorisation,[14] and this serves to indicate that many minority groups are found in situations of disadvantage. However, such stratification can easily result in stereotyping individuals from minority groups.

Housing

The relationship between housing and health and its multifaceted nature can be summed up by a quote from the WHO committee on the public health aspects of housing:[15,16]

> Since the residential environment consists of many elements of the overall environment, with each element capable of exerting individual detrimental effects upon health and well being, it can be deduced that the effect of the residential environment upon health is the sum of individual factors.

Poor housing conditions are still a major threat to public health. The effect of housing may be compounded by those inter-related factors of material income, age, pre-existing illness, and personal behaviour.[13,17,18] The major conditions related to poor housing may crudely be divided into communicable and non-communicable diseases and conditions. These will be additionally influenced by lifestyle and have a greater or lesser effect upon mental, physical and social well-being. Most housing and health studies have focused on the effect of physical health. Ransom made reference to 14 selected European and 24 American studies that focused on some aspect of physical health: eight of the European studies looked at the relationship between housing and tuberculosis, five analysed morbidity and mortality rates, birth rates and infant mortality caused by respiratory disease, and another looked at the height of pre-school children.[16] By contrast, 14 of the 24 American studies dealt with social and psychological aspects. Most found a positive association between housing and health: poor housing correlated with poor health and better housing with better health.

People who are chronically ill or disabled, older people, children, or mothers with young children commonly spend a great deal of their time in the home. Poor housing conditions cause negative health conditions. Physical health may be affected by the transmission of communicable disease. Poor design or overcrowding may result in accidents and injury. Poor housing, overcrowding and noise affect mental health. Housing provides a haven for family life, recreation, rest, sleep and social interaction, and may contribute to a wide range of physical and mental health disorders. Housing is also set in the wider context of the community, which forms identities and infrastructures. For ethnic minority groups in the lower social structure many of these health and social problems will be prominent. Homelessness is a major and increasing problem to some individuals and families in inner cities. Cheaper housing is often found in inner city areas.

Income and employment

Income is the major determinant of standards of living and lifestyle. Low income, certain behaviours, poor housing and environmental amenities had the clearest link with excess burden of ill health.[19] With this association between income and health, it is not surprising to find a strong relationship between unemployment and poor health.[20-22] Although such causal links are sometimes disputed in terms of whether illness results in lack of employment or vice versa, there is no doubt that unemployment is associated with a wide range of ill health. Problems arising include behaviours such as smoking and/or inactive lifestyle, higher risks of psychological disorders (eg anxiety, depression, neurotic disorders, sleeping problems and poor self-esteem), poor physical health, and high mortality. Education is a major influence on employment or the lack of it. The risk of unemployment is higher among those with the least education and in unskilled individuals. Ethnic minority groups experience higher levels of unemployment, low pay, shift work and poor social security rights than the rest of the population.[23] Both the census and the Health Education Authority's survey on health and lifestyle found much higher levels of unemployment especially among African-Caribbean and Bangladeshi people.[24]

Racism and discrimination

Ogunsola writes about the cultural diversity of ethnic minorities, and about the common experiences of racism and how it affects health.[25] Many institutions, the National Health Service included, are not free from racism.[26-28] This may be in the form of direct racism (eg racist abuse), indirect racism or institutional racism (eg an assumption that everyone has equal access to services or employment).[28] Racism also exists between and among minority ethnic groups. All forms of prejudice and racism are disabling both for the perpetrator and the victim.[29] They may lead to blockage of communication between the provider and the receiver, create an atmosphere of rejection, and reduce the chance of concordance. Although a high proportion of people from minority ethnic groups may be disadvantaged socially, have a lower chance of employment and be subjected to racist practices, others enjoy a high standard of living.[30]

Social interaction and peer pressure

Social interaction, support and isolation can influence personal behaviours, for better or worse. Good relationships with relatives, lovers, friends and other members of society are protective factors for good mental health and against the effect of adverse life events. Lack of social support is associated with anxiety, depression, suicide, high blood pressure and excessive use of medication and increased demands on health services.[31] Racism and racial abuse may lead to social isolation and lack of social interaction between individuals and communities. In some minority ethnic groups, elder people and women, especially those from the first generation, may suffer from social isolation with health consequences. However, extensive networks of social support do exist within many minority ethnic communities and will have a positive influence on their health.[32]

Young people's behaviour can be influenced through familial and peer attitude and pressure. In a nationwide survey among children 9–19 years old, conducted in 1989 and 1990, the Health Education Authority (HEA) found that the attitudes and behaviour of family and friends towards smoking, drinking and drug taking appeared to influence the young person's attitudes and behaviour. For example, in a national survey 71% of the young adult regular smokers said that most of their friends smoke, compared with 15% of the non-smokers.[33,34] In Croydon, 56% of teenagers living with adults who drank alcohol regularly were themselves regular drinkers, compared with only 12% of those who lived in a home where alcohol was not consumed.[35] Young people from minority ethnic groups are facing various conflicting pressures and objectives: peer pressure from the majority youth (to be the same), cultural values and religious codes (to be different), racism (you must be different), and self value (we are as good as others).

Information

Information from whatever source has a major role in increasing knowledge, affecting change in attitudes, and changing or modifying behaviour. Although people differ in the extent to which they avail themselves of information, health behaviours can be changed by long-term sustained information campaigns.[36] The main sources of information are parents, friends and relatives, formal and informal education, the media (radio, television, magazines and newspapers) and health professionals. The Office of Health Economics in their survey in 1993 found that for all age groups over 15 years old, the source of information considered to be of primary importance was the general practitioner (GP). Magazines and newspapers scored 16% and television 13%.[37] However, a substantially higher proportion of individuals from professional and managerial social classes obtain health information from newspapers and magazines than from their GP.[36,37] The study suggests that, whilst the media play an important role in providing information, it is necessary for there to be a relationship between that information and the personal situation of the individual if there is to be a change in behaviour.[36] For individuals to change their lifestyles, it is necessary for them to understand the health message and to accept its relevance for their own lives. GP consultation, an interactive process between the patient and doctor, can provide an appropriate opportunity for the interpretation of information according to individual needs.[36] Medical contact can play a useful part in influencing changes in lifestyle such as smoking and drinking.[38,39] The HEA's health and lifestyle survey[24] showed that men from minority ethnic groups were less likely to discuss health promotion with their GPs. While African-Caribbean women have discussed health promotion topics in similar proportion to the general population, south Asian women were less likely to do so. Food, weight loss and physical activity were the main topics discussed by African-Caribbeans and the general public. Less attention was paid by Indians and Pakistanis to physical activity. Bangladeshis were more likely to discuss smoking, child health and heart disease with their GPs.[24] The key source of health information advice is GPs as providers of both advice and leaflets. Availability of relevant health promotion leaflets in appropriate languages and presentation will increase the impact of messages to help people make healthy choices.

Social class itself is sometimes a barrier to the receiving and interpreting of health information. Musick *et al*, for example, found that more than a third of people with cancer living in a deprived and poor area of the United States did not link cigarette smoking with cancer, despite intense and continuing publicity.[40] Such a barrier may lead to delay in seeking medical care in some cases.[41]

Environment

Traditionally, epidemiologists have focused on distinguishing the variations of disease and health between individuals, their communities, their locations and their length of stay in any particular place. These variations are used to identify and determine patterns of ill health. Some of these differences have been put down to genetics, but may equally be determined or precipitated by environment. Environmental factors may impose ways of life and dictate personal circumstances which may lead to choices that could be detrimental to health, for example, access to public transport, parks and open spaces, leisure facilities, safe cycling pathways etc. Such a situation will give little or no room for deliberate choices about healthier options. For some women from minority ethnic groups, their preference to pursue activities such as swimming in a women only environment may not be possible in all residential areas, thus restricting some of their choices. Residents in housing estates in inner cities continually express the need for safe areas for children to play.[42,43] Accident rates are higher in this type of housing. Many parents state that they do not allow their children to play outside because of fear of crime, drugs and danger. This could contribute to the acceptance of a sedentary lifestyle as the norm for these children and young people. An improvement in standard of living can therefore by itself influence individual behaviours and choices in housing, employment, social interaction, and daily living behaviours.

Behaviours and the disease process

Most research on ethnicity and health, with few notable exceptions,[24] focused on specific diseases in particular ethnic groups. Issues of health beliefs, culture, attitudes, experiences and expectations were not an integral part of this research. Few or no links were made between health status and situational and behavioural causes. Many of the risk factors that contribute, directly or indirectly, to the disease process are behavioural and preventable.[44-47] Personal and population behaviours in relation to diet, physical activity, smoking and alcohol do not fully account for social variations in health or premature death. It is, however, important to facilitate people's choice to reduce the prevalence of these potentially health damaging behaviours, recognising that personal, social and economic circumstances may affect the ability of some people to choose to change their behaviours.[12]

Smoking

Smoking is the largest single preventable cause of mortality and accounts for more than a third of all deaths in middle age.[45] In the UK at least 90% of lung cancer deaths, three-quarters of deaths from chronic obstructive lung disease and a quarter of coronary heart disease deaths are attributable to smoking.[44] The risks of smoking apply also to those exposed to passive smoking, as shown by increased respiratory tract infection among children of smoking parents, and lung cancer among people who never smoked but were exposed to passive smoking.[48,49] Experimentation with smoking begins in childhood. The HEA's survey among 9–15 year olds showed that 8% of 9 year olds had had at least one puff of a cigarette, which increased to 38% by the age of 13.[34] However, by the age of 19 smoking patterns and behaviour are similar to those found among the adult population: 25% are regular smokers, and the rates among young women are on the increase, although men at present are heavier smokers than women.[33,50]

Information on smoking patterns and prevalence among the minority ethnic groups is patchy and inconsistent. In general, smoking is more prevalent among the men than the women.[46] The HEA survey found that 40% of Bangladeshi men were regular smokers compared with 19% of Indian men; 18% of the African-Caribbean women were regular smokers while smoking among women from south Asia is either very uncommon[24] or hidden. It is interesting that, while the vast majority of smokers in the general population believed that smoking had some effect on their current

heath, those from minority ethnic groups were more likely to claim
no effect or did not know what effect smoking had.[24] Smoking is a
major lifestyle risk factor for coronary heart disease and stroke
which have been reported to affect certain minority groups disproportionately when compared with the general population. However, the low levels of smoking reported in the HEA health and
lifestyle survey are incongruent with these findings, so consideration
should be given to other risk factors (see Chapter 17).

Alcohol

Alcohol consumption is a major cause of premature deaths and
avoidable ill health.[45] To the individual, and the population, alcohol-
related harm includes physical and psychological ill health, road
traffic accidents, home and work accidents, public disorder,
violence and crime, child abuse, family disputes, and employment
problems.[51] In 1994, 30% of men and 14% of women were reported
as consuming alcohol at above the recommended sensible level of
21 units for men and 14 units for women; 8% of men and 4% of
women were classified as 'problem drinkers'.[50] By the age of 15 over
half have consumed alcoholic drink; 9% of the girls and 6% of the
boys exceeded the limits.[34] By the age of 19, the majority (53%) of
young adults classify themselves as regular drinkers.[33] The majority
of those questioned in the HEA survey agreed that young people
do not know enough about the effects of drinking and half of them
believe that alcohol is dangerous only if 'you get addicted'.[33]

Excessive alcohol consumption may be associated with cardiovascular disease and cancer. Although there is disputed evidence
that moderate alcohol intake may reduce the risk of coronary
heart disease, heavy drinking is linked with hypertension and obesity, leading risk factors in coronary heart disease and stroke. Oral
cancer is also associated closely with high consumption of alcohol.
Marmot et al found that high rates of mouth and larynx cancers
were also experienced by individuals from France, Spain and Italy,
who are generally thought to be high consumers of alcohol[52] (see
Chapter 8).

The evidence about alcohol consumption among minority
ethnic groups is mixed.[53] As alcohol use is forbidden by some
religions, most of the information available is not reliable. People
will not reveal information that might stigmatise them. Most
studies show a lower prevalence of alcohol consumption than in
the general population.[54] Studies in Southall, west London, show
high levels of alcohol-related morbidity among Asians from the

Punjab region.[55] Other research shows that drinking amongst first generation Indian Muslims and Sikhs is higher than in second and third generation adults. This was not the case for white people and African-Caribbeans.[56] These conflicting results demonstrate the importance of understanding different communities.

Diet

A balanced diet has a key role in children's growth and the maintenance of normal physiological functions. Its role in the aetiology of disease is well documented,[57] particularly for cardiovascular diseases and cancers where about 30% of risk is attributed to diet. Unbalanced diets may lead to malnutrition, overnutrition or deficiency diseases. The link between unbalanced and incorrect diet and constipation, obesity and dental caries has been proved. The role of diet in the aetiology of chronic disease such as diabetes, inflammatory bowel disease, intestinal ulcers, arthritis and dementia is the subject of much research. High blood pressure, raised serum cholesterol and diabetes, as the main risk factors (in addition to smoking) for coronary heart disease, are affected by dietary intake. Hypertension, a leading risk factor for stroke, is associated with alcohol intake, obesity, high dietary sodium and low intake of potassium and other minerals.

The high incidence of coronary heart disease among south Asians has been attributed to dietary habits and diabetes,[58–62] and the prevalence of hypertension, obesity and diabetes, which are associated with stroke, are much higher among African-Caribbeans than whites.[62]

Many dietary patterns for minority groups will have changed owing to immigration and the availability of traditional foods. Fat has been added to the Bangladeshi's diet in Britain through the consumption of full-fat milk used to make popular desserts such as rice puddings or mango milk. Another change in the Bangladeshi diet is the availability of relatively cheap cooking oil which, because of its affordability, is used in large quantities. Also, lamb is more often used in Britain and has a higher fat content. Other factors causing changes in the dietary patterns of minority groups include the adoption of Westernised convenience foods, particularly among children, such as chips, burgers, fizzy drinks, cakes and other foods high in fat and sugar.

For African-Caribbeans, rice consumption is very high and will often be mixed with pulses. Staple foods such as yam, plantain and green bananas are high in starch, vitamins, fibre and mineral content. Meat and meat products are consumed moderately and often in 'one pot' meals such as stews or soups. Economic factors may mean that cheaper cuts of meat may well be consumed and have a higher fat content. The use of cheaper saturated vegetable oils in browning meat before cooking or frying foods like fried dumplings is one area for targeting health promotion messages. The availability of traditional foods and their high cost has meant the alteration of cooking methods and content of many African-Caribbean diets. Again, the adoption of a more Westernised diet will have increased the consumption of foods high in fat.

Exercise

Physical activity is part of everyday life. It can take many forms, such as activity at home (housework, gardening, DIY), at work, walking, cycling or leisure exercise and competitive sports. Exercise is associated with the prevention of coronary heart disease, osteoporosis and obesity.[63] The 1994 health survey for England found that 18% of men and women are inactive, with no activity at a moderate or vigorous level.[50] Level of activity declined with age, particularly after the age of 55.

Data on physical activity among minority ethnic groups is scanty. Nevertheless, surveys among south Asian men found lower levels of leisure physical activities than in European men.[64] However, anecdotal evidence suggests that vigorous and regular exercise as a leisure pursuit is on the increase among middle-class minority ethnic groups.

Healthy choices

Health is the accumulative product of the personal, social and economic circumstances in which people live. Communities take the responsibility to protect the health of individuals and the public through various public health and community protection measures. Individuals enhance and maintain good health through the adoption of healthy choices, seeking early medical attention and treatment for illness, and thereby maximising their health potential. Generally speaking, people want health with minimum worry or effort. The majority of people do not want to worry about the food they eat, the drink they consume, the air they breathe, the place where they live, or the behaviours of others that might impinge on them directly and indirectly. Changing lifestyle is a slow process. However, many small changes in lifestyle are practicable and affordable, and may yield high benefits in good health.[65]

Healthy choices are about moderation in behaviour. The human body and mind are not designed to meet the rapid changes in modern living. They need to function and be maintained properly as long as possible, through attention to nutrient requirements, muscular activities, rest, socialisation etc. Responding to natural instincts may not be enough to provide and maintain healthy choices. Information about how to maintain the body and allow the mind to function effectively is essential in a world that is changing rapidly and with ever emerging chemical, biological, physical and technical hazards and risk factors. Such information should be factual, simple and easy to perceive and implement. The authorities and local communities also have a role in promoting and protecting health in areas such as road safety, leisure facilities, physical activity facilities, healthy schools and work places, safe and comfortable houses, social support, and the restriction and/or prohibition of hazards and risk factors (eg restriction of smoking in public places, and prohibition of cigarette advertisements). Improvement in the living standards of people is one of the main influences on the adoption of a healthy lifestyle. Everybody should have the opportunity to attain his or her full potential for health.[12]

Assessing the population's lifestyles

There are many approaches and methods to assess the population's lifestyles. This chapter focuses on two methods: local lifestyle surveys and participatory appraisal. The latter is a method widely used in developing countries.

Local lifestyle surveys

Despite many national surveys on health and lifestyle,[50] some specifically for minority ethnic groups,[24] local surveys are still essential to address local issues and to deliver sensitive and acceptable initiatives and interventions. Local surveys should be designed and conducted in consultation and with input from local communities, to ensure better response and acceptance of the findings.[66] Behaviours and attitudes at population level are dynamic, being in a state of flux and changing over time. Such surveys therefore have to be repeated on a regular cycle of at least three to five years to allow comparative measures in the locality, and to monitor changes, which might influence health.

Designing lifestyle surveys

In order to obtain valid and reliable data, it is essential to get the appropriate design for a local lifestyle survey correct from the start. The same design and methods should be repeatable, with some modification if necessary, to ensure comparability data in drawing any conclusion from trends over many years. Although survey design is beyond the scope of this book, nevertheless it would be of some use to consider in broad terms the points that need to be considered in undertaking such surveys. The aim and the objectives of the survey should be clear and specific. For example, the survey could be comprehensive covering all aspects of lifestyles, or limited to one specific area such as coronary heart disease[50] or sexual health.[67] A survey plan (or protocol) should be developed, addressing the issues of design, methods, consultation, pilot, sample, fieldwork, collection and analysis of data, validation of information, human resources and costs, time scale, and dissemination. It is essential at this stage to consider logistics and the cost of translating questionnaires and other information materials into the languages in common use in the local community, or the use of interpreters for interviewing (Table 1).

Table 1. Designing lifestyle surveys[66]

Objective
Planning (include consultations)
Questionnaire design (include translation)
Self completion
Interview
Examination
Pilot
Sampling
Fieldwork
Return
Pre-checking
Coding ⎫
Data entry ⎭ or bar-code scanning
Editing/data-cleaning
Analysis
Response rate
Report findings
Validation
Dissemination

Methods of conducting lifestyle surveys

In surveying behavioural variables at the population level the methods used are always based on the assumption that: the population is known and well circumscribed; the data are randomly collected; any possible error arising in the process of data collection can be controlled or assessed; and data represent stable and meaningful constructs.[68] Many approaches could be used to assess the lifestyle of any given population or group. The two common approaches are the cross-section and the life-course. The *cross-section approach* is to collect information from individuals, usually a sample, about their history, habits, knowledge, attitudes or behaviour at a single time.[69,70] Methods of conducting such surveys include face-to-face interview, self-completion questionnaire, or telephone interview. Some of these interviews may involve examination of the individual, for example taking blood pressure, serum cholesterol, physical measurement etc. Comparisons could be made between the various components of the sample, for example compare the young with the old, male with female, white with black, Asians with African-Caribbeans and so on. The *life-course approach* traces the lives of members of a single cohort in order to examine changes in lifestyle, knowledge, attitudes and health.[70] Methods may include interviews, self-completion questionnaires, examinations and measurements. The principles of sampling, the effect of non-response, bias, and accuracy of collection and analysis of the data should be adhered to. The individual as the sampling unit (or unit of investigation) should be the unit of analysis.[71] Questions and methods of conducting interviews should be sensitive to the personal and cultural circumstances of both individuals and communities.

Producing questionnaires in the appropriate language is important, as is supplying bilingual interviewers for people who read no languages. Translation of questions is relevant, as many words and phrases do not translate directly or with any meaning into another language. Careful construction and pre-testing of materials and schedules can alleviate many of these problems. In certain circumstances some sensitive issues may be avoided. For example, the HEA survey found that questions on sexual health were not acceptable to many first generation people from south Asian communities.[24]

Participatory appraisal

Participatory appraisal is a method of needs assessment that has been widely used in developing countries. It is also known as participatory rural/urban/rapid appraisal. The method is now widely recognised as a very effective and meaningful way of understanding communities' perceptions of their needs in developed countries and taking joint action based on these needs. Ong *et al*[72] defined rapid appraisal as:

> a method to understand communities' own perceptions of their priority needs. It can be used as a tool for formulating joint action plans between communities and service planners and managers. It can also be used to complement quantitative methods of assessing needs by more in-depth qualitative understanding of socio-cultural perspectives.

Objectives for participatory appraisal are varied but tend to focus on work with deprived or disadvantaged communities.[72–74]

Methods of participatory appraisal

Appraisal tries to involve local people in the process of data collection, surveying, interviewing and observation. Methodologies vary, starting with a review of available secondary data, participant observation and informal interview. Individual interviews include key informants and interest groups. Questionnaire may also be used as well as leaflet mailing which may reveal other contacts. Developing contacts within a community often results in snowball sampling.

Linking and hopefully matching some of the secondary data with information gained from informal interviewing will give a sense of the dynamics of the local community. Focus groups can then be established to take issues raised through the initial interviewing to look at opportunities for and barriers to change, based on people's expression of needs.

Participatory appraisal is very flexible and different methods can be used at any stage, for example: mapping (people draw maps of their community/estate); transecting (people walk through the area discussing with the researcher what they like and dislike); time lines (people record significant events in the history of their community over 5- or 10-year periods, and what has improved or got worse, using diagrams, spider diagrams, Venn diagrams, pie charts, matrix ranking, and social and health ranking).

There are many other methods at the disposal of a participatory appraisal researcher; they have all been devised to elicit information in a non-threatening and non-intimidating way, giving rise to rich qualitative data.

Dissemination and implementation of findings

Resulting information is fed back to the communities and local statutory and voluntary workers via workshops, reports, discussions and meetings. Workshops can also verify and discuss findings and agree action plans.

The feeding of needs assessment data into national and local policy-making bodies, for targeted planning, priority setting, and service changes and development, is an essential part of the process. Findings from research to date demonstrate the importance of socioeconomic determinants of health for some people from minority ethnic groups. With the exception of the HEA survey,[24] which is limited in scope, little research has been conducted to assess lifestyles of minority ethnic groups that lead to better health. Comparative data on all ethnic groups will be of great use to policy development that could lead to benefits for all communities.

Conclusion

Literature review to date reveals the scarcity of research on the lifestyles of minority ethnic groups. It highlights the requirement for both national and local needs assessments to identify current needs and monitor changes in lifestyle behaviours that might influence the health and well-being of these communities. The effect of socioeconomic determinants on the health of people from minority ethnic groups has a very powerful impact role for many, and is disproportionate to the effect on the white population.

References

1   Jacobson B, Smith A, Whitehead M, eds. *The nation's health: a strategy for the 1990s*. London: King's Fund, 1991.

2   Nutbeam D. Health promotion glossary. *Health Promotion* 1986; **1**: 113–27.

3   World Health Organisation. *Ottawa charter for health promotion*. Copenhagen: WHO Regional Office for Europe, 1986.

4   Tones K, Tilford S. *Health education: effectiveness, efficiency and equity*, 2nd edn. London: Chapman and Hall, 1994.

5   Helman CG. *Culture, health and illness*, 3rd edn. Oxford: Butterworth-Heinemann, 1994.

6   Kessing RM. *Cultural anthropology*. New York: Holt, Rinehart and Winston, 1981.

7   Sensky T. Eliciting lay beliefs across cultures: principles and methodology. *British Journal of Cancer* 1996; **74** (Suppl XXIX): S63–5.

8   Spradley JP. *The ethnographic interview*. New York: Rinehart and Winston, 1979.

9   Alasuutari P. *Researching culture: qualitative methods and cultural studies*. London: SAGE, 1995.

10 Whitehead M. *The health divide: inequalities in health in the 1980s.* London: Health Education Council, 1987.

11 Black D. *Inequalities in health.* Report of a research group chaired by Sir Douglas Black. London: Department of Health and Social Security, 1980.

12 Department of Health. *Variation in health: what can the Department of Health and the NHS do?* Report by the variation subgroup of the Chief Medical Officer's Health of the Nation working group. London: Department of Health, 1995.

13 British Medical Association. *Inequalities in health.* Report by the Board of Science and Education. Occasional paper. London: BMA, 1995.

14 Jarman B. Identification of underprivileged areas. *British Medical Journal* 1983; **286**: 1705–9.

15 World Health Organisation. *Public health aspects of housing.* Report of the Expert Committee. Technical report series No. 225. Geneva: WHO, 1961.

16 Ransom RP. *Healthy housing: a practical guide.* Copenhagen: WHO Regional Office for Europe, 1991.

17 Lowry S. *Housing and health.* London: British Medical Journal, 1991.

18 Lowry S. Housing. In: Smith R, ed. *The health of the nation: the British Medical Journal view.* London: BMJ, 1991.

19 Chief Medical Officer. *On the state of the public health 1990.* London: HMSO, 1991.

20 Smith R. *Unemployment and health: a disaster and a challenge.* Oxford: Oxford University Press, 1987.

21 Bartley M. Unemployment and ill-health: understanding the relationship. *Journal of Epidemiology and Community Health* 1994; **48**: 333–7.

22 Benzeval M, Judge K, Whitehead M. *Tackling inequalities in health: an agenda for action.* London: King's Fund, 1995.

23 Oppenheim C. *Poverty: the facts.* London: Child Poverty Action Group, 1990.

24 Rudat K. *Health and lifestyles: black and minority ethnic groups in England.* London: Health Education Authority, 1994.

25 Ogunsola A. *Roots and branches.* Papers for the Open University/Health Education Authority 1990 winter school on community development and health. Buckingham: Open University Press, 1991.

26 National Health Service Management Executive. *Ethnic minority staff in the NHS: a programme of action.* Leeds: NHSE, 1993.

27 Cox J, Bostock S, eds. *Racial discrimination in the health service.* Staffs: Penrhos, 1989.

28 Esmail A, Carnall D. Tackling racism in the NHS: we need action not words. *British Medical Journal* 1997; **314**: 618–9.

29 Fenton S. Racism is harmful to your health. In: Cox J, Bostock S, eds. *Racial discrimination in the health service.* Staffs: Penrhos, 1989.

30 Rawaf S. *For better health: 1992 annual report of the director of public health.* London: Merton and Sutton Health Authority, 1993.

31 Berkman LF. Assessing the physical health effects of social networks and social support. *Annual Reviews of Public Health* 1984; **613**: 413–32.

32 Smaje C. *Health, race and ethnicity.* London: King's Fund Institute, 1995.
33 Rudat K, Ryan H, Speed M. *Today's young adult.* London: Health Education Authority, 1992.
34 Rudat K, Speed M, Ryan H. *Tomorrow's young adults.* London: Health Education Authority, 1992.
35 Williams ES. *Lifestyle of 16–19 year old teenagers in Croydon: results of a survey in 1994.* Croydon: Croydon Health Authority, 1996.
36 Griffin G, ed. *Health information and the consumer.* London: Office of Health Economics, 1995.
37 Griffin JR. *Health information and the consumer.* Briefing paper No. 30. London: Office of Health Economics, 1994.
38 Russell MAH, Wilson C, Taylor C, Baker CD. Effects of general practitioners' advice against smoking. *British Medical Journal* 1979; **ii**: 231–5.
39 Toon P. Inverse care in the inner city: the targeting of GP health promotion resources. In: Griffin J, ed. *Health information and the consumer.* London: Office of Health Economics, 1995.
40 Musick B, Miller M, Nichols C, *et al.* Knowledge and beliefs about cancer in a socio-economically disadvantaged population. *Cancer* 1991; **68**: 1665–7.
41 Kogevines M, Marmot MG, Fox AJ, Goldblatt PO. Socioeconomic differences in cancer survival. *Journal of Epidemiology and Community Health* 1991; **45**: 216–9.
42 Best R. The housing dimension. In: Benzeval M, Judge K, Whitehead M, eds. *Tackling inequalities in health: an agenda for action.* London: King's Fund, 1995.
43 Page D. *Building for communities: a study for new housing association estates.* York: Joseph Rowntree Foundation, 1993.
44 Royal College of Physicians. *Preventive medicine: a report of a working party.* London: RCP Publications, 1991.
45 Secretary of State for Health. *Our healthier nation.* London: Stationery Office, 1998.
46 Department of Health Central Health Monitoring Unit. *Health related behaviour: an epidemiological overview.* London: HMSO, 1996.
47 James W, Kim G, Moore D. Examining racial and ethnic differences in Asian adolescent drug use: the contributions of culture, background and lifestyle. *Drugs: Education, Prevention and Policy* 1997;**4**: 39–51.
48 Colley JRT. Respiratory symptoms in children and parental smoking and phlegm production. *British Medical Journal* 1974; **ii**: 201–4.
49 Wald NJ, Nanchatal K, Cuckle H. Does breathing other people's smoke cause lung cancer? *British Medical Journal* 1986; **293**: 1217–22.
50 Colhoun H, Prescot-Clarke P. *Health survey in England 1994.* London: HMSO, 1996.
51 Faculty of Public Health Medicine. *Alcohol and the public health.* Basingstoke: Macmillan, 1991.
52 Marmot MG, Adelstein AM, Bulusu L. Lessons from the study of immigrant mortality. *Lancet* 1984; **i**: 580–3.
53 Balarajan R, Raleigh VS. *Ethnicity and health: a guide for the NHS.* London: Department of Health, 1993.

54 McKeigue PM, Karmi G. Alcohol consumption and alcohol-related problems in Afro-Caribbeans and South Asians in the United Kingdom. *Alcohol and Alcoholism* 1993; **28**: 1–10.

55 Clarke M, Ahmed N, Romaniuk H, *et al.* Ethnic difference in the consequences of alcohol misuse. *Alcohol and Alcoholism* 1990; **25**: 9–11.

56 Cochrane R, Bal S. The drinking habits of Sikh, Hindu, Muslim and white men in West Midlands: a community survey. *British Journal of Addiction* 1990; **85**: 759–69.

57 Bingham S. Dietary aspects of a health strategy for England. In: Smith R, ed. *The health of the nation: the BMJ view.* London: British Medical Journal, 1991.

58 Balarajan R. Ethnic difference in mortality from ischaemic heart disease and cerebrovascular disease in England and Wales. *British Medical Journal* 1991; **302**: 560–4.

59 McKeigue PM, Marmot MG. Mortality from coronary heart disease in Asian communities in London. *British Medical Journal* 1988; **297**: 390–6.

60 Cruickshank JK. Heart disease in Asians in Britain. *British Medical Journal* 1988; **297**: 683–4.

61 Cappuccio FP. Ethnicity and cardiovascular risk: the variations in people of African ancestry and south Asian origin. *Journal of Hypertension* 1997; **11**: 571–6.

62 Cruickshank JK, Beevers DG, Osbourne VL, *et al.* Heart attack, stroke, diabetes and hypertension in West Indians, Asians and whites in Birmingham. *British Medical Journal* 1980; **281**: 1108.

63 Dargie HJ, Grant S. The role of exercise. In: Smith R, ed. *The health of the nation: the BMJ view.* London: British Medical Journal, 1991.

64 McKeigue PM, Pierepoint T, Ferrie JE, Marmot MG. Relationship of glucose intolerance and hyperinsulinaemia to body fat pattern in South Asians and Europeans. *Diabetologica* 1992; **35**: 785–91.

65 Lockie A. *The family guide to homeopathy.* Harmondsworth: Hamish Hamilton, 1990.

66 Martin J, Rawaf S. *Health and lifestyle in Merton and Sutton.* London: Merton and Sutton Health Authority, 1994.

67 Johnson AM, Wadsworth J, Wellings K, Field J. *Sexual attitudes and lifestyles.* Oxford: Blackwell, 1994.

68 McQueen DV. A methodological approach for assessing stability of variables used in population research on health. In: Dean K, ed. *Population health research: linking theory and methods.* London: SAGE, 1993.

69 Alderson M. *An introduction to epidemiology,* 2nd edn. London: Macmillan Press, 1983.

70 Riley MW. A theoretical basis for research on health. In: Dean K, ed. *Population health research.* London: SAGE, 1993.

71 Altman DG, Bland MJ. Units of analysis. *British Medical Journal* 1997; **314**: 1874.

72 Ong BN, Humphris G, Annett H, *et al.* Rapid appraisal in an urban setting: an example from the developed world. *Social Science and Medicine* 1991; **32**: 909–15.

73 Murray SA, Topson J, Turnbull L, *et al.* Listening to local voices:

adapting rapid appraisal to assess health and social needs in general practice. *British Medical Journal* 1994; **308**: 698–700.

74   Dale J, Shipman C, Lacock L, *et al.* Creating a shared vision of out of hour care: using rapid appraisal methods to create an interagency, community oriented approach to service development. *British Medical Journal* 1996; **312**: 1206–10.

7 | Health promotion – the Sandwell experience

Jenny Douglas
*Lecturer in Health Education and Health Promotion,
School of Education, University of Birmingham*

This chapter will use the World Health Organisation's definition of health promotion as 'the process of enabling people to increase control over and improve their health'.[1] This approach to health promotion aims to reduce inequalities in health by focusing on the structural determinants of health, and emphasises community action to address social and economic inequalities as well as individual action to change lifestyle and behaviour.

The Ottawa Charter has identified five priority areas for action: building healthy public policies, creating supportive environments, strengthening community action, developing personal skills and reorienting health services.[2] Appropriate health promotion programmes, therefore, must be based upon sound information regarding health and lifestyle, socioeconomic and demographic information, cultural and ethnic context. Needs assessment strategies must be developed to take account of these issues by identifying and documenting health experiences and perceptions.

The aim is to examine methods of assessing the health promotion needs of minority ethnic communities in the UK and to identify appropriate health promotion programmes to address these needs. A range of quantitative and qualitative methodologies used to assess health promotion needs in Sandwell will be presented, and there will be an examination of methods of evaluating health promotion programmes in relation to both process and outcomes.

It must be recognised that the minority ethnic communities in the UK are diverse, and particular religious and cultural groups may be further defined in relation to social class and geographical location. Therefore, in promoting their health it is important to acknowledge the range of diversity and difference, and to develop methods and strategies that are able to target and focus on the needs of specific groups and communities.[3,4]

While recognising the differences and diversity among this section of the population, there are common areas of experience. Coronary heart disease, for example, affects Asian communities more than white majority communities, and cerebrovascular disease and strokes are more common in African and African-Caribbean communities (see Chapter 17). The higher mortality rates for coronary heart disease and stroke for people from Asian and African-Caribbean communities are health inequalities that health promotion programmes must address. It is necessary to have a clear understanding of what the inequalities are and how they arise. More specific analysis by ethnic group is needed on the patterns of morbidity and mortality of minority ethnic groups so that further knowledge can be gained on the social, economic and structural factors that affect lifestyles and health.

Common patterns of illness in minority ethnic communities have been documented,[5] particularly in relation to the key areas identified by the government Health of the Nation strategy: coronary heart disease and stroke, cancers, mental illness, HIV/AIDS and sexual health, and accidents.[6] The Health of the Nation strategy places emphasis on developing healthy alliances, but fails to recognise structural and economic factors affecting health and, in particular, the effects of racism and discrimination on the health of minority ethnic groups.[7,8]

In addition to prevailing patterns of mortality and morbidity, individual lifestyles play an important role (see Chapter 6). Religious and cultural norms may to some extent dictate lifestyles, but care must be taken not to assume that all individuals within a religious or cultural group are guided by the same proscriptive or prescriptive practices. Furthermore, lifestyles and cultures are constantly subjected to a wide range of influences and are thus never static.

Whilst culture and individual lifestyle may play an important role in shaping health behaviour, social class and income differences are by far the greatest influence on health status,[9-11] and poverty has a major impact.[9-13] A disproportionate number of individuals from minority ethnic groups in the UK are in the lower socioeconomic groups. This is compounded by experiences of racism and discrimination in employment, housing, health and social care.[14] Aspects of the health experience of minority ethnic communities in the UK are worse than for their white counterparts. For minority ethnic women, gender itself affects health experience and may be a compounding factor in relation to morbidity and mortality.

Thus any framework for assessing and meeting the health needs

of minority ethnic communities must address the complex interplay of environmental, social, cultural, economic, religious and
genetic factors that affect health and health behaviour in this
section of the population. This chapter will give a general account
of the health education programmes that have been developed
over the past decade to address the health needs of minority
ethnic communities, and the specific approaches that have been
undertaken in Sandwell.

Historical perspectives

Early attempts at developing health education programmes for
minority ethnic communities were focused more on concerns
identified by health professionals, with little or no consultation
with the communities themselves. Based on a mainly educative
model, health education materials addressing family planning, respiratory diseases and hygiene were developed and translated into
many languages in the hope that this would result in behaviour
changes. As reflected in the Department of Health's national campaigns, the emphasis later was on dietary advice and antenatal care
with the implementation of the rickets campaign and the Asian
mother and baby campaign in the 1980s.[15,16] More recently it has
become clear that health promotion should be focused on assist-
ing individuals and communities to identify their own health needs
(ie the self-empowerment model).[17,18] Early health education campaigns, which merely reproduced leaflets aimed at white communities in a number of community languages, proved to be ineffective. Often the material was either not targeted at specific health
needs of this section of the population, and was culturally inappropriate, or presented negative images and stereotypes of minority
ethnic communities. Little evaluation was undertaken to ascertain
the effectiveness of early interventions. Such campaigns, with the
exception of a few such as the Asian mother and baby campaign,
were not based on systematic methods of identifying health promotion needs but on the perceptions of health workers. Consequently these initiatives had the effect of blaming individuals or
their cultures for poor health, and did not address social and economic factors. In an analysis of early health education literature
targeted on minority ethnic groups, Bhopal found an emphasis on
birth control, pregnancy and child care, with a dearth of information on chronic diseases such as coronary heart disease and stroke
or on alcohol consumption and smoking.[19] Local campaigns targeting minority ethnic communities were also often carried out in

isolation from the wider health promotion initiatives. Therefore, there was little planned health promotion in minority ethnic communities in areas such as coronary heart disease, cancer, women's health, sexual health and mental health.

Mass media campaigns on HIV/AIDS focused all their attention on white communities with respect to prevention, education and control. Many minority ethnic communities felt that they were not prone to the disease. However, when origins of the disease were discussed or where 'blame' was apportioned, African and black people were targeted.[20,21]

Developing a framework

An ideal model for examining and developing health promotion programmes for black and minority ethnic communities places emphasis on:[2]

- reducing inequalities in health and ensuring equity in health;
- increasing community participation;
- encouraging intersectoral/multisectoral collaboration;
- health promotion and primary health care;
- developing international cooperation;
- promoting a healthy environment.

Any approach to developing health promotion programmes with minority ethnic communities must place emphasis on recognising economic, environmental and political factors which influence health, directly and indirectly.

This model[2] also provides a framework for research[22] to support 'health for all' strategies which place emphasis on the interaction between researchers and policy makers, and outlines that research strategies should:

- describe every aspect of the health of the population so that progress towards targets can be monitored;
- find out what biological factors determine health;
- assess the part that lifestyles play in maintaining or endangering health;
- study the ways in which the physical, biological and social environment determine the health of individuals and populations;
- develop effective and efficient methods of providing people with appropriate care;
- improve policy making, planning and management in programmes for health for all.

Assessing health promotion needs

All individuals in society from all backgrounds need some element of health promotion, to maintain and improve their status of good health, avoid or reduce exposure to risk factors that lead to disease or ill health, recover from an episode of ill health and restore normal functions, or reduce the impact of chronic disease and maximise the quality of life. Therefore, all health promotion programmes should be planned and underpinned by assessing the health needs of the different segments of the population in order to identify the type and nature of interventions that should be developed. The aims and objectives of each of the intervention programmes should be clearly outlined, and the methods and approaches to assess and evaluate the effect of the health promotion activities should be designed at the same stage as the development of the intervention. A range of quantitative and qualitative approaches can be used to assess health status and provide baseline information on populations and communities.

Quantitative data

Quantitative information is required to provide data on prevalence and patterns of illness and conditions in minority ethnic communities, as well as in the rest of the population. Information can be drawn from national and regional routine sources of data, epidemiological information, and specific health and lifestyle surveys. The drawback in relation to minority ethnic communities is that, until fairly recently, such information was based upon country of birth and thus did not provide precise information on the ethnicity of the population. Despite the debate in the health and 'race' literature about whether ethnic groups are adequately defined,[23] the census now provides some data on ethnicity which are available to determine socioeconomic and demographic information on minority ethnic communities in each health district. There is less information regarding mortality and morbidity in minority ethnic communities but this is becoming increasingly available with the requirement for ethnic monitoring of hospital inpatients,[24] a requirement that may be extended to primary care and community health services. This information is essential in identifying the health status of minority ethnic populations, determining their specific health needs and identifying risk factors that may lead to or predispose to a disease process, and providing information required to assess who is healthy and how to maintain and improve further levels of good health. National health and lifestyle surveys have been based upon predominantly white populations[25,26] and there are very few national data on the health and lifestyles of minority ethnic communities apart from a recently published survey by the Health Education Authority.[27]

Qualitative data

Qualitative information on the experiences of health service users, and perceptions of health, is also important and requires the development of a range of methodologies involving open-ended interviews, discussion groups and focus groups, observation and diary keeping[28,29] (see Chapter 3). Some local health and lifestyle surveys have provided information on lifestyle, morbidity and perceptions of health and illness in various minority ethnic communities,[30-32] but there is still only limited information on the experiences of minority ethnic service users outside services like maternity or mental health.

Evaluating effectiveness

Finally, where health promotion programmes for minority ethnic communities have been developed, there are very few published studies evaluating the effectiveness of the interventions and providing examples for other health promoters wishing to develop similar interventions. Often, members of the minority ethnic groups have not been involved in evaluating the interventions. It is essential that they be involved at all stages of needs assessment and evaluation of health promotion programmes, to enable them to identify areas of concern for themselves and be involved in designing appropriate health promotion programmes and evaluating their effectiveness.

Increasing information on innovative programmes and examples of good practice has been drawn together in a database by the ethnic health unit, SHARE of the King's Fund and the Health Education Authority. A valuable information sources guide on 'race' and health has also been compiled by SHARE (Services in Health and Race Exchange).[33]

Assessing health promotion needs: the Sandwell experience

This section will report on a number of initiatives focusing on minority ethnic communities which have been developed by Sandwell Health Authority to assess the baseline information on the health needs of these communities: to produce community-based information on resources for health, to develop the appropriate health promotion programmes and to evaluate the programmes developed.

In 1990 the health authority and the local borough council adopted the 'health for all' charter *Healthy Sandwell 2000,* placing emphasis on reducing inequalities in health. The health authority adopted a strategy for better health for minority ethnic communities in 1991. The strategy, which outlines an action plan and a number of recommendations on health promotion to be undertaken by the health authority and the Family Health Services Authority, is reviewed annually.

Developing an organisational infrastructure

Any health promotion strategy aimed at promoting the health of minority ethnic communities must be part of a wider organisational strategy committed to equal opportunities and making available equal access to health and social care. One of the failures of some health promotion programmes aimed at improving and promoting the health of minority ethnic communities is that they have been organised on an *ad hoc* basis without any organisational support and have been limited purely to information giving.

Local consultation

In Sandwell, during the development and production of both the Healthy Sandwell charter and the strategy for better health for minority ethnic communities, there was wide consultation with a range of statutory and voluntary organisations in the area. Such consultation was carried out through participation in the working party, meetings with various community groups, comments on the draft charter and strategy, and seeking the views of community leaders. Baseline information on services provided to this section of the population was collated to assess progress towards agreed targets.

Community participation

Using different approaches, the involvement of local groups and organisations from minority ethnic communities was developed over a period. Methods included open consultation meetings, meetings and discussions with key individuals and groups, and visits to organisations and groups. The responses to these approaches were excellent. As a result of this, the health promotion unit now has direct contact with a range of organisations in the black voluntary and community sectors, and collaborates with many of them on joint projects.

Smethwick Heart Action Research Project

The impetus for this project arose out of concern for the increased incidence of coronary heart disease and stroke in Asian and African-Caribbean communities respectively. There was little information about the reasons for this in relation to the risk factors which had been identified for mainly white populations. In researching and producing a display on coronary heart disease and stroke in minority ethnic communities, it became clear that further information was needed on lifestyle factors such as smoking, diet, exercise and alcohol intake, and other factors such as stress, socioeconomic and work conditions. The Smethwick Heart Action Research Project, funded by the Health Education Authority as one of eight demonstration projects nationally, was a local demonstration project for Healthy Sandwell 2000. It was a collaborative project between the Health Education Authority, Sandwell health authority and the Family Health Services Authority, the local authority and local minority ethnic community, businesses and religious groups.[34]

The project aimed to identify risk factors for coronary heart disease and stroke for all ethnic groups in Smethwick and then to implement and evaluate strategies to reduce cardiovascular disease through working with local people, practitioners and organisations. The key objectives were to:[35]

- provide baseline data on the lifestyles and behaviour of a sample of the population in Smethwick and examine minority ethnic communities specifically;
- identify key risk factors for minority ethnic communities in Smethwick for coronary heart disease and stroke;
- determine appropriate mechanisms of working with local communities to reduce coronary heart disease;
- disseminate the findings of the project.

This survey was largely quantitative, although qualitative information was collected both through face-to-face interviews and through discussion groups and focus groups held initially to involve minority ethnic communities in shaping the research design. In the initial research, 300 face-to-face interviews were

conducted using a structured questionnaire implemented by interviewers who were matched for ethnicity and language. Individuals
from each of the main communities in Smethwick (African-
Caribbean, Bangladeshi, Indian, Pakistani and white) were selected using a quota sampling method and recruiting interviewees
from community centres and door-to-door recruitment through
street sampling. This method enabled the collection of authentic
information to assess health promotion needs in Smethwick.[36] A
community health profile for Smethwick was also developed.[37]

Developing health promotion programmes

Preliminary analysis of the data identified a number of areas for
development:

- Training of local community workers/lay people to develop
  health promotion projects
- Information on healthy eating with Asian and African-
  Caribbean foods and work with local shopkeepers
- Screening to identify hypertension in African-Caribbean
  communities in conjunction with local black voluntary
  organisations and black churches
- An exercise project with local Asian communities and borough
  leisure services

Health promotion programmes were developed in conjunction
with local people, existing structures in localities, local workers,
voluntary organisations and community groups, and built upon
existing networks.[38] This was important in ensuring that health
promotion initiatives developed were sustainable.

Identifying health promotion information needs

A number of health promotion initiatives developed in Sandwell
were aimed at producing appropriate information for minority
ethnic communities. The development of health promotion information resources for minority ethnic communities and multilingual information has often been based on merely translating information produced for white, English-speaking audiences. This
approach has been confounded by problems often related to poor
translations and the difficulty of undertaking literal translations
where the concepts do not exist in other languages. The approach
in Sandwell has been to start off by identifying information needs
in the first language of the community group and producing

information that is relevant and appropriate. The methodology employed has been to set up focus groups with bilingual facilitators. Information thus collated is used by graphic designers and copywriters working with translators to produce draft materials which are then evaluated by focus groups to ensure that the level, content and information are correct. A number of multilingual leaflets and displays have been developed using this approach: *Healthy hearts* (a display on coronary heart disease); *Women feeling good* (a display on women's health); *Me a parent* (a display on healthy parenting); and *Mental health services and you*. The minority ethnic communities themselves are involved at all stages, from assessing health promotion information needs through to the development and production of materials. Those who are unable to read their own language are helped through the use of diagrams.

Conclusion

This report on some of the Sandwell health promotion unit's programmes to assess the needs of minority ethnic communities is only part of a planned programme of action; health needs assessment has been developed in the areas of women's health, healthy parenting, sexual health and mental health.

Assessing the health promotion needs of the various minority ethnic communities requires a range of methodologies and developing alliances across a wide spectrum of organisations from community and voluntary organisations to academic institutions and commercial design and market research organisations. Existing epidemiological information from national and local sources can be supplemented by small area statistics available from local authority planning departments and statistics collated for other specific programmes. Local studies and reports are also often available from urban programme and community development initiatives within local authorities and health agencies. Local health surveys should employ a range of methodologies to ensure that quantitative and qualitative information is gathered, and minority ethnic communities should be involved throughout the needs assessment process.[39,40]

A number of key areas have been identified as essential in the development of appropriate strategies to meet the health promotion needs of minority ethnic communities:

* Involving local communities in health promotion needs assessment at the outset
* Local consultation on planned health promotion programmes

- Working with a wide range of health workers/community workers/local voluntary organisations/local traders and other local workers
- Developing and supporting local networks so that health promotion programmes and initiatives developed can be sustained
- Development of appropriate training and support to enable health promotion programmes to be sustainable
- Evaluation of each stage of developing health promotion programmes involving local people and communities
- Development of appropriate multilingual, multicultural and multiracial materials in conjunction with local people, based on their information needs, that promote positive well-being using positive images of minority ethnic communities
- Working with a range of other professionals: graphic designers and academic institutions
- Providing a forum for communication between local people, health workers and researchers and health policy makers in identifying strategies and mechanisms for health promotion needs assessment, health promotion programme development and health promotion policy development
- Undertaking action research to identify the appropriate health promotion needs[41]

Key priorities and recommendations for action

Local

- More qualitative and quantitative information on the health status, perceptions of health and health experiences of individuals from minority ethnic communities is needed, and health promotion services should ensure that information from the census and local minority ethnic organisations is collated.[42]
- Clear guidelines for organisations purchasing health promotion and appropriate mechanisms for monitoring and evaluating health promotion specifications in contracts are required.
- Clear specifications in contracts for providers on health promotion issues for minority ethnic communities should be developed.
- Local policies for health of minority ethnic communities must underpin health promotion programmes and strategies.

National

- The Department of Health and the Health Education Authority

(HEA) should give more strategic guidance on developing health promotion programmes with minority ethnic communities.

- There should be centrally held information on current health promotion programmes/projects/materials with minority ethnic communities. This has been initiated with the HEA/SHARE/Ethnic Health Unit database.
- There should be a national database of information on the links between 'race', class, deprivation and gender, as well as culture and genetics on health.

References

1　World Health Organisation. *Health discussion document on the concept and principles.* Copenhagen: WHO, 1984.

2　World Health Organisation. *Health for all targets.* Copenhagen: WHO, 1991.

3　Douglas J. Developing anti-racist health promotion strategies. In: Bunton R, Nettleton S, Burrows R, eds. *The sociology of health promotion.* London: Routledge, 1995.

4　Lethbridge J. Health promotion and education for black and ethnic minority groups. In: Hopkins A, Bahl V, eds. *Access to health care for people from black and ethnic minorities.* London: Royal College of Physicians, 1993.

5　Balarajan R, Raleigh V. *Ethnicity and health: a guide for the NHS.* London: Department of Health, 1993

6　Department of Health. *The health of the nation: a strategy for health in England.* London: HMSO, 1992.

7　Smith R, ed. *Health of the nation: the BMJ view.* London: British Medical Journal, 1991.

8　Ahmad W. *Race and health in contemporary Britain.* Buckingham: Open University Press, 1993.

9　Black D. *Inequalities in health.* Report of a research group chaired by Sir Douglas Black. London: Department of Health and Social Security, 1980.

10　Smith GD, Bartley M, Blane D. The Black report: socio-economic inequalities in health 10 years on. *British Medical Journal* 1990; **301**: 373–7.

11　Townsend P, Whitehead M, Davidson N, eds. *Inequalities in health.* London: Penguin, 1992.

12　Whitehead M. The health divide. In: Townsend P, Whitehead M, Davidson N, eds. *Inequalities in health.* London: Penguin, 1992.

13　Benzeval M, Judge K. *Tackling health inequalities: an agenda for action.* London: King's Fund, 1995.

14　Cox J, Bostock S, eds. *Racial discrimination in the health service.* Staffs: Penrhos, 1989.

15　Save the Children Fund. *Stop rickets campaign.* London: Save the Children Fund, 1983.

16　Bahl V. *Asian mother and baby campaign.* Departmental report. London: Department of Health and Social Security, 1987.

17 Downie RS, Fyfe C, Tannahill A. *Health promotion: models and values.* Oxford: Oxford University Press, 1990.

18 Tones K, Tilford S. *Health education: effectiveness and efficiency,* 2nd edn. London: Chapman and Hall, 1994.

19 Bhopal R. *Setting priorities for health care for ethnic minority groups.* Newcastle upon Tyne: Department of Epidemiology and Public Health, University of Newcastle upon Tyne, 1988.

20 Sabatier R. *Blaming others: prejudice, race and worldwide AIDS.* London: Panos, 1988.

21 Panos Institute. *The third epidemic: repercussions of the fear of AIDS.* London: Panos, 1990

22 Davies J, Kelly M. *Healthy cities: research and practice.* London: Routledge, 1993.

23 Smaje C. *Health, race and ethnicity.* London: King's Fund Institute, 1995.

24. NHS Executive. *Collection of ethnic group data for admitted patients.* Leeds: Department of Health, 1994 (circular EL(94)77).

25 Blaxter M. *Health and lifestyle.* London: Routledge, 1990.

26 Colhoun H, Prescott-Clarke P. *Health survey in England.* London: HMSO, 1996.

27 Rudat K. *Health and lifestyles: black and minority ethnic groups in England.* London: Health Education Authority, 1994.

28 McIver, S. *Obtaining the views of black users of health services.* London: King's Fund Centre, 1994.

29 Douglas J. *Health and social care research: developing appropriate research methodologies with black and minority ethnic communities.* Conference report. West Bromwich: SHARP/Sandwell Health Promotion Unit, 1998.

30 Pilgrim S, Fenton S, Hughes AO, *et al. The Bristol black and ethnic minorities health survey report.* Bristol: University of Bristol Departments of Sociology and of Epidemiology and Public Health Medicine, 1993.

31 Thompson H, Douglas J, McKee L. *Smethwick Heart Action Research Project: results of a health survey with the Afro-Caribbean, Bangladeshi, Indian, Pakistani and white communities in Smethwick.* West Bromwich: SHARP/Sandwell Health Promotion Unit, 1994.

32 Fenton S, Hughes AO, Hine CE. Self-assessed health, economic status and ethnic origin. *New Community* 1995; **21:** 55–68.

33 Presley F, Shaw A. *Race and health: an information sources guide.* London: King's Fund/SHARE, 1995.

34 Thompson H, Douglas J, McKee L. *Smethwick Heart Action Research Project: research process and methodology.* West Bromwich: SHARP/Sandwell Health Promotion Unit, 1993.

35 Malik A, Thompson H, Douglas J, McKee L. *Smethwick Heart Action Research Project: developing heart health initiatives with black and minority ethnic communities.* West Bromwich: SHARP/Sandwell Health Promotion Unit, 1994.

36 Thompson H, Malik A, Douglas J, McKee L. *Smethwick Heart Action Research Project: final report.* West Bromwich: SHARP/Sandwell Health Promotion Unit, 1994.

37 Henry D, Douglas J, Thompson H, Malik A, Khatun M. *Smethwick: a*

community health profile. West Bromwich: SHARP/Sandwell Health Promotion Unit, 1993.

38 Douglas J. Developing with Black and minority ethnic communities health promotion strategies which address social inequalities. In: McLeod E, Bywater P, eds. *Working for equality in health*. London: Routledge, 1996.

39 Ong BN. *The practice of health services research*. London: Chapman and Hall, 1993.

40 Stanfield J, Dennis M. *Race and ethnicity in research methods*. Newbury Park: Sage, 1993.

41 Hart E, Bond M. *Action research for health and social care*. Buckingham: Open University Press, 1995.

42 Nazroo JY. *The health of Britain's ethnic minorities: findings from a national survey*. London: Policy Studies Institute, 1997.

8 | Oral health

Raman Bedi
Professor, National Centre for Transcultural Oral Health, Eastman Dental Institute, University of London

Baseline and trend data on oral health in the United Kingdom have been reported for the past three decades in national dental health surveys by the Office of Population Censuses and Surveys, but questions on race and ethnicity were not included, so these surveys have not provided information on minority ethnic communities. Ethnic background information on users of services is collected by some health authorities. However, the primary source of accessible local data is small-scale studies, published in the dental literature. To date, little is known regarding the self-reported oral health behaviours of the UK's minority ethnic groups.

This chapter reviews the published dental literature and draws conclusions about the oral health of the minority ethnic communities. Some potential research priorities for both purchasers and providers are highlighted.

Background

The first published report on the oral health status of minority ethnic children was in 1970, in a small-scale study involving secondary school children.[1] Since then, a number of studies have been undertaken,[2-11] but they invariably concentrate on dental caries in children attending schools in socially deprived areas.[9,11] They simply confirm the general perception that certain minority ethnic groups have significantly more dental caries than the national average.

Despite the well recognised differences between the various minority ethnic groups in terms of socioeconomic status, lifestyle, genetic predisposition, disease patterns and mortality levels, dental epidemiology has traditionally described ethnic groups as white, Asian and black.[12] However, group descriptors commonly used in dental health studies have been surname, self identification, skin colour and birthplace of individuals.[9,11–14]

The following classifications are used in this chapter:

- 'Asian' includes Indians, Pakistanis and Bangladeshis, whether from the Indian subcontinent or East Africa.
- 'Black' encompasses black Caribbeans, black Africans and black others.
- 'Vietnamese and Chinese' includes Vietnamese refugees and the Chinese who are, principally, from Hong Kong. Not many studies have been conducted on this population group.

The oral health variables in this review are dental caries, periodontal disease, oral cancer, dental anomalies and oral health related behaviours.

Dental caries: primary dentition

Dental caries appear to be polarising in certain population groups, of which minority ethnic groups are commonly quoted as an example.[15] There is also growing awareness that dental decay in the primary dentition is increasing, or at least not improving.[15] Studies examining the primary dentition of Asian children show significantly more caries than in the indigenous population.[9,10] The mean delayed, missing and filled teeth (dmft) scores in Asian children in the UK are 1.5 to twice as high as in children from the white majority population in the sample studies.[9,11]

The Asian population can be subdivided into two groups: those that show a higher caries experience and those whose experience is similar to that of the white group. The latter form part of the Asian non-Muslim and English-speaking population, and the former constitute the rest of this ethnic group, coming from a Muslim background and whose children's mothers spoke English.[9,10]

It is encouraging to note the consistency in the studies of caries in the black community. These show no significant difference in caries experience in the primary dentition from their white counterparts.[2–5,9,16–18] Few studies have been conducted amongst the Vietnamese and Chinese population, but the few data available show a higher level of caries in the primary teeth than in their white contemporaries.[10,11]

Rampant caries

Rampant caries or 'nursing bottle caries' are seen in the primary dentition; this condition has a classic appearance affecting the smooth surface of the anterior teeth and, all too often, a significant number of other primary teeth. Commonly, the child has to undergo a general anaesthetic and multiple dental extraction. According to a recent report, the prevalence of rampant caries within deprived areas of the UK appears to be increasing.[19] Since 1966, three major investigations into the prevalence and severity of dental caries in pre-school children have been conducted in the London inner-city area of Camden;[19-21] the prevalence of rampant caries had fallen from 10% for children examined between 1966 and 1968 to 4% for those seen in 1980, but in 1986/87 regressed to 10% again.[19] When the researchers explored ethnicity as a variable in the Camden survey, the children from an Asian background had a higher prevalence of rampant caries (14%) than the white population (6%).[19] In a larger study conducted in Manchester in 1987/88, the model proposed for identifying high risk groups within the Asian population resident in deprived areas was shown to be consistent for rampant caries.[19,22]

Six hundred and forty-three children were included in the Manchester study; the mean dmft was 2.84 (3.63), with rampant caries affecting 13% of the population.[22] Children were classified into three groups on broad ethnic/facial characteristics; the mean dmft and % age affected by rampant caries for Asians (3.64 and 18%) differed significantly from those of both whites (1.83 and 5%) and African-Caribbeans (1.87 and 7%).[22] When the Asian population was divided into four groups to explore the effects of religion and the mother's ability to speak English (Table 1) it was found that non-Muslim children with English-speaking mothers were less affected than the other three groups.[22] It would appear, therefore, that among the Asian high risk group living in deprived areas, a fifth to a quarter of young children suffer from rampant caries.

Dental caries: permanent dentition

When the permanent dentition is examined, Asians appear to have significantly less caries than their white contemporaries.[16] Even when the Asian population is subdivided by religion and the mothers' ability to speak English, the inequality in caries experience in the primary dentition of young Asian and indigenous schoolchildren is not apparent in the older age group.[16] A comparison between the caries experience in 15-year-old Bangladeshi and indigenous children also shows the dmft of the former group (1.56) to be much lower than that of the white group (3.39).[23]

Table 1. Prevalence of rampant caries according to ethnic group

	Camden study[19]		Manchester study[22]	
	n	% with rampant caries	n	% with rampant caries
White	382	6	178	5
African-Caribbean	40	5	121	7
Asian (total)	85	14	329	18
Muslim*			105	21
Muslim†			102	27
Non-Muslim†			35	23
Non-Muslim*			87	5

*English speaking mother
†Non-English speaking mother

It is encouraging to note that there is a reasonable consensus that no significant difference in caries experience exists in the permanent dentition between the black community and their white counterparts.[16,24,25]

The disparity in dental caries experience between some minority ethnic groups and the white majority community, especially in the primary dentition, suggests that, in addition to ethnicity, socio-economic status, religion and fluency in the dominant language are important risk indicators for the incidence of caries.[11] Poorer dietary education is one reason why Asian children have worse dental health than white children.[8,11,12] Attwell suggests that the Asian communities are adhering to their traditional pattern of eating, but that the children eat sweets as much as the indigenous population and have acquired a taste for other cariogenic foods, including sweetened cordials and carbonated drinks.[26] Bedi, in searching for a social variable that could partially explain inequalities in dental caries in young children, identified the mother's ability to speak English[9] because individuals who were unable to speak the dominant language suffered disadvantages in housing and employment.[9,11] Research by the Adult Literacy and Basic Skills Unit showed that three out of ten UK residents whose mother tongue was not English had real difficulty in understanding or speaking English, while four out of ten could read or write only a little English or none at all.[27] Furthermore, one in five respondents were unable to read or write their mother tongue.[27] This could prevent them from obtaining information on health matters and perhaps increase their reluctance to seek oral care for their children.

The currently available information is too sparse to document adequately the dental caries inequalities in detail between the minority ethnic and the white majority community, particularly among the adult population. The common observation of a difference in caries experience between the primary and permanent dentition in children also leads to the conclusion that other factors besides ethnicity are caries risk indicators.

Periodontal disease (oral cleanliness)

Booth and Ashley found that ethnic group appeared to have a significant influence on plaque, calculus, gingivitis and loss of attachment.[24] Children do not usually have established, irreversible periodontal disease, so researchers have documented oral cleanliness.[9,11] In the primary dentition, results showed that Asian children have a poorer standard of dental cleanliness and gingival condition than other ethnic groups.[10,11] In the study population of Bangladeshi and white children, the gingival condition of the Bangladeshi group was the poorer.[23] In older children, the pattern for oral cleanliness was similar to that in the primary dentition.[16] When the Asian population as a whole was compared with the white population, it had a significantly lower proportion of children with good/fair oral cleanliness.[16] When the ethnic group was subdivided there was no statistically significant difference between the white and Asian non-Muslim English-speaking population in terms of oral cleanliness.[16] However, the Asian high risk groups had a significantly higher proportion of children with poor oral cleanliness.[16]

One of the few studies in adults, of the oral hygiene practices of a group of Asian females, showed that, in terms of time and effort, the subjects were well motivated towards oral cleanliness.[28] The challenge for health workers, therefore, must be to give effective health promotion messages aimed at improving oral cleanliness.

Despite low levels of plaque, African-Caribbeans are more prone to gingivitis, assessed by the presence of profuse bleeding after probing, than their white counterparts.[8-11] This ethnic group also had the highest percentage of clinical attachment loss; further work is required to determine whether this renders them more susceptible to chronic periodontitis.[8] The African-Caribbean group had the highest prevalence and mean number of pockets over 3 mm, but the lowest levels of plaque. This finding may represent developmental differences in gingival maturation or a more hyperplastic response to plaque, and requires further investigation, since deeper pockets provide an ideal environment for anaerobic bacteria associated with destructive periodontal disease.[24]

Little information is available on the oral hygiene of the Vietnamese and Chinese population although a study among 10-year-old children in Greater Glasgow showed no statistical difference between the Chinese and the white population in oral cleanliness.[16]

Oral cancer

Betel-quid chewing has a long history in a number of communities in Asia.[29–34] The ingredients in the betel-quid (pan) vary not only between nations but also between communities and individuals. The major components are the leaf of *Piper betel* L., the nut of *Areca catechu* L., lime and 'katha' or extract of the wood of *Acacia catech*.[34,35] In health terms, the key variable is whether tobacco is added to the above ingredients or not. It has been estimated that there are at least 40 million regular tobacco chewers in the Indian subcontinent.[33] A review of the published literature by the International Agency for Research on Cancer working party[33] concluded that there was sufficient evidence to show that chewing betel-quid containing tobacco was carcinogenic in humans, although there was inadequate evidence to demonstrate that this was also the case for chewing betel-quid without tobacco.[33] This was confirmed by Johnson, and the uncertainty as to whether chewing of betel-quid without tobacco is carcinogenic continues; nevertheless this habit is associated with the development of oral submucous fibrosis.[32]

There has been little systematic research on the prevalence of oral cancer and precancerous lesions among the Asian communities in the UK, despite clear evidence from the medical literature that populations from the Indian subcontinent suffer higher rates of oral cancer than other groups.[32,33]

There has also been little work on the extent to which betel-quid chewing and/or tobacco chewing are practised among the different ethnic groups in the UK.[35–37] Evidence suggests that this practice is more common among the Bangladeshi community.[35–37]

The use of tobacco and betel-quid among Bangladeshi women in West Yorkshire is similar to that of the much larger community in the city of Birmingham.[35] In Yorkshire 95% of women chewed betel-quid and 89% of this group added tobacco, compared with 96% and 81%, respectively, in the Birmingham study. The latter study also found that 92% of Bangladeshi men chewed betel-quid daily, but that only 37% of this group included tobacco in their quid. Smoking was much more common in the male population.[36]

A logistic regression analysis showed that four factors predicted tobacco chewing: gender, age, ability to speak English, and the individual's perception of health.[36] Both betel-quid chewing and the inclusion of tobacco in the quid have widespread social acceptance, irrespective of gender. However, few Bangladeshi women smoke, and this is a generally held social norm, by both genders. The social norms have clear implications for health promotion.

There have been no reported health promotion initiatives in the UK for this population in relation to oral health. It is important to note the changing knowledge and attitude to the use of betel-quid and tobacco in the second generation of this community. There will need to be a clearer understanding of this complex issue by health educators before major health promotion initiatives can be undertaken.

The following observations have been confirmed among the Bangladeshi community in two separate studies:[35,36]

- Betel-quid chewing is widespread.
- Females predominantly engage in tobacco chewing and the frequency of this habit increases with age.
- Tobacco chewing starts in the late teens and early twenties.
- Chewing betel-quid, with or without the addition of tobacco, is perceived to be socially acceptable.

The Birmingham study has led to the construction of a socio-behavioural model that may, in part, explain the widespread practice of tobacco chewing in this community[36] (Fig 1). It illustrates the social pressures on young Bangladeshi women to begin chewing tobacco. The Birmingham study clearly demonstrated that betel-quid chewing starts during the teenage years and that the inclusion of tobacco begins just prior to engagement and marriage.[36] Tobacco chewing is so prevalent among the women that over 80% of the female adult population engage in the habit.[36] It is perceived as having few health risks and is seen as socially acceptable. Refusal to engage in the behaviour is considered deviant by the community and especially by older women; to participate is considered to be socially conforming and appropriate for young women.

Dental anomalies

Double teeth

An extensive review of the literature reveals that the anomaly of conjoined teeth has been described variously as fusion, germination

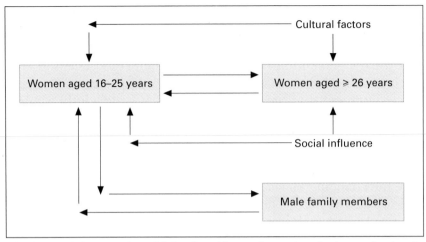

Fig 1. *Sociobehavioural model for the widespread practice of tobacco chewing in betel-quid by women in the Bangladeshi community in the United Kingdom.*

and schizodontia.[38] The authors recommended that the term 'double teeth'[39] be adopted.[38,40] The prevalence of double teeth in the primary dentition, for white schoolchildren, is estimated to be 1.6%.[41] No information is yet available on the prevalence of this anomaly among any minority ethnic group. However, it has been extensively studied in Chinese populations and its prevalence in the Hong Kong Chinese appears to be higher than in the white population in the UK.[42]

Neonatal teeth

Teeth that are present at birth are termed natal teeth; those that erupt during the first month of life are neonatal teeth.[43] Despite their early eruption, both neonatal and natal teeth should be considered as normal teeth that have simply erupted prematurely because they developed in an unusually superficial position.[43] However, they can cause great concern to parents and they have a great deal of associated negative folklore which can stereotype a child as 'unlucky' or a 'bad omen'.[43] In addition to the perceived problems, they can also involve clinical problems, such as mobile or sharp edges. This may necessitate extraction.

The prevalence of natal teeth appears to vary and no accurate figure is available for the UK population, but it is thought to be in the range of 1 in 20,000–30,000. However, among the Hong Kong Chinese the prevalence for natal teeth was found to be 1 : 1,442.[43]

This figure is much higher than would be expected for the white UK community and greater than recent findings for a northern European population.[44]

Evaginated odontomes

This is an enamel-covered tubercle arising from the occlusal surface of a permanent tooth. Its diagnosis is important since fracture of the tubercle is common and invariably leads to the exposure of pulpal tissue and, subsequently, necrosis of the pulp and periapical infection. Although very rare in the white population in the UK, it is frequently seen in the Chinese community. To date there have been no prevalence studies in the UK, but it has been estimated that this anomaly occurs in 3% of Hong Kong Chinese schoolchildren.[45] If this is also true of the Chinese population in the UK, dentists should be trained in its diagnosis and management.[45]

Talon cusps

A talon cusp is a morphologically well delineated cusp projecting from the lingual surface of a primary or secondary anterior tooth and extending at least half the distance from the cemento-enamel junction to the incisal edge.[46] They are rare among the white population. No UK studies have been conducted but high prevalence has been reported in northern India (7.7%) and in Malaysian children.[47,48] The management of these anomalies is complex and loss of the tooth is all too common. If high prevalence were confirmed for particular groups of ethnic minority children, appropriate training should be provided for dentists working in multiracial areas.

Oral health related behaviour

Little information is available on oral health related behaviours in minority ethnic communities. A small local study of dental knowledge, beliefs, attitudes and behaviour among the Asian community in Glasgow showed that they had limited specific knowledge regarding methods for reducing the incidence of caries; 30% could not name any foods known to be detrimental to oral health and only 30% felt that children under the age of 5 years required access to dental services.[49]

The largest adult minority ethnic study undertaken in the UK was completed by Sandwell Health Authority in 1992.[50,51] It attempted to determine the value of using Asian places of worship as a point of contact for disseminating health information. Questionnaires were completed by 1,686 Asian adults (over 16 years old); this represented 72% of the estimate by religious leaders of the size of their congregations.[50] The survey's findings showed that different sections of the Asian population used services differently and each group needed different information; the communication channels that worked best varied depending upon the community involved. A third of all the respondents had experienced dental pain within the past 12 months; the older group were more likely to have experienced pain. Sikh adults were the poorest attenders, with 66% ($n = 611$) not having attended within the past 5 years. Twenty-nine per cent ($n = 480$) of respondents did not have their own dentist; of these, 36% of the Sikh population did not have a dentist, compared with only 9% ($n = 32$) and 13% ($n = 11$) among the Muslims and Hindus respectively. [50,51]

Social deprivation, ethnicity and oral health inequalities

Some authors have suggested that ethnic origin *per se* has no effect on dental disease prevalence but that social deprivation is a major factor, with associated low utilisation of dental services.[18,52] Poverty, deprivation and poor housing influence the health of the community.[53] Inequalities in oral health between the minority ethnic communities and the white population are more understandable in the context of the growing 'underclass' in British cities. Unemployment has always been higher among minority ethnic groups than the white majority population but, as the overall level of unemployment rises, the gap between the two groups widens.[54]

Economic instability affects accessibility and acceptability, as the lower social groups have been shown to underutilise the dental care provided. Services may be inaccessible because resources are inadequate owing to uneven geographical distribution, and studies show that utilisation of health care facilities decreases as distance from a patient's home increases, the underclass being less mobile than the norm.[49,55,56] This was highlighted by a study in which over half of Muslim first generation women and a third of non-Muslim women had never been to the dentist, despite having had at least one pregnancy in the UK and therefore been entitled to free treatment.[57]

A significant relationship has been shown between deprivation, estimated by the uptake of free meals at school, and poor dental health.[58] The lists for free meals were used to identify schools with a high proportion of children with poor dental health and a particular need for oral health promotion programmes.[58]

It is not possible at present to answer the question 'Do minority ethnic groups in the United Kingdom have poorer dental health?' The need for further studies is obvious and priority should be given to minority ethnic studies involving all social classes and the adult population.

Conclusions

The following is a summary of the key points outlined in this chapter:

- Little information is available on the following minority ethnic groups:
  - those who reside outside areas of multiple deprivation;
  - the adult population;
  - the Chinese and Vietnamese populations.

    Small-scale studies have documented children's oral health for the past 25 years. On the whole, these demonstrate inequalities in dental health among Asian children and the white majority population in the primary dentition, but this relationship is not found in the permanent dentition. The levels of oral cleanliness are poorer in the Asian child.
- There appear to be few differences in oral health between the black and the indigenous populations.
- More information is needed on the prevalence of oral cancer among minority ethnic communities.
- There is a need to harmonise descriptions of communities; the ethnic classification used in the 1991 census appears to be the most appropriate for health workers to adopt.
- Variations in oral health among ethnic groups may be better understood as consideration is given to the emerging underclass in British society.

Priority objectives for commissioners and providers of dental services

- To establish baseline information on the oral health status and health-related behaviour of minority ethnic groups both nationally and locally, in order to develop programmes of care that will reduce differences in health status by allocating resources to those in greatest need
- To explore the reasons for non-uptake of dental services by minority ethnic groups, so that services will meet the demands and preferences of minority ethnic groups

- To explore factors and evaluate solutions that encourage regular visits to the dentist, so that minority ethnic groups can derive maximum benefit from the services provided
- To implement ethnic monitoring and to keep under review the interpretation and use of the information gleaned from this process to ensure that services are meeting the needs and are being used by local community groups, within existing resources
- To develop and evaluate methodologies whereby local minority ethnic groups' views of dental services can be obtained so that the preferences of local groups can be voiced and implemented
- To evaluate the effectiveness of oral health promotion directly targeted at minority ethnic groups, so that minority ethnic groups derive maximum benefit from the NHS programmes and services.

References

1 Downer MC. Dental caries and periodontal disease in girls of different ethnic groups: a comparison in a London secondary school. *British Dental Journal* 1970; **128**: 379–85.

2 Beal JF. The dental health of 5 year old children of different ethnic origins resident in an inner Birmingham area and a nearby borough. *Archives of Oral Biology* 1973; **18**: 305–12.

3 Varley TF, Goose DH. Dental caries in children of immigrants in Liverpool. *British Dental Journal* 1971; **130**: 27–9.

4 Whitehouse NH. *A comparative study of the distribution of dental disease among 5 year old children of different racial origin living in Nottingham.* Dissertation for Diploma in Dental Health, University of Birmingham, 1970.

5 Prendergast MJ, Williams SA, Curzon MEJ. An assessment of dental caries prevalence among Gujarati, Pakistani and White Caucasian five year old children resident in Dewsbury, West Yorkshire. *Community Dental Health* 1989; **6**: 223–32.

6 Perkins PC, Sweetman AJP. Ethnic differences in caries prevalence in five year olds in North West London. *British Dental Journal* 1986; **161**: 215–6.

7 Paul PF, Bradnock G. The dental health of Asian and Caucasian four and five year old children resident in Coventry. *Community Dental Health* 1986; **3**: 275–85.

8 Bradnock G, Jadaua SI, Hamburger R. The dental health of indigenous and non-indigenous infant school children in West Birmingham. *Community Dental Health* 1988; **1**: 139–50.

9 Bedi R. Ethnic indicators of dental health for young Asian school children resident in areas of multiple deprivation. *British Dental Journal* 1989; **166**: 331–4.

10 Bedi R, Elton RA. Dental caries experience and oral cleanliness of Asian and White Caucasian children aged five and six years attending

primary school in Glasgow and Trafford, United Kingdom. *Community Dental Health* 1991; **8**: 17–23.

11 Verrips GH, Bedi R. Dental health and ethnic minority groups in the Netherlands, the United Kingdom, Sweden and Norway: a literature review. In: Verrips GH, ed. *Child dental health and ethnicity in the Netherlands.* Leiden: TNO Institute, 1992.

12 Bedi R. Dental health education and ethnicity. *British Dental Journal* 1987; **163**: 32.

13 Office of Population Censuses and Surveys. *County monitors.* London: OPCS, 1992 .

14 Office of Population Censuses and Surveys. Questions on race/ethnicity and related topics for the census. *Population Trends* 1987; **49**: 5–11.

15 Downer MC. The 1993 national survey of children's dental health: a commentary on the preliminary report. *British Dental Journal* 1994; **176**: 209–14.

16 Bedi R, Quarrell I, Kippen A. The dental health of ten year old children attending multiracial schools in Greater Glasgow. *British Dental Journal* 1991; **170**: 182–5.

17 Awath-Behari S. *A comparison study of the dental condition of 5 year old children of different ethnic groups born and brought up in the County Borough of Wolverhampton.* Dissertation for Diploma in Dental Health, University of Birmingham, 1970.

18 Saunder SM, Lunn HD, Francis JF, Sullivan JF. Differences in dental caries in 5 year old children within adjacent districts on the south coast of England. *Public Health* 1991; **105**: 313–8.

19 Holt RD, Joels D, Bulman J, Maddick IH. A third study of caries in preschool aged children in Camden. *British Dental Journal* 1988; **165**: 87–91.

20 Holt RD, Joels D, Winter GB. Caries in pre-school Camden. *British Dental Journal* 1982; **53**: 107–9.

21 Winter GB, Rule DC, Mailer GP, *et al.* The prevalence of dental caries in pre-school children aged 1 to 4 years. *British Dental Journal* 1971; **130**: 271–7,434–6.

22 Bedi R. Ethnicity and rampant caries among 5-year-olds. *Journal of Dental Research* 1989; **68**: 904.

23 Laher MH. A comparison between dental caries, gingival health and dental service usage in Bangladeshi and white Caucasian children aged 7, 9, 11, 13 and 15 years residing in an inner city area of London, United Kingdom. *Community Dental Health* 1991; **7**: 57–163.

24 Booth V, Ashley F. The oral health of a group of fifteen to seventeen year old British school children of different ethnic origin. *Community Dental Health* 1989; **6**: 195–205.

25 Perkins PC. Dental caries in children of 9 and 14 years in three ethnic groups in north-west London. *British Dental Journal* 1981; **150**: 194–5.

26 Attwell SM. *A study of the dental needs of a group of children at nursery schools in the city of Coventry.* Dissertation for Diploma in Dental Health, University of Birmingham, 1974.

27 Adult Literacy and Basic Skills Unit. *A nation's neglect: research into the need for English amongst speakers of other languages.* London: ALBSU, 1989.

28 Jones CV, Srivastava RP, Walsh TF. Oral hygiene practices in a group of Asian females. *Dental Health* 1987/88; **26**: 5–7.

29 Gupta PC, Mehta FS, Pindborg JJ, *et al.* A primary prevention study of oral cancer among Indian villagers: eight-year follow-up results. In: Hakama M, *et al. Evaluating effectiveness of primary prevention of cancer.* IARC scientific publications No.103. Lyon: IARC, 1989: 149–56.

30 Mehta FS, Pindborg JJ, Gupta PC, Daftary DK. Epidemiological and histological study of oral cancer and leukoplakia among 50,915 villagers in India. *Cancer* 1969; **24**: 832–49.

31 Mehta FS, Gupta PC, Daftary DK, *et al.* An epidemiological study of oral cancer and precancerous conditions among 101,761 villagers in Maharashtra, India. *International Journal of Cancer* 1971; **10**: 134–41.

32 Johnson NW. Orofacial neoplasms: global epidemiology, risk factors and recommendations for research. *International Dental Journal* 1991; **41**: 365–75.

33 International Agency for Research on Cancer. *Tobacco habits other than smoking: betel-quid and areca-nut chewing, and some related nitrosamines.* Monograph 37. Lyon: IARC, 1985.

34 Qureshi B. *Transcultural medicine: dealing with patients from different cultures.* Dordrecht: Kluwer Academic Publishers, 1989.

35 Summers RM, Williams SA, Curzon MEJ. The use of tobacco and betel quid ('pan') among Bangladeshi women in West Yorkshire. *Community Dental Health* 1994; **11**: 12–6.

36 Bedi R, Jones PA, eds. *Betel-quid and tobacco chewing among the Bangladeshi community in the United Kingdom: usage and health issues.* London: Centre for Transcultural Oral Health, 1995.

37 Bedi R, Gilthorpe MS. The prevalence of betel-quid and tobacco chewing among the Bangladeshi community resident in a United Kingdom area of multiple deprivation. *Primary Dental Care* 1995; **2**: 39–42.

38 Brook AH, Winter GB. Double teeth: a retrospective study of 'geminated' and 'fused' teeth in children. *British Dental Journal* 1970; **129**: 123–30.

39 Miles AEW. Malformations of the teeth. *Proceedings of the Royal Society of Medicine* 1954; **47**: 817–26.

40 Hagman FT. Anomalies of form and number: fused primary teeth, a correlation of the dentitions. *Journal of Dentistry for Children* 1988; **55**: 359–61.

41 Brook AH. Dental anomalies of number, form and size: their prevalence in British schoolchildren. *Journal of the International Association of Dentistry for Children* 1974; **5**: 37–53.

42 Yuen SWH, Chan JCY, Wei SHY. Double primary teeth and their relationship with the permanent successors: a radiographic study of 376 cases. *Pediatric Dentistry* 1987; **9**: 42–8.

43 Bedi R, Yan SW. The prevalence and clinical management of natal teeth: a study in Hong Kong. *Journal of Paediatric Dentistry* 1990; **6**: 85–90.

44 Flinck A, Paludan A, Matsson L, Holm AK, Axelsson I. Oral findings in a group of newborn Swedish children. *International Journal of Paediatric Dentistry* 1994; **4**: 67–73 .

45 Bedi R, Pitts NMB. Dens evaginatus in the Hong Kong Chinese population. *Endodontics and Dental Traumatology* 1988; **4**: 104–7.

46 Davis PJ, Brook AH. The presentation of talon cusp: diagnosis, clinical features, associations and possible aetiology. *British Dental Journal* 1986; **160**: 84–8.

47 Chawla HS, Tewari A, Gopalakrishnan NS. Talon cusp: a prevalence study. *Journal of the Indian Society of Pedodontics and Preventive Dentistry* 1983; **1**: 28–34.

48 Meon R. Talon cusp in Malaysia. *Australian Dental Journal* 1991; **36**: 11–4.

49 Kay EJ, Shaikh I. Dental knowledge, beliefs, attitudes and behaviour of the Asian community in Glasgow. *Health Bulletin* 1990; **48**: 73–80.

50 Bedi R, Charlton J, Pillai R. *Value of Asian places of worship for collecting health related information.* Sandwell: Sandwell Health Authority, 1992.

51 Bedi R, Charlton J, Pillai R, *et al.* Self reported dental behaviours of the Asian elderly. *Journal of Dental Research* 1993; **72**: 726.

52 Plamping D, Bewley BR, Gelbier S. Dental health and ethnicity. *British Dental Journal* 1985; **158**: 261–3.

53 Hopkins A, Bahl V, eds. *Access to health care for people from black and ethnic minorities.* London: Royal College of Physicians, 1993.

54 Newnhawn A. *Unemployment, employment and black people.* London: Runnymede, 1986 .

55 Smith DJ. *Understanding the underclass.* Policy Studies Institute. Worcester: Billings, 1992 .

56 Morrell DC, Gage HG. Patterns of demand in general practice. *Journal of the Royal College of General Practitioners* 1990; **19**: 331–42.

57 Williams SA, Fairpo CG. Dental attendance patterns and ethnic origin in an inner city area. *Journal of Dental Research* 1988; **67**: 645 .

58 Schou L, Wright C, Wohlgemuth B. Deprivation and dental health: the benefits of a child dental health campaign in relation to deprivation as estimated by the uptake of free meals at school. *Community Dental Health* 1991; **8**:147–54.

9 | Sexual and reproductive health

Ali Kubba
Consultant Community Gynaecologist, Lambeth Healthcare NHS Trust and UMDS Department of Obstetrics and Gynaecology

Family planning is a human right to which all individuals are entitled equal access. Reproductive and sexual health encompasses freedom from the fear and adverse effects of unplanned pregnancy, sexually transmitted infections, and the physical and psychological morbidity of uncontrolled fertility. The minority ethnic population of Great Britain is a heterogeneous group with rich and varied cultures, at various stages of integration with the communities in which they live. There is evidence of poor access to and utilisation of health facilities by these groups.[1]

Set in the context of the need for more appropriate data, this chapter discusses existing studies including experience in southeast London, the role of socioeconomic and religious factors in influencing reproductive decision, the impact of health problems on contraceptive advice, and concludes by setting out a priority agenda for action by commissioners and providers of health care.

Needs assessment

Need for appropriate data

Most services for family planning and reproductive health care are provided by general practitioners (GPs) and community family planning clinics, the former providing about three-quarters and the latter the remaining quarter. In primary care, information is based on practice returns, which show the number of claims for family planning services. This information is virtually useless as it does not reflect the quality, nature or effectiveness of the 'intervention'. There is likely to be some double counting as registering with a GP does not prevent women from obtaining contraceptive and sexual health care from other sources such as chemists and community clinics.

In community family planning services, data collection tends to be better as it is based on the Korner minimum data set requirements. However, information linking ethnicity, fertility and sexuality has been perceived as politically sensitive and therefore no linkage has been attempted. Furthermore, there are currently no mandatory requirements for ethnic group data collection in community services.

Because of the focused nature of the health intervention in community family planning clinics, the data collection is genuinely useful. However, as a consequence of straddling both primary and tertiary services, each with their separate agendas and aspirations, community family planning clinics have been poorly resourced. The under-resourcing and low prioritisation of community reproductive health services are reflected in the level of information technology support systems available; these are often inflexible, limited in range and at times totally reliant on the dedication of individual members of staff.

The community model for data collection can be applied to primary care until a better alternative system becomes available. As the ethos of sexual and reproductive health care is a seamless service covering both primary and secondary care, it is essential for there to be a co-ordinator for needs assessment and data collection across the spectrum and the sharing of information technology. The underpinning of this activity should be total confidentiality for clients. An assurance of confidentiality impacts significantly on the utilisation of a service.

For ethnicity data to be useful, it must differentiate between the first and second (British born) generations.

Existing studies

Most existing studies originate from circumscribed local communities and may not reflect the full range of needs of minority ethnic groups. One of the best studies is McAvoy's work with Asian women in Leicester.[2] In his survey of 235 women the following findings emerged:

- 73% of the sample were able to acquire family planning information as easily as they wanted;
- 41% did not know if their GP provided family planning services;
- over 80% wanted a female doctor;
- few women supported the idea of an Asian-staffed clinic;

- 37% could not read English family planning literature and 5% did not understand it;
- 55% preferred to discuss family planning in their mother tongue;
- 20% wanted information available in the workplace;
- 5% said that maternity hospital staff should be more helpful.

McAvoy and colleagues also identified that Asians made up 22% of the population studied, but accounted for 32% of all births in the city. Their contraceptive use was lower than that of Caucasians but was not affected by religion. Their fertility rate was higher (13% versus 5% for the UK in that year). The study identified that the intrauterine contraceptive device (IUD) was the commonest method used. Thirty-three per cent used the IUD compared with 8% in the general population. Condoms were also popular, whereas vasectomy was very unpopular among Asians.

Woollett and colleagues, in a study of attitudes to contraception of Asian women in east London, found the following:[3]

- positive attitudes to limiting family size and ensuring the spacing of children;
- these women were less likely to use the pill and more likely to use the condom, owing more to fear of side-effects and the perceived negative impact on future fertility than a preference for the condom;
- contraceptive knowledge was related to fluency in English.

Experience in south-east London

West Lambeth is a deprived inner-city district in south-east London with a high minority ethnic population (Table 1). The population is highly mobile within and outside south-east London. A third of patients attending a termination of pregnancy clinic had been resident in the district for under 6 months. Table 2 shows the ethnic group breakdown of the population as a whole and those women who used reproductive health services in 1992. It is clear from this table that black African women are over-represented in both deliveries and terminations of pregnancy. Black Caribbeans again have a high fertility rate and a relatively higher resort to termination of pregnancy. Apart from the latter, African-Caribbeans have similar patterns to Caucasians. Asians are slightly over-represented in both the termination of pregnancy and the delivery figures, but they clearly do not make as much use of the family planning service. This latter observation is echoed in the

Table 1. Percentage mix of the minority ethnic populations of south-east London[4]

	Lambeth	Southwark	Lewisham
Total population	244,834	218,541	230,983
Black Caribbean	12.6 (2nd)	8.3 (7th)	10.1 (4th)
Black African	6.5 (1st)	7.2 (1st)	3.7 (8th)
Black other	2.7	2.2	2.5
Indian	2.1	1.2	1.2
Pakistani	0.8	0.4	0.3
Bangladeshi	0.7 (19th)	1 (13th)	0.3
Chinese	1.3 (3rd)	1.3 (6th)	1 (11th)
Other	3.5	2.9	2.9
Total	*30.2*	*24.5*	*23*

() = rank of the district as % of a total ethnic population in England and Wales.

Table 2. Use of 'reproductive health services' by minority ethnic groups in West Lambeth district

	% of total population* n=244,834	% of deliveries at St Thomas' (1992) n=3,561	% attending community FP clinic (Oct 1990) n=165	% attending a TOP clinic (1992/3) n=183	% attending post-TOP clinic (1992/3) n=133
Black Caribbean	12.6	16.4	18	26	14.6
Black African	6.5	16	5	19.6	33
Asian	3.6	4.8	1	5	25.6
Caucasian	69.8	50.5	65	37	6

FP = family planning; TOP = termination of pregnancy.
*Based on 1991 census

Leicester survey mentioned earlier, where nearly half the Asian women questioned preferred a domiciliary service.

African-Caribbeans appear to access family planning clinics relatively more than other groups, while Africans are under-represented. Africans and, to some extent, Asians appear to be better attenders at post-termination clinics. The latter observation demonstrates the importance of post-abortion services and argues for enhancing their role.

Pregnancy termination services currently fall between acute obstetrics and gynaecology, private clinics and the community. The latter is the natural home for running a pregnancy termination service. This operation often slips through the health service net as a non-event. The system colludes with the client in shutting the mind to the experience of unplanned pregnancy and, indirectly, the need for contraception. Hospitals do not carry post-operative follow-up because of workload pressures, while in the private sector follow-up is offered but not monitored. Post-abortion care is the missing link in the care chain for unwanted pregnancy. Future planning must incorporate a focused approach to post-abortion care wherever it may reside.

In our post-abortion questionnaire, we routinely ask about knowledge of emergency contraception. We noted the replies from 113 women seen in the post-abortion clinic; 54.8% did not know about emergency contraception. Those women were provided with both verbal and written information about emergency contraception. The availability of emergency contraception was also advertised on the local FM radio station. The use of the media is likely to reach those women who do not avail themselves of mainstream services.

The clientele of genitourinary medicine (GUM) clinics may be different from those who use their GPs or local community clinics for sexual health services. In a recent study, 200 women attending the GUM clinic at King's College Hospital were asked about the source of their family planning advice[5] (Table 3). The black Caribbeans surveyed showed a pattern not much different from Caucasians. Many women prefer GUM clinics because of the guarantee of confidentiality. Many of those attending GUM clinics also prefer 'one stop shop' services for family planning and sexually transmitted diseases screening and treatment. However, follow-up appointments are frequently missed. The underuse of 'medical' services by black Africans concurs with the author's own findings from the West Lambeth family planning services (see Table 2).

Table 3. Sources from which patients at a geritourinary medicine clinic obtained family planning advice[5]

Population	Number	GP	Family planning clinic	Chemist
Whites	60	46%	23%	19%
Black Caribbeans	52	44%	27%	13%
Black Africans	8	25%	12.5%	25%

This same study compared the contraceptive usage of whites and African-Caribbeans and found that:

- 7% more African-Caribbeans did not use contraception;
- the IUD and cap methods were not popular with African-Caribbeans;
- the rate of sterilisation in the African-Caribbeans was double that for the Caucasians.

Factors influencing the reproductive decision

The factors that influence choice of family size and use of services are wide and varied, encompassing cultural and religious traditions and socioeconomic circumstances.

Cultural and religious traditions

Cultural misunderstandings on the part of service providers can result in distress for minority ethnic women, and will deter them from using family planning services. An appreciation of these factors is essential if services are to meet the needs of all women, so it is useful to review some of the cultural and religious issues relating to the main minority ethnic groups in Great Britain.[6] Information of this nature is only useful as a basis for finding out from individual women about their personal preferences. Total reliance on cultural and religious information as it appears in handbooks and manuals can result in unhelpful generalisations and racial stereotyping.[7] It is within this framework that the following issues are being raised.

Culture is the sum total of ideals, beliefs, values and knowledge which constitute the shared basis of social actions. Within this context, how men and women see their roles and responsibilities plays a vital part. In Britain family planning is traditionally viewed as women's responsibility; in ethnic minority communities where men are entirely responsible for protecting and providing for their wives, family planning decisions (like other important family decisions) may be made chiefly by the husband/partner. Involving men in the decision-making process will therefore be culturally acceptable to many. It is also important to note that the male/female sex ratio is higher in minority ethnic groups than in the native white population.

The cultural and religious background will also have a bearing on decisions regarding methods of contraception. Many non-Western religions advocate a holistic and natural approach to health and well-being, so there may be a wish not to disturb the balance of nature, and to avoid the use of artificial measures and the 'accumulation' of drugs in the body. For this reason, many people from this section of the population see natural family planning as the most acceptable method of contraception. Family planning programmes, however, do not always cater for this naturalistic perspective, and they rarely incorporate advice on emergency contraception in their natural family planning protocols.

A recent study of African-Caribbeans' attitudes to antihypertensive medicines revealed that tablets were often left off to give the body 'a rest'.[8] Another reason for stopping tablets was the belief that it was dangerous to mix medicines and alcohol. Applied to women on the contraceptive pill, this could lead to increased risk of pregnancy. Interestingly, whilst many women (including those from minority ethnic groups) are concerned about the invasive nature of IUDs and hold the erroneous perception that they have negative effects on health, others may prefer the IUD because they feel reassured by the immediate return of fertility after its discontinuation. The former group may risk an unwanted pregnancy and resort to termination of pregnancy as an alternative to contraception.

The challenge for health professionals is to take care and time to give adequate information and appropriate support to women from this section of the community to help allay their anxieties and assist them in making informed choices and decisions.

The issue of multiple partners should also be considered within a cultural context. In contrast to serial monogamy (where people go through a succession of partners through divorce or separation – a pattern that is increasingly becoming the norm in Britain), in a small section of black and minority ethnic groups polygamous marriages may be practised. Although there are no available data on this at present, it would be necessary to identify whether these two practices influence the number of children women had, and their spacing. The value of this information may be limited in the UK where, aware of the disapproval of polygamy, people may choose not to disclose this type of information to health workers.

Most religions and cultures (including Christianity) are inherently pronatalist, and fertility is largely considered central to a successful relationship. Some Rastafarians follow Old Testament teaching to be fruitful and multiply and replenish the earth. The Vatican prohibition for Roman Catholics is very clear and uncompromising. In Islam, however, there is no equivalent to the Pope or head of the church. Opinions of any religious leader or scholar are simply one's interpretation of the Quran. Though the basis of

Islam is permissibility of what is not forbidden, the interpretation of the religion by some may cause restriction in contraceptive use. In strict religious interpretation, sterilisation is seen as an interference with God's will, but in practice it is an acceptable method in many Muslim societies.

As a reflection of the high value placed on having children in some minority ethnic communities, many women would continue with an unplanned pregnancy even though such pregnancies may be unwanted. The women may fear that an abortion will affect their future fertility – an anxiety expressed by many African-Caribbean women when facing an unplanned pregnancy.

Gender of service provider

In Eastern religions such as Hinduism, Islam and Judaism, physical cleanliness and modesty are important religious obligations for both men and women. This is particularly evident in relationships between the sexes, and there may be strict moral codes governing social interactions.

Mixed discussions about sex and contraception may be extremely embarrassing for all parties and therefore unlikely to achieve much. Women from a number of minority ethnic groups may often prefer services of such an intimate nature to be delivered by a woman only. It is salutary to remember that only 12% of consultant gynaecologists in the UK are women. However, the predominantly female staff in the community reproductive health services could play a role in filling this gap as part of a strategy based on an alliance between primary, secondary and tertiary care.

Although, on the whole, religion is perceived to play a major role in determining uptake and proper use of sexual health and reproductive services, in reality this is moderated by the interplay of cultural and personal perspectives. The dynamics of sexuality, the value and burden of the family, and societal and peer pressures may be so powerful as to marginalise the effect of religion for some individuals. Nevertheless, providers should be aware of religious norms and sensitivities, and provide a service that respects the way of life and beliefs of people whose cultural and religious backgrounds may be different from their own.

Literacy and language skills

Language barriers pose particular difficulties for people who do not speak English. This often leads to lack of knowledge about, and difficulty in accessing, services. Even when services are accessed, the efficacy of the contraceptive consultation is downgraded.

Black and minority ethnic women often have lower literacy and levels of spoken English than men. Many, particularly those who migrated to Britain from rural areas, would not have had access to much formal education in their country of origin. People from the Asian community are particularly vulnerable in this respect. The Health Education Authority black and ethnic minority health and lifestyle survey reported that about a quarter of Indians and almost half of Bangladeshis were unable to read English, and smaller proportions were unable to read any language.[9] Similar work recently carried out among Asian women in south Birmingham revealed that many of those surveyed had no spoken English.

As the proportion of black and minority ethnic people born and brought up in Britain increases, illiteracy and English language skills will be less significant. A survey of patients attending an outpatient department in 1988 at the Dudley Road Hospital, Birmingham, found a significant effect of age on English comprehension, with 60% of 13–28 year olds speaking English, but only 32% of 29–60 year olds doing so.[10] However, the language needs of recent migrants, such as refugees from Ethiopia, Somalia and the former Yugoslavia, is also an important area for consideration. Although many people from these countries may be well educated and have high standards of written and spoken English, the traumatic experiences of civil war and migration are likely to affect English language ability (see Chapter 20).

The young

A major characteristic of minority ethnic populations is their relatively young age structure. This is especially so for Asians. Whereas 20% of UK Caucasians are under 16 years old, the figure for Indians is 32%, for Pakistanis 42% and for Bangladeshis 52%. A two-culture conflict can operate in the lives of many young ethnic minority men and women growing up with parents not born in this country. The conflict is between the strict culture at home and the sexual freedom seen outside their home among their peers. Given that the education system often does not cater appropriately for the needs of minority ethnic children, many will feel alienated. Pregnancy may thus be viewed by some as a way to avoid school or, indeed, to escape home, so sex education and assertiveness training are very important for teenagers in this situation.

Socioeconomic influences

Impact of poverty

Relatively more people from minority ethnic groups live in inner-city areas, where they are more likely to be socially and economically disadvantaged. Deprivation and a high level of mobility combine to reduce the access of this section of the population to information and to services. In areas of Britain with large and highly mobile minority ethnic populations, immigration and refugee policies may frustrate family planning programmes and other health strategies. In inner London this problem presents a challenge to all health care providers.

Immigration laws and the separation of families influence the complex physical, emotional and sociopolitical attitudes to contraception. The effect of the culture of the mother country has already been discussed and, though modified by a number of other factors, it can re-emerge in times of crisis or disillusionment.

Many believe that the main influence on the health status of minority ethnic populations is socioeconomic and environmental. It is said that it is unhealthy to be poor or become poor. Evidence in developing countries shows that, the higher the standard of living of the population, the more the utilisation of family planning, the slogan 'take care of the population and the population will take care of its needs' being universally applicable. Health initiatives have to tackle the external influences on health as well as working through the medical model.

Political influences

A further confounding factor is that foreign and national governments in many Third World countries have funded high-pressure population control programmes. Many minority ethnic people living in Britain will have heard stories about coercive approaches. This has engendered some degree of mistrust in such services:[11]

> Many paternal and apparently sympathetic doctors have persuaded black women to accept an abortion or contraceptive she did not really want, out of concern to control our fertility. And such attitudes are reflected not only through our experiences here in Britain, but in our countries of origin, where myths about the need for population control are used as an excuse for the unleashing of mass sterilisation and birth control programmes on black and Third World women, often as part of the West's aid package.

The emerging migration patterns are likely to cause further confusion. Country of birth may no longer be the country of residence or the country of most recent residence. The societal and peer influence operative along the migration trail may modify the cultural impact on the reproductive decision. Assessing need and cultural awareness of the different ethnic groups are interlinked. To be meaningful they have to span a wide range (older non-UK born individuals and younger ethnic 'British'). Age and immigration patterns affect cultural attitudes within an ethnic group. Geography (country of origin) should not be the main determinant of the approach to an ethnic community. India demonstrates this point with the fact that the Hindus, Sikhs and Muslims have varying cultural and religious practices, which impact on sexual behaviour.

Health service factors

Impact of special health problems on contraceptive choice and reproductive morbidity

A number of clinical syndromes influence the acceptability and safety of contraceptives. Awareness of these conditions and liaison between family planning providers and medical experts would enhance the worth of many interventions. This is a two-way process of peer education as well as raising public awareness. Examples of medical conditions are:

- diabetes is four times more common in Asians than in Caucasians;
- hypertensive disease has a higher incidence in Caribbeans and they are more likely to be diagnosed as having some psychiatric illness;
- sickle cell disease and thalassaemia have obvious implications for the use of a number of contraceptives;
- ischaemic heart disease mortality is 20% higher in Asian men and 29% higher in women.

There are also differences in lifestyle. Smoking is a case in point. A recent study showed that 30% of Caucasian and African-Caribbean pregnant women smoked but only 3% of Asian women did so.[12] Furthermore, studies from Leeds and south-east London suggest that being of a black ethnic group is associated with a higher risk of acquiring gonorrhoea as judged by incidence rates, even after controlling for socioeconomic status.[13,14]

Attitudes of service providers

Health professional attitudes to family size can greatly influence the way in which services are provided and this in turn affects the uptake of services. Whereas children may be both a source of family warmth and economic assets in many developing countries, in industrialised countries such as Britain they are expensive and an economic liability. To parents on a low income, in inner-city areas with poor and few facilities, they may become more of a worry and a drain than a pleasure. In Britain many people hold the view that couples with more than three or four children, unless they are wealthy, are irresponsible and feckless. This view is likely to influence service providers' judgements about, for example, the size of ethnic minority families. Many black and ethnic minority couples who chose to have more children will have felt disapproval. This leads to a poor relationship with service providers.[5]

The above may also be compounded by the unfortunate existence of negative racial stereotyping and myths which often abound in services and jeopardise the dignity and respect of black and ethnic minority people using the services.

Conclusion

The concept of sexuality relates to how people express themselves. This is socioculturally defined and influenced by tradition, customs, religion, level of knowledge and socioeconomic circumstances.

Existing data on the needs and preferences of black and minority ethnic communities in relation to sexual and reproductive health are patchy and of limited scope. This area of health care has been consistently underprioritised, a situation that has been compounded by anxiety about seeming to prey on people's culturally driven reproductive patterns and sexual practices, which hampers research in this area. The information so far available would suggest that the particular needs of this section of the population are not being adequately addressed in the planning and delivery of services.

As applies to the rest of the population, needs assessment for this section of the community should be set within the wider social and political context. Whilst an appreciation of group experiences, values and beliefs is necessary, it is essential also to recognise that people respond to their environment in singularly personal ways and adapt their lifestyle and behaviour to meet changing circumstances, so the importance of treating people as individuals cannot be overemphasised. Of primary importance is the need for service providers to be conscious of the impact of their own cultural sexual norms and attitudes and be careful not to impose them on service users.

Priorities for action

- The paucity of data on the sexual and reproductive health needs of the ethnic population needs to be addressed nationally. A central co-ordinating body may maximise yield.
- Providers of health care should be encouraged to (Table 4):
  - identify the ethnic mix of the communities they serve;
  - involve the communities in health planning;
  - implement a mixture of education and service initiatives;
  - provide information about local services using the right medium and approach;
  - aim to dispel myths and address anxieties.
- Research must avoid stereotyping and generalisation.[7] The purpose is to identify the need for information and education and the appropriate service approach (including an exploration of the specific values of the clinic, GP, outreach and domiciliary services). Research should aim to fill gaps in knowledge and guide practical action in a targeted way,[15] eg emergency contraception for condom users. Research should also identify whether the unmet need is for spacing, delaying or limiting the size of the family, since the contraceptive strategy and targeting is different for these different needs.
- Communication with black and ethnic minority clients should be improved through:
  - effective use of trained interpreters as patients' advocates;
  - translating relevant written educational material;
  - promotion and focus on a positive image of ethnic minority groups;
  - respect for religious and cultural beliefs;
  - use of relevant information and education outlets (radio, television and community groups).
- Sexual and reproductive health services should ideally be provided by trained professionals of the same gender as the client, and with a similar ethnic and linguistic background. The service should be provided in a non-threatening, non-stigmatising manner, and in a 'safe' environment with an unqualified assurance on confidentiality.
- Staff should be trained in racism awareness, and should be assisted and supported to develop antidiscriminatory practices, and skills in cross-cultural communication and counselling.

Table 4. Service issues for sexual health care for minority ethnic groups

- *Information*
  What language?
  Presentation – to be user friendly and sensitive
  What medium?
  Role of outreach
  Making use of community events – to utilise the collective aware-
  ness technique and attract those who individually may be inhibited
  by sexual health messages
- *Use of interpreters/advocates*
  Are linkworkers and advocates employed to address and communi-
  cate difficulties?
  Have they received appropriate training?
  What are their support structures?
- *Acceptability of services*
  Flexibility
  Safe environment
  Female staff
  Race awareness training
  Role of domiciliary services
- *Ethnic minority clinics*
  These are not universally successful. A prerequisite for success is
  networking and involving leaders of the local community. Services
  have to be welcoming, non-patronising and not exclusive to one
  group. However, some clients prefer men only and women only
  clinics.
- *Social and economic regeneration*
  This is the wider political agenda of eradicating poverty and
  unemployment, and improving housing and education.
- *Awareness of the impact of racial discrimination and immigration policies*
  These may separate spouses from each other and from their
  children. On occasion poverty may make the care of children only
  possible in the home country. This leads to emotional trauma,
  ambiguity about birth control and disillusionment of the siblings.
- *Health education and sex education*
  This must be socially and culturally acceptable, and not be seen as
  wanting to change the culture or have a victim blaming attitude.
- *Tackling prejudices in stereotyping and service delivery*
  The most potent example of this is the stereotypical maternity
  health carer who scolds Asian women for having more children
  and recommends or gives Depo Provera[16] without informed consent,
  leading to alienation of the client and rejection of family planning.
  The information and service needs of the ethnic minority population have to be addressed through a plan of action and not
  through a knee-jerk reaction.

- The quality of post-abortion care and postnatal contraception should be enhanced to ensure that the approach is sensitive to the needs of ethnic minority communities.
- Ethnic group monitoring of staff and equal opportunities in employment should apply to all aspects of health care work.

References

1 Firdous R, Bhopal RS. Reproductive health of Asian women: a comparative study with hospital and community perspectives. *Public Health* 1989: **103**: 307–15.

2 McAvoy BR. Asian women: (i) contraceptive knowledge, attitudes and usage; (ii) contraceptive services and cervical cytology. *Health Trends* 1988; **20**: 11–7.

3 Woollett A, Dosanjh-Matwala N, Hadlow J, Djahanbakhch O. The attitudes to contraception of Asian women in east London. *British Medical Journal* 1991; **17**: 72–83.

4 Balarajan R, Raleigh VS. The ethnic populations of England and Wales: the 1991 census. *Health Trends* 1992; **24**: 113–6.

5 Masters L, Nicholas H, Bunting P, Welch J. Family planning in genitourinary medicine: an opportunistic service? *Genitourinary Medicine* 1995; **71**: 334–5.

6 Christopher E. *Sexuality and birth control in community work*. 2nd edn. London: Tavistock Publications, 1987.

7 Fenton K, Johnson AM, Nicoll A. Race, ethnicity and sexual health. *British Medical Journal* 1997; **314**: 1703–4.

8 Morgan M. Lay perspectives, ethnicity and primary care: meeting in memory of Anthony Williams, 1949–1991. *Journal of the Royal Society of Medicine* 1993; **86**: 551–5.

9 Health Education Authority. *Health and lifestyles: black and minority ethnic groups in England*. London: HEA, 1994.

10 Stevens KA, Fletcher RF. Communicating with Asian patients. *British Medical Journal* 1989; **299**: 905–6.

11 Bryan B, Dadzie S, Scafe S. *The heart of the race: black women's lives in Britain*. London: Virago, 1985.

12 Wilcox M, Gardosi J, Mongelli M, Ray C, Johnson I. Birth weight from pregnancies dated by ultrasonography in a multi-cultural British population. *British Medical Journal* 1993; **307**: 588–91.

13 Lacey CJN, Merrick DW, Bensley DC, Fairly I. Analysis of the sociodemography of gonorrhoea in Leeds, 1989–93. *British Medical Journal* 1997; **314**: 1715–8.

14 Low N, Daker-White G, Barlow D, Pozniak AL. Gonorrhoea in inner London: results of a cross sectional study. *British Medical Journal* 1997; **314**: 1719–23.

15 Bhopal R. Is research into ethnicity and health racist, unsound, or important science? *British Medical Journal* 1997; **314**: 1751–6.

16 Ahmad WIU. Policies, pills and political will: a critique of policies to improve the health status of ethnic minorities. *Lancet* 1989; **i**: 148–50.

10 | Addictive behaviours

Adenekan Oyefeso
Senior Lecturer, Department of Addictive Behaviour, St George's Hospital Medical School, London

Hamid Ghodse
Professor, Department of Addictive Behaviour, St George's Hospital Medical School, London

Ethnic minorities are a heterogeneous population with differing values and attitudes.[1] These differences are a result of varying degrees of assimilation into the British culture and generational classification. Qureshi has suggested three generational classes among ethnic minority groups: the first, second and third generations.[2] His classification, however, does not include those who were born in Britain and received their education here. Such individuals have adopted British values, with less than expected of the values of their native culture. Furthermore, there are those who came to Britain as students and continued to live here after completing their studies.

With reference to substance misuse and addictive behaviour, we therefore propose four generational classes: the historical first generation (1GH); the contemporary first generation (1GC); the second and third generations (2G and 3G). The 1GH people are elderly dependent relatives of British residents who migrated to Britain for educational, economic and/or political reasons (ie the 1GC). The 2G people are children of the 1GC; a large proportion of them were born and mostly educated in Britain. The 3G people are children of the 2G, born and receiving their education in Britain; a proportion of this class are children of the 1GC, some of whom are recent migrants and refugees.

This chapter explores the nature of the relationship between cultural background and substance misuse and addictive behaviour in ethnic minority groups, and its impact on service utilisation by this section of the population. It describes different models of needs assessment for substance misuse services in ethnic minority groups.

Substance use and misuse in ethnic minorities

The pattern of substance use in ethnic minorities living in Britain is determined by the degree of assimilation of British values, and the generational class. 1GH ethnic minorities are likely to express the pattern of use that is commonly associated with their original culture. The 2G and 3G are more likely to describe a pattern identical to that observed in the white population, since the majority of members of these classes have assimilated some British values. The pattern described by the 1GC, however, is more likely to be a combination of both patterns, because members of the 1GC have assimilated the values of their original culture as well as British values.

Substance use and misuse in minority ethnic groups can therefore be described from two main perspectives – the historical and the contemporary.

Historical perspective

The substances used and misused by minority ethnic groups are not clearly different from those misused by the white majority.[3] The classes of substance include the opiates (such as opium, heroin, dihydrocodeine and methadone), stimulants (such as cocaine) and other stimulants (such as amphetamines, 'ecstasy' and khat), hallucinogens (such as LSD and psilocybin), central depressants (including barbiturates, minor tranquillisers and other sedatives), inhalants and volatile solvents, alcohol and tobacco. However, there are preferences for certain classes and modes of consumption by different ethnic groups, closely linked to the historical and cultural characteristics of each ethnic group.

The use of opium, for instance, is traditionally associated with the people of the Middle East, Asia and the Western Pacific, especially people of Afghanistan, Bangladesh, Burma, Egypt, Hong Kong, Indonesia, Iran, Macao, Pakistan, Singapore, Sri Lanka, Thailand and Vietnam. The traditional modes of consumption in these populations are by smoking, eating or drinking (for example 'milk shakes' with opium, particularly in north-west Pakistan), and the predominant users, in most parts, are older people in rural areas. In Britain this pattern of use can be associated with the 1GH. The use of heroin (an opium derivative) in these countries is associated with young urban dwellers, and the preferred modes of consumption are smoking and intravenous administration.[4] This pattern is similar to that described among the white and the 1GC, 2G and 3G ethnic minorities.

Cannabis is another drug widely used in certain cultures. It is the most widely misused illicit drug globally, with a long history of use among Indians, Pakistanis, rural Africans and West Indians. However, its mode of preparation and consumption differs from one culture to another. Whereas Africans and West Indians prefer to smoke it, Indians and Pakistanis prefer to take it as an infusion (bhang) or mixed with sweets.[4] These cultural differences in cannabis preparation have given rise to different cannabis forms in the British illicit drug market. The herbal preparations are the least potent. The most potent preparation is hashish, the pure resin of the flowering tops and leaves of the female cannabis plant. Hashish is five to eight times as potent as marijuana.[5]

Khat is a drug traditionally associated with some countries of East Africa such as Kenya, Somalia, Ethiopia, Tanzania, Djibouti, and the Middle East (Yemen). It is a stimulant derived from the leaves and young seedlings of the khat plant. Historically, it was consumed as an infusion, but in recent times in these regions it is widely chewed, a mode of consumption that has become a group activity of some social significance.[6]

In the class of stimulant drugs, cocaine has become the most popular drug of misuse. It is a derivative of the coca plant, noted for its energy and euphoria producing properties. Traditionally, the leaf of the coca plant was chewed by rural dwellers in the high Andean region, an area covering some of Argentina, Bolivia and Peru, but cocaine misuse has become global. Refinement of coca products, including illicit production of crack cocaine, has become a Western phenomenon with widespread social and health implications for urban dwellers of all ethnic groups (except for the 1GH ethnic minorities). Cocaine is consumed by sniffing or 'snorting', smoking and injection.

Reports of widespread use of inhalants and volatile substances outside Western societies have been associated with Mexico and other Latin American countries, and the Sudan. In the West, such abuse has neither a long history nor a cultural context and is usually associated with young children and teenagers (including 2G and 3G ethnic minorities).

The non-medical and recreational use of central depressants is similarly widespread and has neither cultural nor historical specificity. Although alcohol use is a global phenomenon, it may be controlled by religion, especially in the predominantly Muslim countries of North Africa, the Middle East and Asia.

Tobacco, unlike alcohol and the central depressants, has minimal religious or cultural restrictions, except for Sikhs, so it may be the substance with the highest risk to public health in all ethnic groups.

Contemporary perspective

The historical and cultural background of substances and their use and misuse has implications for minority ethnic groups in Britain. It is common to associate ganja smoking with black Caribbeans, khat with East Africans, marijuana with West Africans, hashish and opium with Indians and Pakistanis. Although these stereotypes developed out of historical facts, they do not completely explain substance use and misuse among minority ethnic communities in Britain today.

The use and misuse of, and addiction to, psychoactive substances have grown beyond cultural boundaries. In Britain they depict a classic case of cultural fusion in which the indigenous or native 'values' of an ethnic minority group have become adapted or absorbed by the predominant values of the host culture. Hence, some black Africans residing in Britain have adopted injecting drug use, which is largely uncommon in sub-Saharan Africa for instance. Similarly, black Caribbeans and Africans are now involved in the use and misuse of opiates and cocaine, drugs with which they are not traditionally associated, and use of which is likely to be uncommon among the 1GH minorities.

An understanding of the nature and pattern of substance misuse in minority ethnic groups would therefore call for both cultural specificity (historical perspective) and cultural fusion (contemporary perspective) approaches, including the role of generational class characteristics.

Extent of problem substance use in ethnic minorities

Data on the extent of problematic substance use in Britain are rarely available. This rarity is even more pronounced in minority populations.[7] There is a growing belief that ethnic minorities are less likely to participate in health surveys than their white counterparts.[8] In the Merton and Sutton lifestyle and health survey, for instance, a lower response rate (7.3%) by minority ethnic groups than the census figure (9.1%) was observed.[9]

Consequently, many needs assessment exercises have had to rely heavily on data obtained from agency contacts reported to substance misuse databases and the Home Office addicts index, but these data do not include the 'hidden population' who, for a number of reasons, do not attend services.

There are limitations in using these data to describe extent and pattern of drug use in ethnic minorities. These limitations are related to factors that determine the utilisation of substance misuse services.

Other potential sources of data on extent of substance misuse, such as national, regional and local surveys, by default target people in schools, in employment, and of fixed address. In the light of existing racial inequalities in these areas, such surveys are more likely to exclude minority ethnic people.

Service utilisation in ethnic minority groups

There is a general assumption in Britain that minority ethnic people underpresent to substance misuse services.[8] A recent study[10] has shown that this is partially true. The pattern of presentation to specialist drug services is, like ethnic minority values, not homogeneous. This study, which is a population-based analysis of presentation data as reported to the South Thames (West) substance use database, has revealed that presentation to substance misuse services is influenced by an interaction of ethnicity and sex. Male Chinese and Indians significantly underpresent, while male black Caribbeans and black others significantly overpresent. Among females, the only significant result was reported in female Indians; they underpresent to drug services.[10]

The results of another study investigating changes in presentation rates to services over a 12-month period have shown that changes in each ethnic group are generally influenced by gender and the type of main drug, but in a group-specific pattern.[11]

Determinants of service response in ethnic minority groups

Many factors determine the utilisation of specialist substance misuse services by minority ethnic groups. These factors can be classified into two broad categories: sociocultural and health service related.

Sociocultural factors

Some common sociocultural determinants of service utilisation in minority communities are linguistic limitations, community-specific definition of substance misuse, community values on self-disclosure, and sociocultural protectiveness.

Community-specific definition of substance misuse. Differing cultural perceptions about substance use and related problems influence service utilisation. For instance, among some black Africans, alcohol consumption is part of social and religious life. Alcohol intoxication attracts relatively low sanctions, except when it is accompanied by socially disruptive and harmful behaviour. Alcoholism, however, is socially stigmatised in the same way as mental illness, making it more difficult to establish the concept within this ethnic group.[12] The same applies to problem drug use, with drug addicts generally perceived as mentally ill.

In Asian communities, alcohol use is prohibited or restricted by some of the major religions, so presentation to alcohol services for help may be perceived as a betrayal of faith, and could deter those affected from seeking appropriate help until the situation becomes life threatening. There is evidence, for instance, that in 1979–1983 mortality from chronic liver disease and cirrhosis among men born in south Asia was more than twice the England and Wales average,[13] and mortality for liver cancer was 1.7 times the national average; in these men alcohol consumption was more likely to have accounted for the excess of cirrhosis mortality than hepatitis B.[14]

Linguistic limitations. Many ethnic minorities, especially the 1GH, have problems communicating in, and understanding, English. In the late 1970s, it was estimated that there were 200,000 adults residing in Britain speaking a little English or none at all; most were of Asian origin, with smaller proportions from Cyprus, southern Europe and North Africa.[15] With the rapidly increasing rate of migration into Britain in the 1980s, this estimate may have doubled. The fact that not many agencies have bilingual staff may be a major barrier to access to services for linguistic minorities.

Community values on self-disclosure. Low rates of presentation to substance misuse services in ethnic minorities can also be associated with cultural prescriptions about what may be discussed outside the family. Early socialisation of 1GH of Asian and African origins emphasises the value of family loyalty. The need for this is accentuated in an environment where there is fear of being persecuted or discriminated against by the majority community. Presenting to services where personal details are routinely entered on forms, and kept in files and on computers, for future use may be understandably perceived as vulnerability to further persecution. This perception will be heightened among refugees, whose immigration status is yet to be determined, and among many others whose leave to remain in the United Kingdom has expired. To these people, the Data Protection Act has no relevance.

Sociocultural protectiveness. Service utilisation can sometimes be determined by community values that serve protective functions for members' involvement in substance misuse. These values, which include strong family ties, may result in low prevalence of substance misuse in some minority communities[16] and, consequently, low service uptake. It may be necessary to investigate the nature of these protective factors and how they can be enhanced in order to reduce the prevalence of substance misuse in the entire population.

Also, ethnicity and cultural factors are known to co-vary with genetic factors in predicting alcohol use.[17] For instance, some people of Asian origin homozygous for the mutant of the human class II aldehyde dehydrogenase (ALDH2) isozyme (ie ALDH*2/ALDH2*2) are protected from problematic alcohol use and alcoholism.[18] This is because they are highly sensitive to alcohol and their response to alcohol is similar to an alcohol–disulfiram reaction. For these individuals, low service uptake might be a valid indicator of low prevalence of problematic alcohol use.

Health service related factors

There are three main service-related determinants of utilisation of services in minority communities: availability of resources, physical accessibility and social accessibility.

Availability of resources. Availability has been described as the relationship between the volume and type of existing resources and the requirement for fulfilling the population's health needs.[19] Availability can be assessed in terms of the extent to which specialist substance misuse services are culturally sensitive.

A strong indicator of inadequate sensitivity, for instance, is the assumption that specialist drug services, in both the statutory and non-statutory sectors, were designed mainly for white opiate users in their mid-to-late 20s.[20] Furthermore, until recently, very few specialist substance misuse services had a policy that encourages an understanding of minority community values, traditions and customs. Of those that do, very few proceed to develop focused interventions, communications and support within the target minority ethnic communities.[21]

Physical accessibility. This term describes the relationship between client or need location and the ease of contact with the service. It is sometimes referred to as geographical accessibility when the focus is on service location; temporal accessibility when the focus is on opening time;[19] and structural accessibility when the emphasis is

on type of accommodation and facility. Access to specialist substance misuse services by all clients can be increased when reaching them requires little distance, short travel time and low travel
cost, so provision of transportation and/or payment of fares
usually enhances geographical accessibility. Where feasible,
services are best located *within* communities.

Temporal accessibility focuses on service schedules such as opening time, hours for collecting prescriptions for substitute medication, time, frequency and duration of counselling sessions, waiting
time before first appointment, etc. Increasing temporal accessibility
requires that service providers should have a thorough understanding of users' attitudes and perceptions of, and expectations from,
the service.

Structural accessibility focuses on the perceived adequacy and
convenience of the agency's physical facilities. In some minority
ethnic communities, non-hospital settings are preferred in order
to avoid the stigma associated with consultations within hospital
settings, especially psychiatric hospitals or genitourinary clinics.
Some others prefer private (independent) rather than public settings.[22] Many minority ethnic community members attend appointments with their children owing to the lack of childcare facilities
which would enhance structural accessibility.

Social accessibility. It often happens that, in spite of the availability
and physical accessibility of substance misuse services, minority
ethnic community members are still unwilling to use them. Where
this happens, the primary explanation is one of low service acceptability or poor social accessibility. Social accessibility is a two-way
process that describes the relationship between clients' attitudes
towards providers, as well as those of providers towards the
clients.[19] One measure of social accessibility is the cultural competency of a service, ie its ability to develop and encourage attitudes
that respect rather than show receptivity to different cultures and
people. In order to be socially accessible, and therefore improve
rates of utilisation, substance misuse services would need to be culturally competent, which means that they should *actively* seek
advice from ethnic minority communities and incorporate their
practices with a sense of commitment.[22]

Needs assessment models

If substance misuse services are to meet the needs of local minority
ethnic communities, they need to be adequately resourced, and
remain physically and socially accessible. To achieve these broad

objectives, it is necessary to conduct a needs assessment; this should often involve assessing the needs of the clients as well as the services' needs (eg the capability of the services to meet the clients' needs). The focus of a needs assessment exercise (client centred or service centred, or both) determines the type of method or model of assessment to adopt.

Whatever model is adopted, needs assessment exercises can offer a range of benefits, for both minority ethnic community members and substance misuse services. They can assist agencies in clarifying their philosophy, goals and objectives, and making these sensitive to local needs. They can also help agencies to establish an objective framework for evaluating accountability (ie the extent to which agencies or services are meeting specified objectives). They can provide information that enhances effective client–personnel matching. Brief protocols of some needs assessment models that yield valid results in minority ethnic communities are described below.

Equitable distribution model

This model[23] uses inferential indicators to assess need; their use is necessary because systematic epidemiological data on the extent of problematic substance use among ethnic minority groups in Great Britain are not available. Furthermore, problematic substance use is often not amenable to direct examination or measurement, except in those in contact with intervention agencies. Therefore, needs can be defined as observable social indicators that are presumed to be highly correlated with problematic substance use.

This model, particularly useful for improving service planning and resource allocation, can be implemented in the following stages:

1 Select a number of predictors of substance misuse from a comprehensive review of the literature.
2 Identify reliable sources of routine local data on these indicators.
3 Extract data on indicators for each ethnic group in the catchment area.
4 Calculate for each ethnic group the proportion of the catchment area's total that this figure represents.
5 Sum up the proportions of all indicators for each minority ethnic group, and divide by the number of indicators used. This provides the mean proportion.

If an ethnic group reveals, for example, 10% of the problem, as measured by the chosen indicators, under a principle of equitable distribution it should receive 10% of the resources.

All inferential indicators can have equal weighting, or can be weighted according to the strength of their predictability of problematic substance use, as reported in the literature.

A list of inferential indicators of problematic substance use relevant to this model includes the following:

- substance misuse services utilisation data;
- unemployment;
- drug-related arrests;
- criminal justice system data;
- arrests for driving while intoxicated;
- drug seizures;
- arrests for disturbed behaviour and application of the Mental Health Act;
- morbidity data on conditions associated with drug and alcohol use (hepatitis B and C; tuberculosis; syphilis; liver cirrhosis; substance-related deliberate self-harm; admission to psychiatric hospitals; HIV; alcohol-related motor accidents; substance-related accident and emergency admissions, eg drug overdose and accidents);
- mortality data on conditions associated with drug and alcohol use (hepatitis B and C; tuberculosis; syphilis; HIV; substance-related suicide; liver cirrhosis).

Services utilisation model

This model[9] adapts an indirect method of rate adjustment, commonly used in mortality studies, to estimate the extent to which members of minority ethnic groups under- or over-present to specialist substance misuse services. It relies heavily on data entries to the drug misuse databases which record agency contacts of persons seeking help for substance misuse problems.

This model is useful for determining the extent of demand for specialist intervention, and can be implemented in the following steps:

1 Identify clearly defined ethnic groups and relevant age categories.
2 Extract relevant census data (local, regional or national) on the selected age categories in the defined ethnic groups.
3 Extract relevant contact or presentation data from the drug misuse databases on the selected age categories in the defined ethnic groups, within a specified period.

4   Calculate age-specific presentation rates for each ethnic group (divide the total number of presentations in each age category by the census figure for that age category in each ethnic group).
5   Calculate the number of presentations to be expected in each ethnic group in the chosen sample if it experienced the age-specific presentation rate of the census data (standard population). (Multiply the age-specific rate by the number of presentations in each age category and sum to obtain the expected number of presentations in each ethnic group.)
6   Divide the observed by the expected number of presentations and multiply by 100 to obtain the 'standardised presentation ratio'. If this is greater than 100 it signifies overpresentation, and less than 100 signifies underpresentation; it has a Poisson distribution from which appropriate confidence limits and significance levels can be estimated.

Cultural competency model

Services that are developed to cater for a multiethnic population must be culturally competent. Cultural competency, therefore, needs to be measured against some standards or criteria. One of such standards is termed the 'minority service success' (MSS) rate.[22]

This model evaluates the degree of cultural competency in an agency, in the following steps:

1   Obtain the total population of a catchment area (N).
2   Obtain the total number of clients served by all agencies (TY) in the catchment area within a specified period.
3   Obtain the total population of targeted ethnic minorities in the catchment area (NT).
4   Obtain the actual number (AX) of clients from the minority group of interest served by an agency.
5   Calculate the expected number (EX) of clients from the minority group of interest who could have been served by the agency during the specified period, using the formula:
       $EX = NT \times TY/N$
6   Calculate the ratio of targeted minority clients in the minority group of interest actually served by the agency and those who could have been served during the specified period, using the formula:
       $MSS = AX/EX \times 100$

Demand pattern assessment model

The 'demand pattern assessment' (DPA) model[24] entails the collection of information on demand patterns by evaluating the conceptualisation and prioritisation of substance use in minority ethnic communities.

This model can be used for: examining the nature, extent and pattern of substance use; estimating the nature and extent of problematic substance use, including the numbers and types of current or potential clients served and those at risk of drug and alcohol dependence; identifying new trends in problematic substance use; understanding the communities' perception of and response to needs and problems relating to substance misuse; and understanding communities' perception of, and attitudes towards, existing substance misuse services. It can be implemented using the outline below:

1 Conduct an in-depth interview of a wide range of opinion leaders and key informants in each selected community with focus on socioeconomic, attitudinal and cultural aspects of substance use, including the influence of religion and family relationships. Caution must be exercised as some 'opinion leaders' have denied drug problems in their communities and halted developments. The ethogenic approach should be employed to facilitate data analysis. The most relevant techniques are the synchronic and diachronic analyses.[25] *Synchronic analysis* involves the description of the nature, extent and pattern of substance use within the community at any one time (cross-sectional analysis). *Diachronic analysis* entails the study of stages and processes by which different patterns of substance use are created and abandoned, change and are changed (longitudinal analysis). Diachronic analysis has greater implications for the development of problem-oriented services. The ethogenic approach is also useful in providing a better understanding of sexuality in minority ethnic communities and their perception of HIV/AIDS and attitudes towards safer sex practices.

2 Conduct a questionnaire survey written in the relevant community languages, with items based on the results of ethogenic analyses. Distribute the questionnaires through recognised communication channels within each community. In the case of survey interviews, match the interviewers and interviewees for ethnicity and language.

3 Develop a system of monitoring with relevant interest groups within each community, to assess, prospectively, changes in the nature, extent and pattern of substance use.

Improving availability of data for health needs assessment

Except for the DPA model, the other models rely heavily on routinely collected data, so it is imperative that the quality and completeness of health service data on minority ethnic groups be routinely audited. Other suggestions include:

- Routine screening for drug and alcohol use in general practice and setting up a database for the same, including details of ethnic characteristics.
- Introduction of liaison services between specialist substance misuse services and general hospitals. A model of this is currently being used with success by the drug and alcohol liaison team at St George's Hospital in London, which operates in both in- and out-patient services. Its aims include: assessment of drug/alcohol problems; advice and guidance on substance use, consequences and treatment options; liaison with and referral to other substance misuse services within both the statutory and voluntary sectors; guidance on management of patients with substance use problems, and possible interaction with other treatments; and provision of training for health care workers on the guidelines for early recognition, assessment and treatment of substance use and misuse.[26] The liaison service has tremendous potential for detecting early drug/alcohol problems in ethnic minorities in treatment on medical wards. If appropriately resourced, this service can effectively complement existing data on the nature and extent of substance use and misuse in ethnic minorities by identifying those who have not been detected by existing reporting systems.
- Another level of response must be to make existing services more attractive to this section of the population. There are arguments for a separate service for ethnic minorities.[27] These have been opposed on the grounds that such services will further accentuate the existing perception of racial inequality.[28] What we suggest is an expansion of existing services. The introduction of liaison services such as the drug and alcohol liaison team[18] should be considered. It is necessary also to employ staff from various racial backgrounds to reflect local communities[29] and provide periodic cultural sensitivity training to currently employed agency staff to meet the demands of their catchment area. More choices of substance misuse services should also be made available to minority ethnic communities. In this regard, voluntary sector development in this area should be encouraged.

References

1 Office of Population Censuses and Surveys. *General household survey 1991*. London: HMSO, 1993.
2 Qureshi B. *Transcultural medicine*. London: Kluwer, 1989.
3 Daniel P, Brown A, Jones M, Morgan D. *Problem drug use reported by services in Greater London*. A collaborative report by the regional drug misuse databases. London: St. George's Hospital Medical School, 1993.
4 Arif A. World drug problems and WHO strategies. In: Edwards G, Arif A, eds. *Drug problems in the socio-cultural context: a basis for policies and programme planning*. Geneva: WHO, 1980.
5 Ghodse AH. Cannabis psychosis. *British Journal of Addiction* 1986; **81**: 478–83.
6 Baasher TA. The use of khat: a stimulant with regional distribution. In: Edwards G, Arif A, eds. *Drug problems in the socio-cultural context: a basis for policies and programme planning*. Geneva: WHO, 1980.
7 British Medical Association. *The misuse of drugs*. Netherlands: Harwood Academic, 1997.
8 Abdulrahim D. *Working with diversity: HIV prevention and black and ethnic minority communities*. London: NE and NW Thames Regional Health Authorities, 1991.
9 Rawaf S. *For better health*. Annual report of the director of public health 1992. London: Merton and Sutton Health Authority, 1993.
10 Oyefeso A, Jones M, Ghodse H. *Ethnic differences in pattern of presentation to services for problem drug users in South West Thames Region of England*. Paper presented at the 38th and 21st International Institutes on the Prevention and Treatment of Alcoholism and Drug Dependence, Prague, 1994.
11 Oyefeso A, Jones M, Ghodse H. Ethnic monitoring in specialist drug services: a population-based analysis. *Journal of Substance Misuse* 1996; **1**: 91–6.
12 Babor T. Alcohol: customs and rituals. In: Snyder SH, Lader MH, eds. *The encyclopaedia of psychoactive drugs*. London: Burke, 1986.
13 Office of Population Censuses and Surveys. *Mortality and geography: a review in the mid 1980s*. The Registrar General's decennial supplement for England and Wales. Series DS No. 9. London: HMSO, 1990.
14 McKeigue PM, Karmi G. Alcohol consumption and alcohol-related problems in Afro-Caribbeans and South Asians in the United Kingdom. *Alcohol and Alcoholism* 1993; **28**: 1–10.
15 Smith DJ. *The facts of racial disadvantage*. London: Penguin, 1977.
16 McAdoo HP. Stress absorbing systems in black families. *Family Relations* 1982; **31**: 479–88.
17 Oyefeso A. Sociocultural aspects of substance use and misuse. *Current Opinion in Psychiatry* 1994; **7**: 273–7.
18 Wall TL, Thomasson HR, Schuckit MA, Ehlers CL. Subjective feelings of alcohol intoxication in Asians with genetic variations of ALDH2 alleles. *Alcoholism: Clinical and Experimental Research* 1992; **16**: 991-5.
19 Penchansky R, Thomas JW. The concept of access: definition and relationship to consumer satisfaction. *Medical Care* 1981; **19**: 127–40.

20 Daniel T. Ethnic minorities' use of drug services. *Druglink* 1993; Jan/Feb: 16–7.
21 Oyefeso A. Assessing the needs of problem drug users in a multicultural society. In: *Substance misuse and diverse cultural needs.* Proceedings of the Trent Regional Conference, Derby, 1994.
22 Kim S, McLeod JH, Shantzis C. Cultural competence for evaluators working with Asian-American communities: some practical considerations. In: Orlandi MA, Weston R, Epstein LG, eds. *Cultural competence for evaluators: a guide for alcohol and other drug abuse prevention practitioners working with ethnic/racial communities.* Rockville, MD: US Department of Health and Human Services, 1992.
23 Simeone RS, Frank B, Aryan Z. Needs assessment in substance misuse: a comparison of approaches and case study. *International Journal of the Addictions* 1993; **28**: 767–92.
24 Lengeler C, Mshinda H, de Savigny D, *et al.* The value of questionnaires aimed at key informants, and distributed through an existing administrative system, for rapid and cost-effective health assessment. *World Health Statistics Quarterly* 1991; **44**: 150–9.
25 Harre R. Accounts, actions and meanings: the practice of participatory psychology. In: Brenner M, Marsh P, Brenner M, *et al*, eds. *The social context of method.* London: Croom Helm, 1978.
26 Ghodse AH, ed. *Psychiatry of addictive behaviour handbook.* London: St. George's Hospital Medical School, 1992.
27 Greenwood A. Ethnic minorities' mental health: the case for a specialist unit. *Ethnic Minorities Health* 1993; **4**: i–iii.
28 Parker H. Reply to Anna Greenwood: 'Ethnic minorities' mental health: the case for a specialist unit. *Ethnic Minorities Health* 1993; **4**: i.
29 Esmail A, Carnall D. Tackling racism in the NHS: we need action not words. *British Medical Journal* 1997; **314**: 618–9.

11 | Primary health care

Salma Uddin
General Practitioner, Wallington, Sutton, Surrey

Sheila Webb
Consultant in Public Health Medicine, Bradford Health Authority

Salman Rawaf
Director of Clinical Standards, Merton Sutton and Wandsworth Health Authority, London

Primary health care is a term that is difficult to define. For many, it covers the services provided by general practitioners (GPs) and their teams, general dental practitioners, pharmacists and community nurses. Others widen the definition to include all health care services provided outside hospitals. However, for practical reasons, this chapter focuses on the services provided by GPs and their teams (primary health care teams). The introduction of the 1990 contract for GPs and the National Health Service (NHS) reforms, although maintaining the main characteristics of British primary health care, extended the roles and functions of GPs and their teams.[1-3] Today's GPs not only provide care but also currently purchase secondary care on behalf of the population registered with them (GP fundholders, multifunds, total purchasing projects, GP commissioning groups, locality commissioning, and in the near future 'primary care commissioning groups'). This extension of the role is based on the assumption that, through the 'primary-care led NHS', decisions taken about health care will move closer to patients and local people, and thus be more responsive to their needs.[4,5]

Characteristics of primary health care

Fry described the characteristic features of British general practice as:[6]

- single portal of entry into the NHS (except for accident and emergencies and sexually transmitted diseases);

- direct access to 24-hour availability for registered patients;
- first contact care involving diagnosis, assessment, triage and management or resolution of all defined problems;
- co-ordination of access to local medical and social services for individual patient and family needs;
- gatekeeping function into hospitals through selective referral;
- relatively small and stable population base;
- long-term and continuing generalist, personal and family care within the community, by doctors and health teams, of patients who come to know each other well over the years;
- the content of clinical morbidity and mortality, and of social problems and local needs, will be those occurring in a small population;
- the GP has the opportunity to become the leader, provider and initiator of good health in the local community.

Since the 1970s, GPs have faced many changes and developments, with greater emphasis being placed on general practice as an 'organisation' rather than on the contributions of individual GPs.[4,7,8] This has been in response to the changes in demographic and social trends, advancement in clinical sciences, the population's needs and expectations of health services, the increased competition between primary care providers, and better choices and opportunities demanded by parents, health professionals and managers.[8,9] Nevertheless, primary health care is still underdeveloped, especially in the inner cities, where the larger proportion of minority ethnic groups live with associated problems including: areas of deprivation, higher social needs, unemployment, cultural diversity and population movements.[10,11]

Demands on primary care

General practice care accounts for 95% of contacts that people have with the NHS. The fourth national study of general practice showed that the proportion of people who use GP services at least once during the year increased from 67% in 1955–56 to 78% in 1991–92.[12,13]

People from ethnic minorities, in particular Asians, consult their GPs more than the rest of the population.[14,15] Data from the fourth national general practice study show that consultations were highest among Indian subcontinent ethnic groups, particularly for serious conditions.[12] A higher proportion of ethnic groups of both sexes aged 16–64 years sought medical advice for symptoms, signs and ill-defined conditions compared with white people. Adults in the black African-Caribbean, Indian and Pakistani/Bangladeshi ethnic groups were more likely to consult a doctor than white people for diseases in each of the International Classification of Disease (ICD) chapters, with the exception of neoplasms and mental disorders. Among children, there was no difference between those who were white and those of other ethnic groups in the proportion who attended their doctors for all diseases and conditions.[12] However, older people demand more services from their GPs, especially those of Asian origin.[14,17] Some attribute this to the perceptions of the elderly who consider themselves to be sicker than the white British people.[18]

Cultural attitudes to health

Many factors lead to GP consultations. Most significant among these are the severity of the disease, individual awareness of the possible benefits of health care, health beliefs, socioeconomic factors, accessibility to health care, previous experience with the service, the attitude of professionals towards various ethnic groups, or a combination of these factors. Nevertheless, in general terms some GPs felt that patients from some ethnic groups required longer consultation times, were less specific about their illnesses, were more demanding and tended to be less compliant.[19]

The Health Education Authority's UK-wide survey on health and lifestyle showed that on their last visit to their GP 53% of men and 34% of women consulted for treatment.[17] However, Pakistani and Bangladeshi men are more likely to visit their GP for treatment (60% and 63% respectively). The study showed that attendances for adult health checks, such as blood pressure and cervical smears, are less likely among minority ethnic groups.[17]

A mixture of beliefs in health and health care tend to influence a person's decision to seek medical care. These beliefs, contradictory sometimes, range from a modern understanding of causation of disease and ill health to traditional beliefs of spiritual and cultural origin.[18,20] While some people are brought up on a prevention concept ('better see the doctor in case it may hurt me'), others tend to go to the doctor 'because I might die'. In many cultures, health and illness are determined by 'God's will' and it is believed that human interference can do little.

Asian patients from the Indian subcontinent and the Far East are more likely to present with psychosomatic symptoms, ie vague general symptoms of illness.[15] The Chinese, for example, may attribute ill health to heat and cold;[20] a common cold would require a diet that is hot (and containing meat). Some Africans and West Indians, who believe in voodoo or witch medicine, consider that mental illness or poor health may be attributed to persons wishing them harm. Hindus may attribute ill health to angering their gods. Multiple consultation with alternative practitioners is not uncommon among some patients from minority ethnic groups. GPs and their primary health care teams therefore require a sympathetic understanding of the cultural factors involved in clinical presentations. A sensitive approach to history taking is essential in the care of many minority ethnic groups.

Access to primary care

A high consultation rate among certain ethnic groups is not an indication of better access to primary health care. Ethnic minority women still consult their GPs less than their male counterparts,[15] and lack of access to a female doctor is for many an issue of important cultural and religious significance. However, this preference is identified by most women from all cultures, particularly for gynaecological problems.[21] In a UK-wide survey, less than one in five women see female GPs,[17] though a significant number would prefer to see one. Preference for female doctors is much stronger among south Asian women.

The language barrier is well documented in many studies, and the use of siblings in translating is not uncommon among first-generation immigrants. The use of formal and informal interpreting increases across age bands, and is significantly higher among women. However, while language may be a diminishing barrier among some minority ethnic groups, this is certainly not the case for refugees, asylum seekers and some south Asian groups.

The ethnic origin of GP is perceived as important among some ethnic groups. Over four in five south Asians attend surgeries with an Asian doctor.[17] In service planning and recruitment terms it should not be difficult to meet such expectations and cultural preference in geographical areas with high concentrations of ethnic minorities. Matching some groups, for example Asian patients with a doctor or health professional who speaks the same language, may be difficult in many areas.

Practice based health needs assessment

With the replacement of GP fundholding with primary care 'commissioning' groups (PCGs), all practices, in various geographical configurations, will take direct responsibility to commission a wide range of services for patients registered with them.[4] The driving force for such commissioning will be the 3-year plans for Health Improvement Programmes which will be drawn up in collaboration with health authorities, NHS trusts and local authorities.[4] This is an essential prerequisite for these PCGs to prepare their business plans, respond to their patients' needs and maximise the use of resources available to them. It is expected that PCGs will have the opportunity to become freestanding Primary Care Trusts.[4] Such a shift in commissioning power is seen by many as a marginalisation of the population-based purchasing by the health authorities which takes into account the total need of the population and the major influences on their health.[22] Innovative and robust methods should be developed, for both needs assessment and commissioning, that will incorporate the total district and practice populations' needs and ensure equity and accessibility to appropriate health care. Chapter 2 outlines the theoretical framework for health needs assessment. While a comprehensive needs assessment for any district population is a complex, long-term and continuous process, which requires the expertise of public health physicians and others, simple and practical approaches are needed at practice level. Despite many limitations, increasingly locality and practice based needs assessments are becoming reality.[23–26]

Approaches to needs assessment at locality and practice level

One of the main strengths of British general practice is the long-term relationship between doctors and their patients.[6] This gives GPs a greater opportunity to collect detailed information on patients registered with them. In theory the aggregate of these data will be the basic foundation for needs assessment at practice level, but it is more difficult and requires resources and expertise. Simpler approaches are needed to assess the needs of a practice population. These approaches should be complementary to, rather than instead of, the health authority's district-wide or locality needs assessments. Combining these two levels will give wider opportunities to reach a balance between practice based and population-wide interventions – a challenging role for the new health authorities. While the practice based needs assessment will address the individual needs of those registered with the practice, the locality based assessment will help to determine priorities and service delivery in the geographical area of the practices.

A practical method of health needs assessment at practice level should include both quantitative and qualitative approaches. Chapters 2 and 3 gave some descriptions of these approaches. Caution should be exercised with the interpretation of the collected data at practice level, in particular in relation to prioritisation of services and shifting contracts. The small size of many practices (2,500–10,000 clients) means greater variability in population structure, mortality and morbidity. Many practices, especially those in inner cities, experience a large turnover of registration on their lists (up to 30%). Furthermore, the lack of defined geographical boundaries of the practice population, and the right of GPs to remove patients from their practice lists, make it difficult to obtain consistently reliable data for population-wide interpretations.

Data collection: quantitative approaches

Through collaborative work with the health authority's public health and information departments much of the numerical routine data could be obtained and analysed specifically for the practice population and activities. The practice database could be a valuable source of information from which to assess the practice population's needs, commission health care effectively, and monitor performance. The database covers three areas: patient registration, clinical information and prescribing. Other data on mortality, clinical audit, clinical effectiveness, local hospital activities, housing and environment could be used to supplement the practice data for better decisions as to how to use the resources more effectively to meet identified health needs.

Patient register

The electronic age/sex register provides valuable information about the practice list and the composition of the population served by that practice. One would expect that the practice population is a mirror image of the local geographical population. In some practices this is not the case. Many patients prefer to choose a GP who they believe can respond to their needs. This is certainly true of some ethnic groups who prefer a GP from the same culture and one who speaks their language.[17] Comparing the structure of the practice population with that of the locality and the total district population will provide valuable information on the main problems in relation to specific age groups or gender.

Mapping the practice population, using the postcode of every individual registered with the practice, will provide a clear indication about how patients are scattered.[27] It will enable the practice to predict the likely demand for practice attendance or home visits.

Census and deprivation data provided by the health authority for the practice's locality form an extremely useful set of information to understand the socioeconomic and ethnic composition of the population served by the practice. Deprivation allowances are calculated on the basis of the Jarman index.[28] These allowances are designed to compensate GPs for the extra workload expected in these deprived areas as a proxy for poorer health status. Other annual update information from the health authority and the national statistics office (Office of Population Censuses and Surveys), for example mortality data by diseases, and annual birth rates, will be of use to predict some of the future workload of practices.

Clinical information

The annual consultation rate per person in general practice is between 3 and 4. It is much higher among children (5), the elderly over the age of 70 years (6.5+)[6] and minority ethnic groups (4.2–7.9).[17] General practice is therefore a good source of morbidity data on a small and relatively stable population base. Clinical information could be classified into various groups to calculate the practice workload and the expected referral to hospitals and other specialist services. These groups include obstetric care, gynaecological problems, child health, congenital disorders, ill-defined minor conditions (eg minor trauma, respiratory, gastrointestinal, dermatological, musculoskeletal), specific conditions (eg urinary tract infection, backache, acute throat infection, otitis media, eczema-dermatitis, dyspepsia, constipation, piles, hernia), severe conditions (most of which are emergency cases), chronic conditions (these constitute the bulk of the work in general practice, eg diabetes, asthma, chronic bronchitis, arthritis, hypertension, heart failure, stroke, epilepsy, multiple sclerosis, Parkinson's, thyroid disorders, peptic ulcer, irritable bowel syndrome, chronic renal failure, mental disorders, drug and alcohol misuse), cancers and social problems.[6,29] Patients' chronic disease registers at practice level are useful tools for assessing needs, workloads and outcomes, as well as for planning appropriate management protocols for these patients.[29] Data from health promotion clinics can provide a valuable set of information on patients' lifestyles that influence their current and future health. Call and recall systems for cervical and breast cancer screening are another set of useful information.

Referrals to hospital and specialist services have increased over the years and currently constitute around 10% of all consultations with GPs. The majority of these referrals are for outpatient consultations and diagnostic facilities. Data are obtainable for all outpatient referrals by specialty, inpatient admissions (finished consultant episodes) by diagnosis, domiciliary consultations by specialty, and referral within the practice to the specialist outreach clinics by diagnosis.

Prescribing information

The number of items prescribed by GPs has been increasing over the years. Information on the items prescribed, by age group, by body system using ICD coding (eg respiratory or cardiac) and cost, is available from both the practice computer and the PACT data supplied by the Prescription Pricing Authority. However, since a considerable number of patients do not get their prescriptions dispensed, the PACT data are less reliable. Analysing prescribing data will give an indication of the size of the clinical activities, the main health problems, effectiveness of the therapy, and patient compliance.

Hospital activities data

It would be very useful to obtain data about hospital activities in two possible sets: total activities and those related to the practice. Inpatient and day case data are available through the 'hospital episode statistics' system for a period of treatment under the care of a consultant ('finished consultant episode'). The data will provide patient administrative details, consultant, specialty, clinical details on diagnosis, treatment, operations, and other interventions undertaken. Outpatient data are available by consultant and specialty but are not coded for diagnosis. Similarly, accident and emergency data are analysed by broad specialties. Information on waiting lists and times by specialties is another set of useful data to assess the unmet demands on the services. Furthermore, data on open access to some services, such as radiology, pathology, endoscopy and substance misuse, are also useful in deciding treatment and care plans.

Clinical audit and effectiveness data

Clinical audit should be available from the audit programmes under-taken by the practice, group of practices in the area, and the 'primary care audit groups'. Findings from these audits, as well as those published nationally, could be used to change clinical prac-tices. Effectiveness data, however, are not easy to obtain and inter-pret at practice level, as evidence varies and sometimes conflicts. *Evidence based medicine* (published by the British Medical Journal), the Cochrane Collaboration database of systematic reviews (pub-lished on CD-ROM and updated regularly) and the NHS Centre for Reviews and Dissemination provide excellent summaries of scientific evidence of effectiveness of current interventions, eg *Effectiveness matters*. Evaluation has already shown that evidence based treatment guidelines can improve referrals to secondary care and prescribing.[30]

Other sources of information

Data available from local government on housing, employment (or lack of it), the local economy and environment will help in the process of determining priorities and targeting specific groups of the community.

Data collection: qualitative approaches

This approach, which complements the quantitative data collec-tion, is useful for collecting information on patients' and pro-fessionals' perceptions of health and illness, expectations of inter-ventions and the health services, and experiences with the services (see Chapter 3). Various methods could be employed to capture information in the above three areas: the use of questionnaires, observation, in-depth interviews, focus groups, content analysis, case studies and consensus methods.[31] Qualitative approaches are very useful to elicit the views and the beliefs of the minority ethnic groups served by the practice, to enable GPs and their teams to prioritise services and tailor them sensitively to their clients' needs.

Medical manpower

Although 25% of GP principals were born and qualified overseas,[5] many other GPs from minority ethnic groups were born and qualified in the UK. The UK-wide Health and Lifestyle Survey shows that 79% of clients see a white GP.[17] The African-Caribbeans, however, see equal proportions of white and non-white GPs, and four out of five Asians are registered with an Asian GP. It is essential, in addressing cultural competence, to develop appropriate packages of training in cultural diversity and the health and social needs of various communities with different cultures.

References

1 Department of Health. *Promoting better health.* London: HMSO, 1987.
2 Department of Health. *Working for patients.* London: HMSO, 1989.
3 Department of Health. *The National Health Service and Community Care Act 1990.* London: HMSO, 1990.
4 Secretary of State for Health. *The new NHS – modern and dependable.* London: Stationery Office, 1997.
5 NHS Executive. *GP commissioning groups.* EL(97)37. Leeds: NHSE, 1997.
6 Fry J. *General practice: the facts.* Oxford: Radcliffe, 1993.
7 Gray DP. Twenty-five years of development in general practice. *Health Trends* 1994; **26**: 4–5.
8 Ham C. A primary care market. *British Medical Journal* 1996; **313**: 127–8.
9 Secretary of State for Health. *Choice and opportunity – primary care: the future.* White Paper presented to Parliament. London: Department of Health, 1996.
10 Department of Health, Department of Education. *Report of the inquiry into London's health service, medical education and research.* Presented to the Secretaries of State for Health and Education by Sir Bernard Tomlinson. London: HMSO, 1992.
11 Townsend P, Whitehead M, Davidson N, eds. *Inequalities in health: the Black report and the health divide.* London: Penguin, 1992.
12 Office of Population Censuses and Surveys. *Morbidity statistics from general practice: fourth national study 1991–1992.* London: HMSO, 1995.
13 McCormick A, Charlton J, Fleming D. Who sees their practitioner and for what? *Health Trends* 1995; **27**: 34–5.
14 Balarajan PR, Raleigh VS. *Ethnicity and health: a guide for the NHS.* London: Department of Health, 1993.
15 Gilliam SJ, Jarman B, White P, Law R. Ethnic differences in consultation rates in urban general practice. *British Medical Journal* 1989; **299**: 953–7.
16 Donaldson L. Health and social status of elderly Asians: a community survey. *British Medical Journal* 1986; **293**: 1079–82.
17 Rudat K. *Health and lifestyle: black and minority ethnic groups in England.* London: Health Education Authority, 1994.
18 Ebrahim S. Ethnic elders. *British Medical Journal* 1996; **313:** 610–3.
19 Ahmed WIU, Baker M, Kernohan E. General practitioners' perceptions of Asian and non-Asian patients. *Family Practice* 1991; **8:** 52–6.
20 Helman CG. *Culture, health and illness,* 3rd edn. Oxford: Butterworth-Heinemann, 1994.
21 Preston-Whyte ME, Fraser RC, Beckett JL. Effect of a principal's

gender on consultation with patients. *Journal of the Royal College of General Practitioners* 1983; **33**: 654–8.

22 Funlop NJ. The future purchasing health authorities will have little power to implement strategies. *British Medical Journal* 1995; **310**: 59–60.

23 Scobie S, Basnett I, McCartney P. Can general practice data be used for needs assessment and health care planning in an inner-London district? *Journal of Public Health Medicine* 1995; **17**: 475–83.

24 Hopton JL, Dlugolecka M. Need and demand for primary health care: a comparative survey approach. *British Medical Journal* 1995; **310**: 1369–73.

25 Murray SA, Tapson J, Turnbull L, *et al.* Listening to local voices: adapting rapid appraisal to assess health and social needs in general practice. *British Medical Journal* 1994; **308**: 698–700.

26 Murray SA, Graham LJC. Practice based health needs assessment: use of four methods in a small neighbourhood. *British Medical Journal* 1995; **310**: 1443–8.

27 Gordon A, Womersley J. The use of mapping in public health and planning health services. *Journal of Public Health Medicine* 1997; **19**: 139–47.

28 Jarman B. Identification of underprivileged areas. *British Medical Journal* 1983; **286**: 1705–9.

29 Dawson A, ed. *Chronic disease management registers.* London: HMSO, 1996.

30 Pritchard P, Hughes J. *Shared care: the future imperative?* London: Royal Society of Medicine, 1995.

31 Mays N, Pope C. *Qualitative research in health care.* London: BMJ, 1996.

12 | Genetic services

Jean Chapple
*Consultant in Public Health Medicine, Kensington & Chelsea and
Westminster Health Authority;*

Elizabeth N Anionwu
Dean of Nursing Studies, Thames Valley University

Ethnicity is difficult to define, but any definition includes terms
such as culture, race, colour, language, religion and geographical
origin.[1] The House of Lords has produced a checklist to help establish the meaning of 'ethnic'. Essential factors were considered to
be:

- a long shared history;
- a common cultural tradition.

In addition, some of the following are likely to be present:

- a common geographic origin or descent from a small number
  of common ancestors;
- a common literature;
- a common religion;
- a minority within a larger community.

All these features play an important part in determining needs for
genetic services for people from ethnic minorities.

An individual's genes determine physical characteristics such as
hair, eye and skin colour and biochemical characteristics such as
blood group. Other physical features, such as body build, are inherited, but may be modified by environment, eg diet and exercise.
Although inherited physical characteristics can be altered with cos-
metics and surgery, we cannot yet alter the genetic code which
determines what we look like and how we function. These genetic
traits play some part in each person's ethnic characteristics and will
affect function; for example, they may produce autosomal recessively inherited disorders such as sickle cell anaemia, thalassaemia,

Tay-Sachs disease and cystic fibrosis. These diseases have a different prevalence in different ethnic groups.

Culture and religion also play an important part in determining needs for genetic services. Marriage and childbirth are major life events in any culture, and there are many different practices, customs and beliefs associated with marriage, pregnancy and childbirth in different ethnic groups. These may affect the willingness to accept genetic services, especially when they involve prenatal diagnosis. For example, a woman for religious and cultural reasons may not welcome (and may well not have given true informed consent for) a routine ultrasound scan that reveals she is carrying a foetus with spina bifida. She may feel unable to contemplate terminating the pregnancy. Conversely, she may feel that the time allowed between diagnosis and the birth of an affected child is helpful in preparing for caring for a child with special needs. This exemplifies three basic requirements of genetic services, regardless of ethnic group:

- People must receive non-directive counselling, in language they can understand, on an individual basis, without assumptions made because of their ethnic group, culture or religion.
- Any part of the health service that offers genetic counselling must support the family involved and not damage it.
- A multiethnic and multicultural approach to genetic services is needed to avoid stigmatisation of any group that may be perceived as 'tainted' with a particular genetic problem.

Genetic services have also unfortunately been associated with eugenics – the science of race improvement. Screening programmes targeted to specific ethnic groups may run the risk of being perceived as a means of eugenic control – another reason why a multiethnic approach, emphasising that all ethnic groups have risks of genetic disease, is important.

This chapter will look at:

- general population needs for genetic services;
- needs for screening services for autosomal recessive disorders that have different prevalence in different ethnic groups;
- issues raised by culture and consanguinity;
- training needs of health professionals.

It will cover common disorders caused by single gene defects and congenital malformations. However, numerous and rapid breakthroughs in genetic technology may well have a great effect on the future ability of services to predict the likelihood that an individual will develop one of the common polygenic diseases, such as diabetes or coronary artery disease.

General population needs for genetic services

Genetic risks have two components:

- the probability that a particular disorder will occur;
- the damage and burden that it can inflict.

Clinical genetics deals with both. The aim of clinical genetics is to identify and inform both people with genetic diseases and carriers of genetic disorders in good time, to put their heritable risks into perspective and enable and empower them to make decisions that are right for them and their families.[2]

Table 1 shows the number of patients, and their relatives, with common and other selected genetic diseases who may require advice and testing through a clinical genetics service. The numbers are based on a health authority district with a total population of 250,000 and 3,000 births annually. It does not include people with non-recurrent disorders and malformations, such as Down's syndrome. In total, one out of every 144 births will result in a family being confronted with a child with a serious genetic problem, with 21 new cases each year in the district, 987 people in the district having a genetic disorder, and 5,056 relatives at a one in ten or higher risk of being affected or being carriers.[3]

To satisfy the health needs of people who have or are carriers of genetic disorders, each district must ensure that those who want to avail themselves of genetic diagnosis and counselling have access to high-quality genetic services.

The objectives of genetic services can be summarised as follows:[3]

- to detect and, where possible, exclude risk factors for genetic disorders – in individuals, couples, kindred or specific groups in the population. This might be appropriate:
  - as part of preconception care;
  - during prenatal care;
  - as part of continuing health surveillance during the newborn period, childhood, adolescence and adult life;
- to make accurate genetic diagnoses in those detected as being at risk;
- to assist in the diagnosis of rare genetic syndromes;
- to provide genetic counselling;
- to keep accurate records of genetic data and means of linking the data through confidential family registers;

Table 1. Numbers of patients with some genetic diseases,* and their relatives, who may require advice and testing through a clinical genetics service;[3] the numbers are based on an imaginary district health authority (HA) with 3,000 annual births and a total population of 250,000

Condition	Birth frequency	New cases per year in HA	Approx no. of living patients in HA	Approx no. of unrelated families
Autosomal dominant disorders				
Huntington's chorea	1/3,000	1.0	18	14
Familial polyposis coli	1/8,000	0.4	8	6
Adult polycystic kidney disease	1/1,000	3.0	55	43
Familial hypercholesterolaemia	1/500	6.0	394	355
Tuberous sclerosis	1/12,000	0.25	19	12
Neurofibromatosis	1/2,500	1.2	69	30
Von Hippel Lindau disease	1/1000,000	0.03	1.3	0.8
Retinitis pigmentosa	1/5,000	1.6	36	32
Bilateral retinoblastoma	1/30,000	0.1	8	5
Myotonic dystrophy	1/7,000	0.4	14	11
Autosomal recessive disorders				
Cystic fibrosis†	1/2,000	1.5	25	20
Adrenal hyperplasia	1/10,000	0.3	23	20
Friedreich's ataxia	1/54,000	0.06	2	1.7
Spinal muscular atrophy	1/10,000	0.3	3	2
Phenylketonuria	1/13,000	0.2	18	15
Usher's syndrome	1/27,000	0.1	9	6
Sickle cell disease in African-Caribbeans	1/250			
Thalassaemia		Depends upon ethnic mix of HA and up-take of screening and offer of prenatal diagnosis		
– in Cypriots	1/140			
– in Indians	1/1,000			
– in Pakistanis	1/300			
X-linked recessive diseases				
Duchenne/Becker muscular dystrophy	1/9,000	0.3	8	7
Haemophilia	1/20,000	0.15	11	7
X-linked retinitis pigmentosa	1/7,000	0.43	23	14
Other X-linked eye disorders	1/7,000	0.43	23	14
Fragile-X syndrome‡	1/4,000	0.75	52	49
Other X-linked mental disorders‡	1/4,000	0.75	52	49
Chromosomal disorders				
Unbalanced translocations	1/2,000	1.5	16	16
GRAND TOTAL	*1/144*	*20.8*	*987*	*730*

*Non-recurrent genetic diseases such as Down's syndrome are not included.
†The resources for population screening for cystic fibrosis are so extensive that separate governmental funding is required.
‡These figures describe only severely retarded children.

Table 1. (Continued)

Notes

Birth frequency. Many of these birth frequencies are changing, and those listed here refer to the most recent figures. For example, the birth frequency of Duchenne muscular dystrophy has fallen from 1/6,000 to 1/9,000 as a result of genetic counselling. The birth frequency of thalassaemia in Cypriots has fallen to 0 as a result of antenatal screening, prenatal diagnosis and the offer of selective termination of pregnancy.

Approximate number of living patients. This figure is based on the birth frequency, and the average duration of disease, compared with that in the general population. This too is changing as treatments become more successful.

Number of unrelated families. These numbers are based on experience obtained from family studies. For example, for various diseases, there are 0.42–0.9 families per living index patient; for autosomal recessive diseases the figures range from 0.64 to 0.85, and for X-linked diseases the figures vary between 0.63 and 0.87. The variation depends upon the proportion of cases that are new mutations, and the proportion of affected members of families who are living at any one time.

Approximate number of relatives at risk. These numbers are also based on experience. On average, there are:

- 3 high-risk relatives for each patient with an X-linked disorder in which mutations are common (such as Duchenne muscular dystrophy);
- 6 high-risk relatives for each patient with an X-linked disorder in which new mutations are rare (such as Fragile-X syndrome, haemophilia);
- 6–9 high-risk relatives for each patient with an inherited autosomal dominant disorder;
- 2 high-risk relatives for each patient with a dominant mutation;
- 2 high-risk relatives for each patient with an autosomal recessive disorder;
- 4 high-risk relatives for each patient with a chromosomal translocation.

For diseases of short duration, relatives of dead patients are also counted. These numbers will fall once the genetics department has ascertained all families and there will then be a workload related to the number of new non-familial cases born each year, together with the work necessary to keep old families fully informed and tested with up-to-date techniques.

- to ensure effective, continuing and anticipatory care for those at risk;
- to give training to doctors, nursing and other staff, those specialising in clinical genetics, and especially those training in other specialties and disciplines;
- to provide guidance and support to relevant voluntary bodies;
- to maintain national professional networks to enable these functions to be carried out effectively;
- to monitor effectiveness and quality of services;
- to provide a resource for research and development;
- to provide a source of expert advice for purchasers and providers of services.[4]

It is generally accepted that the regional pattern and organisation of genetic services that has evolved provides the optimum critical mass of clinical and laboratory expertise and activity, with efficient use of specialist staff and resources. It allows expertise in rare disorders to be built up and maintained, and fosters good training, research and development. It also matches the prevalence of common genetic disorders to the numbers of individuals at risk.

Specialist clinical genetics services may be organised at regional level, but are largely an outpatient activity. Peripheral outpatient clinics in health centres and hospitals take the services to patients. Genetic health visitors and associates may take services into people's homes. There is a need to improve equity of access through provision of multiethnic staff speaking some of the key languages, access to interpreters and outreach programmes. For effective service delivery, the regional organisation must be complemented by appropriate expertise and service arrangements at district level, in primary health care and child health services.[5-7]

Need for screening services for autosomal recessive disorders

Diseases that are currently included in programmes for genetic screening are mainly inherited as autosomal recessive disorders. Persons with only one of these recessive genes (a heterozygote) will not be aware that they carry the gene, as their other normal gene compensates for the faulty one.

Each of us carries one or more recessive genes which are potentially lethal or severely damaging if paired with a similar gene. Genes for autosomal recessively inherited disorders are very common in the general population, with extremely high incidence in specific subgroups. Examples include:[8]

- *Thalassaemia:* 3–17% of people of Mediterranean and Asian origin are carriers
- *Sickle cell anaemia:* 8–25% of people of African or African-Caribbean origin are carriers
- *Tay-Sachs disease:* 3–5% of Ashkenazi Jews are carriers, compared with 0.5% of non-Jewish populations
- *Cystic fibrosis:* 4% of white Europeans are carriers.

Carriers who choose a partner within their own ethnic group have a high (3–20%) chance of forming an at-risk couple, so all carriers should be informed and the offer made to test their partners. Table 2 shows the approximate numbers of minority ethnic groups in the UK with specific genetic risk.[8]

A person who develops the signs and symptoms of a recessive disorder must have inherited a faulty gene from each of his or her parents and, therefore, is homozygous for the gene. However, the birth incidence of affected individuals depends on the frequency with which carriers of the same disorder select each other as

Table 2. Approximate numbers of ethnic minorities in England and Wales (based on 1991 census) with specific genetic risks. (From reference 8 and Balarajan R, Raleigh VS. The ethnic populations of England and Wales: the 1991 census. *Health Trends* 1992;**24**:113–6)

African-Caribbean	499,000
African/other black	318,800
Indian	830,600
Pakistani	454,600
Bangladeshi	159,500
East African Asian	220,800
Greek and Turkish Cypriot	193,100
Italian	202,000
Chinese	147,300
Arab	63,000
'Mixed'*	205,000
Jewish	>350,000
Total	*2,953,750*
Total England and Wales population	*49,890,273*
Minorities with specific genetic risks	= 6.5%

* Descendants of marriages between members of white and other groups or between other groups.

reproductive partners. In societies that do not have a culture advocating consanguineous marriages, it is relatively rare for two carriers of the recessive gene for the same disease to have children. In such a society, the birth incidence of the disorder is relatively low, but this can still indicate a large reservoir of carriers of the gene in the general population. Even when two carriers have children, they have only a one in four chance of having an affected child with each conception.

Screening populations for specific genes would theoretically benefit many families, the majority of whom would have had no prior warning through the birth of an affected child that they carried a damaging recessive gene. However, screening has the potential to do more harm[9] than good unless it is set up on a sound theoretical basis, is organised well and is monitored.

We can learn from both positive and negative past experiences of genetic screening in specific ethnic groups about effective approaches to genetic problems.

Lessons to be learnt from existing screening programmes

Beta-thalassaemia

The haemoglobinopathies are the commonest autosomal recessive inherited disorder worldwide. Homozygous beta-thalassaemia is characterised by severe anaemia needing regular blood transfusion and chelation therapy to minimise iron overload which is the usual biochemical cause of death. Carriers can be detected from blood samples by looking for the gene product, an abnormal haemoglobin. It is now possible to offer same day prenatal diagnosis of beta-thalassaemia.[10,11]

Screening programmes to detect thalassaemia carriers have been instituted in several Mediterranean countries with a high prevalence (from 2.4% prevalence of carriers in Latium to 17% in Cyprus). These have resulted in startling reductions in the number of thalassaemia births – reductions of over 95% in Cyprus, 90% in Ferrara (Italy), 60% in Sardinia, 50% in Greece and in Latium (Italy).[10]

Success has been due to a combination of good screening practice being put into effect simultaneously:

- public education among a group with day-to-day knowledge of the effects of the disease in the community; a high prevalence in a small rural community means that most people know at least one person with the disease;
- close involvement of patient groups;
- close involvement of lay and religious leaders;
- involvement of community based medical services;
- availability of effective laboratory screening tests and good laboratory services;
- genetic counselling, prenatal diagnosis and high acceptance of termination of pregnancy, even among patients who oppose on religious and cultural grounds;[11]
- special centres to co-ordinate both prevention and treatment of the disease.

Failure to prevent affected births was due to failure of obstetricians to arrange testing in 26% of 193 thalassaemic infants followed up in the WHO study (1988), patient's delay in contacting the obstetrician in 55%, refusal of foetal diagnosis in 9%, and laboratory error, mainly in heterozygote detection, in 9%. Only 1% of these children were born as the result of parental choice to continue with an affected pregnancy. Four-fifths of the affected children were born because of parental or professional unawareness of the screening programme instead of informed choice.

It is worth noting particular features of some of the programmes. In Latium, screening was offered each year to 13- and 14-year-old schoolchildren; 80% took up the offer with few undue psychological effects. The school programme raised awareness among the rest of the 5 million population. Screening soon spread to the children's relatives and young adults, and has been successful in identifying couples at risk of producing a thalassaemic child before they have an affected child; between 1980 and 1983, 110 out of 161 at-risk couples identified had no affected children prior to the discovery of their carrier status.[12,13]

In Sardinia the target population has been adults of child-bearing age. Health promotion has been provided in a wide variety of community settings, with testing carried out at one hospital.[14] Despite a total uptake of only 22%, targeting and testing of family members of carriers meant that a third of the estimated carriers were detected.

Thalassaemia in Cyprus had proved a great drain on health resources, with 45% of blood supplies being used to treat the disease. Priority has been given to testing couples, and the church encouraged couples to be tested before marriage.[15] Knowledge of the individual's carrier status has a profound effect on reproductive behaviour in Cyprus. The knowledge that first trimester antenatal diagnosis is available and effective allows high-risk couples to have their intended families. Prior to screening programmes, most couples who had had an unforeseen affected child chose to forgo having further children rather than risk having another affected child.[15,16]

In Greece there is a national programme to detect carriers funded by the health ministry. Public education starts in schools as part of the national curriculum. Initial testing is offered to one partner of couples, to save resources, and to pregnant women, so three-quarters of those tested are female. There are over 20 national testing centres and 90% of at-risk couples are now detected prospectively.[17]

In the UK a successful screening programme has been set up for Cypriots living in London. This is an informed, discrete community with active patient groups and the involvement of church leaders and local schools. As an immigrant group from an area where testing was routine, this community was more informed about thalassaemia than the local professionals in a city where thalassaemia is almost unknown in the indigenous population. They pushed for a local service for prospective testing and prenatal diagnosis, which led to a 46% decline in incidence between 1977 and 1981.[18] In contrast, there has been a much slower uptake among non-Muslim and Muslim Asians in Britain. This may be because the minority ethnic groups at high risk are unevenly scattered among a larger population at low risk. These immigrant communities do not have a history of carrier testing programmes in their home country to make them aware of the services that should be available to them.

Language barriers may prevent effective communication. There is evidence that many couples are not counselled in an appropriate language,[19] and a recent survey showed that only four out of 34 haemoglobinopathy counsellors in England and Wales spoke one or more Asian languages.[20] The thalassaemia birth rate in East African Asians in Britain fell only slightly up to 1981 and the rate in the Pakistani community did not fall at all. Consequently, there was only a 21% reduction in thalassaemia major births in Britain by the end of 1981.[21] However, this picture is changing. For example, there is recent evidence that the experience with British Pakistanis shows a population in the process of change, with 'a steady shift towards prenatal diagnosis'.[22]

Sickle cell disease

Sickle cell disease also results in anaemia and painful thrombotic episodes, some producing permanent disability, though clinical severity varies. Carrier status can be detected simply by haemoglobin analysis to look for the gene product, as in thalassaemia. First trimester prenatal diagnosis using gene probes on chorionic villus samples is now possible.

The experience of sickle cell screening in the United States has been a hard learnt lesson in how genetic screening programmes initially resulted in personal damage to some of those tested.[23] In the 1970s the civil rights movement coalesced the black community into an important political entity and sickle cell disease became a political issue, with involvement of President Nixon's office. Legislation was passed rapidly as a result of lobbying by individuals and targeting sickle cell as a disease for concentrated research and other efforts, with little informed public debate.[24] At that time, prenatal diagnosis was not available, so the object of the programmes was to identify carriers but to offer little in the way of reproductive options apart from termination of every pregnancy or not having children at all. This meant that the sickle cell laws were, in fact, eugenic measures. Several states passed laws to make testing compulsory, some at pre-school age, at which reproductive options for carriers cannot be explained adequately.

There was inadequate education of professionals and the public, so a widespread misconception arose that sickle cell trait was a disease state. This led to stigmatisation of carriers, with difficulties in obtaining health insurance and job discrimination. Specific cases of problems caused for individuals can be cited; one child suffered perforation of the appendix because his abdominal pain was falsely attributed to sickle cell disease when he actually had sickle cell trait, and there was delay in the adoption of a child because it carried the trait.[25,26] The 1972 National Sickle Cell Control Act did emphasise that testing should be voluntary, but confused the trait with the homozygous state. Although several mandatory testing laws were repealed by certain states, suspicion remained among the black community.

The main approach has now shifted to secondary prevention by neonatal screening, but services are fragmented, which may reflect organisational problems in health care services in the United States.

In the UK, sickle cell disease has been dealt with chiefly through enthusiastic individuals working with local communities. Initiatives arose as a result of communal efforts in areas where immigration of certain ethnic groups had led to high prevalence.[27,28] The National Health Service did little to meet the needs of sickle cell carriers until the mid-1980s, and there was little understanding of the disease even in high-risk communities. Although black people were screened for carrier and disease status in order to prevent a sickling crisis if they needed an anaesthetic, most were never informed of their status and what the test result meant.[29] This led to missed opportunities for women attending for antenatal care to receive adequate counselling and give fully informed consent for further prenatal tests. In response to these gaps, the first sickle cell counselling centre was established, in Brent in 1979.[30] By 1997 there were over 40 similar counselling centres for sickle and thalassaemia in the UK, most in areas of high prevalence.[31] Services are not yet fully comprehensive, as there is little regional co-ordination and poor links with centres for clinical genetics.[32] Contributory reasons are lack of awareness among health service staff, the relatively recent development of high prevalence communities and their concentration in deprived urban areas. An additional factor has been the failure, until recently, to address the issue at a national level. However, in 1993 the Department of Health published the report of a working party to advise purchasers and providers on services for sickle cell and thalassaemia.[33] More recently the Health Education Authority has also produced guidance for commissioners and providers.[34]

Tay-Sachs disease

About 1 in 30 Ashkenazi Jews are carriers of Tay-Sachs disease, a recessive disorder which causes progressive neurological deterioration and death in children from birth to the age of about 5 years. Before gene probes to detect the disease became available, carriers could be tested for reduced amounts of the gene product, hexoaminidase A, which could also be used for prenatal diagnosis.

In 1970–71 Kaback and colleagues[35] set up a screening programme in California using a community outreach approach to a high-risk Jewish population. The programme used approaches that are now standard for community involvement: liaison with community leaders (in this case rabbis); training lay volunteers to help cope with the intensive education that preceded mass screening in communal centres (schools, synagogues and community centres); and the use of local media (press, radio and television) to give widespread presentations about the programme. Screening started after 14 months of planning, leadership training, manpower development and public education. This is one of the earliest examples of 'cascade counselling', whereby knowledge of the programme, its aims and implications are passed through a community by publicity programmes that lead to word-of-mouth promotion of the scheme. Large programmes need key people to act as advocates for the programme, and these need not necessarily be people who directly benefit themselves. In a study in New Orleans, parents of children in the reproductive age group played an important role by telling their children about the programme and encouraging them to be tested. Discussion with non-professionals was felt to be the most important source of advocacy. A 'Marcus Welby MD' television programme was not perceived as being an advocate but was cited as a source of information by over half of both compliers and non-compliers.

By 1986 over 50 cities in the United States were running screening programmes and more than 350,000 people had been screened; 96% of affected foetuses were aborted and there was an estimated 70–85% fall in the incidence of Tay-Sachs. The highest uptake was in adolescents offered screening in school.[36]

These large community screening projects provide an ideal opportunity to look at the psychological aspects of screening and how these affected compliance. In the Montreal programme in 1977, it was found that 15% of high school students, both tested and untested, found the prospect of screening 'frightening'.[37] Carriers experienced more initial anxiety and worry than those found to be non-carriers, with 46% reporting that they felt 'worried' by being told they were a carrier. All 261 teenage carriers found claimed that they had told their parents they were heterozygotes, and a third of the parents were 'worried' by the news. However, this initial anxiety seems to settle down. Self-image was unchanged in 90% of carriers, diminished in 10% of carriers and enhanced in 10% of non-carriers. The heterozygote students felt that the information they had been given was useful; 95% would want to know the genotype of an intended spouse, 80.4% would marry another carrier, and only 10.6% would reconsider the choice to marry if the intended partner was also a carrier.

This group was followed up 8 years later;[38] 19% reported that they still attached 'worry' to heterozygosity, and only 3% claimed that they would change their marriage plans if their partner was found to be a carrier. Most important, of the 83 ex-students responding, eight could not remember their genotype, but only one of these was a carrier; the other 37 had remembered their carrier status. Nine of the twelve partners of carriers had been tested themselves; carrier status appeared to heighten awareness and increase belief in having a partner tested. This suggests that genetic screening programmes aimed at people well before they are likely to reproduce can be effective. Such programmes allow a long time for people to come to terms with their carrier status and to obtain information about the disease they carry. This contrasts sharply with detection of carrier status in pregnancy.

Phenylketonuria

Phenylketonuria testing provides an interesting example of a screening programme that has been successful over a long period and from which several lessons can be learnt. Phenylketonuria is a term encompassing a variety of autosomal recessive disorders of phenylalanine hydroxylase activity. People with the most severe form of hydroxylase deficiency have less than 1% of normal enzyme activity and can be detected by assaying the effect of the gene product on phenylalanine levels in blood or excess phenyl-keto-acids in urine.[39] It occurs in about 1 in 10,000 births in Britain.[40]

Phenylketonuria differs from the majority of recessive disorders discussed in this chapter in that a special diet low in phenylalanine prevents the build-up of phenylalanine in the brain and subsequent mental retardation. It is therefore eminently treatable and screening has an important part to play in secondary prevention.

Screening takes place in the neonatal period rather than pre-conceptually, as the programmes are focused on finding cases rather than carriers because the disease symptoms are treatable.

In 1969 the Department of Health and Social Security issued a circular recommending that routine neonatal screening be carried out on all newborn infants between the sixth and fourteenth day of life on a heel-prick specimen of blood.[41] The Guthrie technique of detecting raised phenylalanine levels in blood by bacterial inhibition assay is now used in most laboratories to test the samples. A register set up in 1963 has provided excellent monitoring of the programme. Between 1964 and 1974 there was a steady increase in the proportion of infants with phenylketonuria diagnosed as a result of neonatal screening. The great majority of children detected early are within the normal range of intelligence and attend ordinary schools.

Between 1974 and 1978 five babies were diagnosed and registered as having phenylketonuria after the neonatal period. Three resulted from a false negative blood result, one was due to the test paper being lost on the way to the laboratory, and in one the test was not carried out until the baby was 5 months old. This shows the importance of reporting back negative results as well as positive results to health professionals and those being screened directly. As there is a considerable amount of expense in feeding back results to family doctors, community nurses and parents (printing, postage etc), those attending for screening are often told that 'no news is good news'; if they do not hear that they have a positive result, they are to assume that the result is negative and that no further action needs to be taken. The findings of the monitoring process led to feedback of negative results in the phenylketonuria programme, so failure to receive a result means that either a test has not been done (testing is easily forgotten if a baby is seriously ill in the perinatal period) or has been done and lost on the way to the laboratory. It is unfortunate that the lessons from this programme were not learnt by others. In 1985 a similar problem occurred in the cervical cytology programme in the UK; a positive result was not sent out to the woman concerned, so she had assumed that she had no cause for further worry or follow-up. The resulting furore should mean that no screening test in the future is set up without a system for the active reporting of negative results.[42]

With phenylketonuria there is a definite direct advantage to the individual being tested. The test could not be delayed until the child is old enough to give informed consent. As has been discussed previously, the situation is less certain for recessive disorders that are not currently treatable, although there may be some benefits as far as morbidity is concerned in early diagnosis and treatment. In a survey of new mothers to find their attitudes to neonatal screening for Duchenne muscular dystrophy,[43] over 90% of mothers wanted their children to be tested, and there was no significant difference between mothers of boys or girls in thinking that testing would be acceptable. However, only 68% of 201 mothers were aware that their infants were tested neonatally for any disease, implying that informed consent to the programme was not a reality. There is a need for general education about programmes that are already carried out successfully before new genetic screening programmes are started.

Issues raised by culture and consanguinity

There is ample scope for prejudice when different attitudes to consanguineous marriage occur in a society; some cultures see marriage or sexual relations between close relatives as akin to incest, whilst others positively favour consanguineous marriages (uncle and niece, first cousins, first cousins once removed, or second cousins).[22] At least 20% of the world population favours consanguineous marriage, at least 6.5% of couples make such a marriage and at least 8.4% of all babies born are the result of consanguineous parents.[44] This custom is beneficial to women in cultures where this is the norm, but there are social and service implications.[45]

In a consanguineous marriage, both partners inherit a significant number of both normal and pathological genes from their common ancestor(s). This increases the risk of recessively inherited diseases in their children, especially rare disorders, as the chances of one carrier having a child with another carrier of a rare gene causing a disease are very low unless the parents are related.

Consanguinity is often associated with the Muslim religion, though it is uncommon in Indonesia but favoured by Hindus, Muslims and Christians in southern India. Pakistanis have a strong tradition of consanguineous marriage, with 55% of young Pakistanis in Britain marrying a first cousin compared with about 32% in Pakistan.[46] The increased incidence of lethal congenital malformations in British Pakistanis made a large contribution to a perinatal mortality rate of 18/1,000 in 1984 for this group, compared with 12/1,000 in other ethnic groups – a 50% excess.[47-49]

A study in Birmingham showed a considerable excess of chronic disability in the British Pakistani group, practically all within the consanguineous families. A group that made up less than 20% of

Table 3. Theoretical expected increase of genetic risk in a first-cousin marriage[22]

Type of condition	Rate/1,000 births (approx.)	Effect of 1st cousin marriage	Estimated risk in 1st cousin marriage
Lethal or very severe congenital malformation	about 30	× 1.8 approx.	about 54/1,000
Chromosomal	3.2	No increase	3.2/1,000
Inherited:			
dominant	4.0 ⎫	No increase	4.0 ⎫
X-linked	1.5 ⎬ 7.0	No increase	1.5 ⎬ >13/1,000
recessive	1.5 ⎭	× 5 or more	>7.5 ⎭
Total	*30.2*		*>53.2/1,000 = ×1.8*

the population studied suffered 40% of the disability, the overall rate being 2.7 times that found in non-Pakistanis.[47] This highlights the need for the rapid development of appropriate approaches to this problem. Misguided efforts to discourage the cultural norm of consanguineous marriage and blame illness in the child on the parents' blood relationship must be avoided at all costs.

For effective counselling, the woman must understand what is said and must be able to ask questions. At present this means that British Pakistanis should be counselled by a female (ideally a Muslim), in the appropriate language and at home if necessary.[8] The best mediators in the wider community are young British Pakistani professionals who have an insider's view of their own community and culture, as well as professional expertise in counselling from a medical or social service background. Such individuals can approach their own community on health issues, promote the formation of women's and parents' groups, and give guidance to other health professionals.

Other approaches that may prove to be culturally acceptable are:

- population screening for carrier status of thalassaemia, cystic fibrosis etc;
- risk prediction on the basis of pedigree and known cases of genetic disease;
- pre-conception counselling using a careful family history;
- foetal anomaly ultrasound scanning to look for structural malformations in the second trimester of pregnancy.

There is also a need for further research, to include:

- a study of the effects of optimal genetics services on perinatal and childhood mortality and handicap among British Pakistanis;
- national data collection on infant mortality and morbidity by ethnic group rather than by country of mother's birth;
- linking of data from different genetic centres on families with rare conditions.

While carrying out research, explicit care should be taken to neutralise unwarranted and exaggerated perceptions of the genetic disadvantages of consanguineous marriage.

Another difficult issue faced by genetics services is that of foetal sexing. In some Asian cultures the birth of a daughter puts a great financial strain on a family because of the need to supply a dowry on marriage. There is evidence that female infants in India and China may be killed at birth. There are anecdotal reports that in Britain some Asian families opt to terminate a pregnancy where amniocentesis has shown that the foetus is female. The actual incidence in the population and the subscription to this view by other groups (eg to ensure inheritance of goods through the paternal line) remains, and is likely to remain, unknown. It can be argued that this is permissible by law since it may be judged that continuation of the pregnancy would cause 'damage to the ... psychological health of the mother' and thus is covered by the terms of the 1990 Abortion Act. In current British society, where women outnumber men and are increasingly involved in public life and decision making, this cultural view is unacceptable to many members of other cultural groups and the issue remains unresolved and largely hidden in the private medical sector.

Training needs of health professionals

The experience with haemoglobinopathies has highlighted the training needs of health professionals in relation to community genetics for multiethnic populations. Low levels of awareness about sickle cell and thalassaemia have been reported amongst general practitioners[50] and health visitors.[51] The first short haemoglobinopathy counselling course was established in Brent in 1982 and further ones were also set up in Lambeth and Haringey. A course embracing a multiethnic approach to community genetics was set up in 1991 at the Institute of Child Health.[52] By focusing on the issues and dilemmas surrounding the offer of testing and screening for sickle cell, thalassaemia, Tay-Sachs, cystic fibrosis, and

Down's and Fragile-X syndromes, the course addresses many of the topics raised in this chapter. In particular, health professionals are made aware that all ethnic groups are at risk of certain inherited conditions and that these genetic disorders are not narrowly confined to one particular group. This information is also contained in a 23-minute video produced through a grant from the Department of Health.[53] A total of 20 courses were held at the Institute of Child Health, attended by 296 people, mainly midwives, haemoglobinopathy counsellors and community nurses, such as family planning nurses and health visitors. The course appears to have met the needs of the participants, judging from the following anonymous evaluations returned by 292 (98%) of the students: excellent 76%; very good 22%; good 2%. The course has now transferred to the School of Midwifery and Child Health at Thames Valley University and will be running from October 1998.

Key priorities for action

National priorities

- Clinicians and managers need to be made aware of the importance of genetics services to different sections of the community and of rapid developments in the field; they must be particularly aware of sensitive issues, including:
  - the need to counteract a eugenic view of genetics;
  - the need to handle cultural issues, such as consanguinity, with insight and sensitivity;
  - the need to put emphasis on the value of informed choice, which may mean that parents choose to continue with a pregnancy that will result in a child with a disease or disability that is currently not curable; a 'search and destroy' policy to avoid future costs to the health service is unacceptable.
- People must receive non-directive counselling, in language they can understand, on an individual basis, without assumptions being made because of their ethnic group, culture or religion.
- Any part of the health service that offers genetic counselling must support the family involved and not damage it.
- A multiethnic and multicultural approach to genetic services is needed to avoid stigmatisation of any group that may be perceived as being 'tainted' with a particular genetic problem, and to avoid accusations of eugenic control.
- Staffing of genetic services should ensure that staff are from a variety of ethnic groups.
- Efforts should be made to develop appropriate information for

different ethnic groups, in the form of leaflets, videos, presentations etc; these should cover the nature and limits of risk, steps that can be taken to avoid it, how to obtain advice, and the role of clinical geneticists.

- There is a need for further research, to include:
  - a study of the effects of optimal genetics services on perinatal and childhood mortality and handicap among British Pakistanis;
  - national data collection on infant mortality and morbidity by ethnic group rather than by mother's country of birth;
  - linking of data from different genetic centres on families with rare conditions;
  - referral patterns of general practitioners, paediatricians and other staff to look at equity of access for all ethnic groups.

Local priorities

To be effective, genetics services should be developed and maintained on a multidisciplinary and multiethnic basis:

- Each region should develop an organisation, involving both providers (genetics and foetal medicine centres, neonatologists, paediatric pathologists, obstetricians and paediatricians, primary care physicians, public health physicians, health workers involved in family planning, health visitors, midwives, nurses and experts in health promotion) and commissioners. A designated co-ordinator (often but not always a clinical geneticist) should be responsible for bringing these people together on a regular regional basis to improve delivery of both specialist and community genetics services.[8]
- For pre-conception care and prenatal diagnostic services to be delivered effectively, the regional organisation must be reflected at district level and involve general practitioners, maternal and child health workers, and family planning services.[54]
- Genetic screening programmes for carrier status must involve members of the local community, local religious leaders, patient groups and voluntary organisations.
- Genetic screening programmes also require large education programmes, both for health and social care professionals and for members of the local community.
- Efforts should be made to recruit and train geneticists and genetic counsellors from within minority ethnic groups to provide appropriate services in the local community and links from regional genetics centres.

- Efforts should be made to start local support groups for families with members affected by genetic disease; this will facilitate cascade counselling.

References

1 Karmi G, Horton C. *Guidelines for the implementation of ethnic monitoring in health service provision.* London: NE and NW Thames Regional Health Authorities, 1992.

2 Department of Health. *Population needs and genetic services: an outline guide.* London: Department of Health, 1993.

3 Royal College of Physicians of London. *Purchasers' guidelines to genetic services in the NHS: an aid to assessing the services required by the resident population of an average health district.* London: Royal College of Physicians, 1991.

4 Department of Health. *Professional advice for purchasers.* Executive letter EL(91)21. London: Department of Health, 1991.

5 Royal College of Physicians of London. *Clinical genetics in 1990 and beyond.* London: Royal College of Physicians, 1991.

6 British Paediatric Association. *Towards a combined child health service.* London: British Paediatric Association, 1991.

7 British Paediatric Association. *Child health in a changing society,* ed. Forfar HO. Oxford: Oxford University Press, 1988.

8 Royal College of Physicians of London. *Prenatal diagnosis and genetic screening: community and service implications.* London: Royal College of Physicians, 1989.

9 Mant D, Fowler G. Mass screening: theory and ethics. *British Medical Journal* 1990; **300**: 916–8.

10 Bianco I, Graziani B, Lerone M, *et al.* A screening programme for the prospective prevention of Mediterranean anaemia in Latium: results of seven years work. *Journal of Medical Genetics* 1984; **21**: 268–71.

11 Schiliro G, Romeo M, Molica F. Prenatal diagnosis of thalassaemia: the viewpoint of patients. *Prenatal Diagnosis* 1988; **8**: 231–3.

12 Silvestroni E, Bianco I, Graziani B, *et al.* Screening of thalassaemia carriers in intermediate schools in Latium: results of four years work. *Journal of Medical Genetics* 1980; **17**: 161–4.

13 Silvestroni E, Bianco I, Graziani B, *et al.* First premarital screening of thalassaemia carriers in intermediate schools in Latium. *Journal of Medical Genetics* 1978; **15**: 202–7.

14 Cao A, Pintus I, Lecca U. Control of homozygous beta thalassaemia by carrier screening and antenatal diagnosis in Sardinia. *Clinical Genetics* 1984; **26**: 12–22.

15 Angastimotos M, Hadjiminas M. Prevention of thalassaemia in Cyprus. *Lancet* 1981; **i**: 369–70.

16 Zorcolo G, Landis N, Maddeo, *et al.* Beta thalassaemia control. *Lancet* 1986; **ii**: 103.

17 Fessus P. Prevention of thalassaemia and HbS syndrome in Greece. *Acta Haematologia* 1987; **78**: 168–72.

18 Modell B, Ward RHT, Fairweather DVI. Effect of introducing

antenatal diagnosis on reproductive behaviour of families at risk for thalassaemia major. *British Medical Journal* 1980; **i**: 1347–50.

19 Darr A. *The social implications of thalassaemia among Muslims of Pakistani origin: family experience and service delivery.* PhD thesis, University of London, 1990.

20 Anionwu EN. Ethnic origin of sickle and thalassaemia counsellors: does it matter? In: Kelleher D, Hillier S, eds. *Researching cultural differences.* London: Routledge, 1996: 160–89.

21 Modell B, Petrou M, Ward RHT. Effect of foetal diagnostic testing on birth rate of thalassaemia major in Britain. *Lancet* 1984; **ii**: 1383–6.

22 Modell B, Kuliev AM. *Social and genetic implications of customary consanguineous marriage among British Pakistanis.* London: Galton Institute, 1992. Occasional papers, second series, No 4..

23 Rutkow I, Lipton J. Some negative aspects of the State health departments' policies related to screening for sickle cell anaemia. *American Journal of Public Health* 1974: **74**: 217–21.

24 Reilly P. Sickle cell anaemia laws. In: *Genetics, law and social policy*, Ch. 3: 62–86. Boston: Harvard University Press, 1977.

25 Hampton ML, Anderson J, Lavizzo BS, *et al.* Sickle cell non-disease: a potentially serious public health problem. *American Journal of Diseases in Childhood* 1974; **128**: 58–61.

26 Beutler E, Boggs, DR Heller P, *et al.* Hazards of indiscriminate screening for sickling (letter). *New England Journal of Medicine* 1971; **282**: 1484–5.

27 Prashar U, Anionwu EN, Brozovic M. *Sickle cell anaemia: who cares?* London: Runnymede Trust, 1985.

28 World Health Organisation. *The haemoglobinopathies in Europe: a combined report on two WHO meetings.* Copenhagen: WHO, 1988.

29 Sickle Cell Society. *Sickle cell disease: the need for improved services.* London: Sickle Cell Society, 1981.

30 Anionwu EN. Running a sickle cell centre: community counselling. In: Cruickshank JK, Beevers DG, eds. *Ethnic factors in health and disease.* London: Wright, 1989.

31 Anionwu EN. District-based population registers for sickle cell disorders: a role for the haemoglobinopathy clinical nurse specialist? *Child Care, Health and Development* 1997; **23**: 431–5.

32 Anionwu EN. Sickle cell and thalassaemia: community experiences and official response. In: Ahmad WIU, ed. *'Race' and health in contemporary Britain.* Milton Keynes: Open University Press, 1993.

33 Standing Medical Advisory Committee. *Sickle cell, thalassaemia and other haemoglobinopathies.* London: HMSO, 1993.

34 Health Education Authority. *Sickle cell and thalassaemia: achieving health gain.* Guidance for commissioners and providers. London: HEA, 1998.

35 Kaback M, Nathan T, Greenwald S. Tay-Sachs disease: heterozygote screening and prenatal diagnosis: US experience and world perspective. In: Kaback M, ed. *Tay-Sachs disease: screening and prevention.* New York: Alan Liss, 1977.

36 World Health Organisation. *Community approaches to the control of hereditary disease.* Geneva: WHO, 1985.

37 Clow C, Scriver C. Knowledge about and attitudes towards genetic screening among high school students: the Tay-Sachs experience. *Pediatrics* 1977; **59**: 86–91.

38 Zeesman S, Clow CL, Cartier L, Scriver CR. A private view of heterozygosity: eight year follow-up study on carriers of the Tay-Sachs gene detected by high school screening in Montreal. *American Journal of Medical Genetics* 1984; **18**: 769–78.

39 Medical Research Council Steering Committee for the MRC/DHSS Phenylketonuria Register. Routine neonatal screening for phenylketonuria in the UK 1964-1978. *British Medical Journal* 1981; **282**: 1680–4.

40 Modell B. Biochemical neonatal screening. *British Medical Journal,* 1990; **300**: 1667–8.

41 Department of Health and Social Security, Welsh Office. *Screening for the early detection of phenylketonuria.* HM(69)72. London: Department of Health and Social Security, 1972.

42 Editorial. Cancer of the cervix: death by incompetence. *Lancet* 1985; **ii**: 363–4.

43 Smith R, Williams D, Sibert J, Harper P. Attitudes of mothers to neonatal screening for Duchenne muscular dystrophy. *British Medical Journal* 1990; **300**: 1112.

44 Bittles AH. *Consanguineous marriage: current global incidence and its relevance to demographic research.* Research report No 90-186. Michigan: Population Studies Center, University of Michigan, 1990.

45 Khlat M, Halabi S, Khudr A, Der Kaloustian VM. Perception of consanguineous marriages and their genetic effects among a sample of couples from Beirut. *American Journal of Medical Genetics* 1986; **25**: 299–306.

46 Darr A, Modell B. The frequency of consanguineous marriage among British Pakistanis. *Journal of Medical Genetics* 1988; **25**: 186–90.

47 Chitty LS, Winter RM. Perinatal mortality in different ethnic groups. *Archives of Disease in Childhood* 1989; **64**: 1036–41.

48 Balarajan R, Botting B. Perinatal mortality in England and Wales: variations by mother's country of birth (1982–85). *Health Trends* 1989; **21**: 79–84.

49 Bundey S. A prospective study on the health of Birmingham babies in different ethnic groups: interim findings. In: Roberts DF, Bittles AH, eds. *Minority populations: genetics, demography and health.* Proceedings of 27th Annual Symposium, held in 1990, of the Galton Institute. London: Macmillan Press, 1990.

50 Shickle D, May A. Knowledge and perception of haemoglobinopathy carrier screening among general practitioners in Cardiff. *Journal of Medical Genetics* 1989; **26**: 109–12.

51 Choiseul M, May A. Training needs of health visitors in the haemoglobinopathies. *Health Visitor* 1988; **69**: 205–6.

52 Anionwu EN. Genetics: a multi-ethnic approach. *Nursing* 1991; **41**: 9–12.

53 ICH Productions. *From chance to choice.* Video obtainable from the Mothercare Unit of Clinical Genetics & Fetal Medicine, Institute of Child Health, 30 Guilford Street, London WC1N 1EH. Price £30.

54 House of Commons Session (1990–91). Health committee fourth report, Vol I. *Maternity services: pre-conception.* London: HMSO, 1991.

13 | Infectious diseases

Ahilya Noone
Consultant Epidemiologist, Scottish Centre for Infection and Environmental Health, Glasgow

There is a scarcity of literature on the incidence and prevalence of infectious diseases in minority ethnic groups in the UK. Interpretation of this literature is sometimes problematic for, as Bhopal has pointed out, methodological issues in researching ethnic differences in health and disease are yet to be properly confronted by investigators.[1]

Such research may be undertaken on the one hand to quantify and describe the health status of minority ethnic groups as a basis for planning services, on the other to determine the causes, sources and transmission of disease. Definition of the objectives of research on minority ethnic health precedes the development of research methodology. Problems in selection of representative groups bedevil such research, and the categories used in the classification of ethnic groups and the methods of collecting the information often result in inaccurate, imprecise and inappropriate categorisation. A workshop held in 1993 in the United States has provided a useful and detailed account of the limitations of the concepts, measures and uses of these variables, and has produced recommendations for improving this situation.[2]

Associations demonstrated between ethnic groups and infectious diseases result from the effects of, and the interactions between, social circumstances (environmental, socioeconomic or cultural) and individual attributes, the 'social' model of health. To improve the health status of this section of the population it is necessary to determine the factors that result in increased incidence or prevalence of disease in a group, and to identify factors that can be altered. Research and debate on the social context of disease are clearly essential if the health status of communities is to be improved.

For pragmatic reasons, this chapter utilises the 'medical' model of disease (based on relationships between individual character-istics and disease) while acknowledging its many limitations, and examines published data on ethnicity and selected infectious dis-eases in the United Kingdom (UK), namely: tuberculosis, rubella, hepatitis B virus infection, malaria, HIV infection, human T-cell leukaemia lymphoma virus type 1 infection, and sexually trans-mitted diseases. The descriptors of ethnicity which have been pro-vided by the investigators themselves are those used in the text. The emphasis is on the consistency of patterns of association observed in the data, and simple interventions that may reduce the elevated risk of some ethnic groups for selected infectious diseases are described.

Tuberculosis

Surveys of notifications of tuberculosis have been undertaken every 5 years since 1978. These consistently show differences in notification rates between persons whose ethnic group is described as Indian, Pakistani, Bangladeshi, West Indian and white (Table 1). Groups who have their origin in the Indian subcontinent (India, Pakistan and Bangladesh) have notification rates 25–30 times that in the white population, while rates among the group of West Indian ethnic origin are over four times as high. Notification rates for all these groups fell between 1988 and 1993 but differences between ethnic groups remain.[3,4] For the Indian sub-Continent ethnic group the lowest rates are in children born in the UK (Table 2). The highest rates within each group are in those who arrived in the UK within the past 5 years. Most tuberculosis in those born outside the UK is thought to result from infection acquired in home countries where the prevalence of tuberculosis is higher than in the UK – the situation in many countries in Asia and Africa.[5] Tuberculosis may also follow a return visit to the Indian subcontinent, and the risk extends to members of the families born in the UK.[6]

Several factors may contribute to the increased incidence of tuberculosis in some ethnic groups in addition to the higher preva-lence in the country of origin. These include increased exposure to disease within minority ethnic groups in the UK, crowded living conditions and other socioeconomic and environmental factors and culturally determined differences such as diet. Attention has been drawn to the similarity in the clinical presentation of tuber-culosis in patients of Indian subcontinent ethnic origin and persons with HIV infection, and it was suggested that altered

Table 1. Tuberculosis: annual notification rates for newly notified previously untreated patients per 100,000 population in England and Wales, by ethnic group for England[a]

Country	Ethnic origin	1983			1988			1993		
		No. of cases[a]	Population estimate (1,000s)	Rate per 100,000[b]	No. of cases[a]	Population estimate (1,000s)	Rate per 100,000[b]	No. of cases[a]	Population estimate (1,000s)	Rate per 100,000[b]
England	White	1,550	42,994	6.9	1,072	43,938	4.7	1,025	44,632	4.3
	Indian	718	773	178.0	556	800	134.6	546	897	114.7
	Pakistani or Bangladeshi	374	422	169.0	281	541	100.5	461	724	120.1
	Black Caribbean[c]	78	494	30.0	70	464	29.2	49	478	19.4
	Black African[d]	} 156	} 634	} 47.0	37	119	60.4	168	234	135.2
	Other				67	676	12.2	135	795	31.6
	All	2,876	46,164[e]	12.2	2,085[f]	46,829[e]	8.6	2,384	47,772[e]	9.4
Wales	All	126	2,778	8.7	78	2,823	5.3	74	1,874	4.9
England and Wales	All	3,002	48,942	12.0	2,163	49,652	8.4	2,458	50,646	9.2

[a]Number of cases in 6 months.

[b]For calculation of annual rates the numbers of cases in a year in each survey were estimated by multiplying the number of cases in the first 6 months with a scaling factor based on the ratio of cases reported to the OPCS in the first 6 months to the number reported in the whole year. The scaling factors used were: 1.9348 in 1988 and 1.886 in 1993.

[c]Classified as West Indian in 1983 and 1988. [d]Classified as African in 1983 and 1988.

[e]Includes 847,000 in 1983, 296,000 in 1988 and 11,600 in 1993 whose ethnic origin was unclassified and who were distributed among the other groups in proportion to reported figures for calculation of rates. [f]Includes two cases of unknown ethnic origin.

Table 2. Tuberculosis: annual notification rates in the population of Indian subcontinent ethnic origin in England by age, place of birth and years since entry to the United Kingdom[3]

Age (years)	Place of birth and years since first entry	1993	
		Population estimate (1,000s)	Rate per 100,000
< 15	UK	461	34
	Abroad	61	50
> 15	UK	223	83
15–34	Abroad		
	> 15 years	133	53
	11–15 years	74	63
	6–10 years	64	180
	< 5 years	69	440
> 35	Abroad		
	> 15 years	427	105
	11–15 years	54	230
	6–10 years	28	426
	< 5 years	26	1,110
Total		*1,621*	*117*
Directly standardised rate*			132

*Standardised to the 1983 population estimates taking into account age, place of birth, and year of first entry into the UK.

cellular immunity is the common feature in these two groups.[7] The role of 1,25-dihydroxyvitamin D (the storage form of vitamin D) in the immune regulatory function of macrophages has been shown in studies of animal and human cells.[8,9] Lower concentrations of vitamin D than that in the white population occur in some groups from the Indian subcontinent now resident in the UK, and there is also an increased incidence of rickets in these groups.[10,11] Dietary factors associated with vegetarianism have been suggested to account for the higher prevalence of clinical tuberculosis in Hindu members of the Asian group.[12] This latter observation illustrates that cultural characteristics of subpopulations within a larger group may give rise to differences in the incidence of disease.

Notwithstanding the exact mechanism of the increased incidence of tuberculosis among persons of Indian subcontinent ethnic origin, one preventive measure that has been shown to be effective is BCG immunisation. The Department of Health advise that all schoolchildren be offered BCG immunisation routinely at age 10–14 years and that infants at increased risk receive BCG as neonates.[13] The efficacy of neonatal BCG immunisation of Asian babies has been estimated to be of the order of 49% to 64%;[14] that of schoolchildren from the white majority population is of the order of 80%.[15] In the 1988 survey of tuberculosis, 46% of notifications (134/294) in children (ie those less than 15 years old) were of Indian, Pakistani or Bangladeshi ethnic origin and 78% of these (104/134) had been born in the UK (S Meredith, personal communication, 1993). Forty per cent of children from or with parents from the Indian subcontinent whose immunisation status was known, and 74% (17/23) of these under 5 years old, had not received BCG. A survey of district immunisation policies in 1990 showed that 20% of districts, including some with 3% or more of their population originating in the Indian subcontinent, did not offer BCG immunisation to neonates.[16] While 92% of districts were carrying out routine immunisation of schoolchildren, three districts with 3–5% of their population of Indian subcontinent ethnic origin had stopped their schools programme against national policy. Selective immunisation at school entry was offered by some districts, including two of the 15 that had stopped the school programme. The data indicate that there is still room for improvement in BCG immunisation programmes.

Convincing evidence exists, therefore, that some minority ethnic groups have an increased risk of clinical tuberculosis. The specific initiatives that reduce this risk are early diagnosis and effective treatment, BCG immunisation of neonates and schoolchildren, and rapid tracing and appropriate treatment of contacts of cases. Furthermore, screening of new immigrants from high prevalence areas will not only detect active tuberculosis, but more importantly, identify those in whom preventive chemotherapy, as well as BCG, will be effective.

Rubella

Congenital rubella infection is a cause of severe and permanent disability. The proportion of reports of congenital rubella in babies of mothers of Asian and Oriental ethnic origin is greater than would be expected on the basis of their proportion in the population.[17,18] Of 94 reports of congenital rubella in babies received between January 1987 and December 1992, 22% were of children born to mothers whose origin was described on the report as Asian or Oriental.[18] Increased susceptibility to rubella in this group was demonstrated in serological studies of antenatal clinic attenders in London in 1980[19] and in Luton, Leeds and Manchester in 1984.[20,21] Susceptibility of the Asian and Oriental group has declined but is still higher than that of the white population. National policy recommendations are that all children should be immunised with rubella-containing vaccine (MMR) at 12–15 months and again at approximately 4 years, and that women should be screened for rubella antibodies at least in the first pregnancy. However, women who come as young adults to live in the UK from countries where the prevalence of rubella in childhood is low, and/or where there are no childhood rubella immunisation programmes, are at risk of having an affected child. The babies of 15 non-immunised Asian and Oriental women were notified as having congenital rubella in the 3 years to December 1992; 12 of these women had come to the UK as adults. Women who have not had rubella immunisation should be identified, tested for antibodies and immunised prior to pregnancy at the time they first register with a general practitioner.

It has also been noted that the proportion of Asian women tested for contact with rubella in pregnancy is lower than the proportion of non-Asians,[21] a surprising finding in view of the fact that greater parity of the former group would be expected to place them at higher risk of rubella infection resulting from exposure to children. Lack of awareness of the risk, a reluctance to have abortions and late booking are all factors that may account for the lower frequency of tests in a more vulnerable group. These aspects of antenatal care are worthy of further study.

Hepatitis B virus

Chronic infection with hepatitis B virus (HBV) affects at least 5% of the world's population and is the chief cause of cirrhosis and of primary hepatocellular cancer worldwide.[22] Persons with chronic HBV infection are recognised by the presence in their blood of the surface antigen to HBV and are known as carriers. The prevalence of the carrier state varies widely worldwide.[23] In some population groups in south-east Asia and Africa, prevalences of more than 8% have been found. Intermediate levels (2–7%) are found in populations in southern Europe, whereas in western Europe and the US the prevalence is less than 2.0% (Fig 1). Minority ethnic groups resident in the UK include migrants from countries where the prevalence of HBV carriers is high. It is now not uncommon for children from countries where the carrier state is highly prevalent to be adopted by families living in the UK.

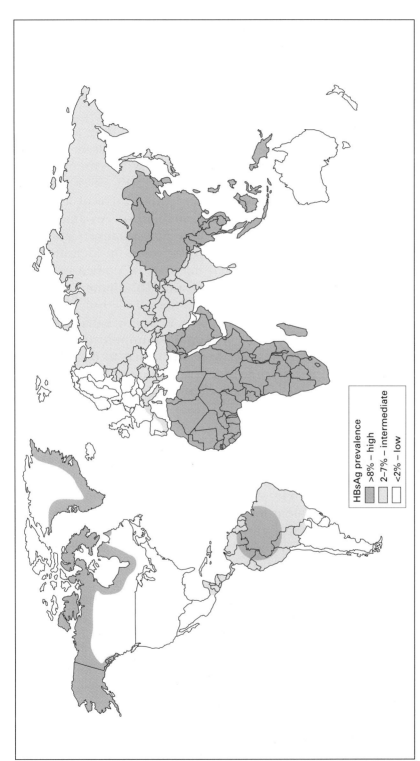

Fig 1. *Global distribution of HBsAg.*

Transmission of HBV infection occurs from carrier mothers to their babies, usually from those carrier mothers in whose blood the 'e' antigen of HBV is also present; 70–80% of babies of such mothers become infected, of whom 80% themselves become carriers. Children infected in the early years of life are at greater risk of becoming carriers than healthy adults who become infected. Such children may also include the siblings of a carrier infant, since HBV infection can be transmitted horizontally between children.

Passive immunisation and a course of HBV vaccine initiated soon after birth have been shown to protect 94% of children of HBeAg positive carrier mothers,[24] and this course of action is recommended in the UK for at-risk neonates.[13] An analysis of reports to the Communicable Disease Surveillance Centre of HBsAg positive women aged 15–40 years, based on identification of non-Caucasian names, suggested that 84% of women were not Caucasian. Nearly 90% of requests for anti-HBV immunoglobulin for passive immunisation of neonates where the ethnic group of the mother was recorded would appear to be for babies who are not Caucasian (J Heptonstall, personal communication, 1993). These mothers and babies are those identified to be at risk by existing antenatal testing practices. It is important to ensure that all mothers and infants at risk are identified by effective strategies. Universal antenatal testing would result in identification of all those at risk regardless of ethnicity.

The health needs of the affected carrier, her spouse and other siblings also have to be met. Oral and written information about the disease, in the appropriate language, should be available to the family. The liver function of the carrier should be monitored and appropriate management instituted. Her spouse will benefit from knowing his HBV status and being advised accordingly. Other children in the family should be investigated to identify any carrier, and to protect uninfected children by immunisation. A similar approach, that is advice, care and management of the whole family, may be required for families with adopted children from countries or institutions (eg orphanages in some countries in eastern Europe) where the prevalence of HBV infection is high.[25] The primary care team has a key role in prevention of HBV infection in families.[26,27]

Malaria

Worldwide more than 100 million clinical cases of malaria are estimated to occur with some 280 million people carrying the parasite each year.[28] Malaria is an important cause of morbidity and mortality among children and young adults in those countries in Asia, Africa and Latin America where the disease occurs (Fig 2).[29] In these countries the hot humid conditions in lower lying areas provide suitable breeding conditions for the Anopheles mosquito, the vector of the malaria parasite.

It is estimated that 38% of the 753,000 visits by UK residents to Africa in 1990, and 41% of the 805,000 visits to India, were by persons visiting family and friends.[30] In 1991 and 1992 nearly 4,000 cases of malaria were reported to the Malaria Reference Laboratory (D Bradley, personal communication). By far the largest proportion of cases occur in the group who travel abroad to visit family and friends. Such cases have been increasing as a proportion of all reported cases: from 26% (501/1,909) in 1978 to 35% (573/1,629) in 1992. *Plasmodium falciparum*, the most serious form of malaria, is most commonly reported, with infection by this species making up 57% (935/1,629) of all malaria cases reported in 1992. The vast majority of cases of *P. falciparum* – 90% (838/935) in 1992 – now occur in persons visiting countries in Africa. In the group who visited African countries in that year, new immigrants and persons visiting family and friends accounted for 40% of cases (359/838), but those visiting family and friends outnumbered new immigrants by four to one. *P. falciparum* also occurs in persons who have visited family and friends on the Indian subcontinent; 39 such cases were reported in 1992. Though the numbers are small, they have tended to increase over the past 6 years. *P. vivax* is the form of malaria most commonly reported in persons who have emigrated from or have visited the Indian subcontinent; it accounted for 70% (359/512) of cases of malaria reported in 1992. The number of cases in persons visiting family and friends outnumber those in new immigrants by five to one.

The incidence of malaria in people visiting countries where the disease is endemic can be considerably reduced by consistent use of antimalarial chemotherapy (for a period that includes at least one week before the visit, the duration of the visit, and 4 weeks after returning), and the adoption of precautions to avoid mosquito bites during travel. The data previously mentioned from the Malaria Reference Laboratory indicate that those who visit family and friends in Africa and on the Indian subcontinent are particularly at risk. They may not seek advice, may not be given advice and/or may not adhere to advice during travel. Some of them believe that they have immunity from living in the area previously, or their family abroad do not take antimalarials so they do

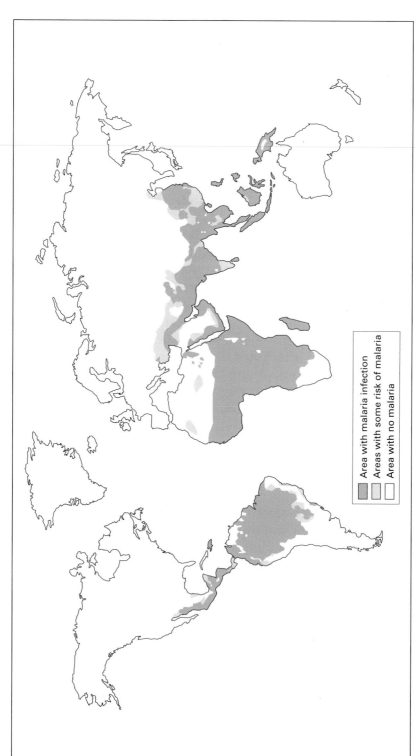

Fig 2. *Global distribution of areas of malaria transmission, 1993.*[29]

not think of it. There is clearly a need to investigate why these infections occur and, in particular, whether pre-travel advice has been sought or given, since the risk of malaria in the countries visited will have changed considerably since some of these persons or their relatives, now resident in the UK, last lived there.

HIV infection

The global HIV epidemic is having a profound impact on the health and survival of many people in many countries in the world and in particular in sub-Saharan Africa (Table 3).[31] World-wide about 13,000 new infections occur each day, giving an annual increase of 20%, but in some developing countries it is in excess of 150% each year.[32] It is estimated that by the year 2000 more than 26 million persons will be infected with HIV, more than 90% of whom will be in developing countries.[33] The prevalence of HIV infection in men and women attending sexually transmitted disease (STD) clinics in some urban areas may be as high as 70% whilst in pregnant women infection rates in some cities approach 30%. Highest levels of infection are usually found in young adult women,[33] and among heterosexual men from African and African-Caribbean origin.[34] The epicentre of HIV pandemic is shifting from Africa to Asia with many countries reporting high incidence of HIV infection. The incidence of new HIV infection in Asia and the Pacific will soon pass that in Africa and is projected to increase into the next century.[35–41] HIV sero-prevalence was 32% in STD clinic attenders in Bombay, India, in 1991[42] and 2.5 times higher among heterosexual African-Caribbeans attending STD clinics in Paris.[34] In some Caribbean countries, HIV prevalence in STD clinic attenders is increasing.[43,44]

Table 3. Estimated number and global distribution of adults and children living with HIV/AIDS; December 1997

Australasia and New Zealand	12,000
East Asia & the Pacific	440,000
Eastern Europe & Central Asia	150,000
Latin America & the Caribbean	1.6 million
North Africa & the Middle East	210,000
North America	860,000
South & South East Asia	6 million
Sub-Saharan Africa	20.8 million
Western Europe	530,000

With the increasing number of HIV infection among women of childbearing age especially in developing countries, the incidence of paediatric HIV infection is on the increase as a result of mother to infant (vertical) transmission. The rates of vertical transmission vary from 15 to 40% in different global areas with the highest in Africa.[45-48] There are many possibilities for the transmission; in utero (antepartum), during delivery (intrapartum), after birth (postpartum), or later through breastfeeding. While maternal viral burden around the time of delivery is the strongest determinant of the risk of disease transmission,[46] many other factors could increase the risk of vertical transmission. Among these are maternal drug misuse, maternal infection and malnutrition.[49] Children living with maternal HIV infection have multiple needs which require dedicated resources from health, education, social services and voluntary sector.[50] With the advances of combination antiviral treatment, the outlook for people with HIV infection has been greatly improved. Indeed, countries with high uptake rates of HIV testing in pregnancy are now seeing a significant decline in paediatric AIDS. As many women do not recognise that they are HIV infected until the baby is born, confidential HIV testing, therefore, should be 'normalised' and offered to all pregnant women as part of routine antenatal care, especially to those living in high prevalence areas.[51-53]

There are longstanding links between the UK and some countries where HIV prevalence is high. Immigrants, refugees and students from these countries come to the UK, their numbers varying from year to year depending on a variety of factors including the political situation in the home countries and immigration restrictions currently in force in the UK. It is not surprising, therefore, that in the surveillance data for England and Wales based on reports to the Communicable Disease Surveillance Centre, HIV infected individuals from countries severely affected by the HIV epidemic are over-represented relative to their proportion in the population. Sixty three percent (1,194/1,881) of people with AIDS reported in the UK by the end of December 1997 who had probably acquired their infection heterosexually abroad were from the 'black African' ethnic group. During the same period, two-thirds (172/261) of children reported with AIDS who had acquired their infection through mother to child transmission were reported to be from the 'black African' ethnic group. The national policy stipulates that an HIV antibody test be offered to all pregnant women attending clinics especially in areas where HIV prevalence is high. This policy is yet to be effectively implemented.

No information on ethnic group is available from the laboratory reporting of HIV infections, but both the AIDS and HIV infection databases include information on the country where the infection was 'presumed to have occurred'. Of HIV infections reported by the end of December 1997 which were probably the result of sex between men and women abroad, 80% were in men and women exposed to infection in countries in Africa. Although the ethnic group distribution of these individuals is not available, it is reasonable to assume that a proportion will be black Africans,[7] and some will be UK residents. This has implications for access to and delivery of care to those affected, and for advising and preventing infection in their friends and relatives. There is undoubtedly a great need for services; sensitivity to the many individual, social, economic, legal and cultural issues is required in providing them.

There are a few reports of the HIV knowledge, attitudes and behaviour of black and minority ethnic groups.[54] The report of a survey of the educational needs of Asian people based on questionnaire completion and on interview concluded that their knowledge was poor and that misconceptions were common (R Shukla, personal communication). The author points to the need for further studies. The national survey of sexual attitudes and lifestyles in the UK includes some preliminary information on sexual behaviour, based on interviews of small randomly selected samples. There is a clear need for further work in this area.[55]

The high prevalence of HIV infection in countries in Africa and among STD clinic attenders in some cities in India has implications for those intending to travel to these countries, including persons from minority ethnic groups visiting family and friends.[56] Strategies for providing effective advice on avoiding HIV infection during travel need to be developed.

Human T-lymphotrophic virus type 1

The human T-lymphotrophic virus type 1 (HTLV-1) has a worldwide distribution but is highly endemic in Japan, the Caribbean, parts of Africa and Melanesia.[40,57,58] The limited number of surveys carried out in the UK suggest that persons of African-Caribbean origin born in the Caribbean and their partners have the highest risk of infection with HTLV-1.[58–64] It is generally accepted that infection is very much less common among UK-born African-Caribbeans.[65]

Transmission of infection occurs by three routes: vertically from mother to child, sexually, and by transfusion of the cellular components of blood.[66] Mother to child transmission is thought to occur mainly through breast feeding. Overall approximately a quarter of children born to infected mothers are themselves infected.[67]

The clinical significance of HTLV-1 infection lies in its association with two distinct disease entities: adult T-cell leukaemia (ATL), and HTLV-1 associated myelopathy/tropical spastic paraparesis (HAM/TSP).[68,69] ATL is a malignancy of mature T cells characterised by leukaemia, hypercalcaemia, bone lesions, skin and lymphatic infiltration. The onset of the syndrome is usually acute and the course rapidly progressive. The lifetime risk of ATL among HTLV-1 infected persons is estimated to be only 2–5%.[70] HAM/TSP is a chronic degenerative neurological syndrome characterised by progressive spastic paraparesis of the lower limbs, bladder and bowel dysfunction, and sometimes sensory abnormalities. The incubation period is 20–30 years in those infected through vertical or sexual transmission; the lifetime risk has been estimated to be about 0.25%.[71]

Vertical transmission of HTLV-1 can theoretically be prevented by screening antenatal patients and the avoidance of breast feeding by infected mothers, but a 'selective' screening strategy would clearly have to be soundly justified. The prevalence of disease is likely to be very low even in mothers of African-Caribbean origin, the vast majority of whom are now likely to be UK-born. Counselling and management of carriers of the virus is now being undertaken at a special clinic set up in London (G Taylor, personal communication).

Other sexually transmitted diseases

Few data are available on the prevalence of other STDs such as gonorrhoea, chlamydia trachomatis, herpes simplex virus type 2, and pelvic inflammatory disease in minority ethnic groups in the UK. Being a member of a minority ethnic group has been identified as a risk factor for STDs and associated risk behaviours in one study from Holland.[72] Data from genitourinary medicine clinics in London[73] and Leeds[74] indicate that the rates of gonorrhoea in black men and women were 10 times higher than those in white persons of the same age and from the same socioeconomic groups.

STD clinics in the UK attended by those at highest risk of infection are the appropriate location for studying the factors that may be associated with increased risk of STD, including ethnic group, socioeconomic status and travel. They are also key sites for implementing preventive initiatives to all those at risk, including members of minority ethnic groups.

Other infections

There are other examples in the literature of increased risk of infectious disease among minority ethnic groups, besides those discussed above. It has been reported that respiratory infections are more common in children from minority ethnic groups; for example children with sickle cell disease have an increased risk of pneumonia.[75] Those with hereditary haemaglobinopathies, therefore, would benefit from pneumococcal vaccine. Current research also suggests that the risk of bacterial meningitis may be increased in some groups (G Urwin, personal communication, 1993). In addition, data on utilisation of health services indicate that there is an increased risk for travel-associated gastrointestinal infections among minority ethnic groups (B Bannister, personal communication, 1993).

Conclusion

Socioeconomic factors are likely to play a part in the more frequent occurrence of some infectious diseases among people from minority ethnic groups. If interventions to improve the health of this section of the population are to be successful, the factors contributing to impaired health status need to be clearly distinguished and the magnitude of their separate effects estimated. In this way, the most appropriate and feasible interventions can be identified and their likely impact assessed. Factors directly related to ethnicity can be separated from those that are socio-economic in origin. In particular, the effect of poverty in increasing the risk of infectious disease in certain communities needs to be examined.

The lack of clarity of definition for minority ethnic groups was alluded to at the beginning of this chapter. There is clearly a need to be more precise about exactly who are the minority ethnic groups with increased risk of infectious disease. Is the risk of tuberculosis, or of rubella, the same in all groups from the Indian subcontinent? Which other ethnic groups are also at risk? Are there subcategories of greater risk defined by socioeconomic status, diet or culturally determined factors, for example? Are refugees from specific areas particularly disadvantaged as regards infectious disease? In addition, the relative risks of infectious diseases for some minority ethnic groups, such as Travellers, Chinese and Vietnamese, have not been studied.

Much of the research on infectious disease and ethnic group has been focused on the health of children. There is now also need for more research on the health of the elderly members of the groups.

The importance of infectious diseases as a cause of morbidity in minority ethnic groups relative to other diseases has not been addressed in this chapter. The impact of the infectious diseases selected for discussion in this chapter may be numerically small, but they have been singled out for consideration because the measures required to alleviate their effects appear clear-cut, simple and likely to be successful if sensitively implemented.

General recommendations

- The methodological basis of research on minority ethnic health, including definitions, should be developed and strengthened.
- Research should be undertaken to clarify the independent role of poverty as a cause of infectious disease morbidity.
- The specific health care needs of some minority ethnic groups, such as travellers, Chinese and Vietnamese, have been neglected and should receive attention. The particular needs of the elderly from this section of the population should also be investigated.

Specific recommendations

- The efficiency of immunisation programmes for the prevention of tuberculosis, rubella in post-partum women and hepatitis B should be improved.
- The antenatal care of mothers whose babies are at risk of congenital rubella or hepatitis B or HIV infection should be evaluated. The care and support offered to families with HBsAg positive members should also be appraised and improved where necessary.
- There is an urgent need for preventive and care services for HIV-infected persons and their families, from black and minority ethnic communities, that are accessible and acceptable to the communities affected.

Acknowledgements

I am grateful to the following people for their help in providing data and/or advice: Barbara Bannister, David Bradley, Amanda

Durante, Roger Feldman, Henika Konforti, Sara Meredith, Ahmed Hamid, Julia Heptonstall and Gillian Urwin. They are, however, not responsible for the views expressed!

References

1   Bhopal RS. Future research on the health of ethnic minorities: back to basics; a personal view. In: Ahmad WIU, ed. *The politics of 'race' and health.* Bradford: University of Bradford, Race Relations Research Unit, 1990.

2   Centers for Disease Control. Use of race and ethnicity in public health surveillance. Summary of the Centers for Disease Control/ Agency for Toxic Substances and Disease Registry Workshop. *Morbidity and Mortality Weekly Report* 1993; **42**: RR-10: 1–17.

3   Kumar D, Watson JM, Charlett A, *et al.* Tuberculosis in England and Wales in 1993: results of a national survey. *Thorax* 1997; **52**: 1060–7.

4   DeCock KM, Low N. HIV and AIDS, other sexually transmitted diseases, and tuberculosis in ethnic minorities in United Kingdom: is surveillance serving its purpose? *British Medical Journal* 1997; **314**: 1747–51.

5   Sudre P, ten Dam G, Koichi A. Tuberculosis: a global overview of the situation today. *Bulletin of the World Health Organisation* 1992; **70**: 149–59.

6   McCarthy OR. Asian immigrant tuberculosis: the effect of visiting Asia. *British Journal of Diseases of the Chest* 1984; **78**: 248–53.

7   Davies PDO. Vitamin D and tuberculosis. *American Review of Respiratory Diseases* 1989; **139**: 1571.

8   Bar-Shavit Z, Noff D, Edelstein S, *et al.* 1,25-Dihydroxyvitamin D_3 and the regulation of macrophage function. *Calcified Tissue International* 1981; **33**: 673–6.

9   Rook GAW. Role of active macrophages in the immunopathology of tuberculosis. *British Medical Bulletin* 1988; **44**: 611–23.

10   Henderson JB, Dunnigan MG, McIntosh WB, *et al.* The importance of limited exposure to ultraviolet radiation and dietary factors in the aetiology of Asian rickets: a risk-factor model. *Quarterly Journal of Medicine* 1987; **241**: 413–25.

11   Hunt SP, O'Riordan JLH, Windo J, Truswell AS. Vitamin D status in different subgroups of British Asians, *British Medical Journal* 1976; **ii**: 1351–4.

12   Finch PJ, Millard FJC, Maxwell JD. Risk of tuberculosis in immigrant Asians: culturally acquired immunodeficiency? *Thorax* 1991; **46**: 1–5.

13   Department of Health, Welsh Office, Scottish Office Department of Health, DHSS (Northern Ireland). *Immunisation against infectious disease.* London: HMSO, 1996.

14   Rodrigues LC, Gill ON, Smith PG. BCG vaccination in the first year of life protects children of Indian subcontinent ethnic origin against tuberculosis in England. *Journal of Epidemiology and Community Health* 1991; **45**: 78–80.

15   Hart PDA, Sutherland I. BCG and vole vaccines in the prevention of tuberculosis in adolescence and early adult life: final report to the Medical Research Council. *British Medical Journal* 1977; **ii**: 293–5.

16 Joseph CA, Watson JM, Fern KJ. BCG immunisation in England and Wales: a survey of policy and practice in schoolchildren and neonates. *British Medical Journal* 1992; **305**: 495–8.

17 Miller E, Waight PA, Vurdien JE, *et al.* Rubella surveillance to December 1992: second joint report from the PHLS and National Congenital Rubella Surveillance Programme. *Communicable Disease Report* 1993; **3**: R35–40.

18 Miller E, Waight PA, Vurdien JE, *et al.* Rubella surveillance to December 1990: a joint report from the PHLS and National Congenital Rubella Surveillance Programme. *Communicable Disease Report* 1991; **1**: R33–8.

19 Peckham CS, Tookey P, Nelson DB, *et al.* Ethnic minority women and congenital rubella. *British Medical Journal* 1983; **287**: 129–30.

20 Miller E, Nicoll A, Rousseau A, *et al.* Congenital rubella in babies of south Asian women in England and Wales: an excess and its causes. *British Medical Journal* 1987; **294**: 737–9.

21 Miller E, Waight P, Rousseau SA, *et al.* Congenital rubella in the Asian community in Britain. *British Medical Journal* 1990; **301**: 1391.

22 Hoofnagle JH. Chronic hepatitis B. *New England Journal of Medicine* 1990; **323**: 337–9.

23 Sobeslavsky G. Prevalence of markers of hepatitis B virus infection in various countries: a WHO collaborative study. *Bulletin of the World Health Organisation* 1980; **58**: 621–8.

24 Beasley RP, Hwang L-Y, Lin C-G, *et al.* Prevention of perinatally transmitted hepatitis B virus infections with hepatitis B immune globulin and hepatitis B vaccine. *Lancet* 1983; **ii**: 1099–102.

25 Hershow RC, Hadler SC, Kane MA. Adoption of children from countries with endemic hepatitis B: transmission risks and medical issues. *Pediatric Infectious Disease Journal* 1987; **6**: 431–7.

26 Masters N, Livingstone A, Cencora V. Hepatitis B: prevention in primary care. More community based policies needed. *British Medical Journal* 1989; **298**: 908.

27 Cencora V, Challoner F, Gooch S, *et al.* Immunisation of neonates at risk of hepatitis B. *British Medical Journal,* 1988; **297**: 481.

28 World Health Organisation. World malaria situation in 1989. *Weekly Epidemiological Record* 1991; **66**: 157–64.

29 World Health Organisation. World malaria situation in 1993. *Weekly Epidemiological Record* 1996; **71**: 37–9.

30 Department of Employment. *International passenger survey 1990.* London: DoE, 1991.

31 World Health Organisation. AIDS data at 30 June 1995 and the current global situation of the HIV/AIDS pandemic. *Weekly Epidemiological Record* 1995; **70**: 193–200.

31 World Health Organisation. AIDS data at 30 June 1995 and the current global situation of the HIV/AIDS pandemic. *Weekly Epidemiological Record* 1995; **70**: 193–200.

32 Tarantola DJ, Mann JM. Global expansion of HIV infection and AIDS. *Hospital Practice* 1996; **31**: 63–6.

33 Quinn TC. Global burden of the HIV epidemic. *Lancet* 1996; **348**: 99–106.

34 Meyer L, Couturier E, Brossard Y, *et al.* Trends in HIV infection among sexually transmitted disease patients in Paris. *AIDS* 1996; **10**: 401–5.

35 Umenai T, Narula M, Onuki D, *et al.* International HIV and AIDS prevention: Japan/United States collaboration. *Journal of Acquired Immune Deficiency Syndrome Human Retrovirology* 1997; **14** (Suppl 2): S58–S67.

36 Corwin A, Simanjuntak CH, Ansari A. Emerging disease surveillance in Southeast Asia. *Annals of Academy of Medicine of Singapore* 1997; **26**: 628–31.

37 Srikanth P, John TJ, Jeyakumari H, *et al.* Epidemiological features of acquired immunodeficiency syndrome in southern India. *Indian Journal of Medical Research* 1997; **105**: 191–7.

38 Lindan CP, Lieu TX, Giang LT, *et al.* Rising HIV infection rates in HO Chi Minh City herald emerging AIDS epidemic in Vietnam. *AIDS* 1997; **11** (Suppl 1): S5–S13.

39 Dore GJ, Kaldor JM, Ungchusak K, Mertens TE. Epidemiology of HIV and AIDS in the Asia-Pacific region. *Medical Journal of Australia* 1996; **165**: 494–8.

40 Tajima K, Soda K. The epidemiology of AIDS/HIV in Japan. *Journal of Epidemiology* 1996; **6** (Suppl 3): S67–S74.

41 Yu ES, Xie Q, Zhang K, *et al.* HIV infection and AIDS in China, 1985 through 1994. *American Journal of Public Health* 1996; **86**: 1116–22.

42 Mehendale SM, Shepherd ME, Divekar AD, *et al.* Evidence of high prevalence and rapid transmission of HIV among individuals attending STD clinics in Pune, India. *Indian Journal of Medical Research* 1996; **104**: 327–35.

43 *IXth international conference on AIDS.* Berlin 1993; abstract no PO-C03-2617.

44 Figueroa JP, Ward E, Morris J, *et al.* Incidence of HIV and HTLV-1 infection among sexually transmitted disease clinic attenders in Jamaica. *Journal of Acquired Deficiency Syndrome Human Retrovirology* 1997; **15**: 232–7.

45 Klirsfeld D. HIV disease and women. *Medical Clinic of North America* 1998; **82**: 335–57.

46 Kotler DP. HIV in pregnancy. *Gastroenterology Clinic of North America* 1998; **27**: 269–80.

47 Nourse CB, Butler KM. Perinatal transmission of HIV and diagnosis of HIV infection in infants: a review. *Irish Journal of Medical Sciences* 1998; **167**: 28–32.

48 Law MG, Downs AM, Brunet JB, Kaldor JM. Time trends in HIV infection among pregnant women in Europe. *AIDS* 1998; **12**: 211–6.

49 Vials A. Review of the literature on prevention of early vertical transmission of the HIV virus. *Midwifery* 1997; **13**: 216–20.

50 Mok J, Cooper. The needs of children whose mother have HIV infection. *Archives of Disease of Childhood* 1997; **77**: 483–7.

51 Mercey D. Antenatal HIV testing. *British Medical Journal* 1998; **316**: 241–2.

52 De Cook K, Johnson AM. From exceptionalism to normalisation: a reappraisal of attitudes and practice around HIV testing. *British Medical Journal* 1998; **316**: 290–3.

53 Royal College of Paediatricians and Child Health. *Reducing mother to child transmission of HIV infection in the United Kingdom.* Recommendations of an Intercollegiate Working Party for enhancing voluntary confidential HIV testing in pregnancy. London: RCPCH, 1998 (Abstract in *BMJ* 1998; **316**: 1333).

54 Haour-Knipe M, Dubois-Arber F. Minorities, immigrants and HIV/AIDS epidemiology. *European Journal of Public Health* 1993; **3**: 259–62.

55 Johnson AM, Wadsworth J, Wellings K, Field J. *Sexual attitudes and lifestyles.* London: Blackwell Scientific Publications, 1994.

56 Blattner WA. Retroviruses. In: Evans A, ed. *Viral infections of humans,* 3rd edn. UK: Plenum Press, 1989: Ch. 21, 545–92.

57 Wiktor SZ, Blattner WA. Epidemiology of human T-cell leukaemia virus type 1 (HTLV-1). In: Gallo RC, Jay G, eds. *The human retroviruses.* London: Academic Press, 1991. Ch. 9, 175–92.

58 Tosswill JH, Ades AE, Peckham C, *et al.* Infection with human T cell leukaemia/lymphoma virus type 1 in patients attending an antenatal clinic in London. *British Medical Journal* 1990; **301**: 95–6.

59 Tedder RS, Shanson DC, Jeffries DJ, *et al.* Low prevalence in the UK of HTLV-1 and HTLV-11 infection in subjects with AIDS, with extended lymphadenopathy, and at risk of AIDS. *Lancet* 1984; **ii**: 125–7.

60 Salker R, Tosswell JHC, Barbara JAJ, *et al.* HTLV-1/11 antibodies in blood donors. *Lancet* 1990; **336**: 317.

61 Banatvala JE, Chrystie IL, Palmer SJ, *et al.* Retrospective study of HIV, hepatitis B, and HTLV-1 infection at a London antenatal clinic. *Lancet* 1989; **ii**: 798.

62 Cruickshank JK, Richardson JH, Morgan OStC, *et al.* Screening for prolonged incubation of HTLV-1 infection in British and Jamaican relatives of British patients with tropical spastic paraparesis. *British Medical Journal,* 1990; **300**: 300–4.

63 Mowbray J, Mawson S, Chawira A, *et al.* Epidemiology of Human T-cell leukaemia/lymphoma virus type I (HTL-I) infections in a sub-population of Afro-Caribbean origin in England. *Journal of Medical Virology* 1989; **29**: 289–95.

64 Brennan M, Runganaga J, Barbara JAJ, *et al.* Prevalence of antibodies to human T cell leukaemia/lymphoma virus in blood donors in north London. *British Medical Journal* 1993; **307**: 1235–9.

65 Cruickshank JK. HTLV-I infection in Britain. *British Medical Journal* 1990; **301**: 442.

66 World Health Organisation. Virus diseases. Human T-cell lymphotropic virus-1 (HTLV-1). *Weekly Epidemiological Record* 1992; **67**: 213–7.

67 Sugiyama H, Doi H, Yamaguchi K, *et al.* Significance of postnatal mother-to-child transmission of human T-lymphotropic virus type-1 on the development of adult T-cell leukaemia/lymphoma. *Journal of Medical Virology* 1986; **20**: 253–60.

68 Hinuma Y, Nagata M, Misoka M, *et al.* Adult T-cell leukaemia: antigen in an ATL cell line and detection of antibodies to the antigen in human sera. *Proceedings of the National Academy of Sciences USA* 1981; **78**: 6476–80.

69 Gessain A, Bouin F, Vamant JC, *et al.* The G antibodies to human

T-lymphotropic virus type-1 patients with tropical spastic paraparesis. *Lancet* 1985; **ii**: 407–9.

70   Murphy EL, Hanchard B, Figueroa JP, *et al.* Modelling the risk of adult T-cell leukaemia/lymphoma in persons infected with human T-lymphotropic virus type 1. *International Journal of Cancer* 1989; **43**: 250–3.

71   Kaplan JE, Osame M, Kubota H, *et al.* The risk of development of HTLV-1-associated myelopathy/tropical spastic paraparesis among persons infected with HTLV-1. *Journal of Acquired Immune Deficiency Syndrome* 1990; **3**: 1096–101.

72   Hookyas C, van der Velde FW, van der Linden MMD, *et al.* The importance of ethnicity as a risk factor for STDs and sexual behaviour among heterosexuals. *Genitourinary Medicine* 1991; **67**: 378–83.

73   Low W, Daker-White G, Barlow D, *et al.* Gonorrhoea in Inner London: results of a cross sectional study. *British Medical Journal* 1997; **314**: 1719–23.

74   Lacey CJN, Mervick DW, Bensley DC, *et al.* Analysis of the socio-demography of gonorrhoea in Leeds. *British Medical Journal* 1997; **314**: 1715–8.

75   Melia RJW, Chinn S, Rona RJ. Respiratory illness and home environment of ethnic groups. *British Medical Journal* 1988; **296**: 1438–41.

14 | Women and children

Zarrina Kurtz
Consultant in Public Health Medicine, South Thames Regional Health Authority, London

Health in infancy and childhood is the basis for the health of the population as a whole. Because of the risks for certain health problems in minority ethnic groups, there are particularly important needs for preventive and early interventions in children and young people from these groups. In addition, a very high proportion of people from minority ethnic communities living in this country are young. Their health and lifestyle will have a significant impact on their future health as adults, and the health and understanding of health matters of their mothers is likely to have a significant influence on both.

The issues addressed in the other chapters in this book are all of at least as much significance to minority ethnic women as to men. This chapter focuses more specifically on a further set of issues which are of particular relevance to women (particularly those relating to reproductive health) and children.

Demography and socioeconomic characteristics

The ethnic minority groups in Britain are a disproportionately young population. According to the 1981 census, 3.9% of the total population came from a household whose head was born in the New Commonwealth or Pakistan, but 6.2% of those aged under 16 and 7.4% of children under the age of 5 years. These proportions have grown so that according to the 1991 census, in which ethnic group was recorded on the basis of self-classification, the minority ethnic population made up 5.9% of the total and 9.7% of children both under the age of 16 and under 5 years of age[1] (Table 1). Almost without exception, the age profile of each ethnic minority group is younger than that of the indigenous population for both males and females, with about 50% of Bangladeshi, Pakistani and

Table 1. Age distribution (females) for England and Wales (%)[1]

Age (years)	Total	White	Black Caribbean	Black African	Black other	Indian	Pakistani	Bangladeshi	Chinese	Other Asian	Other
0–4	6.3	6.0	7.2	11.9	19.9	8.7	13.3	15.6	6.8	7.6	16.5
5–14	11.6	11.1	12.5	16.1	27.4	18.9	27.5	29.7	13.9	14.2	24.1
15–24	13.4	13.2	16.2	18.7	21.7	17.0	20.0	21.0	18.5	15.1	17.7
25–44	28.5	28.2	35.6	42.7	25.2	35.4	27.0	23.1	43.2	46.0	28.3
45–64	21.4	21.9	23.7	9.4	4.7	15.9	10.8	9.8	13.8	14.6	9.7
65+	18.7	19.6	4.9	1.2	1.3	4.1	1.4	0.8	3.9	2.6	3.6

mixed origin groups aged under 16 years. The age distribution of those of West African, African and Indian origin, however, is not very different from that of the total population of Great Britain.[2] Recent detailed analysis of the 1991 census has shown that non-random undernumeration has led to underestimation of the numbers of young male adults in ethnic minority populations, particularly among black people, and of people living in inner city areas who also move frequently, among whom ethnic minority groups are over-represented.[3] However, the 1995/6 population estimate based on the labour force survey shows that children under 16 represent 33.4% of all ethnic populations (compared with 20% of the white population), and over 45% among Pakistani, Bangladeshi and mixed origin groups.[4]

Almost three-quarters of the minority ethnic population in Britain live in metropolitan counties, concentrated in inner city areas;[4,5] more than two-fifths live in Greater London.[6] In inner London, minority ethnic groups make up almost a quarter of the total population and over half the school population.[7] In Inner London Education Authority schools in 1989, 19.9% of primary and nursery school pupils and 14.1% of secondary school pupils were not fluent in English. Eighty-four different languages were spoken as a first language.[8] However, the geographical distribution of different ethnic groups varies across the country, so there are substantial concentrations of groups from a relatively homogeneous background in some places, such as Bangladeshis in Tower Hamlets, while others, although numerous in total, are more dispersed, for example the Chinese.[9]

In 1990, 79% of all people in minority ethnic groups under the age of 25 had been born in the UK, compared with only 12% of those aged 25 or over. The proportions born in the UK vary among different ethnic groups; for example, 98% of 25-year-olds of West Indian origin were born here compared with 72% of Pakistanis or Bangladeshis.[6]

Minority ethnic children are disproportionately found in families living in deprived circumstances, with their parents unemployed or low paid, their housing overcrowded and lacking amenities, and with difficult access to public services including education.[10] Black households are three or four times more likely than white to become statutory homeless.[11] African-Caribbean children and those of mixed parentage are more likely to be admitted to local authority care than are white or Asian children.[12]

Average household size varies according to ethnic group. White households tend to contain fewer persons on average (2.45) than all ethnic minority households (3.40), among which households headed by a Pakistani or a Bangladeshi are the largest, with an average of 5.12 persons per household, while West Indian households average only 2.67 persons.[6]

Fertility rates, except in Caribbean-born women, are higher than in UK-born women. Births to all mothers born outside the UK constituted 11.6% of all births in 1990.[13] It can be seen from Table 1 that there are also higher proportions of women in the child-bearing age groups than in the white population, and correspondingly very low proportions who are old and very old.

Women's health

General health

A special review, undertaken to identify the health issues of people from different ethnic groups in the five key areas of the government's Health of the Nation strategy, highlights the particular patterns of mortality and morbidity in women in England and Wales. The information, based on data for 1979–83, suggests that minority ethnic people, including women, have worse experience of coronary heart disease, cancers, mental illness and HIV/AIDS. These areas are addressed in detail in Chapters 17, 18, 19 and 13 respectively.

Pregnancy and childbirth

In view of the relatively high birth rate, maternity services are of great importance for the health of both women and children from particular minority ethnic groups living in this country. Birth outcome is generally less favourable, as summarised in a review of issues for the health of people from minority ethnic groups in the government's strategy for health in England;[9] minority ethnic babies experience higher perinatal mortality than the babies of UK-born mothers (Fig 1). Perinatal mortality, defined as stillbirths and deaths in the first week of life, for Pakistani babies is almost double that for babies of UK-born mothers. Some of the causes underlying these variations are: differences in the uptake and quality of antenatal and obstetric care, maternal health and nutrition, marriage and childbearing patterns, lower birth weights and a higher incidence of congenital abnormalities in some groups (Fig 2). Asian, African and Caribbean women are at higher risk of diabetes and hypertension.[14] Many Asian women have not been

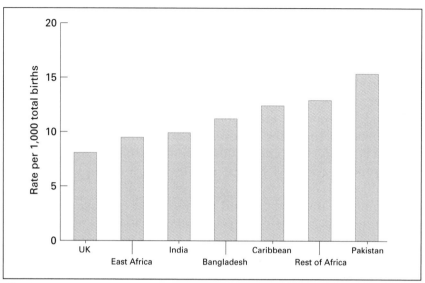

Fig 1. *Perinatal mortality, by mother's country of birth; England & Wales, 1988–90.*[9]

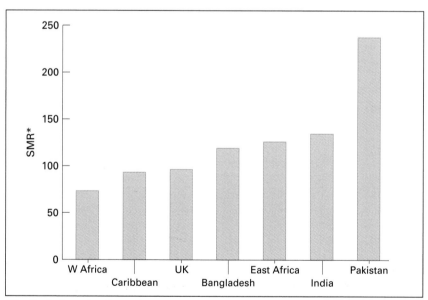

Fig 2. *Infant deaths and stillbirths from congenital abnormalities, by mother's country of birth; England & Wales, 1981–5.*[9]
*All mothers, England and Wales = 100

immunised against rubella, having come to this country as young adults, so they are at greater risk of contracting rubella in pregnancy. The poor health of Pakistani infants is particularly worrying, especially the high rate of congenital abnormalities seen in these babies (Fig 2). Pakistani mothers generally have a low social class distribution and make less use of health services during pregnancy. Consanguinity, high fertility and childbearing late into the reproductive period could also be contributory factors.

There are marked variations between health authorities in perinatal outcome for ethnic minorities (Fig 3). Moreover, differences between the rates for overseas-born and UK-born mothers are much greater in some health authorities than in others. These geographical variations suggest that there are examples of 'good practice', which could be propagated more widely.

All mothers, their infants and families need effective and appropriate antenatal, obstetric and postnatal care. There is now available a comprehensive and up-to-date guide to what is known about effective care in pregnancy and childbirth.[15] However, the professional and lay views of what is needed are likely to be particularly divergent in relation to people from minority ethnic groups. In no field more than in childbirth are religious and cultural considerations so profound.

It is also important to remember that the minority ethnic populations are socially, culturally and economically heterogeneous,

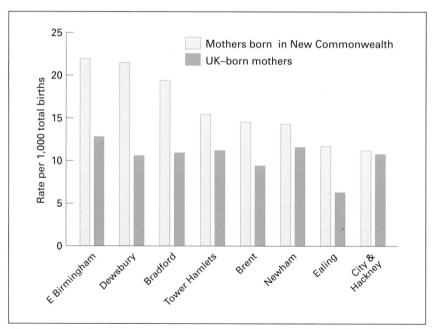

Fig 3. *Perinatal mortality in selected district health authorities; England & Wales, 1982–5.*[9]

with varying health problems and requirements. For instance, although perinatal mortality is high in Caribbean and Pakistani babies alike, the underlying factors appear to be quite different. There are marked differences in perinatal mortality even *within* the Asian community.[16] Access and acceptability are at least as important for women from ethnic minorities as the capability of the health service to provide effective care. Language and cultural barriers often further compound difficulties with access.[17] Difficulties will also arise if women are in temporary accommodation or move frequently and thus do not receive consistent primary care services. Recent immigrants, refugees and 'travellers' may need targeted outreach services.[18] It is of note that in inner city areas, where the majority of minority ethnic families live, primary care services tend to be poorer than in more affluent neighbourhoods.

An expert group[19] reporting in 1993 stressed the importance of informed choice – that pregnant women should understand the issues and choices and decide for themselves such questions as the type of care they would wish, the sort of professional they would wish to carry it out, the place of delivery and the degree of intervention, based on the following principles of good maternity care:[19]

- The woman must be the focus of maternity care. She should be able to feel that she is in control of what is happening to her and able to make decisions about her care, based on her needs, having discussed matters fully with the professionals involved.
- Maternity services must be readily and easily accessible to all. They should be sensitive to the needs of the local population and based primarily in the community.
- Women should be involved in the monitoring and planning of maternity services to ensure that they are responsive to the needs of a changing society. In addition care should be effective and resources used efficiently.

The impact of cultural, religious, racial and socioeconomic background is becoming increasingly well recognised. In the implementation of *Changing childbirth*, the requirement for informed choice means that families who are not fluent in English, or in the established procedures in this country for health education, screening, risk assessment, and care during labour and after the baby's birth, have particular needs for appropriate and detailed information, often with a large counselling component, offered with skilled and ethnic sensitivity.

An information booklet issued by the Catholic bishops of England, Ireland, Scotland and Wales, for example, strongly advises mothers not to accept testing for conditions such as Down's syndrome where, if the foetus is found to be affected, the possibility of terminating the pregnancy is likely to be raised.[20] The issues with regard to counselling and screening services for genetic conditions are described more fully in Chapter 12.

A recent study in the US found that in prenatal care black women were given 20% less counselling to give up smoking and 30% less to give up alcohol. Poorer women were more likely to be given advice about smoking and drugs, with rich women more likely to be given information about alcohol and breast feeding. The study measured what women recalled, which is ultimately what is most likely to be linked to health behaviour changes, not what providers report of their practice.[21] Whilst the antenatal period is a crucially important opportunity for promoting the health of the mother, the baby and the whole family, the education of both boys and girls at a young age is fundamental. There is concern that health education is not adequately provided throughout the education system in this country, and that for children from minority ethnic groups messages related to sex education, nutrition and child rearing often conflict with those from their parents. It is felt that there is a general lack of regard in British schools for the particular needs of pupils from this section of the population. This is further compounded by the fact that their parents are less likely to be actively involved or hold positions of responsibility within the education system, such as acting as parent governors.[22]

Women are usually the main influence on the lifestyle of their young children and of their husbands. Thus, much depends on their effectiveness in gaining access to health education and to primary care for child health surveillance. In addition to language, cultural and socioeconomic factors, which may place barriers against satisfactory access, racism may also be important. Asian mothers living in certain areas find themselves hardly able to leave the house because they are likely to suffer aggression and violence. There are also many instances that demonstrate racism within the health care system.[23] Studies have shown that general practitioners are reluctant to take patients from certain ethnic groups on to their lists. In Leicestershire it was found that a higher proportion of general practitioners with many Asian patients are not on the obstetric list than those with a largely non-Asian practice population. Late enrolment into formal antenatal care was found to be because of doctors' as well as patients' behaviour.[24]

Children's health

All children need services that will enable them to reach their maximum potential within the resources available. Useful general guidelines for the assessment of needs are now available.[25] There may be particular needs for children from certain ethnic groups in the following areas but, once again, guidelines about the requirements of these children for good quality services have been published.[26]

Infant feeding and nutrition

A series of studies of feeding habits and nutrition in the under-5s in the Bangladeshi community in Tower Hamlets was carried out by the children's department at the London Hospital and the community child health services. In 1983 the diets of some Bangladeshi infants and children were found to be deficient in vitamin D and iron.[27] In 1985, comparison of weaning practices with the Tower Hamlets infant feeding policy revealed an urgent need for effective education on all aspects of infant feeding in the Bangladeshi community.[28] In 1989, although Bangladeshi infants were on average lighter than Caucasian infants, no evidence was found that they were undernourished.[29] The first national survey on infant feeding in Asian families has shown that the incidence of breastfeeding among Asians is higher than among white mothers.[30]

As a result of screening in children aged 1–4 years in an inner city practice in Bradford, iron deficiency was found in 25% of children from ethnic minorities – a significantly higher percentage than in their peers.[31] Nearly 70% of eligible children were screened. All parents welcomed this programme and subsequent treatment.

Growth is perhaps the most important single measure of the overall health of children. There has been a national trend towards taller children, but this ceased between 1979 and 1986. Representative national studies have consistently shown that shorter height is found in children from lower social classes,[32] inner cities and ethnic minority groups, with the exception of African-Caribbean boys and girls.[33] Until recently, reference curves for growth standards have been based only on white populations. Revised reference curves for black and ethnic minority children are now being developed.[34]

Immunisation

A number of studies have examined factors influencing the uptake of immunisation among children from ethnic minority and white families. One such study, carried out over four school terms in Bloomsbury during 1990–91, showed that only 56% of all entrants to primary schools in the district health authority were fully immunised (defined as a completed primary course of DPT and polio with a booster, and protection against measles from measles vaccine and/or MMR).[35] Asian children (27% of the sample) were less likely to have been fully immunised than other groups; 50 of the 54 children with no immunisations were of Asian origin. Among African children (12% of the sample), 34% were living in temporary accommodation, as were 22% of Bangladeshi children, compared with 5% of children of UK origin. The most common reason given for inadequate immunisation (in 41 of the 54 without immunisation) was that the child was a recent immigrant. The vast majority of children (93%) were registered with a general practitioner, but 11% (17/153) of children living in temporary accommodation were not registered, compared with 1% of those in permanent accommodation.

English was not the main language spoken at home for 39% (555) of all the primary school entrants in Bloomsbury. The main language for 57% of these families was Bengali, but 43 other languages were mentioned. An interpreter was available for the school health interviews for 205 of the 555 children from families where English was not the main language spoken at home, although the nurses expressed some difficulty with language for a further 79 children. Only 18 (1%) of the children attended the school health interview unaccompanied by a parent or other adult.

A study in Glasgow, however, found that immunisation uptake was slightly higher in children with Asian names, identified from the computerised child health register, than in children with European names matched for sex and postcode sector.[36] This was accounted for by better uptake of pertussis vaccine. Health visitor contacts were also found not to differ between the ethnic groups.

Asian and white parents attending two child health clinics in Nottingham were both found to be deficient in their knowledge about infectious diseases and immunisation, but the former were particularly unaware of diseases that could affect their families both in the UK and on trips to the Indian subcontinent.[37]

Tuberculosis

The high rates of tuberculosis found in children of Asian origin born in Britain are well known. The incidence is lowest in white children (under 15 years of age) at 3.6/100,000 compared with children of Indian origin at 72/100,000, and children of Pakistani and Bangladeshi origin at 95/100,000.[38] Based on notifications of tuberculosis in Bradford in 1980–82, the incidence in Asians was 20 times greater than for white people. Incidence was high in the central wards of the city with high Asian concentration, where nearly half the Asians lived in overcrowded housing (5.1 per household compared with the district norm of 2.2).[39] The residents of these wards were also more likely to be unemployed, without a car, and living in older, unmodernised housing. This study highlights the role of socioeconomic and environmental factors, which were acknowledged to be all-important in the aetiology of tuberculosis when the illness was more common in previous centuries. These factors must remain important in prevention and treatment, although the assumption has been that Asians have a genetic predisposition to tuberculosis or are importing the disease to Britain (see Chapter 13).

The findings from a study in the Leeds metropolitan district were rather different. Between 1982 and 1986, the rates of tuberculosis and anti-tuberculosis chemoprophylaxis in Asian children were similar to those in white children. Very few children from ethnic minorities had active disease.[40]

Dental health

Children in social classes IV and V have the most dental and oral disease, and are least likely to have dental care. Children from some minority ethnic groups have either higher or similar disease rates, but receive less treatment than their peers.[41] For example, a high prevalence of dental caries in deciduous teeth was found in Vietnamese children in comparison with children of other origins living in the same three London boroughs.[42] It was considered that social class fully accounts for the high caries rate in Vietnamese children.[40] The children had a relatively low caries experience in permanent teeth, in common with what is found in studies in other parts of the world (including the USA). A high caries experience was found in children from families who had spent a longer time in this country, which gives cause for concern and indicates a need for preventive programmes for this ethnic group[43] (see Chapter 8).

Accidents

Accident rates have been shown to vary little overall between children from minority ethnic families and white families,[44] but there are ethnic differences in the incidence of certain types of accidental injury such as severe burns and scalds, probably as a result of cultural differences in methods of cooking,[45] exacerbated by poor housing and overcrowding.

Child abuse

There may be difficulties in access to appropriate health care for children from minority ethnic families suffering child abuse. This is because 'as a form of social deviance, child abuse is subject to the definition of various audiences rather than being intrinsic to the act. What is termed abuse varies between cultures and subcultures'.[46] The definition in law is not clear, particularly in defining neglect. Health professionals have considerable discretion in deciding what is or is not a probable case of abuse. Lack of knowledge of minority cultures and traditions, such as differences in upbringing, may present problems. Parental authority is often given greater value in many ethnic minority cultures, and this can lead to errors in professional judgement when abuse is suspected.[47] One study reported minimal differences between nurses working in the USA and in the UK in their attribution of child abuse, although the differences might have become statistically significant with a larger sample size.[46]

Consistent with other reports, it could not be said that minority ethnic groups are more tolerant of abuse or neglect, or whether similarities in attribution of abuse are due to a common culture among health care practitioners or to the larger culture in which health care systems exist.[47] However, in dealing with suspected child abuse, supportive and sensitive attitudes among all professionals are essential to increase understanding of cultural differences in the meaning of behaviours and in approaches to alleviating stress. More experience and training in ways of working with families from different ethnic groups is required for all those working with children. In this field, differences in approach between the health and social services may compound the difficulties, as may the independent difficulties of these families in accessing social services.[48-50]

The issue of female circumcision raises complex practical, moral and ethical issues for professionals. This traditional practice among certain communities is illegal in the UK. It is often felt that lack of action by health service workers to prevent circumcision of young girls is an expression of comfortable racism.[51] Steps taken to stop the practice may be regarded as evidence of lack of cultural sensitivity and unwanted authoritarian interference.[52]

Chronic illnesses and disability

Few studies have examined access to health care for children with chronic illness from ethnic minority families. A paper from Canada relating to immigrant Chinese families argues that social organisation and ideology of health care services generate particular illness experiences.[53] Immigrant families find the ideology of their new environment dissonant with their customs for managing illness, which often leads to non-compliance and ineffective treatment. Health professionals explain non-compliance by the obvious fact of cultural differences, but it can be argued that it should be understood in terms of institutional practices that exclude families from participating in care taking.

The increasing provision of home care services may encourage practitioners to negotiate culturally acceptable care with parents. It has been shown in this country that ethnic minority families are disproportionately less likely than white families to be involved in respite care schemes, probably because of poor communication of information about the services, concerns about how black and ethnic minority children will be looked after, and the unavailability of ethnic minority carers and professionals.[54]

Mental health

In the Netherlands it has been found that delinquency is more common in immigrant teenagers. Although immigrant children attend primary schools, many drop out after the age of 12, possible reasons including language barriers to learning and lack of encouragement from teachers and parents.

Children experience greater cultural pulls than their parents, and their difficulties often show up at school. There is considerable uncertainty as to whether the most helpful approaches are available to children of black and minority ethnic communities who tend to be disproportionately excluded from school, taken into the care of the local authority and placed in residential schools for children with emotional and behavioural difficulties.[55]

Despite the stresses of living in a new environment, there is little hard evidence that immigrants have higher levels of psychiatric morbidity than the indigenous population in most European countries. However, studies are made difficult in that psychiatric disturbances and emotional disorders often present differently in migrants.

Drug and alcohol misuse is increasing in immigrant populations (see Chapter 10). Problems are aggravated by poor access to psychiatric care and because immigrants often prefer to consult other members of their community before seeking professional help. Counselling is also mistrusted.[57]

Conclusion

In the assessment of needs, homogeneity among different ethnic groups should not be assumed. As with the white majority, minority ethnic communities are diverse in terms of religion, culture, language, race and, most important, personal experience. There will also be differing expectations about health and health care services. For example, a small study was commissioned by the Wandsworth Community Health Council on the assumption that closure of the South London Hospital for Women, which is staffed by women, would mean that Asian women in particular would not have access to maternity services from women doctors.[58] The findings showed that white, Asian and African-Caribbean women all preferred hospital to home birth. There was no particular preference for a woman doctor among the white women or among the Asian women, who just wanted a good doctor; although not especially concerned, about half the African-Caribbean women expressed a preference for a woman doctor.

In assessing health care needs, it is important that ways be found and consistently supported to identify the needs of minority ethnic women and to develop the appropriate service responses. Local linkworkers are a key resource. However, there is a need for such services to be well resourced and evaluated, and for better levels of training and support for this group of health workers.[59]

Advances in our understanding of the health care needs of women and of children from minority ethnic groups are hampered by a lack of routinely collected data about their use of services. The introduction of ethnic group monitoring into the National Health Service (NHS) as part of the minimum data set for inpatients in April 1995 will go some way towards improving the information base. The opportunity to monitor the use of maternity services will be important. It is also likely that ethnic group will soon be collected as part of the Confidential Inquiry into Stillbirths and Deaths in Infancy. This will add to the picture in this most important area for ethnic minority health.

The continuing lack of data about the use of primary care and community services is of serious concern in exploring the needs of women and children from different ethnic groups living in Britain. An important code of practice is available for the improvement of services in primary care,[60] and the Children Act 1989 is a force for improvement in all aspects of children's lives. The latter sets out the requirement to take account of the child's religious persuasion, racial origin and cultural and linguistic background.[61] These codes and the findings of special studies highlight the equal importance, with comprehensive and relevant routine data collection, of comprehensive and relevant routine community consultation, for assessing needs.

The difficulty for some services in communicating with groups or individuals for whom English is not their first language is now being imaginatively tackled by computer-generated translations which can be accessed appropriately for different linguistic groups.[62,63] It is important once again to use a number of sources such as the Muslim Women's Helpline and the findings of both qualitative and quantitative research. There is also now a good deal of useful research information, such as that from some Asian women speaking about depression,[64] and that which highlights the fundamental role of environmental, social and cultural conditions in the risk of sudden infant death syndrome.[65]

It is becoming increasingly clear that the assessment of needs for health care across all fields must be recognised as a complex undertaking if the considerable resources of the NHS are to be used effectively and not wasted. We should be encouraged that so much has been learned so fast in the particularly complex field of the health of people from ethnic minorities, but it is essential to pursue actively further knowledge and understanding.[66]

References

1 Balarajan R. *Ethnic diversity in England and Wales.* An analysis by health authorities based on the 1991 census. London: NIESH, 1997.

2 Haskey J. The ethnic minority populations of Great Britain: their size and characteristics. *Population Trends 54.* London: HMSO, 1988.

3 Soni Raleigh V, Balarajan R. Public health and the 1991 census. *British Medical Journal* 1994; **309**: 287–8.

4 Drever F, Whitehead M, eds. *Health inequalities.* Decennial supplement. London: HMSO, 1997.

5 Balarajan R. On the state of health in inner London. *British Medical Journal* 1986; **292**: 911–4.

6 Smyth M, Browne F, eds. *General household survey 1990.* London: HMSO, 1992.

7 Hunter J. Educational priority indices RS 1254/89. ILEA Research and Statistics Branch (1989) and School Rolls from DES Form 7. In: *Education statistics 1988–89.* London: ILEA, 1990.

8 Sinnott J. *ILEA language census RS 1261/89.* Inner London Education Authority Research and Statistics Branch. London: ILEA, 1989.

9 Balarajan R, Soni Raleigh V. *Ethnicity and health: a guide for the NHS.* London: Department of Health, 1993.

10 Bradshaw J. Racial disadvantage. In: *Child poverty and deprivation in the UK.* London: National Children's Bureau, 1990.

11 Association of Metropolitan Authorities. *A strategy for racial equality in homelessness.* Report of Local Authority Housing and Racial Equality Working Party. London: AMA, 1990.

12 Rowe J, Garnett L, Hundleby M. *Child care now: a survey of placement patterns.* London: British agencies for adoption and fostering: 1989.

13 Office of Population Censuses and Surveys. *Population trends 65.* London: HMSO, 1991.

14 Cappuccio FP. Ethnicity and cardiovascular risk: the variations in people of African ancestry and South Asian origin. *Journal of Human Hypertension* 1997; **11**: 571–6.

15 Enkin M, Keirse M, Chalmers I, eds. *A guide to effective care in pregnancy and childbirth.* Oxford: Oxford University Press, 1989.

16 Balarajan R, Soni Raleigh V. Variations in perinatal, neonatal, post-neonatal and infant mortality in England and Wales by mother's country of birth 1982–85. In: Britton M, ed. *Mortality and geography: a review in the mid-1980s, England and Wales.* OPCS series DS No. 9. London: HMSO, 1990: 123–37.

17 Baxter C. *Race equality in health care and education.* London: Bailliere Tindall, 1997.

18 Durward L, ed. *Traveller mothers and babies: who cares for their health?* London: Maternity Alliance, 1990.

19 Expert Maternity Group of the Department of Health. *Changing childbirth.* Part 1. London: HMSO, 1993.

20 Catholic Bishops' Joint Committee on Bio-ethical Issues. *Antenatal tests: what you should know.* London: Catholic Truth Society (publisher to the Holy See), 1989.

21 Kogan MD, Kotelchuck M, Alexander GR, Johnson WE. Racial disparities in reported prenatal care advice from health care providers. *American Journal of Public Health* 1994; **84**: 2–8.

22 Contact a Family. *The educational needs of ethnic minority children who have disabilities and special needs.* Conference report. London: Contact a Family, 1989.

23 Foster MC. Health visitors' perspectives on working in a multi-ethnic society. *Health Visitor* 1988; **61**: 275–8.

24 Clarke M, Clayton DG. Quality of obstetric care provided for Asian immigrants in Leicestershire. *British Medical Journal* 1983; **286**: 621–3.

25 British Association for Community Child Health. *Services for children: a model for purchasers and paediatricians.* Discussion paper. London: British Paediatric Association, 1994.

26 Slater M, ed. *Health for all our children.* London: Action for Sick Children, 1993.

27 Harris RJ, Armstrong D, Ali R, Loynes A. Nutritional survey of Bangladesh children aged under 5 years in the London borough of Tower Hamlets. *Archives of Disease in Childhood* 1983; **58**: 428–32.

28 Jones VM. Current infant weaning practices within the Bangladesh

community within the London borough of Tower Hamlets. *Human Nutrition: Applied Nutrition* 1987; **41A**: 349–52.

29 Davies AG, Wheeler E. Analysis of the weights of infants of Bangladesh origin attending two clinics in Tower Hamlets. *Child Care, Health and Development* 1989; **15**: 167–74.

30 Thomas M, Avery V. *Infant feeding in Asian families.* London: Stationery Office, 1997.

31 James J, Evans J, Male P, Pallister C, *et al.* Iron deficiency in inner city pre-school children: development of a general practice screening programme. *Journal of the Royal College of General Practitioners* 1988; **38**: 250–2.

32 Department of Health. Children's growth and nutrition. In: *On the state of the public health 1988.* London: HMSO, 1989: 74–81.

33 Garrow JS (chairman). Committee on medical aspects of food policy. Third report of the sub-committee on nutritional surveillance: executive summary. *Reports on Health and Social Subjects, No. 33.* London: HMSO, 1988.

34 Chinn S, Price LE, Rona RJ. Need for new reference curves for height. *Archives of Disease in Childhood* 1989; **64**: 1545–53.

35 Bedford HE, Masters JI, Kurtz Z. Immunisation status in inner London primary schools. *Archives of Disease in Childhood* 1992; **67**: 1288–91.

36 Bhopal RS, Samin AK. Immunisation update of Glasgow Asian children: paradoxical benefit of communication barriers? *Community Medicine* 1988; **10**: 215–20.

37 Morgan S, Aslam M, Dove R, *et al.* Knowledge of infectious diseases and immunisation among Asian and white parents. *Health Education Journal* 1987; **46**: 177–8.

38 Medical Research Council. Tuberculosis in children in a national survey of notifications in England and Wales, 1987–9. *Archives of Disease in Childhood* 1992; **57**: 734–41.

39 Froggatt K. Tuberculosis: spatial and demographic incidence in Bradford, 1980–82. *Journal of Epidemiology and Community Health* 1985; **39**: 20–6.

40 Cundall DB, Pearson SB. Inner city tuberculosis and immunisation policy. *Archives of Disease in Childhood* 1988; **63**: 964–85.

41 Williams SA, Gelbier S. Access to dental health? An ethnic minority perspective of the dental services. *Health Education Journal* 1988; **47**: 167–70.

42 Todd R, Gelbier S. Dental caries prevalence in Vietnamese children and teenagers in three London boroughs. *British Dental Journal* 1990; **168**: 24–6.

43 Editorial. Our children's teeth. *British Medical Journal* 1989; **298**: 272.

44 Alwash R, McCarthy M. Accidents in the home among children under 5: ethnic differences or social disadvantage? *British Medical Journal* 1988; **296**: 1450–3.

45 Vipulendran V, Lawrence JC, Sunderland R. Ethnic differences in incidence of severe burns and scalds to children in Birmingham. *British Medical Journal* 1989; **298**: 1493–4.

46 Levinson RM, Graves WL, Holcombe J. Cross-cultural variations in the definition of child abuse: nurses in the United States and the UK. *International Journal of Nursing Studies* 1984; **21**: 35–44.

47 Qureshi B. Multi-cultural aspects of child abuse in Britain. *Journal of the Royal Society of Medicine* 1989; **82**: 65–6.

48 Qureshi B. Paediatric problems in multi-ethnic groups. *Maternal and Child Health* 1987; **12**: 15–20.

49 Stubbs P. Developing anti-racist practice: problems and possibilities. In: Blagg H, Hughes JA, Waltam C, eds. *Child sexual abuse: listening, hearing and validating the experiences of children.* Harlow: Longman, 1989.

50 Channer Y, Parton N. Racism, cultural relativism and child protection. In: Violence against Children study group. *Taking child abuse seriously: contemporary issues in child protection theory and practice.* London: Unwin Hyman, 1990.

51 *Female genital mutilation: proposal for change.* London: Minority Rights Group International, 1992.

52 Ladjali M, Rattray IW, Walden RJW. Female genital mutilation: both the problem and the solutions rest with women. *British Medical Journal* 1993; **307**: 460.

53 Anderson JM. Ethnicity and illness experience: ideological structures and the health care delivery system. *Social Science and Medicine* 1986; **22**: 1277–83.

54 Poonia K, Ward L. Fair share of (the) care? *Community Care* 1990; No. 796: 16–18.

55 Inner London Education Authority Equal Opportunities Sub-Committee (Schools). *Suspensions and expulsions from school 1986/87.* Research and Statistics Branch of the ILEA. Report by Education Officer. London: ILEA, 1988.

56 Wallace SA, Crown JM, Berger M, Cox AD. Child and adolescent mental health. In: Stevens A, Raftery J, eds. *Health care needs assessment.* Second series. Oxford: Radcliffe, 1997.

57 Annis J. Migrants need better mental care. *British Medical Journal* 1992; **304**: 275.

58 MacDonald L, 1996 (unpublished).

59 Hoare T, Thomas C, Biggs A, Booth M, Bradley S, Friedman E. Can the uptake of breast screening by Asian women be increased? A randomised controlled trial of a linkworker intervention. *Journal of Public Health Medicine* 1994; **16**: 179–85.

60 Commission for Racial Equality. *Race relations code of practice in primary health care services for the elimination of racial discrimination and the promotion of equal opportunities.* London: CRE, 1992.

61 Lane J. What role has the law played in getting rid of racism in the lives of children? *Children and Society* 1993; **7**: 164–82.

62 Fuller J, Baylar A, Sanders M, Waithe C. Bilingual Health Advocacy Project..

63 Ethnic Minority Word-Processing and Translation Services for Health Care. Trident Health Ltd, Computer Consultancy, London SE1, 1993.

64 *The sorrow in my heart: sixteen Asian women speak about depression.* London: Commission for Racial Equality, 1993.

65 Davies DP, Gantley M. Ethnicity and the aetiology of sudden infant death syndrome. *Archives of Disease in Childhood* 1994; **70**: 349–53.

66 MacKenzie KJ, Crowcroft NS. Race, ethnicity, culture, and science. *British Medical Journal* 1994; **309**: 286–7.

15 | Learning difficulties

Carol Baxter
Senior Lecturer,
University of Central Lancashire, Preston

People with impaired intellectual capacity are neither physically nor mentally ill. Assessment of the need for care and support of people from this section of the population falls primarily within the remit of the education and social welfare agencies. However, as with the rest of the population, people with learning disabilities also become ill or have longstanding medical conditions and will, from time to time, require the services of health professionals. It is essential therefore that health professionals be drawn into the debate and to increase their awareness and skills when working with this client group.

This chapter explores the factors that contribute to the incidence of learning difficulties in minority ethnic populations.[1] The process of assessing people's intellectual capacity in order to ascertain the degree of disability is examined, followed by an exploration of the processes involved in individual care planning and the issues that need to be taken into account to ensure that the processes are effective in determining the levels of support required.

Incidence and prevalence

There is no national information on the prevalence of learning difficulties among minority ethnic communities, but local studies have provided useful information. The prevalence of learning difficulties among ethnic minority children appears to be higher than among white children. Information from some northern mill towns is particularly revealing. In Rochdale, for example, although only 5.5% of the population are Asian, they make up 40% of all the children attending the development therapy unit and 35% of the children receiving portage.[2] A Manchester study revealed more of each type of severe disability.[3] In Oldham, Asian babies make up

18% of births, yet over a third of the under-5s (double the expected rate) have severe learning difficulties.[4] In Camberwell, children with severe language impairment were significantly over-represented among children born to parents from the New Commonwealth.[5]

Aetiology and contributing factors

There has been a long-running debate about the cause of the apparently higher prevalence of learning difficulties in some minority ethnic communities. Factors that have been suggested as relevant are a higher incidence of congenital rubella syndrome and a higher frequency of first-cousin marriages.

Congenital rubella

The incidence of congenital rubella is two to three times higher in Asian than in non-Asian births in England and Wales.[6] There may be two reasons for this. Rubella immunisation rates may be low among Asian girls at school in the UK, if information about the immunisation and the need to return consent forms is not translated or interpreted. However, immunisation take-up in Bradford among Asian infants was higher than among non-Asians, perhaps because it was given during routine baby clinic visits.[7] Also, the relatively few young Asian women who come to Britain after the age of routine rubella immunisation in schools may be susceptible to infection if they have not been exposed to rubella in their country of origin. A similar situation existed for African-Caribbean women coming to Britain in the 1960s.

Consanguinity

The issue of first-cousin marriages is far more emotive and controversial, and has contributed much to an approach that 'blames the victim'. First-cousin marriages may increase the risk of autosomal recessive conditions, but many of these conditions are so rare that 50% consanguinity would be required before significant numbers would appear in the population. In the few studies that have carefully explored the association between consanguinity and congenital malformation no significantly high correlation has been established.[8-12] It seems clear that congenital rubella syndrome and first-cousin marriages cannot completely explain the higher than expected proportion of ethnic minority infants with learning difficulties.

Poverty

Most congenital abnormalities, including learning impairment, have causes present during the pre-conception period, at conception and during the early weeks of pregnancy. These include poor housing, environmental pollution, inadequate and inappropriate education, and other forms of deprivation that have an indirect effect on the outcome of pregnancy. Ethnic minority communities have lower incomes than the white community;[13] the correlation between poverty and perinatal mortality is well established.[14] In areas with high rates of learning disabilities, there are also high perinatal mortality rates. There is also substantial evidence that perinatal mortality and morbidity rates are higher among babies whose mothers were born in the New Commonwealth and Pakistan.[15]

Antenatal services

Maternity services are known to influence pregnancy outcome. Several studies have identified a problem of racial inequality in access to antenatal services. A study in Leicester showed that only 64% of Asian mothers had over 5 months of antenatal care,[16] and in a Bradford study 60% of Asian mothers, compared with 20% of their non-Asian counterparts, had less than 4 months of antenatal care.[17] Other studies have highlighted the low uptake of maternity services by African-Caribbean women.[18] The main reason for underuse of services is their culturally inappropriate and unwelcoming nature.[19]

Diagnosis of certain abnormalities between weeks 8 and 16 of pregnancy is a routine part of antenatal care. Counselling during this period is of particular importance so that prospective parents have the opportunity to discuss any genetic risks and make informed decisions regarding their pregnancy, but pre-conception and antenatal genetic counselling is almost unheard of among ethnic minority families; where it does occur in minority communities it has been principally for specific blood disorders such as sickle cell anaemia and thalassaemia. The following case illustrates that the skills and expertise necessary for sensitive and effective work with ethnic minority families are gravely lacking in the health services:[20]

Mohinder and Pargan Singh are well into middle age and are not first cousins. Of their five grown up children, three are handicapped. The couple are dedicated Sikhs and devoted parents. I asked them whether, if they had known that they stood a good chance of having more handicapped children after their first, it would have altered the size of the family they chose to have. Astonished, they both asked if one could tell whether a child would be handicapped and said that had they been aware of the risk, they would have sought medical advice.

Assessment procedures

Over the past 20 years there has been a growing body of opinion that inappropriate procedures might be contributing to the disproportionate numbers of ethnic minority children assessed as having moderate learning difficulties and being placed in special schools.[21,22] More recently, similar anxieties have been expressed about the over-representation of ethnic minority children in schools for those with severe learning difficulties. In 1986, parents were worried that their children had been assessed in English, saying that they would have been able to carry out the required tasks if the assessment had been in their own language.[23] There is a major concern that children for whom English is a second language are being disproportionately placed in schools and units for children with severe learning difficulties. A report by Her Majesty's Inspectorate in 1983, on a school in Bradford for pupils with learning difficulties, noted that 23% of these children spoke English as a second language, often with delayed speech and language,[24] whereas an Inner London Education Authority report found that no particular ethnic minority group was over-represented in special schools overall.[25]

Statementing is a statutory requirement for identifying the educational support required by children with special needs, including those with learning difficulties. The important role of parents in this process has been recognised by the 1981 Education Act which provided a framework within which parents would have rights of involvement throughout assessment procedures resulting in the 'statementing' of their children. However, it is still difficult for many parents to understand the complex and highly bureaucratic assessment and review procedures, or to make full use of their rights. For parents from ethnic minority communities, involvement is made even more difficult.

Formal letters proposing assessment or annual reviews may not be translated for, or understood by, parents.[26] The onus is often on the parent who does not speak English to find an interpreter, who will usually be a family member or a friend not necessarily well versed in educational terminology or procedure. This is of increasing concern to families.[27] Parents may believe that 'special' education is of 'better quality' than that in general schools.[28]

If the 1981 Education Act is to be taken seriously, service providers have to enable all parents to participate. The Advisory Centre for Education recommends that authorities should:[29]

- ensure that a 'competent bilingual professional' is involved in the proceedings throughout;
- translate all materials used;
- arrange meetings where parents who have children with learning difficulties can meet and discuss common concerns.

Adopting these recommendations would go some way towards addressing the problems of the educational system to involve ethnic minority parents who have children with learning difficulties.

A number of ideas for improving the current situation emerged at a conference, including the following:

- Parents should be seen as partners in the education of their children.
- Statementing reports should be produced in the parents' first language, in addition to English.
- Professionals are often not aware of, or sensitive to, the needs of bilingual pupils; more bilingual staff are needed within schools.
- People with disabilities need to be consulted on educational issues.
- Tests and assessment procedures are not free of cultural bias; it is important for this to be kept in mind and to be eliminated as far as possible when reviews are taking place.
- Tapes should be produced in different languages to explain the statementing procedure to parents.[30]

In the field of assessment generally, there have been moves towards more holistic procedures. Approaches such as 'getting to know you' and 'shared action planning' look at all aspects of an individual's life. The aim is to shift power from professionals to the individuals themselves by involving them in their own assessment. These changes are welcome, especially if they take into consideration the particular needs of ethnic minority people with learning difficulties, whose position is doubly disadvantaged.

Efforts must be made to ensure that:

- 'a child is not taken to have a learning difficulty because the language or form of language of his home is different from the language of instruction in his school' (para 70 DES circular 1/83 Assessment and Statements of Special Education Needs);
- interpreters are used where people's mother tongue is not English;
- all procedures are looked at critically for cultural bias and stereotypes;
- the part that racism plays in ethnic minority people's lives, and how it can affect performance, is recognised and considered during assessment;
- bilingual children and adults, or those who do not speak English, have the opportunity to express themselves in their first language;
- new, more appropriate and flexible assessment approaches are developed, including better ways of involving parents.

Individual care planning

People with learning difficulties usually have to rely on others to plan their lives. Individual care planning has its origins in the movement to recognise that each person is unique and should receive assistance according to his or her individual needs, regardless of severity of handicap. Individual care planning provides a systematic approach to support and care for people with learning difficulties, designed to enable them to achieve short- and long-term goals in their lives appropriate to their wishes, needs and circumstances.

In discussions with people with learning difficulties and their families, and with service providers, a number of issues that need to be addressed before individual care plans can be assumed to be appropriate to the needs of a multiracial and multicultural society have been identified.

Working with families

Individual care plans often focus heavily on the individual, taking far less account of his or her place in the dynamics of the family. In many ethnic minority communities, the collective spirit of families and communities is more highly valued than the personal autonomy and individualism encouraged in white British society. For ethnic minority adults with learning difficulties, this difference in emphasis may be very important; although services may recognise that adults with learning difficulties still need the support of their families, the model of 'normal' family patterns and dynamics held by service providers is likely to be more appropriate to white families.

The idea of 'training for independence' is one example of how ethnic minority families may be alienated by services. The goals of training for independence identified within individual care planning (eg learning skills so that the individual may ultimately be able to live alone) can conflict with the tradition of extended family living which some ethnic minority families may prefer. White service providers are rarely skilled at (or confident about) working with families from ethnic minority communities whose norms, circumstances and experiences may differ significantly from their own.

Who sets the agenda?

Individual care plans are usually initiated by service providers to deal with issues or situations that they view as important or in need of discussion. The priorities and concerns of families and individuals are likely to be submerged in this service-led approach.

Power relationships

A fundamental premise of individual care plans is that service users, their families and service providers should be involved on an equal basis, but such an equal partnership is unlikely to be achieved given the unequal status of consumers and professionals, exacerbated by the status differentials between black and white people and the language and cultural differences. These factors are seldom taken into account by existing services. Unless conscious and practical efforts are made to redress the inequalities, the involvement of black families and individuals in the system of individual care plans is in danger of being one of submissive acceptance and gratitude.

Communication difficulties

Communication difficulties can greatly reduce the benefits of individual care plans for people with learning difficulties from ethnic minority communities. Key participants do not always appreciate the background and experiences of service users and their relatives, or speak the same language. Interpreters are rarely made available (working through interpreters in situations involving detailed negotiations may be unsatisfactory anyway).

Conflicting views

Service providers and service users may hold different ideas about appropriate directions for the future care of their family members. Conventions may differ as to what is appropriate for discusion within and outside the family. The idea of talking about personal family matters and feelings and discussing their relatives with 'strangers' may be unusual, if not unacceptable, for some people. There may also be differences in what can be discussed between men and women. For example, a man may feel it inappropriate or religiously improper for him to discuss the personal and intimate physical care of his adolescent daughter. He may feel embarrassed when relating to female service providers. The situation can be aggravated by choice of venues or times for meetings.

Ethnic minority families, especially women and mothers with young children, may feel intimidated and isolated at the prospect of a meeting with a large number of white professionals in an environment in which they do not feel at ease, so they may not voice their concerns. Many ethnic minority people are used to, more comfortable with, and function more effectively on a one-to-one basis in such matters. Indeed, most parents of any ethnic group would prefer such an approach. In these circumstances, there is a real risk that ethnic minority service users and their families may become merely passive recipients of plans and services alien to their wishes and needs.

Cultural stereotyping

There has been recent interest in cultural information about ethnic minority people to inform the process of individual care plans. This has not always worked to the advantage of black and ethnic minority people with learning difficulties for several reasons. Much of the existing literature has tended to promote the misconception of minority traditions and lifestyles as different, 'backward' and 'bizarre'. Service providers often resort to cultural stereotypes and generalisations. For example, sweeping statements about what Sikhs, Hindus or Muslims think invariably ignore other factors such as social class, age and gender. This will be detrimental to the provision of good services for the individual service user.

Preoccupations with culture often result in service providers attributing every problem to, and basing all decisions on, cultural differences. This 'blaming the victim' approach diverts attention from underlying similarities in the needs of individual service users and their families for information, advice, support, and sensitive and appropriate services.

Role of black keyworkers

Black and ethnic minority service providers often find themselves in circumstances where they assume the role of key person for people of their own ethnic group with learning difficulties. They are expected to act as a voice outside the system whilst being part of that system – a position that may result in conflict with their managers. Not all black workers will be able to meet this challenge. It has to be recognised that this situation demands skills that are not always easily acquired.

Holistic approaches to assessment

New, more holistic approaches to assessing people with learning difficulties are to be welcomed. Approaches such as 'getting to know you'[31] and 'shared action planning'[32] aim to look at all aspects of an individual's life, placing the individual very much at the centre of the stage and trying to find out what his or her life has been like in the past, is at the present and could be in the future. A specific aim is to shift power from professionals to the individuals themselves by involving them in their own assessment. The focus is on building up a whole picture of the person. The dynamic nature of people's lives has to be acknowledged; emphasis has to be placed on their speaking up for themselves wherever possible, facilitating satisfying lifestyles and relationships.[33]

The inadequacies of assessment procedures become even more apparent when applied to ethnic minority children with learning difficulties. Such tests are based on the assumption that individuals will identify with images based on white middle-class lifestyles and experiences. Racial stereotyping, inappropriate cultural approaches, and language or communication difficulties further decrease the value of traditional assessments for ethnic minority children.

Assessment procedures are based on white British norms, which may bear little relationship to the everyday life of the ethnic minority person and his or her family. Unfamiliarity with test-taking procedures may result in the child being poorly motivated to carry out the test. Unfamiliar testing equipment or instruments may also produce inaccurate results, such as the use of stories that depict white suburban lifestyles and the use of farm animals to test recognition when children are used only to an urban lifestyle.

References

1 Baxter C, Poonia K, Ward L, Nadirshaw Z. *Double discrimination: services for people with learning difficulties from black and ethnic minority communities*. Based on research from the Norah Fry Research Centre at the University of Bristol, funded by the King's Fund Centre and the Commission for Racial Equality, from July 1988 to November 1989. London: Hodder and Stoughton, 1990.

2 Whitfield S. Principal Educational Psychologist, Rochdale Portage Service. Personal communication, December 1988.

3 Akinsola HA, Fryer T. A comparison of patterns of disability in severely mentally handicapped children of different ethnic origins. *Psychological Medicine* 1986; **16:** 127–33.

4 British Association of Social Workers. Special Interest Group on Services for People with Mental Handicap. Newsletter No 7, January, 1987.

5 Wing L. Prevalence of different patterns of impairments in immigrants. In: Wing JK, ed. *Recent research in social psychiatry*. London: MRC Social Psychiatry Unit, Institute of Psychiatry. Unpublished report, 1969.

6 Miller E, Nicoll A, Rousseau S, *et al*. Congenital rubella in babies of South Asian women in England and Wales: an excess and its causes. *British Medical Journal* 1987; **294:** 737–9.

7 Baker MR, Banderanayake R, Schweiger MS. Difference in rate of uptake of immunisation among ethnic groups. *British Medical Journal* 1984; **288:** 1075–8.

8 Rao PSS, Inbaraj SG. Inbreeding effects on foetal growth and development. *Journal of Medical Genetics* 1980; **17:** 27–31.

9 Terry PB, Bissenden JG, Condie RG, Mathew PM. Ethnic differences in congenital malformations. *Archives of Disease in Childhood* 1985; **60:** 866–8.

10 Rosenthal M, Addison GM, Price DA. Congenital hypothyroidism: increased incidence in Asian families. *Archives of Disease in Childhood* 1988; **63:** 790–3.

11 Kumar D. Associate Specialist, Centre for Human Genetics, Sheffield Health Authority. Personal communication, 1990.

12 Pearson M. Ethnic differences in infant health. *Archives of Disease in Childhood* 1991; **66:** 88–90.

13 Brown C. *Black and white Britain: the third PSI survey*. London: Gower, 1984.

14 Townsend P, Phillimore P, Beattie A. *Health and deprivation: inequality in the north*. Beckenham: Croom Helm, 1988.

15 Balarajan R, Botting B. Perinatal mortality in England and Wales: variations by mother's country of birth. *Health Trends* 1989; **21:** 79–84.

16   Clarke M, Clayton DG. Quality of obstetric care provided for Asian immigrants in Leicestershire. *British Medical Journal* 1983; **286:** 621–3.
17   Lumb KM, Congden PJ, Lealman GT. A comparative review of Asian and British born maternity patients in Bradford 1974–1978. *Journal of Epidemiology and Community Health* 1981; **35**: 106–9.
18   Larbie J. *Black women and maternity services: a survey of 30 young Afro-Caribbean women's experiences and perceptions of pregnancy and childbirth.* London: Training in Health and Race, 1984.
19   Pearson M, ed. *Racial equality and good practice: maternity care.* Cambridge: Health Education/National Extension College, 1985.
20   Boram B. Asian handicaps. *New Society* 1987; 10 March: 22–3.
21   Coard B. *How the West Indian child is made educationally subnormal in the British school system.* London: New Beacon Books, 1971.
22   Tomlinson S. *Education subnormality: a study of decision making.* London: Routledge and Kegan Paul, 1982.
23   Chaudhury A. *ACE special education advice service for the Bangladeshi community.* London: Advisory Centre for Education, 1986.
24   Tomlinson S. Asian pupils and special issues. *British Journal of Special Education* 1989; **16**: 119–22.
25   Inner London Education Authority (ILEA) Research and Statistics. *Characteristics of pupils in special schools.* London: ILEA, 1984.
26   Rehal A. Involving Asian parents in the statementing procedure: the way forward. *Educational Psychology in Practice.* 1989; 189–92.
27   Contact a Family. *Reaching black families? A study of Contact a Family in Lewisham and the relevance of services for black families who have children with learning disabilities and special needs.* London: Contact a Family, 1989.
28   Chaudhury A. How special is special? *Issue* Spring, 1988.
29   Advisory Centre for Education. *Asian children with special needs.* London: Advisory Centre for Education, 1989.
30   Abrol S. Curriculum and culture. *Special Children.* 1990; February: 8–10.
31   Brost M, Johnson T. *Getting to know you: one approach to service assessment and planning for individuals with disabilities.* Wisconsin: Wisconsin Coalition for Advocacy, 1990.
32   Brechin A, Swain J. *Changing relationships: shared action planning with people with a mental handicap.* London: Harper and Row, 1987.
33   Brechin A, Swain J. A share of the action for consumers. *Community Living* 1988; March/April: 20–1.

16 | The elderly

Samad Samadian
Consultant Physician & Honorary Senior Lecturer
(Care of the Elderly), St Helier Hospital, Carshalton/
St George's Hospital Medical School

The circumstances of older people in Britain have been the focus of considerable research, but in much of it older people have been treated as a homogeneous group defined only by age. This approach is not helpful with older people from minority ethnic groups, most of whom are in Britain as a result of immigration or are the children of migrants. Some may have spent their entire working lives in Britain and have now reached retirement; others may have come to be near children. The levels of cultural and social integration may vary between different groups, and indeed between individuals. This chapter focuses on the health and social care needs of minority ethnic elders.

The ageing process

The definition of 'ageing' has long been debatable. Some suggest that ageing is a continuous process starting at conception; others contend that it is a discrete phenomenon only apparent in advanced age and should be treated separately from the developmental phase.[1] Although the writings of Hippocrates included much about old age, little is included in modern textbooks, where basic parameters of normality have usually been obtained from white middle-class (usually male) medical students with little or no attention given to changes that occur with age. Whatever the definition, ageing is characterised by loss of adaptability of an individual organism over time; homoeostatic mechanisms usually become less sensitive, less accurate, slower and less well sustained. Ultimately the individual is unable to adapt to some challenge from the external or internal environment. Organ systems age differently and there is also considerable variation in the rate of decline within each individual. There are two important consequences of this process: lack of uniformity in the biological age of different organs and increasing divergence between one individual and another.[1] A debate also exists about the 'age of ageing' or at what average age the individual passes the invisible frontier of failure to cope with the expected workload or responsibility of the indigenous culture. The question also arises as to whether there can be such a standard age.

One observer in the United States considered 35 years to be the crucial age for the onset of deterioration in adaptability and unproductiveness. Another study suggests 30 years as a lower limit for ageing in this respect,[2] which is very different from the legal established retirement age in, say, Britain where eligibility for the state pension starts at 65 (until recently 60 for women). Old age, as far as it equates with retirement, is a modern phenomenon. It is only in the 20th century that the majority of each age cohort expects to reach the point where they become pensioners. Even the definition of 'pensioner' is a relatively modern one, given that it rests on the notion of a universal old-age pension.

A Nigerian study found that some people equated 'old' in women with the menopause, yet in the same area men were not regarded as old until they reached 80 years old.[3] A last point on ageing is that a number of students of the subject have detected, cross nationally, a similarity in the process and effects of ageing in diverse cultures, even though there are varying cultural patterns of chronological onset and deterioration.

Demography

The numbers of minority ethnic elderly people living in Britain have increased steadily over the past three decades. The 1971 census indicated that there were 26,400 people of pensionable age born in the New Commonwealth and Pakistan living in Britain. The 1981 census gave an estimated figure of 87,117 – just under 1% of the total elderly population. The 1991 census indicated that 3% of the people who classified themselves as being from a minority ethnic group were over the age of 65; the figure for the white majority population was 17%. The age structure of the ethnic minority population is such that a substantial increase in the proportion of elders is expected over the next 20–30 years.[4]

Patterns of disease and medicine of old age

The aged are survivors. The melancholy stereotype is not true of all old people, but it needs only to be the fate of 10%, as indeed it is, for an enormous demand to be unleashed for medical and social services. There is little information on minority ethnic elders' perception of symptoms and presentation of disease. However, the fact that ageing is universal would mean that certain aspects of disease, hence presentation in old age, will be 'culture free'.

The first aspect that will be discussed is 'multiple pathology' of very late life. This consists of four major disabilities: immobility, disability, incontinence and intellectual impairment. These four 'giants of geriatrics' have four common properties: they have multiple causes, destroy independence, cannot be treated and need human helpers. These giants are not, however, exclusive to all old people.

The second problem of old age is non-specific or insidious presentation, rapid deterioration if untreated, and high incidence of secondary complications of disease and treatment.

The third and most important aspect is a greater inter-relationship of problems in old people than in the younger population. Physical, social, emotional and environmental events are experienced in close association, so disturbance in any one dimension is likely to be reflected in one or more of the other dimensions.

For minority ethnic people there are obviously other problems, namely communication, cultural attitudes to medicine, concepts of rehabilitation, diet and community care. However, it would be naive to think of the problems of ethnic minorities as being mainly lack of knowledge of the English language, different customs and beliefs, or some 'exotic illness'. The problem resides with jeopardies. The double jeopardy hypothesis[5] predicts an adverse interaction between becoming older (the first jeopardy) and belonging to an ethnic minority with cultural and racial discrimination (the second jeopardy). In addition, there is a further effect of economic and social disadvantage which compounds the consequences of first and second jeopardy, ending in triple jeopardy.[6,7]

Although British studies have not set out the test for double jeopardy in the way outlined by American writers,[5] it is too early to make conclusive statements about this hypothesis in relation to the Asian and African-Caribbean elderly in Britain. However, there is indirect evidence that older people from ethnic minority communities in Britain suffer an additional burden of inequality in relation to health.[7] Younger Asians and Caribbeans are already suffering as much illness and require as much medical treatment as significantly older white people[8] (see Chapter 19), so there is evidence of premature ageing among this section of the British population.

Morbidity and mortality

Disablement is common among the elderly. About two-thirds of all disabled people are over the age of 65.[9] Not only does the prevalence of handicap increase markedly with advancing age but so too does the proportion of individuals in each group who are severely handicapped.[10] There has been little systematic study of disability in ethnic minorities. However, it should not be so different from that in the indigenous population, except that Asians and African-Caribbeans need as much medical treatment as older groups of whites.

Elderly Asians, like their indigenous counterparts, become frailer as they become older, with the level of incapacity rising sharply over the 75-year age group.[11] In a comparative study in Leicestershire, the Asian elderly were similar to their indigenous counterparts in capacity to perform basic activities of daily living unaided.[12]

In cardiovascular disease the mortality of immigrants reflects the pattern in the country from which they come. Immigrants from France, Spain and Italy (lower rate countries) have a low standardised mortality ratio from ischaemic heart disease.[13] Those born in East Africa and the Indian subcontinent have higher mortality from coronary heart disease than the white population.[14] Myocardial infarction is roughly twice as common in Asian patients presenting to hospital and only half as common in African-Caribbean patients, compared with national rates[15] (see Chapter 17). The extent of myocardial damage tends to be greater in Asians. Coronary trauma seems to occur prematurely and its progress is faster.[16] The usual risk factors are generally not higher in south Asians than in the general population. The incidence of stroke is also higher than that for the indigenous population.

In the native British population the prevalence of non-insulin dependent diabetes in those aged over 40 is about 5%.[17] Prevalence in south Asians is 4–5 times higher, reaching 30% by the age of 65.[18] Osteomalacia is considerably more common in Asian patients, probably owing to the composite effects of lack of sunlight, consumption of chappatis, a diet low in vitamin D, and genetic differences.[19] Although the reasons are not clear, it is believed that chappati flour is high in phytic acid, which is known to obstruct the absorption of vitamin D. Tuberculosis incidence is much higher in south Asians than in any other group in the United Kingdom. In adults, the notification rate is 40 times higher in south Asians than in the native population[20] (see Chapter 13).

Old age is a time of mental as well as physical vulnerability. For some senior citizens, age brings a loss of faculties, senility, and dementia – an organic illness that causes progressive mental impairment through failure of blood supply to the brain cells, or through a complex syndrome of disease processes relating to the chemistry of the brain. The earliest and most significant symptom of dementia is severe loss of short-term memory, with consequent inappropriate behaviour, disorientation and loss of ability to care for oneself. It is arguable that their experiences of racism and discrimination, resulting in depression and anxiety, make minority ethnic elderly particularly vulnerable.

The incidence of dementia is likely to increase as the size of the minority ethnic population grows. In deciding whether or not an elderly person is suffering from dementia, interviewers must develop questions and methods that test memory and intellect without being ethnocentric and irrelevant to a person who does not share the same experience or background as the interviewer. Questions that are culturally biased about current affairs and important events and people can put ethnic minority elders at a disadvantage.

Psychogeriatric service provision for the indigenous elderly is uneven in quality and in the allocation of resources. Provision for minority ethnic senior citizens is often worse, partly because there may be reluctance to refer people who need help, sometimes because of inadequate training. This means that doctors are unable to respond to different modes of presentation.[21] There are no simple or easy solutions, but health care practitioners must be better informed and know where to seek help and advice.

Socioeconomic status

It is generally accepted that poverty is a fact of life for many elderly people. Because they are over-represented in unskilled and semi-skilled occupations, minority ethnic elders are less likely to generate higher pensions. They are more vulnerable to unemployment and redundancy and, having held low income jobs for much of their working lives, many have not been able to save towards their retirement, so many live on minimum state pensions. More recently arrived migrants, for example Ugandan Asians, the Vietnamese and Bangladeshis, are unlikely to have paid enough National Insurance contributions to qualify for a full state pension, but are eligible for other state benefits. In a study of African-Caribbean

and Asian old people, less than half of the Asian elderly interviewed received any pension, but 78% of the African-Caribbean
elderly did.[22] Those who live with their families may be particularly
badly off, being ineligible for certain benefits. Where elderly parents have recently joined their children they are also unlikely to
receive any pension, and are therefore totally dependent on their
families. Bureaucratic procedures and immigration controls which
require proof of a claimant's age or right of abode also serve to
restrict access to benefits to which people may be entitled.

Minority ethnic senior citizens are often unaware of available services or their entitlements. Even if they know about financial entitlements, they are often unaware of other related benefits. Language is a major concern for non-English speaking elders, since
access to information and benefits depends on a person's ability to
read and speak English and to deal with complicated regulations
and their explanations. In a recent study it was found that 88% of
the Asian elderly interviewed did not speak English.[22] As in other
areas of service provision, statutory bodies such as the Department
of Social Security have been slow to provide information in
appropriate languages, simplify the English used, or provide
interpreters.

Social networks

There is no such thing as independence; everyone is dependent
on others. Rather, there is relative acceptance and tolerance.
There are some general patterns to the social network around
each individual, but each network is different and to understand
disease in old age it is essential that the social network be studied
and understood. This network is mainly based upon the immediate
family, neighbours, health and social care workers in the voluntary
and statutory sectors. Each social network is unique to the individual. Requests come through others for help when the
tolerance level of the network changes and acceptance changes to
rejection. The level at which rejection appears is dependent upon
the inherent strengths and weaknesses of individuals in the
network. Some refer too early, some too late and some not at all.

The breakdown in the care system has nowhere been more
cruel and tragic than in the collapse of the traditional extended
family system in which the elderly remain always part of the stable
community unit ordered by kinship. Evidence as to the breakdown
of the traditional system comes from many places. A prevalent host
community myth, for example, concerns the supportive role of the

extended family: 'they look after their own'. This is a powerful means of ignoring the needs of single people and couples.

A survey in Birmingham demonstrated that almost a third of African-Caribbeans and 1 in 20 Asian elders lived alone, with a quarter living as couples.[23] The myth of extended family care is one reason why domiciliary services and community nursing services are so seldom provided for Asian elders. Further myths are to do with the services used. If ethnic minorities do not use a service it is often assumed that they do not need it. The rationale is that the services are open to all, irrespective of race and culture, and that people will inevitably use them if they are required. The reality, however, is that services were often not used because they were seen as inaccessible and inappropriate, and living with families does not necessarily mean that the service support was not needed.[24]

Residential services

It is apparent from the limited available research that day centres or residential homes primarily designed for elderly people from the white majority population are inappropriate for many minority ethnic elders. Indeed, rather than providing a 'haven' for some minority ethnic people, placement in these residential homes has only served to increase their sense of loneliness and isolation. The racist views held by some white residents do not disappear simply by virtue of the fact that they are senior citizens. Lack of understanding by staff often means that when a minority ethnic elder arrives support will not be readily given and the need for it is not appreciated.[21]

Black and Asian minority elders are more often following other communities, eg the Jewish and Polish communities, by expressing a preference for sheltered housing schemes that reflect the customs, language, food, lifestyle and beliefs of their communities. Unfortunately the understanding and recognition of their right to be provided for as they wish is not always forthcoming from the planners, policy makers and service providers. Yet there is little doubt that where such schemes exist the elders benefit from sharing cultural, linguistic and social experiences.[23] Such schemes can also be cost effective – by reducing the pressure on health and social services – but there is a gap between what policy makers consider to be adequate provision and what minority ethnic elders need and want. This gap is unlikely to close so long as there is no effective consultation between the policy makers and the communities.

Conclusion

The needs of the elderly are the responsibility of both health and social services, and greater cooperation and coordination between the two services is essential. The framework under which health and social care is provided in Britain has changed dramatically in the 1990s. The introduction of the internal market into the National Health Service, and the corresponding changes made to the delivery of social services by community care legislation, produced an environment that is supposed to be more responsive to the needs of patients and clients.

There is one negative aspect of the reforms that is likely to affect older people from minority ethnic communities in much the same way as they affect the elderly population as a whole. Together with the stress on competition and quasi-markets, there is an emphasis on self-reliance in matters of health and welfare. The multiple pathology of old age, and the difficulty in distinguishing between health and social needs, could mean increased difficulties for all older people, as people live longer and demand more services and for much longer periods. This means that more functions of the welfare state come under the 'means tested' eligibility criteria of social services and income support. Not only are these services stigmatised but, given the relative lack of wealth, minority ethnic elders may be further disadvantaged. If to all of this are added the impact of migration and the ensuing language and cultural barriers, then the impact of social policies can be very negative.

However, creating a distinction between commissioners and providers is designed so that needs can be clearly recognised and solutions easily organised. In theory this should benefit older people from ethnic minorities, given that their specific social and cultural needs can be articulated and met. The emphasis on the establishment of a mixed economy of welfare could lead to services being provided by the minority groups themselves as commissioners using their new-found freedom to finance those who best meet needs. This is obviously more likely to occur in the area of social services than in health care, but it points to a potentially positive outcome of the reforms. This, however, begs the question of whether such services should be separate from the mainstream services or be integrated with them. Although evidence of the former is slowly emerging, more research is required. It would seem that, to facilitate individual choice, a range of alternatives would be the ideal. The 'integrated care' approach proposed in the White Paper *The new NHS* is based on partnership between health and social services as well as other local agencies.[25] Such an approach will, it is hoped, examine all possible alternatives to provide quality and effective care based on population and patient needs.

References

1   Hall DA. *The biomedical basis of gerontology.* London: Wright, 1984.
2   Tout K. *Ageing in developing countries.* Oxford: Oxford University Press, 1989.
3   Ekpen Y. *Report on study of elderly Nigerians.* Birmingham: Centre of West African Study, University of Birmingham, 1986.
4   Office of Population Censuses and Surveys. *1991 Census.* Monitor. London: OPCS, 1992.
5   Norman A. *Triple jeopardy: growing old in a second homeland.* London: Centre for Policy on Ageing, 1985.
6   Dowd JJ, Bengston VL. Ageing in the minority population: an examination of the double jeopardy hypothesis. *Journal of Gerontology* 1978; **33**: 427–36.
7   Ebrahim S. Ethnic elders. *British Medical Journal* 1996; **313**: 610–3.
8   Nazroo J. *Ethnicity and mental health.* London: Policy Studies Institute, 1997.
9   Harris AL. *Handicapped and impaired in Great Britain.* London: HMSO, 1971.
10 Andrews K. *Rehabilitation of older adults.* London: Edward Arnold, 1987.
11 Donaldson LJ. Health and social status of elderly Asians: a community survey. *British Medical Journal* 1986; **293**: 1079–82.
12 Clarke M, Clarke S, Odell A, Jagger C. The elderly at home: health and social status. *Health Trends* 1984; **16**: 3–7.
13 Marmot MG, Adelstein AM, Bulusu L. *Mortality in England and Wales.* OPCS Studies of Medical and Population Subjects No. 47. London: HMSO, 1984.
14 Harding S, Maxwell R. Differences in mortality of migrants. In: Drever F, Whitehead M, eds. *Health inequalities.* Decennial supplement. London: HMSO, 1997 .
15 Hughes LO, Cruickshank JK. Ischaemic heart disease in people of subcontinent origin. In: Cruickshank JK, Beevers DG, eds. *Ethnic factors in health and disease..* London: John Wright, 1989: 257–62 .
16 Hughes LO, Raval V, Raftery EB. Coronary disease in Asians: an ethnic problem. *British Medical Journal* 1989; **298**: 134–50.
17 Forrest RD, Jackson CA, Mudkin JS. Glucose intolerance and hypertension in North London: the Islington diabetes survey. *Diabetic Medicine* 1986; **3**: 338–42.
18 McKergue PM, Marmot MG. Mortality from coronary heart disease in Asian communities in London. *British Medical Journal* 1988; **297**: 903.
19 Metabolic bone disease in Asians. *British Medical Journal* 1976; **2**: 442–3 (editorial).
20 MRC Tuberculosis and Chest Disease Unit. National survey of

tuberculosis notification in England and Wales 1978–1979. *British Medical Journal* 1980; **281**: 895–8.

21 Larbie J, Mares P, Baxter C. *Training handbook for multiracial healthcare.* Cambridge National Extension College, 1987.

22 Barker J. *Black and Asian old people in Britain.* England: Age Concern, 1984 .

23 Bhalla A, Blackmore K. Elders of the ethnic minority groups. AFFOR. A survey of 400 elderly Asians, Afro-Caribbeans and white people in Birmingham, 1981.

24 Lindesay J, Jagger C, Hibbet M, *et al.* Knowledge, uptake and availability of health and social services among Asian Gujarati and White elderly persons. *Ethnicity and Health* 1997;**2**:59–69.

25 Secretary of State for Health. *The new NHS: modern and dependable.* London: Stationery Office, 1997.

17 | Heart health

Elizabeth E M Kernohan
Director, Clinical Epidemiology Research Unit,
University of Bradford
and Deputy Director of Public Health, Bradford Health Authority

The terms ischaemic heart disease (IHD) and coronary heart disease (CHD) are used interchangeably. They essentially refer to a disease acquired by people during their lifetime caused by a number of factors of which smoking, unhealthy diet, diabetes, lack of exercise and raised blood pressure are the most important (see later). The disease leads to thickening of the coronary arteries and deposition of cholesterol in plaques in the arterial lining. The narrowing reduces the blood flow to the cardiac muscle, preventing the normal response to increased demand on the muscle during exercise or stress. The shortage of oxygen experienced by the heart muscle can give rise to a classic form of heart pain known as 'angina' or to gradual death of heart muscle leading to heart failure. The sudden disintegration or rupture of a cholesterol plaque causes a very sudden reduction in the flow of blood, leading to death of some or most of the heart muscle – an acute myocardial infarction or heart attack – which in severe cases is fatal. Medical intervention can improve the symptoms and even dilate or replace the coronary arteries to improve the blood flow. However, such procedures will only provide relatively short-term relief if the disease itself, the build up or atheroma, is allowed to progress.

Inherited characteristics, and possibly poor development or nutrition around the time of a person's birth, may increase the susceptibility to CHD in later life. However, there is growing evidence that not only can a healthy lifestyle prevent the onset of CHD, even when the disease is already established, but alterations in lifestyle can prevent the disease progressing or even reverse it. It is for this reason that both CHD and its manifestations are suitable for a preventive approach (see Chapter 6).

There are striking differences in the patterns of deaths from CHD in the African-Caribbean, south Asian and white populations

in the UK (and, worryingly, evidence of increasing health inequalities).[1-4] The standardised mortality ratio* (SMR) for the
African-Caribbean population started from a low base 20–25 years
ago and continues to fall. For the south Asian population the SMR
started at a high level in the early 1970s, about 30% above the
national levels, and has continued to rise. In the white population
the epidemic is now waning, some 10 years after the decline in
other high-rate countries.

This chapter is based on a CD-ROM search of over 7,000 references on heart disease, which narrowed to around 30 with specific
reference to minority ethnic groups. To balance this international
and largely USA-based perspective, I will also cover the methods,
findings and implications of work I have been directly involved
with in Bradford over the past 10 years.

What is meant by heart health?

The general term 'heart health' is used here in an attempt to
reflect the importance of issues outside the National Health
Service in the prevention of this disease. Also it is important to
focus on the long lead-in time (usually estimated at 15–20 years)
for this type of condition, during which the individual is healthy,
albeit perhaps at increased risk. In terms of prevention it is
frustratingly late once the person has developed symptoms and the
opportunity costs are relatively higher.

As the whole area of prevention around CHD is multifaceted,
three categories of prevention will be used throughout this
chapter, in their traditional public health meaning:[5] primary,
secondary and tertiary prevention.

Primary prevention is a population-based approach, best thought of
in terms of keeping people, and particularly the young, heart
healthy. This includes social and fiscal policies (provision of leisure
facilities and price of tobacco as examples, respectively), and
lifestyle education through curriculum development in schools.

Secondary prevention is an approach for those who are at most risk
of developing the disease or in the early asymptomatic period. This

---

*The standardised mortality ratio (SMR) adjusts for the age structure of the pop-
ulation. The expected value is 100. If the SMR is higher than this, there is a higher than expected number of deaths. So, if SMR = 120, there is a 20% higher than
expected number of deaths. Similarly, if the SMR is lower than 100, the health
experience is better.

subpopulation will be in their mid-30s and older. Secondary prevention involves screening for risk factors, and giving appropriate advice, counselling and treatment to minimise the risk of developing the disease or its progression.

Tertiary prevention is for people with established disease, having classic angina (pectoris) or a history of myocardial infarction. It should include effective intervention at the personal level such as stopping smoking and/or weight loss to minimise the sequelae of the disease, and optimum management by general practitioners and hospital consultants, including effective drugs such as aspirin, statins and angiotensin converting enzyme inhibitors. It may also include interventions such as angiography (pictures of the heart's blood supply) and heart surgery.

Why are we interested in this area of health experience?

Heart disease is worthy of exploration for a number of reasons:

- It is the major killer in the UK, and will remain a major cause of death well into the next century.
- Much is now known about the lifestyle and risk factors that predispose a group of similar individuals to the disease.
- The waning of the epidemic in many populations in different parts of the world indicates that death and morbidity can be reduced.
- Services for heart disease are very expensive, especially at the surgical and intervention end of the spectrum.
- There are different levels in the incidence of CHD among minority ethnic groups; this needs exploration, explanation and education of these populations and of health professionals.
- There is a very significant amount of distress and morbidity caused both directly and indirectly by heart disease.
- Heart health is a particularly fascinating area to study because of the dramatic changes this century and because it adds to our understanding of the genetic/environment or nature/nurture debate
- Much of the effort to improve heart health will also improve health in the areas of stroke, cancers and mental health/well-being.

Which groups in the population are we talking about?

The total population of Great Britain is 54.88 million (+2% for

national underestimate).[6] The ethnic origin of the population resident in England, Scotland and Wales was asked for the first time in
the 1991 census.[6] By 1995 it was estimated that, out of 51.2 million
people in England and Wales, 3.2 million assessed themselves as
ethnic minorities.[4] The percentage of ethnic groups in England
and Wales in 1995 was as follows:

White	93.7	Black Caribbean	0.9
Indian	1.7	Black African	0.6
Pakistani	1.1	Black other	0.2
Bangladeshi	0.4	Chinese	0.2
		Other groups	0.9

Epidemiology of CHD, with special reference to ethnicity

International data

In the USA, people from minority ethnic groups suffer excess
deaths well above the levels experienced by whites from a number
of specific causes. For instance, in 1986 the overall age-adjusted
mortality was 1.5 times that of whites;[7] for cardiovascular disease
the SMR was 150 and for diabetes it was 240.

A study of deaths over 3 years in New York City showed that in
Harlem the SMR was 223.[8] Harlem has a 96% black population,
with 41% of people living below the poverty line. Almost all the
excess mortality was among those under 65 years old, with a SMR
in this age group of 291 for males and 270 for females. The main
causes of these excess deaths were CHD (23.5% of the excess; SMR
223), cirrhosis of the liver (17.9% of the excess; SMR 1050) and
diabetes (3.7% of the excess; SMR 543).

Blacks have a higher incidence of both obesity and heart disease
in the USA.[9] Against an overall prevalence of obesity in adults of
25%, black women have a particularly high prevalence of 44%. A
telephone interview study of 4,790 people in New York State
examined socioeconomic and other multiple risk factors across
ethnic groups.[10] The main finding was that ethnicity and education
were independently associated with behavioural risk factors for
CHD, including smoking, lack of exercise, obesity and knowledge
about blood pressure and cholesterol. In general, blacks had less
favourable risk factor profiles and levels of knowledge after
adjustment for educational attainment.

The 'know your body' programme in the District of Columbia
began in 1983.[11] After 2 years of intervention, aimed at reducing
CHD risk factors among black students, there was a favourable

impact on systolic and diastolic pressures, cholesterol, fitness and smoking. Also, health knowledge and attitude towards smoking were significantly shifted in a favourable direction. This approach is based on the findings of other studies which stated that 48% of black children in the Bronx, New York, had one or more risk factors for heart disease at 9 years old. As children age, they are more likely to develop multiple heart disease risk factors, so early intervention would be an important component of primary prevention strategy.

Another interesting publication from the USA looks at tertiary prevention of CHD:[12]

> Increasing competition in the medical market place and the advent of hospital prospective payment have increased concern about potential threats to patient access and quality of care.

Of the 140,000 admissions to Massachusetts hospitals in 1985 for circulatory disease or chest pain, 78% were analysed. Despite the fact that age- and sex-adjusted admission rates for whites and blacks were similar, whites underwent one-third more coronary catheterisation and twice as many coronary artery bypass grafts and coronary angioplasties. This was after controlling for age, sex, income, primary diagnosis and the number of secondary diagnoses. These findings led the authors to conclude:[12]

> If medical decisions are being made on the basis of race we need to understand more about the complex interaction between physician and patient that leads to this inequality and the implications of those patterns for the appropriateness and efficiency of medical care.

Previous studies on surgical interventions for CHD had been limited by not combining a population and hospital based approach as in this study, which removed extraneous factors such as differential referral or admission patterns – so-called confounding variables.

National data

The national trends in the UK over the past 20 years are summarised in Table 1.[13,14] In this period the overall mortality in England and Wales fell by 5% in men and 1% in women. This is in contrast to an increase in mortality for the group with the highest SMR at the outset. In 1970–72, the SMRs were 128 and 129 in males and females born in the Indian subcontinent; these increased to 136 and 146, increases of 6% and 13% respectively.

Table 1. Standardised mortality ratios for ischaemic heart disease at ages 20–69 in England & Wales residents, by country of birth

Ethnic group	Sex	1970–2	1979–83	% change
Indian subcontinent	M	128	136	6
	F	129	146	13
African	M	116	113	–3
	F	78	97	24
Caribbean	M	49	45	–8
	F	89	76	–15
England & Wales	M	105	100	–5
	F	101	100	–1

The African Commonwealth population shows a mixed pattern:

- for males, a higher SMR of 116, falling by 3% to 113;
- for females, a lower SMR of 78, which rises by 24% to 97.

The Caribbean Commonwealth population, conversely, starts from lower bases:

- for men, an SMR of 49, which falls by 8% to 45;
- for women, an SMR of 89, which falls by 15% to 76.

However, by 1991–93 CHD still accounted for the largest proportion of deaths among men born in East Africa (SMR 160) and the Indian subcontinent (SMR 150).[4] The class divide again manifested itself with significantly higher mortality among manual classes.[4]

Local data

Of the half million population in Bradford, 13.6% are from minority ethnic groups;[15] The majority of these are of south Asian* origin.[16,17] An unpublished update of trends among the predominantly Pakistani Muslim Asian population in Bradford (Table 2) shows similar evidence of increasing inequality between the white majority and Asian minority populations. These trends had been predicted 8 years ago in the early analysis in 1988,[18] based on the epidemiological evidence at that time. In the early 1980s, the

---

*South Asian refers to people from Pakistan, India and Bangladesh either originating from these countries or second or subsequent generations.

age- and sex-specific rates for the south Asian and white residents were similar. By the early 1990s, however, there had been a considerable decline in the death rates in the white population, but either an increase or a slower decline in the Asian population. These findings for the Bradford population are similar to the predictions for the Leicester Asian population,[19] but for different reasons. The Leicester authors have assumed a constant differential of mortality between the Asian and non-Asian populations at 1.4, and applied this to known demographic changes by the year 2008. The Bradford data have *not* taken demographic trends into account, which will further worsen the mortality rates for the south Asian population and increase the CHD deaths differential. This reinforces the need for a strong preventive approach at national level;[20] this will be covered in the last section.

Risk factor profile comparisons by ethnicity

The risk factors for coronary heart disease, which together explain about 50% of the risk, are:[21] smoking; family history; raised cholesterol; diabetes; lack of exercise; raised blood pressure; ageing; male

Table 2. Death rates from ischaemic heart disease (ICD 410-4) in Bradford's Asian and non-Asian populations, by age and sex per 100,000 population

Period	Age 45–54	Age 55–64	Age 65+
Asian men			
1980–84	222	958	2,404
1990–92	415 (+87%)	655 (–32%)	1,522 (–37%)
Asian women			
1980–84	60	350	1,060
1990–92	52 (–20%)	281 (–20%)	1,091 (+3%)
Non-Asian men			
1980–84	340	940	2,550
1990–92	176 (–48%)	568 (–40%)	2,030 (–20%)
Non-Asian women			
1980–84	80	280	1,690
1990–92	46 (–43%)	196 (–11%)	1,420 (–16%)

Source: Kernohan EEM, Dews HG. Unpublished work, 1996.

genotype; poverty; excess or no alcohol; diet; insulin resistance/ central adiposity. These factors are all relevant at the primary and secondary prevention levels. In particular, diabetes and poverty are important for the Asian population and hypertension in the lower risk African-Caribbean population. Dietary advice needs to be carefully tailored to religious subgroups, as there is a wide variety of the profile of nutritional intake among different minority ethnic groups.

There is increasing support in the literature for the insulin resistance theory[22–25] which, if accepted on a balance of probability, would suggest that, in addition to control of diabetes, control of obesity (particularly central) and increased physical exercise should also be addressed within this group.[26,27]

The remaining risk factors have either a neutral or a heart healthy effect on minority ethnic communities.

What is being or still needs to be done nationally and locally?

There is a lot of good work already in progress around the country on CHD with specific reference to the needs of minority ethnic people. This includes:

- culturally sensitive 'look after your heart' (LAYH) courses;
- the creation of an ethnic health task force chaired by Baroness Cumberlege;
- ethnic minorities literature review bulletins;
- local initiatives such as media coverage through Zara Dhyan Dein and the establishment of the Bangladeshi women's smoking project in Keighley, West Yorkshire.

As ever, there remains much to do to raise the health experience based on current knowledge and to ensure that ethnic minority populations also achieve the national Health of the Nation targets for CHD[28] and the more recent target proposed in the Green Paper *Our healthier nation.*[29] Strategies to reduce CHD among minority ethnic groups should be aimed at reducing the risk and providing more appropriate and accessible treatment. Such strategies should not just focus on reducing the differentials in CHD morbidity and mortality between the minority and the general populations.[30] There is sufficient evidence that poorer groups and some ethnic minorities may not receive equitable access to services.[30] Some specific suggestions for further action are offered below, with a proposed lead organisation(s) at both national and local levels, adapted from *The nation's health: a strategy for the 1990s.*[31]

Primary prevention

National

- Social policy on poverty, unemployment. (Office for National Statistics (ONS) to monitor)
- Health promotion to maintain advantageous lifestyles in black and Asian ethnic minorities. (DoH to lead)
- Heart health promotion in schools curriculum/PSE content. (Department for Education and Employment to lead)
- Dietary advice (eg NACNE, COMA) needs to be tailored for religious or cultural subgroups in the UK. (DoH to lead)
- Facilitate the healthy choice becoming the easy choice (particularly regarding agricultural, transport and leisure policies).

Local

- Non-discriminatory employment and housing policies. (Local authority (LA))
- Collaborative work with schools to monitor lifestyles in schoolchildren and influence PSE curriculum. (LA)
- Directors of public health to identify trends in ethnic minority groups for CHD for publication in their annual reports; consider separate targets for ethnic minority populations for districts with large numbers of ethnic minority populations. (Health authority (HA))
- Culturally sensitive health promotion to continue to be developed. (HA, Primary care groups (PCGs))
- Staff training to focus on cultural and religious issues about CHD prevention/lifestyles in areas with significant numbers of ethnic minority people. (HA, PCGs, NHS Trusts).

Secondary prevention

National

- Outcome-based contracts for the screening and counselling of the high-risk population. (NHS Executive to lead)
- Continued publication of knowledge about risk factors in the high-risk groups. (DoH, R&D)

Local

- Commissioning authorities to encourage LAY! ('look after yourself') and LAYH culturally sensitive classes. (HA, PCG's)
- Consideration to be given to ensure adequate availability of interpreters and health advocates. (HA, PCG's, NHS Trusts)
- Local media coverage of risk factors and knowledge for

minority ethnic communities. (HA, local press, radio and television)

Tertiary level

National

- National allocation of Research & Development funding for CHD and stroke to give adequate weight to studies and practical methods of improving both the knowledge base and effective interventions for minority ethnic people for CHD. (R&D)
- Consideration should be given to systematic recording of names on death tapes from ONS in sentinel districts to enable longitudinal trends on second and third generation Asians to be monitored and to plan service needs appropriately; however, with proper legislation, ethnicity could be included on the death certificate. (DoH/ONS)

Local

- Clinical audit to study differences in investigations, treatments and survival by ethnic groups. (local audit)
- Local CHD and stroke groups specifically to address the needs and monitor treatment rates of the minority ethnic communities as appropriate. (Directors of public health)
- Planning of services to include representatives from minority ethnic groups in all commissioning authorities with more than 1% from these populations. (HA)

These suggestions are not comprehensive, but offer a reasonable start for districts wishing to embark on a specific preventive approach to CHD for their ethnic minority populations. During a period of instability and change, it is important that there be tangible commitment to reducing inequalities and increasing the voices of the minority ethnic groups in decision making. For areas where good things are already happening, this must become part of the norm. In other areas, a few good things starting to germinate would be an important start:

> We would consider our effort a success if more people began with the understanding that implementation, under the best of circumstances is exceedingly difficult. They would, therefore, be pleasantly surprised when a few good things really happened.[32]

Acknowledgements

I would particularly like to thank my colleagues in the Public Health Department and general practitioners in Bradford with whom I have worked on these issues. As always, thanks to Janice Joyce for her patience and quality of typing, and to Dr Rawaf's 'team' for their comments.

References

1   *Variations in health.* Report of the variations sub-group of the Chief Medical Officer's Health of the Nation working group. *What can the Department of Health and NHS do?* London: HMSO, 1995.

2   Modood T, Berthoud R, Lakey J, *et al. Ethnic minorities in Britain: diversity and disadvantage.* Fourth national survey of ethnic minorities. London: Policy Studies Institute, 1997.

3   Cappuccio FP. Ethnicity and cardiovascular risk: the variations in people of African ancestry and South Asian origin. *Journal of Human Hypertension* 1997; **11**: 571–6.

4   Harding S, Maxwell R. Differences in mortality of migrants. In: Drever F, Whitehead M, eds. *Health inequalities.* Decennial supplement. London: HMSO, 1997.

5   Dever GEA. Epidemiology in health services management. Rockville, Maryland: Aspen, 1984.

6   *Great Britain 1991 census.* Health Area Monitor, CEN 91 HAM 16. London: Office of Population Censuses and Surveys, 1993.

7   Windom RE. From the Assistant Secretary for Health. *Journal of the American Medical Association* 1989; **262**: 196.

8   McCard C, Freeman HP. Excess mortality in Harlem. *New England Journal of Medicine* 1990; **332**: 173–7.

9   McGinnis JM, Ballard-Barbash RM. Obesity in minority populations: policy implications of research. *American Journal of Clinical Nutrition* 1991; **56**(6 suppl): 1512–4S.

10 Shea S, Stein AD, Basch CE, *et al.* Independent associations of educational attainment and ethnicity with behavioural risk factors for cardiovascular disease. *American Journal of Epidemiology* 1991; **134**: 567–82.

11 Bush PJ, Zuckerman AE, Theiss PK, *et al.* Cardiovascular risk factor prevention in black school-children: two-year results of the 'know your body' program. *American Journal of Epidemiology* 1988; **129**: 466–82.

12 Wenneker MB, Epstein AM. Racial inequalities in the use of procedures for patients with ischaemic heart disease in Massachusetts. *Journal of the American Medical Association* 1989; **261**: 253–7.

13 Marmot MG, Adelstein AM, Bulusu L. *Immigrant mortality in England and Wales 1970–78: causes of death by country of birth.* London: Office of Population Censuses and Surveys, 1984.

14 Balarajan R, Bulusu L, Adelstein AM, *et al.* Patterns of mortality among migrants to England and Wales from the Indian subcontinent. *British Medical Journal* 1984; **289**: 1185–7.

15 Kyle D. *The health of the nation: the health of Bradford 1993.* Annual health report of the director of public health. Bradford: Bradford Health Authority, 1993.

16 *1991 census: Yorkshire region.* CEN 91 HAM 14. London: Office of Population Censuses and Surveys, 1993.

17 *1991 census update.* Bradford: Bradford Metropolitan District Council, 1993.
18 Kernohan EEM. *The health of Bradford 1987.* Annual report of the director of public health. Bradford: Bradford Health Authority, 1988.
19 Lowy AGJ, Woods KL, Botha JL. The effects of demographic shift on CHD mortality in a large migrant population at high risk. *Journal of Public Health Medicine* 1991; **13**: 276–80.
20 Gupta S, de Belder A, Hughes LO. Avoiding premature coronary deaths in Asians in Britain. *British Medical Journal* 1995; **311**: 1035–6.
21 Poulter N, Sever P, Thom S. *Cardiovascular disease: risk factors and intervention.* Oxford: Radcliffe, 1993.
22 McKeigue PM, Shah B, Marmot MG. Relation of central obesity and insulin resistance with high diabetes prevalence and cardiovascular risk in South Asians. *Lancet* 1991; **337**: 382–6.
23 Hughes LO, Cruikshank J, Wright J, *et al.* Disturbances of insulin in British Asian and white men surviving myocardial infarction. *British Medical Journal* 1989; **299**: 537–41.
24 McKeigue PM, Ferrie JE, Pierpoint T, Marmot MG. Association of early-onset coronary heart disease in South Asian men with glucose intolerance and hyperinsulinemia. *Circulation* 1993; **87**: 152–61.
25 Cappuccio FP, Cook DG, Atkinson RW. Prevalence, detection and treatment of diabetes in different ethnic groups in south London. *Canadian Journal of Cardiology* 1997; **13** (suppl B): B196–7.
26 Olefsky JM, Reavan GM, Farquhar JW. Effects of weight reduction in obesity: studies of carbohydrate and lipid metabolism. *Journal of Clinical Investigation* 1974; **53**: 64–76.
27 Kovisto VA, Yki-Jarvinen H, DeFronzo RA. Physical training and insulin sensitivity. *Diabetes/Metabolism Reviews* 1986; **1**: 445–81.
28 *The health of the nation: a strategy for health in England.* Key area handbook: Coronary Heart Disease and Stroke. HMSO, 1992.
29 Department of Health. *Our healthier nation.* London: Stationery Office, 1998. (Cm 3852).
30 NHS Centre for Reviews and Dissemination. *Ethnicity and Health.* Report No. 5. York: CRD, 1996.
31 Smith A, Jacobson B. *The nation's health: a strategy for the 1990s.* London: Health Education Authority, 1988.
32 Pressman JL, Wildavsky A. *Implementation how great expectations in Washington are dashed in Oakland or, why its amazing that federal programs work at all, this being a saga of the Economic Development Administration as told by two sympathetic observers who seek to build morals on a foundation of ruined hopes.* Berkeley: University of California, 1984.

18 | Breast cancer

Tanya Hoare
Department of Health Care Studies,
Manchester Metropolitan University

The high incidence of breast cancer is a major public health concern. It is the second most common female malignancy throughout the world, and the single commonest cause of female cancer deaths.[1-4] Breast cancer is not confined to Western industrialised societies, since more than half the cases occur in developing countries.[5,6]

It has been suggested that overemphasis of differences between minority ethnic groups and the white population has not had a real impact on improving public health.[7,8] Much research on minority ethnic health in this country has focused on diseases specific to these groups and less on the more common causes of morbidity and mortality.[7-9] The major health issues of the whole population, such as breast cancer, may well be broadly the same for minority ethnic groups.

The UK has one of the highest mortality rates for breast cancer in the world;[4] it is one of the diseases for which targets have been set in *The health of the nation*[10] and the more recent *Our healthier nation*. While advances in treatment continue to be explored, the current direction for improvement in prognosis lies with secondary prevention, ie screening for early detection.

In assessing the health needs of women from minority ethnic groups in the UK, the fundamental issues to be addressed are whether they are disadvantaged either with respect to the incidence of breast cancer or in the uptake of screening. Such investigations not only raise awareness of differences between populations but also emphasise similarities. Obtaining such information is currently hampered by the fact that valid data on ethnic origin are not recorded in routine health records in the UK. Furthermore, until the 1991 census, which included a question about ethnic group, there had not been adequate demographic information to allow the investigation of rates.

Health professionals need to be aware of the patterns of breast cancer, environmental risk factors and factors affecting screening. This information allows the recognition of any unmet needs and the planning of appropriate strategies for health services and health education.

Breast cancer

International variations

There are wide variations in the incidence of breast cancer throughout the world,[1] with approximately a 6-fold difference between North America and many parts of Asia. As can be seen from Fig 1, the highest rates in the world are found in the USA and Canada, followed by Western Europe.[1-6]

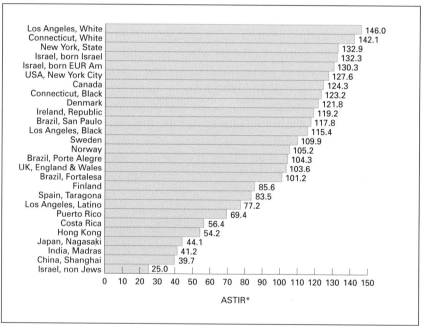

Fig 1. *International variations in breast cancer incidence.* Age-standardised truncated incidence rates (ASTIR)* for female breast cancer in selected cancer registries around 1980. (Source: *Cancer incidence in five continents.* Vol V. Lyon: IARC, 1987).
*ASTIR are calculated restricting the data to the age range 35–64 years, and each 5-year age-group within such an age range is given the weight appropriate to the world standard population, thus facilitating comparisons between different communities as rates at the extreme age groups are eliminated. Reproduced (with permission) from reference 6.

The lowest incidence of breast cancer is observed in Oriental Asians (Chinese and Japanese women) and Arabic populations, and low rates are also found among women from the Indian sub-continent.[1,3,5] There is a 2–3-fold difference in incidence between the latter group and women in the UK. Intermediate incidence levels are found in South America, Latin America and Eastern Europe, although there are areas of high incidence in Brazil.[1,2,5,6] Although there are fewer data available for African countries it appears that, while incidence rates are substantially less than for the developed world, it remains one of the commonest forms of cancer.[3]

International comparisons of incidence are hampered by the lack of population-based statistics from many parts of the world, and only proportional rates are available in many developing countries. The latter express cancer frequency as a proportion of all cancers for the group studied. Information is particularly valuable therefore from the old established Bombay Cancer Registry and from Japan, one of the most developed and affluent countries in the world, but geographically distant from the West. Although cancer mortality rates are more widely available than incidence data, they are influenced by the success of treatment, so information on incidence is preferable.

Increases in the incidence of breast cancer have been consistently observed throughout the world.[5] Countries that began with the highest rates (North America and Western Europe) are still in the lead, where factors associated with the disease have been more prevalent in these industrialised countries for longer.[5] It will be interesting to monitor changes in the developing world as lifestyles are influenced by adaptations to the Western pattern.

Migrant studies

Studies of Japanese migrants to Hawaii and the rest of the US have shown how trends in breast cancer shift towards those of the host population in subsequent generations.[11,12] Second and subsequent generation Japanese women living in the US no longer exhibit the low incidence found in Japan and have rates the same as the rest of the US, strongly suggesting that environmental or lifestyle factors are involved in the aetiology of the disease. Similar findings have been shown for migrant groups to Australia and Israel.[3,13,14] Migrant studies provide the strongest evidence that changes in lifestyle such as reproductive patterns and dietary habits influence cancer incidence. Such findings have important implications for women from minority ethnic populations in the UK and for public health physicians involved in planning their care.

Incidence in the UK

The majority of older minority ethnic women are first-generation migrants to this country[15] and would be expected to show the incidence of their country of origin. Since data on ethnic origin are not recorded by cancer registries in the UK, the few studies that have been undertaken to investigate this have used proxy measures.[16–20] These have studied Asian populations, defined as people originating directly or indirectly from the Indian sub-continent, for two main reasons. First, these populations can be identified on the basis of name, which is recognised as an accurate way, at the present time, of identifying people from India, Pakistan and Bangladesh.[5,21–23] Underenumeration of Asian women by this method owing to cross-cultural marriage is unlikely since this is currently estimated to be low in Britain,[18,24] but in the future the method could be less useful. Second, the Asian population is numerically the largest minority ethnic group in the UK.[15]

It would appear that the incidence of breast cancer among Asian women in the UK is approximately half that of the indigenous population. The incidence in Asian women in west Scotland, where the registry covers 57% of the Scottish population, is much closer to that found in Bombay than in the UK overall.[17] A low incidence of breast cancer was found among 'Asians' in Bradford and Leicestershire, based on standardised cancer registration ratios.[16] A retrospective study using 'hospital activity analysis' looked at cancers in blacks, whites and Asians attending a Birmingham hospital,[19] and found low rates of breast cancer in minority ethnic women. These studies did not have adequate population data for the Asian population, relying on 'place of birth' information from previous censuses. Now that denominator data are available from the 1991 census, it is important to investigate cancer incidence rates further, to provide baseline information for measuring the public health problem, and to monitor changes in the population.

Relevance of risk factors for minority ethnic women

Age

Throughout the world, age-specific incidence rates for breast cancer increase steeply up to about 45–54 years, after which they continue to increase, albeit at a somewhat slower rate.[5] In parts of the world where the disease is relatively uncommon, incidence rates level off after the menopausal age, or even decline.[5]

In the study of-hospital activity, it was found that Asian women presented at an earlier age than white women (but had more advanced disease).[19] Confounding factors could be the younger age structure of the Asian population in the UK, and higher parity. The study of Bradford Asians also indicated an increase in breast cancer in the younger age groups.[16] While the incidence of breast cancer may be rising, age-specific rates may not show the same increase over all ages.[3,25] This requires verification in the various population groups.

Reproductive and menstrual experience

There is evidence that early menarche, late menopause, low parity and late age at first birth are related to increased risk of breast cancer.[3] Age at menarche is affected by childhood nutritional status, and the improved socioeconomic conditions for migrants to this country could result in its decrease.[6] Age at first birth appears to have an independent effect on breast cancer risk and is the most important reproductive factor.[3] Women having their first birth at an early age enjoy a considerably reduced risk of breast cancer.[3,26] The apparent protective effect of high parity has been reported to disappear when age at first birth is taken into account,[3,5,27] although the evidence from different parts of the world is conflicting. An increase in the age at first birth may occur in minority ethnic women through adaptation to differing social influences and improved contraceptive availability.

Evidence for a reduced risk of breast cancer due to lactation is inconclusive.[3] While breast feeding is usual practice in the Indian subcontinent, it is reported to be disappointingly uncommon among Asian mothers in the UK.[28]

There may be an increased risk of breast cancer due to oral contraceptive use at an early age or before first pregnancy,[6] but it is not known how this relationship affects ethnic minority women. An increase in oral contraceptive use in the Third World has been reported.[6]

Race and social class

Data from the US have shown a 30% higher incidence of breast cancer among white women compared with black or Hispanic women in the same area.[3] The relationship, however, is confounded by differing ages at first birth, which is at least partly responsible for this social variation.[5] Consequently, as circumstances among the ethnic groups alter, incidence rates are reported to be rising more rapidly among black than white women.[3]

Similarly, socioeconomic indicators themselves are unlikely to account for the higher incidence reported in most countries among women of higher socioeconomic status. In England and Wales, for example, higher rates have been shown in social class I than class V,[4,29] and these differences are attributed to factors such as age at first birth. Furthermore, using alternative social indicators such as housing tenure and car access, there were no differences in mortality between the more and less disadvantaged groups on either scale.[30]

Diet related factors

Dietary practices have increasingly become the focus of attention in studies of breast cancer and a conflicting variety of information has been produced.[3,31,32] Much of the evidence has been derived from correlation studies between incidence and mortality with *per capita* intake of total fat and other dietary factors.[3,31] Breast cancer is more common in countries consuming a Western diet,[33,34] and the low Japanese rates are thought to be a reflection of lower dietary fat consumption.[12] Japan is one of the most affluent and developed countries of the world, yet breast cancer incidence is among the lowest. The lower breast cancer rates in Asian women from the Indian subcontinent are consistent with their lower intakes of meat products;[17] their total fat intake has been reported as comparable to that of the indigenous UK population although the fat in the Asian diet is mainly derived from dairy (butter) products.[17] There is no consistent evidence currently available on the influence of dietary factors on breast cancer, and it is an area about which it is notoriously difficult to obtain valid information.

Summary

- The incidence of breast cancer among minority ethnic women is two to three times less than that of the indigenous UK population, and reflects the rate in their country of origin.
- Although breast cancer incidence is proportionately lower among minority ethnic women, since breast cancer is a common disease it remains a substantial public health problem.
- It is likely that breast cancer will increase among various minority

ethnic women owing to changing exposure to risk factors, demographic changes and adaptation to differing lifestyles.

- Data on ethnic groups' origins are not collected by UK cancer registries; ethnic monitoring in routine health records would greatly facilitate surveillance studies.

Breast cancer screening

The National Health Service breast screening programme was introduced in the UK in 1988,[35] the target population being women 50–64 years of age. Women of this age group who are registered with a GP are invited to have an examination by mammography every 3 years, and women aged 65 and over may request it. Breast screening has not been shown to be effective in women under the age of 50.[35] The aim of the screening programme is to reduce the very high mortality from breast cancer in this country, and targets for the year 2000 and beyond have been set in the Health of the Nation report[10] and *Our healthier nation*. A crucial factor in achieving the target is the maintenance of a high attendance rate for screening, of at least 70%, in both the incident and prevalent screening rounds.[35] This, in turn, is dependent on the acceptability of the service to all women, and to maximise attendance it is important that the needs of women, including those from minority ethnic communities, are met. According to the Chief Medical Officer's annual report for 1996, 65% of women aged 50–64 resident in England had been screened at least once in the previous 3 years.[36]

There are several issues to consider for the breast screening of minority ethnic women:

- are they less likely to attend for screening than others?
- where attendance is low, the identification of barriers;
- implementation of strategies to meet any unmet need.

Uptake of screening

Reports from the UK, both before and after the introduction of the national screening programme, have examined social class differences in attendance rates,[37–39] but there are very few studies that have investigated this in relation to ethnicity. Based partly on anecdotal evidence, it is generally believed that attendance for breast screening is low among minority ethnic women. Most of the information about uptake of screening is obtained from studies of Asian populations, for the reasons outlined in the section on breast cancer.

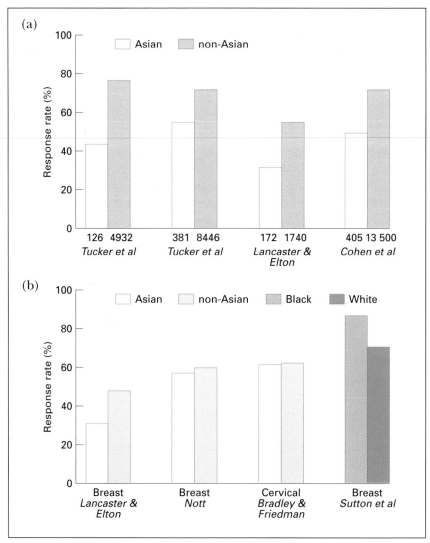

Fig 2. (a) *Breast screening uptake: response by ethnic group.* **(b)** *Screening uptake: response by ethnic group accounting for socioeconomic group.*

Although very few studies have precisely quantified the difference in uptake of breast screening among Asian women compared with the indigenous population,[40–44] some investigators have suggested that uptake is substantially less among Asians.[40–42] Typically, uptake of around 50% is reported for Asian women compared with around 73% for non-Asians (Fig 2a). However, the interpretation of these differences is possibly confounded by variation in the distribution of such factors as social class.

These reports of uptake may be for several months of screening, covering many different types of area, and are not necessarily comparing like with like. For example, it is well known that screening uptake varies markedly in different areas.[36,39,45] It can be argued that area of residence, the type of area that people live in, regardless of ethnic origin, reflects what can be broadly termed socioeconomic group. When comparisons have been restricted to relatively homogeneous areas, eg socially disadvantaged parts of inner-city areas, Asian women have not been shown necessarily to have a lower attendance for either the breast[42,43] or cervical[46] screening programme, as shown in Fig 2b. These studies were conducted for Pakistani Moslem populations.[42] One study showed that uptake by black women was higher than that for white women in the same area of inner London.[46]

It would appear that the uptake of screening by Asian women may be low, but not necessarily lower than among women of similar socioeconomic groups.[48] The study of cervical screening[46] is interesting since it was restricted to women of 50–64, who are no longer receiving antenatal care. Earlier reports of lower uptake of cervical screening among Asian women[30,49] were made before the introduction of the call/recall scheme, when low response might not be surprising. Furthermore, the comparisons may have been confounded by the same factors described above. The finding that black women do not seem to be disadvantaged with respect to screening attendance[42] may result from their relative integration in the community. Familiarity with health services could also account for the finding that the uptake of breast screening is related to the length of time that Asian women have lived in this country.[50,51] Asian women, regardless of their country of origin, who had lived here for over 5 years were significantly more likely to attend for screening than those who had arrived more recently. The value of these investigations is that they emphasise an important fact that may be overlooked when considering minority ethnic groups: there must be awareness not only of the differences between various groups but also of the similarities between some groups and the indigenous UK population.

Acceptability

Are there common problems that make it difficult for all women to accept an invitation for screening, and are there additional difficulties for minority ethnic women? It is frequently supposed that cultural factors are a cause of non-attendance for women from minority ethnic backgrounds, but it is important to establish the relative importance of these factors if a genuine assessment of needs is to be made. The most effective means of promoting their participation may be related to accessibility and organisational aspects of the service rather than to attitudes and beliefs.

A major reason for non-attendance for screening is common to all women in the population. It is recognised that inaccurate health authority registers, from which screening invitations are derived, are a problem, especially in inner cities were invitations are frequently sent to addresses at which the women no longer live.[52-56] Up to 35% of invitation addresses were shown to be inaccurate in south-east London,[51] and a study in central Manchester found that 49% of Asian non-attenders were no longer resident at their given address.[56] Many of the latter had returned to the Indian subcontinent and some had only been visitors to the UK.[55]

A prior notification list is sent to GPs for checking addresses and eligibility before screening invitations are sent out. Not all GPs amend this list before its return to the health authority, and not all patients keep their GPs updated,[55,56] but it is essential that both realise the importance of correct information if women are to receive their invitations.

Inaccurate registers are compounded for Asian women by either their return, or extended visits of months or even years duration, to the Indian subcontinent. In central Manchester, one-third of the Asian non-attenders who were resident at the invitation address were making lengthy visits, often of unknown duration.[55,56] Another study found that over a quarter of invited Asian women were either temporarily (on visits) or permanently (not resident) unable to respond to the screening invitation.[50,51]

An appreciation of minority ethnic naming systems by health professionals could have an impact on response to screening invitations. Asian women may use a title such as Begum or Bibi, equivalent to Mrs or Miss. Health authorities add 'Mrs' or 'Miss' to names and then screening offices may abbreviate them. As can be seen from the example in Table 1, this has the effect of sending an invitation to 'Mrs, Mrs'.

When several Asian women live in the same house it is not surprising that a major problem faced by radiographers is whether a woman, if she attends, is indeed who they think she is. Women apparently well outside the screening age range attend, with implications for radiation hazards for young or pregnant women.

There is a range of attitudinal factors affecting attendance for screening by minority ethnic women.[55,57] A recent report has

Table 1. Example of systems for naming patients

GP record	Health authority list	Screening office abbreviation
Jane Smith	Mrs Smith, Jane	Mrs J Smith
Soraya Bibi	Mrs Bibi, Soraya	Mrs S Bibi
Fatima Begum	Mrs Begum, Fatima	Mrs F Begum

described the knowledge and beliefs about health, cancer and screening among selected black, Asian and Chinese women.[58] Where invitations are received, an overriding problem for Asian women has been shown to be a lack of comprehension about the concept of screening apparently well women for the detection of disease.[55,56] Women, and their families, see themselves as fit and well and can see no reason for a medical invitation to improve their health.[55,56] Illness may be perceived as a situation in which symptoms exist and then treatment is sought. With a low level of literacy among some minority ethnic women,[50,51] where someone else is required to read and explain the invitation, the issue may not be given priority.[54,55] This 'gatekeeper' effect results in women being unaware of the invitation.[55-57] There appeared to be less apprehension about the procedure and its result among Asian women than others;[55] when communication is also a concern, accompaniment beyond the home may be the norm for many minority ethnic women.[55-57]

Meeting the need

There has been little evaluation of strategies designed to increase understanding about screening and promote attendance. Despatch of health education material, translated into various languages, along with breast screening invitations varies considerably between screening offices. Even where such leaflets are used, attendance may remain disappointingly low,[42,50,51] suggesting that written information is not sufficient to meet the needs of some minority ethnic women.

Personal visits, with leaflets or a video, to Asian women's homes in Leicester were shown to be effective in persuading those who were resident, and who had never had a cervical smear, to have a smear.[49] That study was, however, conducted before the introduction of the call/recall scheme, so it is not surprising that almost none of the control group went for a smear. Furthermore, the authors concluded that this type of intervention would not be feasible in practice for all invited Asian women. A randomised controlled trial of an Asian population in Oldham who were invited for breast screening found that linkworker visits explaining about screening were unsuccessful.[50,51] In this study, women in the intervention group were visited at home by linkworkers and given a brief talk and encouragement in their own language about screening, whereas the control group received no visits. There was no difference in attendance between the two groups.[50,51] However, in a randomised controlled trial in inner London, training general practice receptionists proved to be effective in improving breast screening uptake, especially among Indian women.[59]

Accessibility to the target population was a problem in the breast screening study. This also resulted in an ineffective outcome for a scheme to visit all non-attenders for cervical screening in Liverpool,[60] although this may be less of a problem for Asian populations.[61] It may well be that a more long-term approach of health education for all sections of the minority ethnic community is the only appropriate strategy. A training package has been developed for this.[62] However, it must be remembered that screening uptake by minority ethnic women has been shown to increase with length of stay in this country.[50,51]

It is important to realise that for any intervention to have an impact it must cover all the target population, and must therefore be practicable. When action is proposed to increase uptake, it is important that the outcome measure be defined and evaluated. Interventions are not without costs, and the resources used in the personal visits in the above studies could be deployed in other ways to increase coverage.

Acceptability and attendance are affected by:

- women not being at invitation address;
- women on extended visits to the Indian subcontinent;
- families not passing on information;
- lack of understanding about screening:
  - did not know what invitation was for;
  - did not understand how screening could improve health;
  - apprehensive about procedure and result;
  - communication;
- accessibility to service.

Conclusion

A health service that meets the needs of people from minority ethnic populations must have information about both the scale of a problem and its relative importance to the rest of the population. Information about the absolute scale determines whether there is a major health concern, and relative differences are useful for planning purposes. Women from minority ethnic groups in the UK currently appear to have a two to three times lower incidence of breast cancer and so do not constitute a high-risk group in the whole population. Breast cancer is a common disease, however, so it remains a major public health issue. The incidence in minority ethnic groups is likely to rise towards that of the host population,[33] and there is no justification for a lack of effort in carrying out health education programmes about breast awareness in these communities.

Attendance for screening among minority ethnic women may well be low, but not necessarily lower than for women of similar socioeconomic groups. There should therefore be concern about why attendance is low, in relation to both social deprivation and ethnicity. Recognition of the relative importance of factors affecting attendance is vital if a valid assessment of the health needs of women is to be made. As initiatives to promote the uptake of health services compete for scarce resources, it is essential rigorously to evaluate the effectiveness of actions and strategies so that resources can be used effectively. To do so requires judgement based on valid and reliable information. It is important to understand these issues if we are to improve the delivery of health care and plan appropriate services for all sections of society. Taking into account such ethnic differences is important in achieving a successful implementation of the government's strategy to develop cancer services, and the Healthier Nation contract on cancer.[64]

References

1   Parkin DM, Muir C, Whelan SL, *et al.*, eds. *Cancer incidence in 5 continents.* Vol VI. Lyon: International Agency for Research on Cancer Publications, 1992.

2. Parkin DM, Laara E, Muir CS. Estimates of the worldwide frequency of sixteen major cancers in 1980. *International Journal of Cancer* 1988; **41**: 184–97.

3   Boyle P. Epidemiology of breast cancer. *Baillières Clinical Oncology* 1988; **2**: 1–53.

4   Cancer Research Campaign. *Facts on cancer* No. 6, 1991; No. 6, 1996.

5   Kalache A. Risk factors for breast cancer, with special reference to developing countries. *Health Policy and Planning* 1990; **5**: 1–22.

6   Kalache A, Horton D. Breast cancer in the developing world: an unaddressed challenge. *Breast* 1992; **1**: 124–8.

7 Sheldon TA, Parker H. Race and ethnicity in health research. *Journal of Public Health Medicine* 1992; **14**: 104–10.

8 Bhopal RS. Future research on the health of ethnic minorities: back to basics – a personal view. *Ethnic Minorities Health* 1990; **1**: 1–3.

9 Bhopal R. Is research into ethnicity and health racist, unsound, or important science? *British Medical Journal* 1997; **314**: 1751–6.

10 Department of Health. *The health of the nation: a strategy for health in England.* London: HMSO, 1992.

11 Buell P. Changing incidence of breast cancer in Japanese-American women. *Journal of the National Cancer Institute* 1973; **51**: 1479–83.

12 Nomura AM, Lee J, Kolonel LN, *et al.* Breast cancer in two populations with different levels of risk for the disease. *American Journal of Epidemiology* 1984; **119**: 496–502.

13 McMichael AJ, Giles GG. Cancer in migrants to Australia: extending the descriptive epidemiological data. *Cancer Research* 1988; **48**: 741–6.

14 Melnik Y, Slat PE, Katz L. Breast cancer in Israel 1960–75. II. Effects on age and survival. *European Journal of Cancer* 1980; **16**: 1017–23.

15 Balarajan R. *Ethnic diversity in England and Wales.* An analysis by health authorities based on the 1991 census. London: NIESH, 1997.

16 Barker RM, Baker MR. Incidence of cancer in Bradford Asians. *Journal of Epidemiology and Community Health* 1990; **44**: 125–9.

17 Matheson M, Dunnigan MG, Hole D, *et al.* Incidence of colo-rectal, breast and lung cancer in a Scottish Asian population. *Health Bulletin* 1984; **43**: 245–9.

18 Donaldson L, Clayton D. Occurrence of cancer in Asians and non-Asians. *Journal of Epidemiology and Community Health* 1984; **38**: 203–7.

19 Potter JF, Dawkins D, Pandha HS, Beevers DG. Cancer in blacks, whites and Asians in a British hospital. *Journal of the Royal College of Physicians of London* 1984; **18**: 231–5.

20 Harding S, Maxwell R. Differences in mortality of migrants. In: Drever F, Whitehead M, eds. *Health inequalities.* Decennial supplement. London: HMSO, 1997.

21 Donaldson LJ, Taylor JB. Patterns of Asian and non-Asian morbidity in hospitals. *British Medical Journal* 1983; **286**: 949–51.

22 Sillitoe K. Ethnic origin: the search for a question. *Population Trends* 1978; **13**: 25–30.

23 Nicoll A, Bassett K, Ulijaszek S. What's in a name? *Journal of Epidemiology and Community Health* 1986; **40**: 364–8.

24 Jones PR. Research report: ethnic intermarriage in Britain. *Ethnic and Racial Studies* 1982; **5**: 223–8.

25 Department of Public Health Medicine, North Western RHA & Centre for Cancer Epidemiology. *Breast cancer in the North Western region.* North West Regional Health Authority, 1993.

26 Kalache A, Vessey MP. Risk factors for breast cancer. In: Baum M, ed. *Clinics in oncology: breast cancer.* London: Saunders, 1982: 661–78.

27 MacMahon B, Cole P, Lin TM, *et al.* Age at first birth and breast cancer risk. *Bulletin of the World Health Organisation* 1970; **42**: 209–21.

28 McAvoy B. Women's health. In: McAvoy BR, Donaldson LJ, eds. *Health care for Asians.* Oxford: Oxford University Press, 1990.

29 Kogevinas N, Goldblatt P, Pugh H. *Socio-economic status and breast*

cancer in England & Wales: time trends in incidence, survival and mortality. LS Working Paper No. 63. London: OPCS, 1989.

30   Smith J, Harding S. Mortality of women and men using alternative social classification. In: Drever F, Whitehead M, eds. *Health inequalities.* Decennial supplement. London: HMSO, 1997.

31   Boyd NF. Nutrition and breast cancer. *Journal of the National Cancer Institute* 1993; **85**: 6–7.

32   Giovannucci E, Stomter MJ, Colditz G, *et al.* Comparison of prospective and retrospective assessments of diet in the study of breast cancer. *American Journal of Epidemiology* 1993; **137**: 502–11.

33   Hems G. The contribution of diet and childbearing to breast cancer rates. *British Journal of Cancer* 1978; **37**: 974–82.

34   Hargreaves MK, Buchowski MS, Hardy RE, *et al.* Dietary factors and cancer of the breast, endometrium and ovary: strategies for modifying fat intake in African American women. *American Journal of Obstetrics and Gynecology* 1997; **176**: S255–64.

35   Forrest P. *Breast cancer: the decision to screen.* London: Nuffield Provincial Hospitals Trust, 1990.

36   Department of Health. *On the state of the public health.* Annual report of the Chief Medical Officer 1996. London: HMSO, 1997.

37   Hunt S, Alexander F, Roberts M. Attenders and non-attenders at a breast screening clinic: a comparative study. *Public Health* 1988; **102**: 3–10.

38   French K, Porter A, Robinson S, *et al.* Attendance at a breast screening clinic: a problem of administration or attitude? *British Medical Journal* 1982; **285**: 617–20.

39   Vaile M, Calnan M, Rutter D, *et al.* Breast screening in three areas: uptake and satisfaction. *Journal of Public Health Medicine* 1993; **15**: 37–45.

40   Tucker A, Gale AG, Roebuck EJ. Breast cancer and screening Asian populations. *British Journal of Radiology* 1991; **65**: Congress supplement.

41   Cohen MEL, Turnbull A, Kapera L. Significant variations in breast tissue patterns between Asian and Caucasian women resident in southern Derbyshire. *Breast* 1992; **1**: 158.

42   Lancaster G, Elton P. Does the offer of cervical screening with breast screening encourage older women to have a cervical smear test? *Journal of Epidemiology and Community Health* 1992; **46**: 523–7.

43   Nott M. Personal communication, 1991. (Windsor & Slough Breast Screening Service)

44   Rudat K. *Health and lifestyle: black and minority ethnic groups in England.* London: Health Education Authority, 1994.

45   Hollyyoak V. Uptake of breast screening may be influenced by practice specific factor. *British Medical Journal* 1995; **310**: 1004.

46   Bradley A, Friedman E. Cervical cytology screening: comparison of uptake among Asian and non-Asian women in Oldham. *Journal of Public Health Medicine* 1993; **15**: 46–51.

47   Sutton R, Bickler G, Saidi G, *et al.* Prospective study of predictors of attendance for breast screening in an inner-city area. *Journal of Epidemiology and Community Health* 1994; **48**: 65–73.

48   Hoare TA. *Ethnic minorities and breast screening.* UKCCCR/NHSBSP

Publication No. 28. Breast Screening Acceptability Workshop: Research & Practice, 1993.

49 McAvoy B, Raza R. Can health education increase uptake of cervical smear testing among Asian women? *British Medical Journal* 1991; **302**: 833–6.

50 Hoare T, Thomas C, Biggs A, *et al. A randomised controlled trial of an intervention to increase the uptake of breast screening among Asian women.* Centre for Cancer Epidemiology report No. 100. Manchester: Christie Hospital NHS Trust, 1992.

51 Hoare T, Thomas C, Biggs A, *et al.* Can the uptake of breast screening be increased? A randomised controlled trial of an intervention. *Journal of Public Health Medicine* 1994; **16**: 179–85.

52 McEwan J, King E, Bickler G. Attendance and non-attendance for breast screening at the south-east London breast screening service. *British Medical Journal* 1989; **299**: 104–6.

53 Doyle Y. A survey of the cervical screening service in a London District. *Social Science and Medicine* 1991; **32**: 953–7.

54 Beardow R, Overton J, Victor C. Evaluation of the cervical cytology screening programme in an inner-city health district. *British Medical Journal* 1989; **299**: 98–100.

55 Hoare TA, Johnson CM. *Non-attendance for breast screening among Asian women: whose problem?* Centre for Cancer Epidemiology report No. 96. Manchester: Christie Hospital NHS Trust, 1991.

56 Hoare T, Johnson CM, Gorton R, *et al.* Reasons for non-attendance for breast screening among Asian women. *Health Education Journal* 1992; **51**: 157–161.

57 Hoare TA, Thomas C, Biggs A, *et al. Survey of non-attenders for breast screening.* CCE Report No. 101, Centre for Cancer Epidemiology report No. 101. Manchester: Christie Hospital NHS Trust, 1993.

58 McAllister G. *Ethnic minorities and breast screening.* Development Worker Project. Final report. Department of Health, 1992.

59 Atri J, Falshaw M, Gregg R, *et al.* Improving uptake of breast screening in multiethnic population: a randomised controlled trial using practice reception staff to contact non-attenders. *British Medical Journal* 1997; **315**: 1356–9.

60 Carter J, Ellerby SE. Increasing the uptake of cervical smear testing among Asian women. *British Medical Journal* 1991; **302**: 1152.

61 Hoare TA, Johnson CM. Increasing the uptake of cervical smear testing among Asian women. *British Medical Journal* 1991; **302**: 1540–1.

62 *Communicating messages to ethnic minority women.* Information package produced for NHS breast screening programme, 1993.

63 Department of Health, Welsh Office. *A policy framework for commissioning cancer services.* Report by the expert advisory group on cancer to the Chief Medical Officers of England and Wales. *Guidance for purchasers and providers of cancer services.* London: Department of Health, 1995.

64 Secretary of State for Health. *Our healthier nation: a contract for health.* London: Stationery Office, 1998.

19 | Mental health

S P Sashidharan
Professor of Community Psychiatry, University of Birmingham

Martin J Commander
Senior Research Fellow, University of Birmingham

This chapter sets out some of the problems, priorities and strategies in identifying the mental health needs of minority ethnic groups, specifically those of non-European origin, living in the United Kingdom. We examine the increasing importance being attached to health needs assessment in the context of changes in the National Health Service, and argue that in relation to minority ethnic communities the current approaches to needs assessment are unlikely to alter the mental health service experience of these groups. The problems of definition and related conceptual issues around what constitutes mental health needs are on a par with the lack of uniformity in defining ethnicity, race or culture, especially when related to health. The conflict of interests between providers of mental health services and users of such services is well recognised, but the views of the minority ethnic communities and users of the service continue to be ignored in the assessment of needs and in setting priorities in care. We argue that this problem requires special strategies within the needs assessment programme. The chapter develops some of the more salient themes from current debates around ethnicity and mental health on the basis of data from work undertaken in inner-city Birmingham, with emphasis on service use. We conclude by arguing that the mental health needs of black people in the UK require a fundamental reappraisal of current principles in service provision, including shifting the balance of care from professionally based institutional practices to the community.

Relevance of ethnicity in mental health needs assessment

The health needs of the minority ethnic communities in this country are well known.[1] The health status of minority ethnic groups is also well documented.[2] Furthermore, differential patterns of morbidity and iniquitous service use are recognised within minority groups.[1-4] Socioeconomic and 'ethnic' or 'cultural' factors that underlie such discrepancies have been investigated, while less attention is paid to institutional and nosocomial factors in the appropriate recognition of health needs. It would appear that services available in the black community have remained largely inflexible in responding to needs.[4,5]

In the provision of mental health care, for example, factors that determine the production of pathology are perhaps less important than those that influence the definition and subsequent recognition of such pathology. This is certainly true when we try to provide an understanding of the discriminatory nature of health care, as experienced by the black community.[5,6]

In this context, the relevance of needs assessment as currently understood within the central planning, local commissioning and providing of mental health services for minority ethnic groups requires a critical review. For example, there is little in the current procedures around needs assessment and commissioning to suggest that the needs of the black community will be more appropriately recognised and dealt with within the National Health Service.[7] In particular, the plethora of procedures and reforms introduced in the area of mental health care over the past 8 years, such as the 'care programme approach', do not appear to have brought about any significant changes in the experience of black people in relation to psychiatry. If anything, the emphasis being placed on greater control and supervision of psychiatric patients through 'supervision registers' and 'supervised discharge' may lead to a greater entrenchment of ideas of coercion and compulsion in the treatment of black patients. Similarly, the introduction of market forces to health does not appear to have led to an increased awareness of the needs of this section of the community.

Problem of definition

One of the most crucial problems in this area is establishing what constitutes a mental health need. The difficulties in defining mental illness or mental disorder, and the lack of consensual agreement on who requires mental health care, are problems that have bedevilled psychiatry for decades. Within psychiatry there are no reliable or acceptable criteria against which disease or disability can be validly measured and the need for health or social care

agreed.[6,8] Such problems associated with disease or needs definition are clearly more pronounced and intractable in minority
ethnic groups.[9] Largely this is because the process of delineating
mental disorder from mental health is socially constructed and
sanctioned. The boundary between what is seen as disease or
dysfunction on one hand and mental health on the other is often
an arbitrary one, depending on cultural, historical and political
factors.

Cultural factors play a far more significant role in the recognition of mental disorders than they do in the case of physical illnesses.[10] What may be considered as a departure from normative
behaviour or an alteration in emotional and psychological well-
being in one culture may not have the same meaning when
applied to another cultural context. For example, our ideas about
depression or anxiety are crucially determined by the emphasis
placed on culturally and socially incongruent emotional response
in a Western European context. The validity of such categories of
mental disorder in a non-European setting has been questioned
on the basis of cross-cultural studies.[8,10,11] Furthermore, the univer-
sality of psychiatric categorisations, the relevance and validity of
diagnostic groups such as schizophrenia for example, are further
problematised within non-medical approaches to the understanding of human distress. The question being posed here is not merely whether the expressions of mental disorder are culturally or otherwise variant, but whether the very concept of mental illness has
any validity outside particular discourses and specific social and
cultural milieux.

Mental illness as a cultural category

If mental illnesses are cultural categories (ie attribution of pathological significance to certain forms of deviant behaviour in a given
culture, based largely on prevailing notions of normality), then the
dangers of applying such explanatory models to the experiences of
different cultural groups, without any acknowledgement of cultural
differences, are obvious. For example, the use of Western psychiatric norms within non-Western cultures often leads to what Kleinman calls the 'category fallacy', that is the imprecise and often falla-
cious re-creation of a Western model of explanation in a
non-Western setting.[10] Such cultural biases, inherent in psychiatric
diagnoses and nosology, as well as in psychiatric practice, are often
made visible through critical approaches like the new cross-cultural
psychiatry.[12] Whilst the implications of this are obvious when

Western psychiatric practice is exported and made available, for example in Third World settings, the critical weaknesses within psychiatric practice and theory are equally important in the study of non-European people living in the West. Based on this, the applicability of our current diagnoses and approaches to understanding the mental health experiences of black people in this country demand reassessment and revision.

Another problem in the assessment of mental health needs of black people is the uncomfortable overlap between psychiatric practice and the maintenance of social order.[13,14] It is well recognised that those who are seen as most in need of psychiatric care in this country are also those who are structurally and politically disadvantaged, such as women, the unemployed, the low paid, immigrants, and those from minority ethnic groups.[15] The complex relationship between these sociodemographic groups, poverty, the production of ill health, access to service and the experience within psychiatry is often difficult to specify.[16] As in the criminal justice system, for example, the over-representation of these population groups within psychiatric care reveals the normative values and correctional functions of psychiatry. To argue that the high levels of service utilisation by black people accurately predict a need for psychiatric care would make sense only if the social control aspects of psychiatry are dismissed as irrelevant. Therefore, to equate mental health need with epidemiological estimates of treated morbidity could be highly misleading and, unlike in the estimation of medical needs on the basis of demand for treatment, psychiatric treatment conceals social and political biases independent of psychiatric illness. This is particularly relevant to minority ethnic groups, especially the African-Caribbean people who are often inducted into psychiatry through coercive means.[4,11,17]

Towards comprehensive mental health needs

Given the significant problems associated with the validity and reliability of psychiatric diagnosis, and because of the unequal nature of institutional psychiatry as experienced by various minority groups, needs assessment based on diagnosis or service usage is likely to be incorrect. The differential experience of psychiatry by minority ethnic groups, when compared with the majority, makes any attempt to define their mental health needs especially daunting. Our argument is that the established practices of needs assessment, for example based on professional opinion or service evaluation, would be highly misleading when applied to minority groups.

An additional problem is that most of what we know about the mental health of black people in this country is based on service usage at specialist level, and the lack of research or empirical data relating to the more common mental health experiences within the black community will hamper comprehensive needs assessment.[1] The usual premise in health needs assessment is that observations from institutional or specialist care will inform us of morbidity patterns in the community at large. However, such a relationship between specialist care and what may be happening in the community at large cannot be assumed to be true for the mental health of minority ethnic groups. It is recognised that there is a general problem with establishing the nature of psychiatric morbidity at different levels in the pathway to psychiatric care.[18] More specifically, there may be qualitative differences in the presentation of mental illness in the general population and at primary care.[11] A related problem is that the normative concepts and experiences of mental health within different minority groups are not established with any certainty.[19] Therefore, a service-led approach (based on institutional experiences) is unlikely to further our understanding about the nature and extent of mental health problems in the black community. It can be argued that the validity of professional opinion in relation to mental health or illness is likely to become increasingly problematic as we move further away from the hospital setting, given that our current definitions about what constitutes mental illness are largely derived from hospital practice. Consequently, the concept of needs assessment becomes increasingly tentative if needs and their assessment are understood from an exclusively medical or institutional perspective.

Defining ethnicity

The definition of ethnicity or race, like the definition of what constitutes mental health need or mental illness, is equally problematic and it is often difficult to identify a reliable or valid set of criteria on the basis of which such demarcations of population groups could be achieved. Recently there has been increasing acknowledgement of the need to desegregate the terms race, ethnicity and culture, which until now have been viewed as synonymous within health and social sciences.[20] This debate allows, perhaps for the first time in contemporary discourses on race and ethnicity, the possibility of a more complex and historically informed analysis of the relationship between health status and cultural categories.

In a similar vein, the uniformity that is often assumed in relation to 'ethnic minorities' or 'Asians' or 'African-Caribbeans' begins to fall apart when the mental health needs of these populations are examined. There is, for example, increasing evidence of the variability and heterogeneity of mental health needs among subgroups within such communities, as well as differential patterns of relationship with service providers. Unfortunately, current discourses and programmes established under the general theme of ethnicity and health fail to acknowledge these difficulties. If we view both mental illness and ethnicity as uniform, reliable and valid categories, which could be defined, applied and measured in the same way as other indices of health status or determinants of ill health or disability, any attempt to provide a uniform strategy to establish mental health needs, applied across minority ethnic groups, is bound to fail.

Conflicts in determining mental health needs

Another problem that is often overlooked in the assessment of health care needs in general, and in minority ethnic groups in particular, is the conflict of interests between users and providers of health care services. Nowhere is it more explicit than in the area of mental health care.[21] On the one hand, the professional views of the commissioners and providers are largely based on the notion that there is continuing and often unrecognised health care need which is best addressed by more health care interventions. On the other hand, the views of the majority of mental health service users appear to be that they need less in the form of treatment and more preventive and supportive strategies to deal with what are primarily seen as social problems.[22] In fact, the link between the discriminatory conditions under which the minority ethnic groups live and the mental health consequences of this are more readily acknowledged in these communities than amongst service providers at large. In addition, while the black users and their carers are more aware of the iniquitous nature of mental health services and institutional responses, professional positions remain largely unaltered. Furthermore, the views of the community are further interpreted as evidence of pathology within ethnic minority people.[15] It is inevitable that such a conflict, in perceptions and ideology, will lead to divergent views on what constitutes the priorities in mental health care for the minority groups.

Epidemiologically based mental health needs assessment

Some of the issues outlined above can be further highlighted by an examination of service utilisation data. The epidemiology of mental disorders in the minority ethnic groups in this country is under-researched. What constitutes present knowledge in this field is primarily a product of hospital statistics. The relevance and validity of such information is highly problematic. This, however, has not deterred psychiatrists from pursuing ethnic patterns of mental illness, largely consistent with earlier theories based on racial types.[5,23] Such an approach continues to generate much argument about the robustness of the research findings and, more important, about the ideology of psychiatric research in relation to ethnicity.[16,24]

In the context of specifying the mental health needs of minority ethnic groups, it will be of interest to identify some of these patterns of service use. We present findings from an epidemiological survey carried out in west Birmingham, an area with a substantial minority ethnic population. The main aim of the study was to provide estimates and determinants of psychiatric morbidity at all levels of psychiatric care, from the general population to specialist setting. One of our hypotheses was that reliance on hospital data alone would distort the understanding of the overall mental health needs of minority groups because of powerful selection factors that operate in determining entry into care and in defining mental disorders, so any assessment of mental health needs based on such easily measurable service activity will be

Table 1. Period prevalence rates by ethnicity (Goldberg & Huxley 'pathways to care' model): depressive and neurotic disorders

		Asians		Blacks		Whites	
		Rates	Ratio	Rates	Ratio	Rates	Ratio
LEVEL 4	Psychiatric services total*	29		20		46	
Filter 3	Decision to refer		38.2		18.1		16.8
LEVEL 3	Primary care	1,108		361		771	
Filter 2	Conspicuous case recognition		2.7		3.7		2.0
LEVEL 2	Primary care total	2,943		1,341		1,542	
Filter 1	Decision to consult		1.3		1.6		1.8
LEVEL 1	Community	3,720		2,140		2,740	

Rates/10,000/1 month
*Includes only those using specialist mental health services with case register diagnoses of depressive or neurotic disorders.

biased and is unlikely to provide a true picture on the basis of which rational allocation of resources could be made.

Our results show that reliance on hospital or service utilisation data alone will not give a true picture of the extent or nature of mental health needs in the community (Table 1). In our study, mental health problems (excluding severe mental illness) were not only more common among Asians but Asians were also more likely than either blacks or whites to consult their GPs. However, at the GP level, white people were more likely than either Asians or blacks (for whom case recognition was particularly poor) to have their mental health problems recognised.[25] When it came to referral to the specialist service, black people were more likely than the other two groups to pass through the interface between primary and secondary care (filter 3), and those referred were largely designated as having severe mental disorder.

Asians, in contrast, were under-represented in overall prevalence rates for treated mental disorders, including psychosis and affective disorders (Table 2). African-Caribbeans are over-represented in these categories, except for affective disorders where their risk in comparison with the whites is on a par with that of Asians.[26]

We also confirmed the trend for African-Caribbeans to have a greater risk of hospital admission than others, especially for psychosis, and the magnitude of such risk is greatest for compulsory admissions. However, on the basis of these data, or similar findings from hospital based studies, it would be inappropriate to conclude that any specific pattern of mental health need has been established, any more than it could be argued that Asians as a group underutilise service or African-Caribbeans have increased

Table 2. Period prevalence rates by ethnicity: all diagnoses

		Asians		Blacks		Whites	
		Rates	Ratio	Rates	Ratio	Rates	Ratio
LEVEL 6	Compulsorily detained inpatients*	1		14		3	
Filter 5	Section under Mental Health Act		6.0		1.5		4.0
LEVEL 5	Psychiatric inpatients	6		21		12	
Filter 4	Decision to admit		16.0		10.5		12.3
LEVEL 4	Psychiatric services total	96		220		148	

Rates/10,000/1 month
*Includes only those using specialist mental health services with case register diagnoses of depressive or neurotic disorders.

mental health morbidity compared with whites. Alternative explanations are possible, such as: Asians indeed have lower levels of what psychiatrists consider to be treatable illnesses and African-Caribbeans are more likely than whites to be referred to service, irrespective of their mental health needs. Similar findings were reported from the fourth national survey on ethnic minorities,[11] from which it was also concluded that those born or educated in Britain had much poorer mental health than their counterparts who migrated to Britain at an older age.[11] The only way to pursue these competing hypotheses would be to shift the focus of research to the population at large or to the use of primary care service and evaluate the experience of black users, once they have been inducted into psychiatric care. Until such studies are undertaken, which we argue are a prerequisite for appropriate needs assessment, there must remain doubts about the nature and extent of provisions for mental health care in minority ethnic groups.

Conclusion

There are no compelling reasons to think that the current interest in needs assessment will by itself herald a renewed engagement in the area of health and ethnicity. This is particularly true in mental health care where the current theories and practices appear to discriminate against this section of the population. One of the major problems in this context is the continued reliance on culturally specified notions about what constitutes mental health need and the use of indices of institutional care, which merely reflect the problems of conventional practice. In establishing mental health needs in minority ethnic groups, the most productive strategy for commissioners and providers of services would be to extend the current needs assessment exercise to include black service users and carers, and to abandon the reliance on hospital based statistics alone.

References

1 Cochrane R, Sashidharan SP. Mental health and ethnic monorities: a review of literature and implications for services. In: *Ethnicity and health*. York: NHS Centre for Reviews and Dissemination, 1996.
2 Ahmed W, ed. *Race and health in contemporary Britain*. Buckingham: Open University Press, 1993.
3 NHS Executive Mental Health Task Force. *Black mental health: a dialogue for change*. London: Department of health, 1992.
4 Wilson M. *Mental health and Britain's black communities*. London: King's Fund, 1993.

5   Fernando S. *Mental health, race and culture.* London: MIND, 1991.
6   Littlewood R, Lipsedge M. *Aliens and alienists: ethnic minorities and psychiatry.* Harmondsworth: Penguin, 1989.
7   Wing JK. Mental illness. In: Stevens A, Raftery J, eds. *Health care needs assessment.* Oxford: Radcliffe, 1995.
8   Kleinman A. Anthropology and psychiatry: the role of culture in cross-cultural research on illness. *British Journal of Psychiatry* 1989; **151**: 447–54.
9   Littlewood R. Psychiatric diagnosis and racial bias: empirical and interpretive approaches. *Social Science and Medicine* 1992; **34**: 141–9.
10 Kleinman A. *Rethinking psychiatry: from cultural category to personal experience.* New York: The Free Press, 1998.
11 Nazroo J. *Ethnicity and mental health.* London: Policy Studies Institute, 1997.
12 Littlewood R. From categories to contexts: a decade of the new cross-cultural psychiatry. *British Journal of Psychiatry* 1994; **156**: 308–27.
13 Mercer K. Black communities' experience of psychiatric services. *International Journal of Social Psychiatry* 1984; **30**: 22–7.
14 Black Health Workers and Patient Group. *Psychiatry and the Corporate State, Race and Culture* 1983; **25**: 505–12.
15 Cochrane R. *The social creation of mental illness.* London: Longman, 1983.
16 Smaaje C. *Health, race and ethnicity: making sense of the evidence.* London: King's Fund, 1995.
17 Davies S, Thornicroft G, Leese M, *et al.* Ethnic differences in risk of compulsory psychiatric admission among representative cases of psychosis in London. *British Medical Journal* 1996; **312**: 533–7.
18 Thornicroft G, Brewin CR, Wing J. *Measuring mental health needs.* London: Gaskell/Royal College of Psychiatrists, 1992.
19 Belippa J. *Illness or distress?* London: Confederation of Indian Organisations, 1991.
20 Senior PA, Bhopal R. Ethnicity as a variable in epidemiological research. *British Medical Journal* 1994; **309**: 327–30.
21 Chamberlin J. *On our own: patient-controlled alternatives to the mental health system.* London: MIND, 1988.
22 Institute of Race Relations. *Community care: the black experience.* London: Institute of Race Relations, 1993.
23 Sashidharan SP. Afro-Caribbeans and schizophrenia: the ethnic vulnerability hypothesis re-examined. *International Review of Psychiatry* 1993; **5**: 129–44.
24 Sashidharan SP, Francis E. Epidemiology, ethnicity and schizophrenia. In: Ahmad WIU, ed. *'Race' and health in contemporary Britain.* Buckingham: Open University Press, 1993.
25 McCormick A, Fleming D, Charlton J. *Morbidity statistics from general practice.* Fourth national study 1991–1992. London: HMSO, 1995.
26 Commander MJ, Sashidharan SP, Odell SM, Surtess PG. Access to mental health care in an inner-city health district. II. Association with demographic factors. *British Journal of Psychiatry* 1997; **170**: 317–20.

20 | Refugees

Ghada Karmi
Visiting Professor, University of North London

Within the health service the subject of refugees has not tradition-ally been viewed with interest. Doctors in Britain, whether working as general practitioners (GPs) or in hospital, are not formally trained in the health care of migrants and refugees.[1] They know little about the legal status or rights of refugees and many do not realise that they are entitled to NHS services. There is anecdotal evidence that some GPs are unwilling to accept refugee patients, who are regarded as a burden requiring excess time and facilities. There is a pervasive view that refugee issues are boring and low status, and that refugee health care is primarily a charitable activity better suited to the paramedical and social services. Furthermore, it is widely thought that refugees constitute for the health service a peripheral concern which does not require special attention. Worldwide the numbers of refugees and asylum seekers have increased dramatically over the past decade, and now constitute a problem of enormous magnitude for the countries where they seek refuge. This increase is mainly felt in the poor countries of Asia and Africa: only 5% of the world's 18.8 million refugees seek asylum in the industrialised world.[2] Britain and the rest of Europe are feeling the strain as well. In Western Europe, 540,000 asylum seekers were registered in 1991 – nearly twice the 1989 figure and more than three times that of 1987. The conflict in the former Yugoslavia has led to the largest refugee crisis since the Second World War, and all European countries are affected by it.[3]

Britain scores ninth on the list of Western European asylum coun-tries, with a ratio of 1 refugee to 4,962 inhabitants (in Sweden the ratio in 1989 was 1 in 100),[2] but here too the refugee flows have increased dramatically. Since 1988 the number of refugees arriving in the UK has gone up by 500%; in 1996 the Home Office recorded 28,000 asylum applications, excluding dependants but including a growing proportion of unaccompanied refuge children.[4] In 1993

there were 22,370 applications for asylum and about 250 unaccompanied refugee children were admitted here, though the latter
figure is not exact.[5] The conflict in the Balkans has added to this
picture; in the 3 months between September and December of
1992, some 300 Albanian refugees arrived in Britain from Kosovo
every week.[6] Greater London is the major destination for refugees.
Over 90% of all asylum seekers in Britain settle there. In 1989 the
now disbanded London Strategic Policy Unit estimated that there
were 127,930 refugees in London, but exact numbers are difficult to
obtain because there is no official source of local statistics. In 1992 it
was estimated that there was a total of 116,000 asylum seekers in the
North London health regions, mostly living in inner city districts.[7]
These numbers have certainly increased since then and did not in
any case include people from Bosnia. Other major refugee centres
are Brighton, Lothian and Strathclyde, Merseyside, Tyneside,
Cardiff and South Wales, the West Midlands (with the biggest numbers at 4,000–5,000), and Greater Manchester.[5] The numbers (Fig 1)
are not in any sense overwhelming and should pose no problem,
but the reality is that refugees present the health and social services
with particular challenges out of all proportion to their actual
population size. Their health care, far from being marginalised,
should be the subject of special attention and interest.

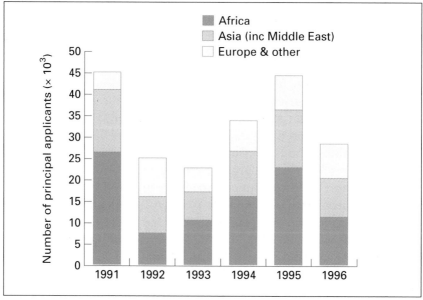

Fig 1. Applications for asylum, 1991–1996 (Source: Home Office 1997)

Health problems of refugees

Since refugee health has traditionally not featured as an important part of health care, it is not surprising that the information available on these health issues in the countries of resettlement is haphazard and has tended to focus on specific areas. The best covered of these is the psychological aspect, which is not unexpected since many refugees suffer from the stress of insecurity and the effects of persecution, often having been tortured or physically abused.[8] There are also physical health problems related to the countries of origin and the experience of becoming a refugee. In addition to all this, refugees will encounter difficulties of access to the services because of language problems and unfamiliarity with British systems.[9] They are likely to face the health consequences of unemployment and poverty. All these factors are accentuated in the case of unaccompanied refugee children, many of whom end up with poorly resourced local authorities which cannot properly cope with their special problems.[10]

Thus, the health problems and hence needs of refugees are a complex mixture of physical, psychological, social and legal factors which requires a proper response from the health and social services. This has hitherto not been forthcoming in Britain and the approach to refugee issues has been largely negative. Refugees are viewed as passive and helpless, in need of charity and unable to participate for themselves in the provision of health care. But nothing could be further from the truth. It has been argued that refugees are extraordinary people, resilient survivors who suc-ceeded in escaping from intolerable situations.[11] Many of them are educated and competent and would not have left their countries if they had had a choice. All this argues, therefore, for a positive approach to refugee health issues that recognises refugees' strengths and recruits them in their own health care.

Physical health

Because the final health picture in refugees is a complex of physical, psychological and environmental factors, it is difficult to classify their health problems in purely physical terms. However, a useful classification of refugee health problems has been produced that divides the refugee situation into a number of stages and these will ultimately define the service needs of refugees.[12] This classific-ation poses a series of questions. First, before becoming refugees, were the people rural or urban dwellers? Second, what was their nutritional status in the home country and what was the type of disease to which they were exposed? Third, what were their previous lifestyles, culture and education? This will shape the refugees' acceptance and expectations of health care practices in the new environment. Fourth, what caused the refugee crisis, and was this political conflict or famine, or both?

Each of these possibilities will have health implications. The young and the elderly are likely to be the most vulnerable, but women refugees also carry a disproportionate share of the problems of displacement.[13] They invariably have the care of the children, have often been sexually abused in prison, in flight, or as a part of torture, and are often faced with greater responsibilities due to the breakdown in traditional family and community structures.

As far as refugees in Britain are concerned, there is little information on their physical health when they arrive since there is no systematic health screening here. Routine screening at the port of entry would be helpful in identifying the epidemiology of physical conditions among asylum seekers and lead to appropriate action that treats both the incoming refugee and the host population. While this has been the practice in several other countries for some time, most notably Australia[14] and North America,[15] Britain has lagged far behind.

As things stand, asylum seekers (and other migrants) entering the country are assessed by immigration officers and it is only at their discretion that some are referred to the port health authorities. Since immigration officers are not trained health professionals, the process is haphazard and will of necessity miss out some cases. Small, unpublished surveys of groups of refugees coming into Britain have suggested that the problems vary in incidence and type depending on the particular group. There is no overall physical refugee health problem as such, though some common experiences will dictate a similar outcome. For example, many refugees will have undergone physical hardship, often extreme, during their flight from the zone of persecution or war. Before reaching Britain they may also have had stopovers in several countries where they suffered further privation and exposure to infection, hunger and disease. In Somalia, for example, high mortality rates were reported among civilians and refugees due to famine, malnutrition and preventable infectious disease.[15] This would argue for a far more rigorous screening policy for refugees at the ports of entry into Britain to assess the prevalence and severity of these health hazards. It is certainly the impression of infectious disease experts in London that the recent rise in reported cases of tuberculosis is in part due to the high incidence of this disease in the refugee population.[16] The situation is aggravated by the lack of adequate health care services available to refugees in the countries of transit.

Anecdotal evidence suggests that a proportion of refugees arrive with diseases endemic in their countries of origin. Cases of malaria, hepatitis B and HIV/AIDS have been reported, but their true incidence in refugees in Britain is unknown. In 1993 the Refugee Council appointed a special worker for asylum seekers with HIV and AIDS in recognition of the special difficulties that this group might face when trying to get treatment. During a conference on refugee health held in London in 1992, Olatunbosun and Hirst reported on the problems refugees face in revealing their infection with HIV; this is bound up with fears of losing their asylum application and even fear of asking for tests.

Physical torture plays an important part in the causation of ill health in refugees. Depending on the type of torture employed, refugees have been left with a variety of physical disabilities. These commonly include the after effects of burns, musculoskeletal disorders, and damage to the genitals, especially in men. This may lead to a bewildering variety of symptoms, impossible to unravel unless the health professional is already aware of the possibility of torture. Most refugees will not admit to having been tortured and may consult the doctor repeatedly with vague and undefined symptoms that defy diagnosis. These will frequently be aggravated by psychological stress, thus making the final presentation even more complicated. The separate subject of stress in refugees is important and will be dealt with in more detail below.

Little is known about drug and alcohol use among refugees in Britain. It is reported that Vietnamese arrivals to Britain from refugee camps in Hong Kong exhibited a drug problem, which led to the establishment of a special hostel in 1992 for the treatment of severe addiction. Somali refugees seem also to have imported khat with them, a drug new to Britain. This is a plant cultivated in East Africa and Yemen and has mildly stimulant properties. It is said to cause depression and psychosis when used in large doses. Whereas in the home countries it has widely accepted social use, it has become addictive over here. Refugee groups put this down to the high level of unemployment and social problems among refugee men.[17] The use of khat is not illegal in this country, and there is as yet no significant lobby working to ban its importation.

Mental health

There is a considerable literature on the mental health of

refugees,[8,18] in striking contrast to the dearth of material on other health aspects. All refugees are likely to experience some form of psychological disturbance as a result of their experiences. The effects of displacement on the mental health of refugees can be profound. Many asylum seekers, already traumatised, are subjected to a hostile reception from the authorities or even detention at the port of entry. The problem is often then exacerbated by a long wait for a decision on their asylum application. In 1987 the British Refugee Council, as it was then, estimated that it took the Home Office an average of 53 weeks to deal with such applications, but many people had to wait for 18 months and sometimes for longer than 2 years.[19]

Several factors have been identified as significant in the development of mental illness in displaced persons:[20] language difficulties, family separation, hostility from the host population, and traumatic experience prior to displacement. The way in which refugees cope with this mixture of factors is dependent on individual adaptability and what may be termed psychological strength. Many refugees cope well with the trauma of flight from their home country but are more vulnerable to pressures and problems in the new society in which they have sought refuge.

Knowledge of the language and familiarity with official systems can be of enormous help and, conversely, lack of these will aggravate existing problems and cause increased stress. Adaptation to a new environment is known to be stressful for all migrants, including those who wish to move from one country to another.[21] Several aspects are involved. Individuals have to learn to adapt to the new culture while shedding their own. The successful balance between these two determines the psychological outcome. The adaptation strategy employed may lead to assimilation, integration or separation/marginalisation, and the behavioural shift necessary to accomplish any of these will influence the degree of cultural stress. The stress manifestations that can result, include anxiety, depression, feelings of alienation, and a variety of psychosomatic symptoms. On occasion the stress may lead to suicide.[22]

Many refugees lack a sense of identity with the new society they live in and are unable to form a clear relationship with it. This derives from what has been described as a form of bereavement among exiled individuals.[23] They lose positive reinforcement of the self which normally comes from a person's roots, status within the original society, and emotional support there.

Adapting to a new environment requires an understanding of the new values and relating one's own identity to these in order to find a place within the society of adoption. Refugees are probably the group least able to do this, since their sense of identity and security will have been profoundly affected by variable periods of violent uprooting and displacement in circumstances of persecution. This leads to stress and grief, the expression of which is often misinterpreted as 'post-traumatic stress disorder',[8,24] especially in refugees from non-Western societies. Misdiagnosis of the true causes of this form of stress may lead to inappropriate treatment and aggravate the original condition. Cultural understanding is essential for therapists trying to deal with these patients, and the explanations of refugees themselves for their symptoms are more important than preconceived views which therapists may have.

To this catalogue of misfortunes faced by refugees must be added the effects of hostility on the part of the host population. While there are well publicised reports in Europe, especially Germany, of extreme forms of rejection of refugees by their 'hosts', the picture in Britain is less clear. Refugee groups have complained repeatedly that their members face discrimination in housing, health and social services, and newspapers have given publicity to the sufferings to which refugees in government detention centres are subjected.[25] Discrimination, whatever its extent, will in any case be aggravated by refugees' powerlessness in the face of language difficulty, ignorance of British systems, legal uncertainties and lack of money. The difficulties that refugees experience will be exacerbated by the knowledge that they have merely fled from one form of persecution to another. Instead of resolving their problems, the new country will have presented them with new ones that will increase their feelings of stress and isolation.

The question of racism in the provision of mental health services has frequently been raised with regard to ethnic communities.[26] There is evidence to show that Afro-Caribbean people are over-represented in the compulsory admission statistics to mental hospitals in Britain, and it has been suggested that this is more connected with racism than an actual increase in psychiatric morbidity.[27,28] However, it is not unusual that compulsory admission becomes necessary because psychiatric symptoms are not detected and properly dealt with at an early stage of the illness. There is also anecdotal and case-study evidence to indicate that racism may occur in the diagnosis and treatment of refugees. The use of Western diagnostic criteria may be inappropriate for many refugee groups, and a cultural understanding of their societal values and norms will be crucial for the provision of effective treatments and services. The findings of the fourth national survey of ethnic minorities suggest that Western assessment of psychiatric illness is inappropriate for use among culturally different groups.[29] Here again, involving refugees themselves in the mental health care of their communities should prove of value.

Informal surveys of refugees arriving in Britain have revealed that a majority of them suffer from stress, anxiety or depression. The refugees attributed most of these problems to events in their home country, but also to unemployment and uncertainty about their future in Britain. They mentioned money problems, feelings of isolation and difficulties with housing. Most reported feelings of homesickness, but these tended to decrease as time passed. Refugees who were in employment and spoke good English experienced significantly less of these feelings. A study in Lewisham in London found high levels of stress and anxiety among refugees;[28] about one-third of the sample said they wanted some form of counselling. Another study among Eritrean refugees reported that two-thirds were suffering from severe depression;[30] the causes cited for this included loneliness, alienation from British culture, lack of support and lack of skills to help them settle in Britain, and it was these factors rather than the pre-exile experiences that were the more significant.

The psychosocial effects on refugees of violence deserve special mention. This is one of the main themes in the life histories of refugees with serious somatic and psychological consequences,[31] yet few health professionals in this country are trained to care for such conditions. A training course set up by the author in 1991 for London GPs with refugee patients, which included special sessions on the mental health of refugees, was very poorly attended.[1] A pre-course postal questionnaire comprising questions about GPs' competence in refugee health care and their need for further training was sent to 600 London GPs. The majority of respondents believed that they had low competence in this area and expressed an interest in attending a specialist training course, particularly on torture and psychological trauma. Of the 3,906 GPs invited to the course, which was tailored to suit their needs as identified through the questionnaire survey, only 33 registered to attend. This low response could not be attributed to lack of publicity for the course, and it was concluded that the health care of ethnic minorities in general and refugees in particular remained for most GPs a low-priority professional topic. This is a matter of concern, since failure to recognise and treat refugee patients who have been victims of violence early enough can lead to long-term psychopathology.[32]

Access to health care services

There is a widely held view among refugee groups and some health professionals that refugees have problems of access to health services.[9] This poor access is likely to be responsible for their health difficulties, rather than any excess incidence of physical or mental disease. Although most refugees are registered with a GP, anecdotal reports suggest that they have difficulty in getting the time and attention they need, especially in relation to psychological problems. In recognition of this, some health authorities have appointed a worker to coordinate GP activity with refugees. The problems of access derive from a number of key factors. First among these is the lack of English language competence, which means that refugees cannot describe their health problems or ask for the services they require. This leads to the need for interpreters, which can be expensive and difficult to arrange, and this in turn leads to a reluctance to provide this service. Informal interpreters, such as children or other relatives, then become the norm, which is unsatisfactory. To avoid the problem, many refugees may desist from consulting for minor ailments, which then become chronic and more difficult to treat.

Lack of awareness of refugee cultures by health professionals leads to superficial stereotyping of groups and deters from learning about them. This is often compounded by ignorance of refugees' legal rights and a belief that 'they are lucky to get what they can'. There is a plethora of anecdotes about the insensitivity and misunderstandings in the health service, especially in primary care. Many refugees complain that GPs are unsympathetic, have no time to listen to them, and only want to treat one problem at a time, thus failing to understand the complexity of the refugee experience. GPs tend to prescribe medicines rather than spend time diagnosing and investigating the causes of symptoms with which refugees present. Because of the tendency towards somatisation in refugees, this omission is more serious than it might be for other patients.[33] It has to be said that GPs working in inner city 'refugee areas' are under considerable constraints and themselves require support and resources.[34]

Many refugees do not know their rights to health care, and this impedes their access to services. In a study of Somali and Eritrean refugee women in Haringey, many of those receiving income support were paying for their prescriptions, unaware that they were exempt from payment.[35] Those living in temporary accommodation were often not registered with a GP at all. Likewise, many believed that not having refugee documents meant that they were not entitled to GP or other health services. Refugees from non-Western countries are unfamiliar with Western medical concepts and with the range of treatment on offer. This applies especially to counselling and psychotherapy services, which are not formalised in non-Western societies, and where emotional support from the family and other members of the community is perceived as the most appropriate solution for psychological problems.

There is little firm information on refugees' access to health care in this country. The foregoing account has made a theoretical case for why access to this group of patients might be restricted. But we know next to nothing about refugees' uptake of preventive services, of primary or secondary care, or psychiatric services. Refugee elders, small numerically but with special needs, do not feature in any surveys or official figures on community care. This dearth of information is in part due to the way in which routine statistics are collected in Britain, without any indication of ethnic origin of the service user. It is also a reflection of the low priority hitherto accorded to this area of health care. This approach will have to be abandoned if service needs of refugees are to be properly assessed.

A number of local, often small-scale, projects for refugees have been set up to respond to their needs. These have attracted modest funding from statutory health bodies. For example, the Department of Health provided funding in 1993 for small projects with the Somali community. The Regional Health and Ethnicity Programme has funded a number of refugee projects in the two North Thames regions. The Medical Foundation for the Care of Victims of Torture is a charitable organisation responding to refugees' mental health needs; local specialist clinics on the same lines are badly needed for refugee groups with mental stress. There are also a number of interpreting and advocacy projects for ethnic minorities, many of which include refugees. Unpaid volunteers are often recruited to provide this service and the overall situation is unsatisfactory. Among the larger initiatives in health authorities, two merit attention: the Vietnamese mental health project at Tooting and the Haringey refugee development project at Enfield and Haringey Health Authority. The Vietnamese project is concerned with improving mental health services for refugees from Vietnam, and the Haringey project aims to conduct needs assessment on five major refugee groups in the district.

Need for a national strategy

For the reasons set out above, I believe that the specific health needs of refugees require special attention; in Britain today there is no comprehensive health and service strategy to cater for them, the current situation being *ad hoc* and unsatisfactory. On entering the country, migrants and asylum seekers are randomly referred for health screening according to the judgement of the immigration officer, who is not medically trained. Thereafter, those who have not been detained at the port of entry, pending clarification of their status, are supposed to receive health care in the health district where they will reside.

Many do not stay at the address to which they first go and are lost to follow-up by the public health services. No outreach services exist to trace them and offer them help. The initiatives set up to provide refugee health care are the result of random interest in some health authorities, and many of these duplicate each other's work since there has hitherto been no coordination of work in this field.

In order to provide appropriate services for this important group, we need to take several steps. First, assemble accurate refugee statistics at local level (the current situation whereby health districts have no exact demographic figures on their refugee populations is unsatisfactory and makes provision of services unnecessarily difficult). Second, ensure equality of access by refugees to the services. Third, provide appropriate training for staff in refugee health. The participation of refugees themselves in all these areas is essential.[36] Such a response by the NHS will require intersectoral coordination, extra funding and, above all, commitment.

There is much official comment on the necessity of providing equality of access to our ethnic population, of which refugees form a part,[37,38] but these good intentions need to percolate downwards into the service as a whole. Furthermore, proper health provision for refugees will not be cheap and, in today's economic and political climate, increased public spending will not be popular.

A health care strategy that draws all these strands together is urgently needed. Such a strategy should include a code of practice for screening at the ports of entry into Britain, and a plan for the aftercare of refugees in primary and secondary care. Examples of good practice are already appearing and should be incorporated into national guidelines. One GP practice in central London has begun, with health authority help, to run a separate walk-in service

for refugees who are not registered with a GP.[39] This includes a
health visitor and interpreters and is proving highly successful.
The clinic now attracts refugee patients from surrounding practices who find the facilities useful, and the experiment has raised
the question of whether a separate service for refugees, with
specially trained staff, might be the method of choice for treating
this group of patients. This and similar questions should form part
of a national debate on refugee health, in which refugees
themselves should participate.

If the issue of refugee health care is not addressed in this way,
refugees will continue to be seen as a burden and a problem for
the health service. Initiatives will be duplicated in different parts
of the country, which is wasteful of effort and expense. For a long
time, the problem of refugees was ignored in the hope that it
would somehow go away. Given the explosion in the flow of displaced people from areas of conflict throughout the world, such
an attitude is a luxury that no one can any longer afford.

References

1 Karmi G. Educating London doctors in migration and health: a new
   initiative. *International Migration* 1992; **30**: 131–9.
2 US Committee on Refugees. *World refugee survey 1989 in review.* Washington: US Committee on Refugees, 1990: 30–4.
3 Burke A, Macdonald G. The former Yugoslavia conflict. In: Cranna
   M, ed. *The true cost of conflict.* London: Earthscan, 1994.
4 Home Office. *Asylum statistics UK 1996.* London: Government
   Statistical Service, 1997.
5 The Refugee Council. Statistics obtained from the Home Office, 1994.
6 The Refugee Council. *Refugees from Bosnia, Serbia and Croatia.* London: Refugee Council, 1992.
7 Karmi G, Awiah T. *Refugees and the National Health Service.* London:
   NW/NE Thames Regional Health Authorities, 1992.
8 Silove D, Sinnerbrink I, Field A, *et al.* Anxiety, depression and PTSD
   in asylum-seekers: association with pre-migration trauma and post-
   migration stressors. *British Journal of Psychiatry* 1997; **170**: 351–7.
9 Department of Health. *On the state of the public health.* Chief Medical
   Officer report for 1991. London: HMSO, 1992.
10 Jockenhovel-Schiecke H, ed. *Unaccompanied refugee children in Europe:
   experience with protection, placement and education.* Frankfurt: European
   Standing Committee on Unaccompanied Refugee Children, 1990.
11 Muecke MA. New paradigms for refugee health problems. *Social
   Science and Medicine* 1992; **35**: 515–23.
12 Dick B. Disease of refugees: causes, effects and control. *Transactions of
   the Royal Society of Tropical Medicine and Hygiene* 1984; **78**: 734–41.
13 Bonnerjea L. *Shaming the world: the needs of women refugees.* London:
   Change and World University Service, 1985.

14 Reid JC, Goldestein GB, Keo L. Refugee medical screening in NSW: refugee welfare versus public risk? *Community Health Studies* 1986; **10**: 265–74.

15 Forbes S. *The refugee health care system.* Background paper on policies, programs and concerns. Washington DC: Refugee Policy Group, 1982.

16 McEvoy M. Personal communication,1993.

17 Black P. Khat is legal, it's addictive and it's destroying our men's lives. *Voice* 1993; August 24: 14–5.

18 UNHCR (Refugee Policy Group). *Selected bibliography on refugee health.* Geneva: UNHCR, 1991.

19 British Refugee Council. *Setting for a future: proposals for a British policy on refugees.* London: BRC, 1987.

20 Holtzman WH, Bornemann TH, eds. *Mental health of immigrants and refugees.* Austin: University of Texas, 1990.

21 Berry JW, Kim U, Minde T, *et al.* Comparative studies of acculturative stress. *International Migration Review* 1987; **21**: 491–512.

22 Karmi G, Abdulrahim D, Pierpoint T, *et al. Suicide among ethnic minorities and refugees in the United Kingdom.* London: Health and Ethnicity Programme, 1992.

23 Munoz L. Exile as bereavement: socio-psychological manifestations of Chilean exiles in Great Britain. In: *Mental health and exile.* Seminar Report. London: World University Service, 1978.

24 Eisenbruch M. From post-traumatic stress disorder to cultural bereavement: diagnosis of Southeast Asian refugees. *Social Science and Medicine* 1991; **33**: 673–80.

25 *The Independent* March 25: 1994. There have been numerous other articles on the same subject in *The Guardian.*

26 Fernando S. *Race and culture in psychiatry.* London: Croom Helm, 1988.

27 McGovern D, Cope R. First psychiatric admission notes of first and second generation Afro-Caribbean. *Social Psychiatry* 1987; **22**: 139–49.

28 Balloch S, Bright J. *Refugees in the inner city.* London: Centre for Inner City Studies, Goldsmith College, 1993.

29 Nazroo J. *Ethnicity and mental health.* London: Policy Studies Institute, 1997.

30 Michael TT. Research report on an exploratory study of psychological factors among Eritrean refugees. *Refugee mental health.* October 3 Seminar paper. London: Healthy Islington 2000, 1990.

31 Barker R, ed. *The psychological problems of refugees.* London: British Refugee Council and European Consultation on Refugees and Exiles, 1983: 14–21.

32 National Institute of Mental Health. *Mental health services for refugees.* US Department of Health and Human Services, 1991: 205–18.

33 Mumford DB. Detection of psychiatric disorders among Asian patients presenting with somatic symptoms. *British Journal of Hospital Medicine* 1992; **47**: 202–4.

34 Department of Health. *Making London better.* London: Department of Health, 1993.

35 Bernard-Jones S. *Qualitative assessment study of Somali and Eritrean refugee women in Haringey.* London: Haringey Health Authority, 1992.

36 Dick B, Simmonds S. Primary health care with refugees: between the idea and the reality. *Tropical Doctor* 1985; **15**: 2–7.
37 Department of Health. *Press release H92/351*. London: Department of Health, 1992.
38 Department of Health. *Press release H93/723*. London: Department of Health, 1993.
39 Moghissi A. London general practitioners. Personal communication, 1994.

Part 2

CONSUMER EXPERIENCES

21 | The MACHEM experience

Gilroy Ferguson

Clinical Consultant, Personal Performance Consultants UK Ltd,
Manchester
Former Chair, Manchester Action Committee on Healthcare for
Ethnic Minorities

The Department of Health recognises that 'the health of minority ethnic communities needs to be given careful attention'. The Chief Medical Officer's report for 1991 pointed out that the National Health Service (NHS) must address the particular needs of ethnic minorities living in this country and take positive steps to eliminate discrimination.[1]

Although minority ethnic people have lived in Britain since the 17th century, most have settled here since the 1950s and 1960s. As they have become a significant part of British society different patterns of illness, disease and health care needs have become apparent. This has to be seen in the context of Western medicine, being essentially Eurocentric. The illness pattern among minority ethnic people in the UK may not have changed significantly over the years but, owing to the absence of adequate research and the sparsity of systematic data collection and clinical observation within the predominantly white medical establishment in Britain, illnesses may appear to be new or dramatic in their presentation. More recently, as the 1991 report indicates, there is increasing evidence that, when compared with the indigenous white population, people from different racial and cultural backgrounds show different patterns of illness and have different patterns of health needs. It is apparent that in order to maintain health standards the NHS needs to understand the differences and to appreciate the need to enable equitable access to the range of health care facilities that exist. It is also important for health authorities and trusts to recognise that addressing the issue of unequal access to health care is not giving preferential treatment to minority ethnic groups. Like other citizens of this country, minority ethnic people are entitled to expect a service that is in keeping with that outlined in the

Patient's Charter.[2] The delivery of health care on the basis of equal
opportunities is therefore necessary to achieve and sustain racial
equality within the health care services.

This chapter sets out to describe the work of the Manchester
Action Committee on Healthcare for Ethnic Minorities
(MACHEM), and its role in the assessment of needs and in
influencing policies affecting the health care of the local ethnic
minority population.

The Manchester context

In discussing examples of good practice in assessing consumers'
experiences, the question of prioritising the different needs will
inevitably arise. For the purpose of this chapter, this discussion will
be presented within the context of the needs of the ethnic
minority communities.

In 1986 the North Western Regional Health Authority
(NWRHA) sought to address issues concerning the health care of
minority ethnic people in the region by issuing guidelines to the
health authorities on how best to implement its strategies.
Although the NWRHA's initiative ought to be commended, it was
clear that the first problem encountered was that the guidelines
were issued without consultation with people from minority
ethnic communities, particularly those from the Caribbean who
had long lived within inner city areas and many of whom were
specifically encouraged to migrate to England to work in the
NHS and other public utilities. Naturally, many from those communities felt that their views were not considered important.
After a series of community based meetings and assistance from
some local elected representatives and the Community Health
Council, a group of people representing a variety of disciplines
and backgrounds came together and formed the organisation
MACHEM which received its first funding through joint finance
arrangements in Manchester in 1991. A full-time manager was
appointed in September 1993 to complement a staff team
comprising a full-time administrator and two part-time
development workers. The organisation therefore relies heavily
on the commitment and skills of its voluntary members.

As a voluntary organisation and a registered charity, the main
aim that MACHEM is constituted to meet is its commitment to
working towards the promotion of equity and the elimination of
discrimination on the grounds of race or religion in the fields of
social care, health care, community care and employment in these

areas. In furtherance of this aim, it seeks to work with agencies in the statutory and voluntary sector.

Why was it essential for an organisation with the above specific aims to be established in Manchester?

At that time, the minority ethnic population made up about 12% of the total population of Manchester, with African-Caribbean people a significant proportion. In the 1991 census, 16% of people classified themselves as being from a minority ethnic community, of which 5% are African-Caribbean.

Because of the diverse ethnic groups within the 12%, it was important to have an organisation that could reflect as broad a view as possible about health needs as they affect this section of the population. Furthermore, as most of these communities lived within the inner city areas, with associated social deprivation and unemployment, it was recognised that neither health nor local authorities were responding appropriately to their needs.

The purpose of setting up MACHEM was twofold:

- to act as a group to raise awareness of the specific health care needs of these diverse communities;
- to participate actively in setting up mechanisms to ensure processes for consultation at policy level within the three health districts and the local authority.

Why does MACHEM consider itself an authority on health needs assessment in minority ethnic communities?

MACHEM's membership is about 70 people comprising a diverse number of community groups and individuals. This provides a well established network through which information about the needs of the different groups within the community may be obtained. Using this information, MACHEM is in a position to communicate these needs, and identify and advise on potential ways of delivering services. Effective ways to influence policy development and initiatives come about through an understanding of its own membership. That is in itself consultation, a process whereby one can see the emergence of good practice.

Mechanisms for raising awareness

When the organisation was formed there was no mechanism in place whereby the needs of minority ethnic people could be identified and acknowledged at policy level. Unlike the more organised larger white groups, the black voluntary sector comprised a number of small individual groups, many unfunded with no formal corporate structure. Many people from minority ethnic communities felt that the 'white groups' were not representing their needs, so MACHEM decided to develop a strategy for representative consultation at the highest level, by establishing relations with ethnic minority working parties within the local authority, social services and health departments. MACHEM also recognised that, because of the level of inequities and inequalities,[3] it would have to meet with officers at the highest level in the decision-making process. Negotiations succeeded in gaining the commitment by executives to attend such meetings to discuss and agree ways in which ideas on needs could be incorporated into their health care strategies. Once the mechanisms were in place and discussions began, it also became evident that equal opportunities policies in employment needed to be developed in the first instance in order to put in place ways of delivering health care on an equitable basis and to begin to address the issue of appropriate personnel to deliver such care.

MACHEM raised awareness in health authorities of the need for specific steps to be taken to address the particular health needs of the different groups. In addition to the regular district working party meetings, subgroups were set up to look at specific issues at ward, department and personnel level. Examples of how this process was developed with resultant positive outcomes are as follows.

Mental health

The topic of mental health and African-Caribbean people has been a constant source of concern, not only in Manchester but also elsewhere. There is substantial evidence to demonstrate that young black people using the statutory psychiatric services are three times more likely than their white counterparts to be diagnosed as suffering from some sort of psychosis (see Chapter 19). As a consequence, many black people perceive the psychiatric system as divesting them of their right to effective and appropriate treatment, so it alienates them.

MACHEM has constantly sought to identify areas where a more structured approach could be developed for providing appropriate mental health services for black people. It has suggested a rationalisation of services, incorporating voluntary groups providing vital mental health services in the community into the overall service.

Over a considerable time the organisation has pointed out that services for minority ethnic people should not be marginalised by short-term funding, and so at greater risk at times of financial stringency within departments, but should be assimilated into the mainstream. The African-Caribbean Mental Health Project, which is based in the Zion Community Resource Centre in Hulme, works to provide a limited complementary mental health service for young African-Caribbean people with psychiatric problems. In its discussions with providers, MACHEM suggested that there is a potential for developing a partnership with the health trust. Although as yet no clear strategy has been developed, the Manchester health authorities purchasing plan for 1994/95 states:[4] 'Voluntary sector projects which service those with mental illness should be continued on mainstream funding.' Suggestions were put forward by MACHEM for a more integrated approach to the provision of mental health services. Such integration includes, as indicated above, official recognition and incorporation of the African-Caribbean Mental Health Project within a package of mental health services provided by Central Manchester Healthcare Trust and negotiations with the psychiatric social work services. This will ensure that the three agencies work together in meeting the specific needs of African-Caribbean people with mental health problems. MACHEM has also recommended that the community psychiatric nursing services, psychology services and day-centre services should form part of this review. In accordance with these proposals MACHEM has further suggested that Central Manchester Healthcare Trust should, in collaboration with these agencies, provide drop-in facilities in the community with 24-hour access and staffed by the three agencies and volunteers. This would ensure that carers and relatives feel that they can receive the support that they need before a crisis point is reached.

Appropriate staffing is essential to the delivery of effective mental health services to African-Caribbean people. MACHEM has proposed that, where there are problems of recruiting African-Caribbean staff, a scheme should be devised to provide trained lay workers and that the new community care arrangements could be used as a vehicle for this purpose. A further recommendation by MACHEM would involve health promotion units engaging in the provision of information on mental health issues concerning African-Caribbean people.

MACHEM acknowledges that in Manchester the health authorities and Central Healthcare Trust are faced with constant demands

for new and specific services, sometimes with little or no additional
financial resources. Yet the 1991 report on the health of central
Manchester indicates that, when compared with other cities, it has
one of the poorest health records. Within this context, mental
health care for black people has been shown to be less than appropriate to their specific needs. This factor has also been recognised
in the health authorities' purchasing plan for 1994/95:[4]

> There are unmet needs for mental health services among members of
> ethnic minorities. Some mental health services are not sensitive and
> appropriate to the needs of ethnic minority people. The services must
> be appropriate and responsive to the needs of all users, including
> members of ethnic minorities.

The recently published plan also admits that this is not just a local
issue and refers to the task force recently set up by the government
to identify how these services should be improved.

In summary, it can be said that in Manchester there is a wide
range of mental health services provided, and in many ways the
trusts and health authorities can take some comfort in the variety
of services offered. There is, nevertheless, the historical problem
of limited services to meet the specific needs of minority ethnic
people. Admittedly some action has been taken to attempt to make
the services more diverse. In response to the concerns expressed
by its members, MACHEM recommended a full review of mental
health services across the city, with particular emphasis on the
needs of black people. It is indeed encouraging that Manchester
Purchasing Consortium has stated in its plan for 1994/95, in
respect of acute psychiatric inpatient service, that a joint commis-
sioner/provider working group will be set up to propose short-
term and long-term solutions.

Diabetes

There is a high incidence of diabetes among middle-aged and
elderly African-Caribbean people. Both national and local figures
substantiate this: mortality rates are 3–4 times higher than the
national average for Caribbean born people.[5-7] As the following
three initiatives identify, another important area of work to which
MACHEM has made significant input has been in addressing the
issue of diabetes in the African-Caribbean communities in Manchester. First, working closely with the statutory services and the
African-Caribbean elderly care group in central Manchester,
MACHEM identified ways in which it could play a role in influencing the dietary behaviour of the people who attended the African-

Caribbean luncheon club. Working with the African/Caribbean luncheon club, community Dietitian, health promotion unit and the family health care facilitator, an application was made to the 'look after your heart' national project for funding to support an initiative aimed at improving dietary practice among this section of the population. Whilst encouraging maintenance of the traditional diet, the objective was to encourage modification in order to reduce the contributory factors to the development of both diabetes and coronary heart disease. As an example of good practice, this initiative offered the potential for effecting change through a collaborative approach between community and statutory groups, and enabling the development of a more long-term objective to disseminate dietary information to the wider African-Caribbean community. Second, working collaboratively with Manchester University's research department, health promotion unit, primary health care facilitator and locality project for elderly African-Caribbean people, MACHEM set in motion a much more systematic way of developing and disseminating appropriate information for people with diabetes.

The third example relates to care of the elderly. MACHEM played an advisory role in the development of a locality team, which sought to provide a multidisciplinary view of community provided nursing support services for minority ethnic people. The key objective of this initiative was to identify shortfalls in services, and to determine ways for assessing needs and improving access to existing and developing services.

As a consequence, strategic planning problems were identified between different localities, and the necessity for cross-boundary sharing of health care resources to meet needs was also identified. Because of the specific services that elderly African-Caribbean people, in particular, receive in some areas, many people cross boundaries to use the facilities provided (such as those of the Afro-Caribbean luncheon club/care group). Hence, it seemed perfectly practicable to develop a model arrangement for interdistrict/interlocality cooperation in enabling people to use the resources. In choosing to travel distances to reach a luncheon club, individuals are making definite statements about their needs for the culturally appropriate food and the activities within the group. The logistical problems were mainly focused on budgetary controls and allocations within specific boundaries. Hence, although nursing resources could be used quite effectively between the localities, constraints through statutory regulations prevented this from taking place.

Linkworker service

Another of the more obvious gaps in health care services that became apparent to MACHEM was the need for a linkworker service in central Manchester. Suggestions were put forward to Central Manchester Health Authority for such a scheme. In June 1990 a district linkworker coordinator was appointed and, under the management of St Mary's Hospital, undertook the task of assessing the extent to which language barriers prevented members of minority ethnic communities from receiving full and adequate health care services. The study carried out by the linkworker coordinator, with support from MACHEM, highlighted the need for provision of translating and advocacy facilities for, among others, its Somali outpatients. The report, recommending four part-time posts, was accepted in 1991 and appointments were made. MACHEM, through its joint meetings with Central Manchester Health Authority, regularly requests evaluation reports on the uptake of the service, and it soon became evident that the male Somali linkworker appointed was unable, because of religious and cultural reasons, to meet the needs of the female Somali community. Further negotiations resulted in a female Somali linkworker being appointed.

MACHEM is aware that this part-time service is inadequate to meet all the demands placed on it and that funds limit the extension of this particular service. Discussions with two of the districts have therefore resulted in the establishment of a bank of interpreters. MACHEM assisted in the completion of bids for funding for this complementary scheme and has played a major role in the training programme for interpreters.

Catering

A MACHEM initiative was successful in bringing the three health authorities' catering groups together. This resulted in a city-wide forum being established to coordinate ethnic minority meals throughout the city's hospitals. This collaborative working has led to cross-fertilisation of ideas and has enabled uniform progress to be made. Manchester's hospitals are now in a position to offer Halal, Kosher and Caribbean meals on most menus, with progress also in the provision of Chinese meals. Although, on the surface, this may appear to be a very basic outcome, it is nevertheless important for the qualitative experience of patients. Furthermore, this initiative has helped to clarify two main misconceptions. First, it was assumed that because Caribbean people speak English they are familiar with English food and that this was adequate for their needs. Second, it was assumed that addressing issues such as dietary needs would incur additional expenditure. Third, ignoring the changing patterns of food choice in the general population, it was assumed that meals once provided will only be chosen by the particular groups for whom they were initially intended.

Other issues

Other issues that MACHEM has successfully brought to the attention of both commissioners and providers have concerned:

- payments on an equitable basis for religious representatives of all faiths who are required to visit hospital patients;
- the provision of appropriate facilities to meet religious requirements.

Advice has also been given on suitable signposting throughout the hospitals.

Employment of minority ethnic staff

From its inception, MACHEM focused on employment issues as a major part of its consultative processes with the health authorities. It was found necessary to appraise and make recommendations regarding equal opportunities, not only in service delivery but also in employment and training practices. A great deal of work was involved in the actual formulation of 'equal opportunities' policies, and the organisation was able to negotiate and advise on equal opportunities issues generally. This resulted in the authorities becoming more conversant with the legislative requirements to implement good practices in areas such as recruitment and selection procedures.

Having a clear set of objectives, MACHEM is represented on each of the employment practices subgroups and has been able to advise on the principles of increasing the numbers of minority ethnic people in employment through, for example, positive action measures. There is an enormous amount yet to be done to enhance equal opportunities in employment throughout the health districts. Monitoring of the workforce and new applications in certain disciplines have highlighted immense under-representation of minority ethnic people at all levels within the NHS. We continue to suggest ways to improve this; advertising using local centres and using the ethnic minority press are some of the measures recommended.

There are several important elements of great concern to MACHEM and which, together with educational/training colleges/universities, trusts and health authorities, it will strive to address, for example:

- The apparent low numbers of people from minority ethnic communities who are entering a variety of the health professions, such as speech therapy, chiropody and physiotherapy
- The under-representation of people from these communities at higher levels within the NHS, and the tendency of minority ethnic doctors to be channelled towards psychiatry, geriatrics and mental handicap services, denying them opportunities and experiences in the more attractive and lucrative acute specialties
- Opportunities, or lack of them, for training minority ethnic staff to improve their promotion prospects
- Commitment to the training in equal opportunities for all staff within the NHS.

It has to be appreciated that people who have worked in any large bureaucratic organisation for lengthy periods of time would expect to move up the career ladder. Black people, particularly African-Caribbean, have worked in the NHS constantly since the 1950s and 1960s, yet proportionately they still remain largely at the lowest levels.

Successful negotiations have resulted in the creation of two 'equal opportunities' officer posts. However, whilst we acknowledge that this is a step forward, there is evidence to suggest that these posts have resulted in a concentration of equal opportunities responsibilities on those individuals. Good practice in applying equal opportunities throughout service delivery, and recruitment and selection procedures, should be the responsibility of all managers and staff in all departments, and there is concern about the lack of a systematic approach to training in equal opportunities throughout the work force. This will remain a high priority for MACHEM and the district working parties for some considerable time.

Conclusion

Health services are essential in maintaining a healthy population. It is important, therefore, that the NHS be appropriate and accessible to all sections in this multiracial society. In order to achieve this, the NHS has to recognise that racial discrimination exists throughout its services and that tackling it is essential to achieving and maintaining a service accessible to all. There is little doubt that ethnic minority patients have different experiences of using the health service from people in the white majority population. Its nature and make-up, when one considers assessment in health needs, makes MACHEM unique. The organisation, whilst not having the human and financial resources to undertake empirical and large-scale quantitative research projects, has on tap members from a variety of communities who can speak with authority on the health difficulties experienced by their members and identify areas where statutory authorities are not meeting these needs. MACHEM is the only black voluntary organisation in Manchester providing a forum for minority ethnic individuals to discuss these shortfalls with decision makers in the health services.

The way forward

MACHEM is a relatively young organisation. Despite being inadequately resourced, it has developed good practices in assessing needs and experiences of people from minority ethnic communities using health services, as documented in this chapter which also gives a flavour of the effectiveness of MACHEM in enabling some of the needs to be addressed.

It is MACHEM's belief that many of the difficulties faced by people from minority ethnic communities are due to insensitive delivery of services. There are also issues surrounding the low numbers of minority ethnic people entering a variety of health disciplines, together with the lack of equal opportunities training throughout the workforce and, in particular, for managers responsible for recruitment and selection of staff.

In looking to the future, there are also major areas of study relating to these communities that MACHEM would like to see addressed, for example the higher than national average incidence of strokes (76% higher in men and 110% higher in women), hypertension (4 times higher in men and 7 times higher in women) and diabetes (rate of mortality 3–4 times the national average).

Other areas that we would like to see developed include, in the first instance, a feasibility study of the need for provision of an outreach worker for African-Caribbean communities. It is evident that patois is widely used and that speakers of patois can face real difficulties in accessing health care services. We are equally concerned about access problems faced by people from the Somali community. Therefore, in conjunction with Manchester Health Authority, we have submitted a proposal to the Department of Health to train three bilingual workers from the community who would be briefed on the main provisions of health services in the appropriate areas.

MACHEM is aware of the proposals for the amalgamation of the health authorities in Manchester and Salford and community health services throughout the city to form two large bodies. This will, in itself, bring new health care management, distribution and access problems. However, there will also be benefits, particularly for minority ethnic people in the sense that services will be based on city-wide strategies rather than, as at present, localised pockets of service developments directed at minority ethnic communities.

Such a development offers positive potential and the opportunity for effective consultation and thus assessment of health needs of minority ethnic people, so enabling the climate for 'health for all' to move nearer practical reality rather than just declarations of intentions.[8]

References

1 Department of Health. *On the state of the public health.* Annual report of the Chief Medical Officer for 1991. London: HMSO, 1992.
2 Department of Health. *The patient's charter.* London: Department of Health, 1991.
3 Department of Health. *On the state of the public health.* Annual report of the Chief Medical Officer for 1994. London: HMSO, 1995.
4 Manchester Health Authorities. *Draft purchasing plans 1994/95.* Manchester: The Health Authorities, 1994.
5 Department of Health. *Ethnicity and health: a guide to the NHS.* Heywood (Lancashire): Department of Health, 1993.
6 Raleigh VS, Kiri V, Balarajan R. Variations in mortality from diabetes mellitus, hypertension and renal disease in England and Wales by country of birth. *Health Trends* 1997; **28**: 122–7.
7 Cappuccio FP. Ethnicity and cardiovascular risk: the variations in people of African ancestry and south Asian origin. *Journal of Human Hypertension* 1997; **11**: 571–6.
8 World Health Organisation. *Targets for health for all.* Copenhagen: WHO, 1985.

22 | The Asian experience

Tanzeem Ahmed
Director, Confederation of Indian Organisations, UK

The consumer movement has gathered momentum in recent times. Government charters have given some recognition to consumers by providing yardsticks by which to measure the quality of service provision and mechanisms for complaining. Legislation has also made it mandatory to consult with consumers. The NHS and Community Care Act 1990 and *The new NHS* place a legal duty on service commissioners and providers to plan and deliver more appropriate services to improve the health of their populations. However, despite this recent and previous legislation and the changing nature of social and welfare services, consumers from minority ethnic communities have had little impact on this process of change. This chapter draws upon the findings of two pieces of research carried out by the Confederation of Indian Organisations (CIO): one in the area of mental health and the other in health promotion activity in Asian voluntary groups and health needs of the community. ('Asian' is used throughout rather than the more explicit 'South Asian'.)

Health needs assessment

Many researchers and practitioners have highlighted the complexities of health needs assessment (see Chapter 2). Suffice it to say here that language, culture, religion and health beliefs are significant factors in the process and those involved must avoid a simplistic view when assessing communities.[1]

It appears that many health professionals, including those designing policy and setting priorities, are ill informed on the health needs of minority ethnic communities, and hence set priorities that may be at variance with the needs of local communities. Effective needs assessment can only be carried out against a background of careful analysis of the health status of ethnic minorities. Furthermore, it is of little use to assess health needs without careful consideration of how these needs will be met through current services and how future developments will take account of them.[2]

Consultation

Current health care provision is based on Western medical concepts, which have proved to be inadequate for the needs of minority ethnic communities. To address these inadequacies, services need to be planned in consultation with this section of the population. Consultation is not a simple task and there are no hard and fast rules governing how this should be carried out. Some degree of flexibility will be required. There are, however, some general guidelines, including:

- the need for certain procedures and mechanisms to be in place that will allow for interactive dialogue;
- professional boundaries as well as power relationships need to be overcome;
- issues such as the language used, and the need for the venue for the consultation to be appropriate;
- consultation should be a continuous process that informs policy and planning and is not a 'one off';
- procedures for feeding back the outcome of consultation must be put in place;
- the health care needs of minority ethnic communities must be represented by the communities themselves or those who are most in touch with their needs;
- representation must be apparent at the very initial stages of policy development, and a clear strategy for the involvement of the community must be incorporated.

In our experience, the extent of consultation with the community is inadequate. In a study conducted by the CIO exploring the health promotion activities within the Asian voluntary sector, it was identified that two-thirds of the groups in the sample (often the most well known and recognised in the borough) had never been directly consulted in the planning of local services.[3]

Whose needs?

Given that the provision of health services is based on the needs of the majority population, needs of minority ethnic communities that differ from those of the white majority are often regarded as special and have resource implications. Fear of backlash from the majority population deters many policy makers from prioritising this area of work. On the contrary, however, the needs of ethnic minorities do not assume a special place or call for privileged services. They should be viewed in the same light as the well recognised inequalities in access that exist for other disadvantaged groups in Britain. As a first step in addressing these inequalities, commissioners of health care will need to stipulate rigorous compliance with equal opportunities policies in their contracts/service agreements with providers. These contracts/service agreements will then need to be carefully monitored.

Barriers to service uptake

Small localised projects, as well as researchers, have succeeded in raising awareness of the barriers to access that have hindered the uptake of many services by ethnic minorities. Such barriers are now well documented and include:

- language and communication difficulties;
- lack of appropriate information;
- lack of sensitivity to cultural and religious needs;
- racism in service delivery;
- negative past experiences;
- lack of confidence in the ability of services to understand and meet needs.

The community's responses

Inadequacies of provision and limited access have led to many communities setting up voluntary groups to fill the gaps in service provision and to counteract neglect and discrimination by statutory agencies. As locally based organisations, they have the appropriate skills and experiences to share with the statutory sector. Whilst offering services that are meaningful and appropriate to their communities, voluntary organisations can only go some way in service provision. They are constrained by insecure funding, inadequate premises, lack of equipment, shortages of staff and lack of training and support.[3] Voluntary organisations operating within these limitations cannot therefore offer an alternative to the National Health Service. Health providers must explore the potential for joint initiatives with the voluntary sector and adopt strategies to develop collaborative partnerships.

The community's experiences with the health services

Mental health: hidden needs

The work of the CIO in the area of mental health illustrates some of the issues in the health care of minority ethnic communities. Its involvement in mental health arose out of concerns raised by members of the Asian communities as well as professionals working in the area. It was felt that there was a widespread problem of hidden distress in the communities for which there were few outlets for expression. For the Asian communities, experience of psychological services was characterised by an underuse of available preventive services. Asian people therefore tended to reach crisis situations before receiving statutory care.[4]

The CIO wished to explore further the area of hidden distress. A small-scale survey to elicit the views and experiences of 98 randomly selected individuals was carried out. Although the findings cannot be generalised to the Asian communities as a whole, they provide useful insights to the perceptions of some of the members of the communities.[5]

It was found that the statutory care received by individuals in the sample had a negative effect on them. Rather than improving the mental health condition, quite often the conditions were made worse. Difficulties arose due to communication problems, inappropriate treatment and lack of training received by professionals in treating people from the Asian communities.

Communication

It is especially difficult for those who cannot communicate in English to take part in their diagnosis in any meaningful way. In cases where interpreters were used, the difficulty of putting concepts and beliefs familiar in one culture into the language of another has led to misinterpretation. The need to communicate personal, individual experiences using familiar words and intonations of voice is lost in a three-way interaction process. This is further complicated when interpreters are unfamiliar with the mental health jargon, which is often used. In addition, concepts cannot be isolated from the cultural and religious beliefs in which they are embedded, and lose their meaning in the process of interpretation.

Inappropriate treatment

It is clear from both anecdotal evidence and various research papers available in this area that treatment offered to Asian users was often totally inappropriate, resulting from a failure of professionals to understand the presenting problems. Cases were reported in which culturally appropriate behaviour of Asians, such as in times of grieving, was misinterpreted as symptomatic of psychological disorder. For instance, when a woman broke her bangles following the death of her husband it was misinterpreted as attempted suicide arising from manic depression. In another case a woman who asked a spiritual healer to carry out special prayers to take away the spirit of a dead husband was misdiagnosed as having hallucinations symptomatic of schizophrenia.

Asians are more likely to receive medication and electro-convulsive therapy than their white counterparts and are more frequently diagnosed in psychotic categories;[6] in particular, they are not likely to be referred to psychotherapy or counselling.

It is extremely difficult for a professional who does not share an understanding of the conceptual framework and life experiences of a client to make a diagnosis that reflects an understanding of the presenting problem. The limited use of Western medical models for understanding, diagnosing and treating mental health problems in the Asian communities must therefore be acknowledged.

Limitations of professional training

At present the training of professionals does not equip them with the skills and knowledge increasingly required in a multicultural society. Current literature available on mental health problems in the Asian communities offers simplistic explanations, often based on stereotypes:

- a belief that members of Asian communities are not 'psychologically minded' and lack the capacity for psychological insight necessary for certain therapeutic interventions;
- there is a stigma attached to mental distress in the Asian communities which prevents members from expressing symptoms of distress, and hence mental health problems are not acknowledged;
- mental health problems do not reach services because they are taken care of within the extended family network.

Beliappa's community survey revealed that the emotionally distressed did not 'somatise' their distress and were able to recognise the psychosomatic nature of their problems;[5] these people did present their physical symptoms to their GPs but the latter were unable to detect the underlying psychological distress. This is supported by the finding that both Asian GPs and those from the white majority communities were less successful at recognising symptoms of distress in Asian patients than in their white counterparts.[7] One lady in the sample illustrates this:

> I am fit now, but for years I was suffering with aches and pains, sleeplessness and lack of appetite ... I could see that all this was caused by stress. I had three miscarriages because of this ... my experiences in my marriage led to physical ailments ... They [doctors] would treat me for physical problems, gave me pain killers, but never bothered to find out what the problem was.

Beliappa's data demonstrated that emotional difficulties are recognised but are not classified as pathological. Instead, individuals use a holistic model and link such experiences within a normative structure of roles and expectations.[5]

The high number (23%) of people in Beliappa's sample reporting the experience of mental distress suggests that people are prepared to talk about emotional distress as long as the context is safe. Hence, the stigma surrounding mental distress is similar in all communities and does not exist to a greater extent in Asian communities.

With regard to the stereotype of the extended family network supporting the individual members, it was found that only 13% of the sample saw the family as a viable means of support, and then only for concerns relating to health and child care.

Beliappa's study showed that lack of appropriate referrals and adequate preventive services for the Asian communities means that those in distress cope with their problems using internal resources such as prayer (44%) and crying (10%). Some members turn to religious healers and other alternative sources for help. The inadequacy of available structures leads those in distress to crisis situations.

An issue for planners of services is that those experiencing distress are hidden from service providers and official figures misrepresent the extent of the problem. The need to target the non-users of services is clearly represented in the case of mental health. It is more cost effective to prevent conditions arising at the primary care level than to treat conditions when they occur often requiring greater resources at the point of secondary care. Prevention and health promotion must be seen as a major component of policy.

Health promotion

To plan health promotion for a heterogeneous group of people with a different knowledge base, linguistic skills and health beliefs is a truly challenging task. This was apparent in the CIO's study into the health promotion activity in Asian voluntary groups which explored the effectiveness of different means by which information is delivered to the Asian communities.[3] It also aimed to gain insight into the health information needs of different user groups, linguistic communities and those with varying language and literacy skills. (This research was again primarily focused on the Asian communities.)

It appears from some studies that health knowledge in minority ethnic community groups is poor.[8,9] In addition, it is suggested that knowledge of aspects of health and social services is also poor.[10] This is reflected in the CIO's study in which out of a sample of 98 users (of Asian voluntary organisations) the majority demonstrated a general lack of awareness of health issues. The users identified a range of areas in which information was required. Over half the sample (58) had needed some health information in the past 2 years and had taken steps to find this information. However, the information that they obtained was not always satisfactory and was often inappropriate because it did not take account of cultural and religious factors. In general there was a lack of good quality information available in translation.

One reason for this lack of appropriateness of information is that health promoters are not always well informed of the health beliefs and information needs of minority ethnic communities. The health care priorities identified by health promoters do not match those of the communities. Health promotion may also be in danger of relying on negative stereotypes of minority ethnic communities and imparting Western ideologies. This practice is the result of the poor quality of training available in the area of race and health.

At present, available health education material is uncoordinated and lacks the strategic approach required for effective dissemination. This lack of coordination has resulted in duplications, gaps and anomalies in materials that are being produced and a poor use of available resources.[11]

The CIO's study highlights the relevance of taking into account the priorities of different user and linguistic groups. It was found that health priorities differed according to age, gender and disability, and varied among linguistic communities. For example, joint problems and cancer were the main health concerns of the Gujarati respondents. Bangladeshi respondents were more concerned about blood pressure (high and low) and diabetes. Blood pressure was also a main health concern for the Tamils. Punjabis reported more health concerns related to physical disabilities and mental health.

Similar variations were observed with regard to the users' perception of the most effective means of receiving health information. The respondents found it difficult to identify any one method of receiving health information as the most effective. The usefulness of a particular medium depended on the purpose it was being used for, the nature of the information and the linguistic abilities of the audience. Within this sample there was an overwhelming demand for information to be produced in English and the mother tongue (85% of the sample wanted bi- or multi-lingual information). The identification of Asian radio for communicating health information is significant in this context and was prioritised by women and the elderly to a larger extent. Since Asian radio has become more established it offers scope and potential for disseminating information on various areas of concern.

Conclusion and recommendations

This chapter has drawn together some of the issues relating to the importance of consulting consumers. It is clear that current health care provision is based on Western medical models, which do not reflect the beliefs, values and attitudes to health held by minority ethnic communities. In order to make health care more responsive to the needs and priorities of users from these communities, it is important to broaden approaches and move away from perspectives based on stereotypes.

Research has shown that various barriers still exist in relation to access to health care. It is clear in the case of mental health that such barriers have led to an underuse of existing preventive services and has meant that certain health conditions remain hidden from service providers.

The dissatisfaction with current service provision has led to many voluntary organisations setting up services to assist their users by providing various health activities and health information themselves. The efforts of voluntary organisations need to be recognised and supported with resources. These organisations are most in touch with the people they are serving and are offering accessible, relevant and appropriate services. However, despite their strengths, voluntary groups cannot offer alternative services to statutory care as they lack the infrastructure and the resources required to do so. It is therefore essential that existing services take on board the recommendations that are being made by so many researchers, community workers and health care professionals, so that we achieve quality and equality in service delivery. In particular, there is a need for:

* addressing the barriers to access to services;
* more comprehensive training of professionals in race and health;
* better systems of consulting consumers;
* broadening approaches to health care and health information production and dissemination.

It is high time that health care providers accepted some of these recommendations and also accepted their responsibilities to all consumers of health care. The new statutory requirements, for health authorities to improve health and trusts to improve quality, enshrined in the White Paper *The new NHS*, will provide greater opportunities to address needs and improve services to all communities including minority ethnic groups.[12]

References

1   Modood T, Berthoud R, Lakey J, *et al. Ethnic minorities in Britain: diversity and disadvantage*. Fourth national survey of ethnic minorities. London: Policy Studies Institute, 1997.

2   Bhopal R. Is research into ethnicity and health racist, unsound, or important science? *British Medical Journal* 1997; **314**: 1751–6.

3   Webb-Johnson A. *Building on strengths: inquiry into health activity in the Asian voluntary sector*. London: Confederation of Indian Organisations, 1993.

4   Commander MJ, Sashidharan SP, Odell SM, Surtees PG. Access to mental health care in inner-city health districts: II. Association with demographic factors. *British Journal of Psychiatry* 1997; **170**: 317–20.

5   Beliappa J. *Illness or distress? Alternative models of mental health*. London: Confederation of Indian Organisations, 1991.

6   Shaikh A. Cross-cultural comparison: psychiatric admission of Asian and indigenous patients in Leicestershire. *International Journal of Social Psychiatry* 1985; **31**: 3–11.

7   Bal SS. Psychological symptomatology and health beliefs of Asian patients. In: Dent H, ed. *Clinical psychology: research and development*. London: Croom Helm, 1987.

8   Bhopal RS. Asians' knowledge and behaviour on preventative health issues: smoking, alcohol, heart disease, pregnancy, rickets, malaria prophylaxis and surma. *Community Medicine* 1986; **8**: 5–21.

9   Kay EJ, Shaikh I, Bhopal RS. Dental knowledge, beliefs, attitudes and behaviour of the Asian community in Glasgow. *Health Bulletin* 1990; **48**: 73–80.

10 Smith NJ, McCulloch JW. Immigrants' knowledge and experience of social work services. *Mental Health Society* 1977; **4**: 190–7.

11 McAvoy BR, Raza R. Can health education increase uptake of cervical smear testing among Asian women? *British Medical Journal* 1991; **302**: 833–6.

12 Secretary of State for Health. *The new NHS: modern, dependable.* London: Stationery Office, 1997.

23 | The African refugee experience

Richard Mugisha
Ex-Caseworker, Uganda Community Relief Association, London

Sarah Nansukusa
Co-ordinator, Uganda Community Relief Association, London

As identified in Chapter 20, being a refugee can lead to physical and mental health problems. Adjusting to life in a strange country presents an enormous hurdle. Whatever their age, sex, family situation or cultural origin, coming to terms with the often traumatic experience of the past, the pain of separation and loss, and uncertainty about what lies ahead, can be a lifetime struggle;[1] this is intensified by the dearth of opportunities to improve their situation in Britain. This chapter focuses on African people who are refugees in the UK. Quoting from the direct experiences of individuals, it bears testimony to the urgent need to address the special health needs of this section of the population.

Africans in Britain

The total number of Africans in Britain is not clear. In the 1991 census 205,400 people (0.4% of the population) described themselves as Black Africans.[2] Most African visitors, private patients and business people do not usually stay longer than 6 months at any one time. The Africans who live in Britain today could be divided into three categories: government and privately sponsored students, migrant workers, and refugees; this is in addition to those born in the UK.

In flight from religious or political persecution, many Africans came to this country as refugees in the 1970s and 1980s. Despite the British government's restrictions on asylum seekers and immigrants in the 1990s, the crises born of the end of the Cold War and subsequent uncertainties for life safety have continued to send Africans, notably from Ghana, Sudan, Rwanda, Sierra Leone and Zaire,[3] to this country.

African refugees come to the UK for several reasons. Some of the reasons are fear of persecution, to join relatives and friends to establish a platform to enable them to fight against non-democratic regimes at home. For some, as English is the only language they speak, Britian is one of the obvious choices. A good number do not have many options and are driven by circumstances. It should be noted, however, that only a small proportion of African refugees seek asylum in Britain and, indeed, in Europe. Figures compiled by the Refugee Council from reports by the United Nations High Commission for Refugees, the World Bank, the United States Committee for Refugees and the European Consultation on Refugees and Exiles in 1991 showed that Malawi (southern Africa), with a GNP *per capita* of US$190, was host to 823,000 refugees whereas Britain, where it was US$14,375, hosted 101,300; the ratio of refugee to population was 1:10 and 1:566 respectively.[4]

The Asylum and Immigration Appeals Act 1993 and the Asylum and Immigration Act 1996 include several regulations that affect the health needs of asylum seekers. All applicants for asylum are subject to fingerprinting; those failing to comply are liable to summary arrest. Applicants have to demonstrate a 'reasonable likelihood' of serious risk of prosecution in the country or territory to if they are sent back. The operation of a number of detention centres to 'control' the situation has been rejected by the medical profession and human rights activists.[5] The 1996 Act contains new immigration offences, powers and penalties. Restrictions were imposed on employment and entitlement to benefits;[6] under section 9, housing authorities must not let accommodation to persons subject to immigration control unless permitted by the Secretary of State.[6,7] Asylum seekers are now only entitled to assistance or accommodation under the homelessness legislation, if they claim asylum on arrival.[8] As long as these restrictions are in force, assessing the health needs of African refugees will remain a problem.

African refugees are among the poorest of the poor in Britain, where a large proportion are living on a state benefit owing to unemployment.[9] A research report by the Uganda Community Relief Association in 1993 revealed that 34.2% of Ugandans living in London were unemployed though available for work (Table 1), and only 8% were getting unemployment benefit, suggesting that few had been employed for long enough to qualify for it. The same report[7] indicated that 38.7% continually move and 26.1% were in accommodation that was in disrepair, damp, overcrowded and with no proper heating. A quarter of respondents lacked sole use of sanitary and cooking facilities (a much higher proportion than in

Table 1. Employment status of 368 Ugandan refugees[7]

Full-time employment	65	17.7%
Part-time employment	45	12.2%
Self-employed	7	1.9%
In training	24	6.5%
Available for work	126	34.2%
Not available for work	20	5.4%
Full-time student	29	7.9%
Part-time student	40	10.9%
Other	12	3.3%

the general population), mostly in privately rented accommodation with high rents and high electricity/gas bills (Table 2).
Social services housing was slightly better than privately rented
accommodation. Though the report was about Ugandan refugees,
it reflects the general situation of other African refugees.

Experiences of the National Health Service

Attitude and stigma

Owing to the high prevalence of HIV in their communities,
Africans suffer from discrimination, racist abuse, unemployment
and isolation, and there is much stereotyping which affects access
to health services. Such services may also be perceived as culturally
inappropriate and health professionals as insensitive to the needs
of refugees. According to Western media and analysts, half of

Table 2. Proportion (%) of homes with features rated as poor/deficient[7]

	Social housing	Privately rented
Overall	9.6	16.3
Heating	17.0	21.5
Damp	24.5	24.6
Noise	22.1	19.0
Repair	21.9	29.0
Rent	16.0	26.7
Electricity/gas	30.4	40.3
Neighbours	17.6	14.1

Uganda's population, for example, will be HIV positive by the year 2000.[10]

One of the major consequences of this view has been that patients from this region are sometimes tested for HIV without being informed, or pressured to have the test as in the typical case of a woman admitted to a London hospital while in labour:[10] allegedly the consultants had a policy of treating all Africans and Afro-Caribbeans as high-risk groups for HIV infection, so she was isolated from other mothers and the nurses and doctors wore extensive barrier clothing; she was in fact HIV antibody negative.

Often, service providers believe that HIV positive patients come from Africa to Britain for free treatment. Patients are often treated as scroungers who should feel privileged to be receiving medical treatment here:[11] an HIV positive Ugandan was isolated and ignored after admission to a London hospital, the nurses did not want to enter his room, food was left at the door for him to collect, and his medication was delayed.

Relevant prior health information given to service providers is sometimes ignored, as in the case of a pregnant woman who had been circumcised when a child in Somalia and had informed the staff of this, explaining that labour would require specialist assistance, but when her labour was induced she recalls there being chaos and panic when the duty staff realised that she was infibulated. The information that she had provided appeared not to have been recorded, or may have been misunderstood owing to language difficulties.[11]

Communication between consumers and service providers

Although the 1996 Asylum and Immigration Act gives all refugees, including asylum seekers, full entitlement to hospital and health services through a general practitioner (GP) under the same arrangements as for UK residents,[6,12] very few people from this section of the population are aware of what services exist in the health sector. Many are not registered with GPs, have never heard of social workers, and those who have do not use their services regularly. For example, in an assessment study of health needs of Somali and Eritrean women in Haringey it was found that 30% of the sample had no access to GPs. Of this 30%, some chose other routes, such as through the accident and emergency department of a hospital. Others had to find ways of dealing with their problems within their own communities and existing personal networks.[11]

Language barrier is one of the factors that hinder access to services. In the above study, it was found that those who spoke English reasonably well felt that they were able to identify what service provision existed using appropriate community contacts and key professionals such as social workers and health visitors, but those whose English was poor had not developed trusting relationships and found the situation daunting.[11]

In some cases it is not clear whose responsibility it is to provide information about availability of interpreters. One woman was told by a receptionist that she should only come if she brought her own interpreter, so on a subsequent visit she brought along a family member, but they were then told that they had to be able to write English as well, which neither could do. They were given to understand that the responsibility ultimately rested with the patient to find someone suitable otherwise the GP would not be prepared to see them.[10] Many of these and other problems in obtaining access to health services were highlighted by the Chief Medical Officer as early as 1991.[13]

Language difficulties prevent many refugees from understanding information provided, so there is no point in availing of services. A person may develop a complicated situation that may further puzzle service providers, as in the case of a refugee, living alone in London and speaking little English, who was diagnosed as having tuberculosis resulting from AIDS and in hospital for over a month during which time he could not speak to anyone in his own language. Without a translator, he became extremely withdrawn and depressed, lack of human communication adding to his poor health, and he was finally placed in a homeless person's hostel, where there was unconcealed hostility to people with AIDS.[14]

A wide range of information materials has been produced with the aim of effectively reaching out to minority ethnic service users, especially in the area of HIV and AIDS,[4] but there is a degree of reluctance to make use of them: they are mostly in English; most target groups do not identify themselves with the materials; even those who have a basic knowledge of English cannot, because of inappropriate images, tell whether a leaflet has anything to do with them. Information on videos would be more appropriate if it were properly presented, but there is a problem of dissemination, they tend to be expensive, and group viewing is not easy to arrange. Television pictures of people dying from AIDS in Africa have led to a measure of apathy among people at whom video materials are targeted.

Perception of the health service role

The latest immigration legislation is aimed at reducing the number of foreigners seeking to enter the UK and stay for a long time.[15] In the process of restricting immigration, however, the state puts all possible statutory sectors into use, not excluding the health service. It is possible, for instance, that if medical inspectors of immigrants at the ports of entry consider that an entrant subject to immigration control is likely during a stay in the UK to require medical treatment for AIDS, or for illness associated with HIV infection, the person should provide an estimate of the cost of such treatment so that the immigration service may decide whether the entrant has the means to meet the cost of treatment during the period of stay envisaged.

However, owing to the fact that they seek political asylum, refugees cannot be refused entry immediately. Those who have HIV infection are therefore able to use the NHS. It is for this reason perhaps that in their first months after arrival refugees do not get easy access to GP services. Some of them have to wait until the Home Office issues a letter indicating that they have been allowed to stay in the country or have been granted temporary stay as asylum seekers. This is so despite the health authorities' statutory obligation that, once a person is residing at a temporary address, GPs should, if approached, register that person on a temporary basis for up to 3 months.[13]

The African refugees' experience has shown that social workers tend to be less sympathetic to their traumatic endurance. They also sometimes perceive that they play the role of immigration officers and are thus more interested in problems that led to the consumer's flight to the UK, and not likely to play an advocacy role. It is unclear as to who speaks on the person's behalf if the social worker does not.

Intervention by the health service in consumers' immigration matters delays service provision and discourages open discussion of health problems. There have even been reports of African mothers being induced into allowing their babies to take part in anti-HIV treatment trials because they are afraid of being deported if they refuse.[11]

Waiting lists

Despite the Patient's Charter,[17] which sets a maximum waiting time for elective medical treatment (currently 18 months), it appears from the experience of African refugees that they fare considerably worse. One of the authors (RM) is personally aware of two refugee women who were on waiting lists for an operation in a London hospital for 6 years before resorting to alternative means of treatment.

Cultural differences

Lack of understanding of the social and political background of patients often means that health professionals cannot deliver an adequate and culturally sensitive service.[18,19] One professional stated in a letter: '….this group seems to be very isolated and very unwilling to accept the support of the kind we generally offer our patients'.[16] In this case, the doctors sought help from 'experts', but there are instances where service providers do not pay adequate attention to details.[20]

Service providers may mistakenly assume that poor command of the English language signifies general lack of knowledge.

Conclusion and recommendations

The issues raised above are not new. They have been of increasing concern over the past few years. There are now numerous reports putting forward more recommendations than can possibly be implemented.[7] The following paragraphs highlight the essential issues that should be taken into account by purchasers and providers.

African refugees face many disadvantages, especially unemployment, poverty and poor housing. The Ugandan community experiences very high levels of unemployment despite the fact that many people are highly qualified.[7] Without the ability to break into the mainstream employment the community will remain trapped in poor circumstances and will be unable to develop. The housing situation is equally bad.[21]

The immigration authorities, at best, doubt the validity of applications for asylum and, at worst, keep refugees in detention until their case is dealt with. With the Asylum and Immigration Act 1996 now in force, there is an increase in the number of asylum seekers in detention centres,[4] so ways need to be found of reaching these detainees.

There is a need for the NHS to be more sensitive to the needs of refugees and play less of an immigration service role. So long as refugees continue to encounter such interviews in the health service sector, they will not feel comfortable enough to be open and to use the service with confidence. Ways of improving this situation should be explored.

Many African refugees will have experienced a deterioration of the health services in their country of origin; the use of traditional medicine is therefore on the increase.[21] Greater emphasis should be placed on identifying and building on those practices that may be helpful.

There should be a particular emphasis on African women's needs. Women are less likely to be educated and are often totally dependent on men for support and information. Action should be taken to address the double deprivation due to refugee status and gender.

As a complement to the usual approach of supplying leaflets, alternative methods of disseminating information should be investigated. Emphasis should be put on finding ways of informing newly arrived people about what services exist, how to access them, and at what cost, if any. The government funded Haringey Refugee Consortium currently advises refugees in that borough on education and employment opportunities. They also conduct English classes for speakers of other languages. The consortium is mainly staffed by refugees and other people from minority ethnic communities. The NHS needs to explore the possibility of conducting health promotion lessons in such a setting.

Members of the various African communities are adequately qualified or are capable of being so. The possibilities for harnessing their skills as a resource in the community should be explored; employment as community health workers, interpreters and advocates are some of the options.

Many African doctors currently have difficulty entering British medical practice, yet they would play a key role in providing services to African communities. Action should be taken to ensure that African doctors are adequately represented in the NHS.

Finally, there is a need for a national study of the situation of African refugees in the UK. Its findings should eventually contribute to wider efforts to change or mitigate the new asylum laws, which treat asylum seekers as 'guilty until proved innocent'.

The above list is by no means exhaustive. This chapter has outlined the situation of African refugees in the UK. Their experiences within the NHS highlight the issues that need to be addressed in health needs assessment. There is the capacity, if the political will exists, to make the necessary policies.[21]

References

1   Silove D, Sinnerbrink I, Field A, *et al.* Anxiety, depression and PTSD in asylum-seekers: association with pre-migration trauma and post-migration stressors. *British Journal of Psychiatry* 1997; **170**: 351–7.

2   Office of Population Censuses and Surveys. *1991 census.* London: OPCS, 1992.

3   Home Office. *Statistical bulletin: asylum statistics.* London: Government Statistical Service, 1993, 1994, 1995, 1996.

4   House of Commons. Treatment of persons who claim asylum. In: *Asylum and Immigration Appeals Act 1993.* London: HMSO, 1993: 1,3.

5   Bunce C. Doctors complain about treatment of asylum seekers in Britain. *British Medical Journal* 1997; **314**: 393.

6   *The Asylum and Immigration Act 1996.* London: HMSO, 1996.

7   Bell J. *Ugandan refugees.* London: Community Development Foundation, 1993: 15.

8   Refugee Advisers Support Unit. *The Asylum and Immigration Act 1996: what it means, related measures and timetable.* London: Refugee Council, 1996.

9   Jones T. *Britain's ethnic minorities.* London: Policy Studies Institute, 1993.

10   Bhatt C. *AIDS and the black communities.* London: BHAN, 1991: 18,19,46.

11   Bernard-Jones S. *Qualitative needs assessment study of Somali and Eritrean refugee women in Haringey.* London: Haringey Health Authority, 1992: 5,7,12,18.

12   Refugee Advisers Support Unit. *Refugees and access to health services.* London: Refugee Council, 1996.

13   Department of Health. *On the state of the public health 1991.* Annual report of the Chief Medical Officer. London: HMSO, 1992.

14   Dada M. *Multilingual Aids.* London: Health Education Authority, 1992.

15   Montaquim A. African babies in controversial experiment. *Weekly Journal,* July 1993.

16   Bradbeer C. HIV and AIDS in Africans in the UK (letter). London: St. Thomas' Hospital, 1991.

17   Secretary of State for Health. *The patient's charter.* London: HMSO, 1991.

18   Helman CG. *Culture, health and illness,* 3rd edn. Oxford: Butterworth-Heinemann, 1994.

19   Coleman V. *The health scandal: your health in crisis.* London: Mandarin Paperbacks, 1989: 213.

20   Enns A. The clocks have stopped in Uganda. In: Dodge CP, Wiebe PD, eds. *Crisis in Uganda: the breakdown of health services.* Oxford: Pergamon Press, 1985: 53.

21   Maitland JM. *Is health in East Africa dependent on democracy and human rights?* Paper at seminar on human rights and democracy in East Africa, Vaxjo University, Sweden, August 1991.

24 | The Chinese experience

Pui-Ling Li
Chairman, London Chinese Health Resource Centre

The Chinese population is the third largest minority ethnic community in the UK, but the health care needs of this community are among the least well researched. This chapter looks at some of the barriers to access to the National Health Service (NHS) faced by the Chinese community. Lack of a shared language between health professionals and the Chinese population is only one such barrier; others are the failure of NHS providers to acknowledge the working patterns of the majority of Chinese adults, and a lack of awareness among health professionals of the health beliefs and expectations of Chinese people. The work of the London Chinese Health Resource Centre, one initiative to bridge the gaps between primary and secondary care and the Chinese community, is outlined, and arguments are clearly stated for such provision to be incorporated into mainstream provision with adequate funding.

The Chinese community

The 1991 census confirms that, of all the minority ethnic groups, the Chinese showed the least geographical concentration.[1] Even in London, where 38% of the Chinese population lives, there is no clustering. This distribution across the country has meant that it is the least likely community to receive appropriate resources from individual NHS providers and commissioners. The lack of information on the demographic, health and social status of the community was noted in a 1985 government report.[2] Ten years later, there is still little published literature on the Chinese population, but that does not mean that little has been done by individuals to address their health and social needs.

Access to health care

The Chinese community experience difficulties similar to those of other minority ethnic communities in accessing the NHS.[3] Linguistic difficulties and the absence of culturally appropriate services have led to the presentation of many health problems as crises. For example, it took a young woman 5 years to discover that the reason for her infertility was an operation she had 'consented to' with the understanding that it was the only option she had for curing her persistent anaemia and excessive blood loss. Her family spoke very little English and believed that the medical team must know best, but 5 years later a Chinese-speaking general practitioner at the London Chinese Health Resource Centre[4] explained to her, for the first time, that she had undergone a hysterectomy. For workers with minority ethnic communities these disasters not only occur but also are sadly common.

A frequently held belief among purchasers and providers is that such difficulties could be solved if people learnt the English language. However, it is not so simple; to overcome barriers to access, health workers need an understanding of the health beliefs and the historical background that led to migration to Britain. This would explain much of the current social structure, the demographic characteristics, the patterns of employment and the needs of a community.

Historical background

First to arrive in the early 19th century were Chinese seamen employed on British merchant ships, who settled in major port areas such as Limehouse in east London, Liverpool, Cardiff and Bristol. Dispersal from these areas later occurred as a result of the development of the laundry business. However, the number of Chinese people in Britain remained small at only about 400 in 1900. Until the 1950s, Chinese migrants tended to be professional people, students and nurses from various parts of the world.

In the late 1950s and 1960s, larger numbers arrived as a result of the collapse of agriculture in the rural parts of Hong Kong, and the discovery at the same time of a market for Chinese catering in Britain. This group accounted for 75–80% of the Chinese population in Britain. The key dialects are Hakka and Cantonese. Most had received little formal education and had little or no knowledge of English. Men came with the intention of returning to Hong Kong upon retirement. Two factors influenced the timing of the arrival of their wives and families: the emergence of the Chinese take-away food business in the late 1960s provided both an outlet for family labour and accommodation for the families;

increasingly restrictive immigration legislation then encouraged
them to bring dependants from Hong Kong before it became too
late.

Approximately 90% of the Chinese population in Britain work in
the catering business. Economic needs have led to fragmentation
of families and dispersal of the community. The romantic ideal of
an extended family, working and supporting each other, is very
much a thing of the past. Business viability often means families
having to seek geographical locations where there is little direct
competition with others, and this precludes the collective settle-
ment of the community in one area. The ensuing cultural vacuum
and isolation have left the majority of the community with little
means to express their needs. The proportion of Chinese that are
professionals is growing but still very small, perhaps 2–3%.

Integration into British society

Chinese people work long and unsociable hours in the catering
trade. A typical working day for a waiter starts at 11 am and finishes
at 1 am, with a break on some days from 3 to 5 pm; there is usually
one day off a week. Not only do workers have very little leisure
time, their periods of relaxation do not correspond to those of the
wider society. It is difficult to step out of this cycle of social deprivation. Alternative forms of employment are not a possibility without
the ability to speak English. As a result, many or some Chinese
elderly people who may have spent their entire working lives in this
country can only manage little more than sign language.[4]

In the past two decades, the most important change is the
increasing proportion of British-born Chinese, who by 1981 made
up a quarter of the community. This group is beginning to emerge
from the education system with different skills and aspirations
from their parents. They may be less likely to be involved in catering and be involved in the mainstream British employment sectors.
This will increase the community's feeling of being permanently
settled in Britain. However, as Chinese migration is continuing,
particularly owing to potential political changes in Hong Kong, the
community as a whole in Britain will continue to have difficulties
for some time.

Experiences with health services in Britain

To bridge communication barriers, members of the Chinese
community have to use friends and children as interpreters, so the

former have to forgo the luxury of confidentiality. Consequently, there is a great deal of under-reporting of illnesses which are of a sensitive nature, for fear it gets round the community, or owing to a feeling that it is too embarrassing to be discussed via a third person. In the absence of help from an adult, most state agencies use children as interpreters, forgetting that the child may not be able to speak Chinese fluently. Greater importance is the question of whether it is fair to place a child in a situation that both parent and child may find embarrassing or distressing, such as the interpretation of gynaecological problems or prognosis of cancer. The child will undoubtedly lack knowledge of appropriate medical terms in both languages. It is very easy for misinterpretation and misunderstanding to occur, and in some of these cases the consequences will be serious. Children who are proficient in both languages may be taken out of school on a regular basis to interpret for the community. The shift in power to the child that comes with such a responsibility can affect the parent–child relationship and lead to family conflicts; a child who is normally 'in charge' will understandably find it hard to relinquish this power when the parents exert their parental role.

The London Chinese Health Resource Centre

Individuals have volunteered their own time and resources to deal with the community's health care needs over a number of years. In 1985 specific recommendations were made concerning the health care needs of the Chinese community,[2] but funding for some of these did not become available until 1988. One development was the establishment in 1988 of the London Chinese Health Resource Centre, the first Chinese organisation to tailor health services to the needs of the community using a range of methods for their delivery.

The models used by the centre

Universal health needs. The model embraces the definition of health adopted by the World Health Organisation, which defined health as a 'state of complete physical, mental and social well being and not merely the absence of disease or infirmity'.[5] Central to the range of methods used by the centre in meeting the health needs of the Chinese community is 'enabling' the community 'access' to the NHS. This universal health need, irrespective of the ethnicity of the community, should be addressed by health service orientated actions as well as community specific approaches.

Health service orientated actions. The promotion of greater awareness and understanding among health care providers and purchasers is a significant part of the centre's work. The aim is to encourage the provision of trained health interpreters/advocates, the targeting of existing resources to meet the health needs of minority ethnic communities, the promotion of innovative employment practices to achieve the ethnic mix of health service workers that reflects better the population they serve, and the implementation of equal opportunity policies.

Community orientated actions. The centre undertakes a range of projects across London to promote greater awareness among the community of the structure of the NHS and the methods of access. These include a regular professional training programme for members of the community to become health interpreters/ advocates. Several projects concentrate on the development of community participation, empowerment and the promotion of self-help to address the social aspects of health.[6]

Community specific health needs

Patterns of illness and disease differ between minority ethnic groups and from those of the white population.[7] For the Chinese community, it was important for the centre to provide health care with which the community can immediately identify. There was a need to consult the community before the provision of other more unfamiliar forms of health care, such as the use of health promotion seminars and telephone health lines.

The key service that the centre offers is the Sunday surgery run by bilingual Chinese doctors who are full-time employees in the NHS. Sunday was chosen, as this is the only day off work for the majority of the community. The functions of the surgery are similar to general practice but investigations and treatments are not prescribed. It is fundamental to the principles of the centre that the NHS should not be replaced but that patients are 'enabled' to use it. Consequently, good rapport and close working relationships have been fostered with patients' general practitioners. The Sunday surgery illustrates two key issues in health care provision to minority ethnic communities: the cultural and social aspects of a community must be taken into account.

The centre also undertakes needs assessment research for purchasing authorities. Central resources are required to research further ethnically specific clinical conditions, eg the higher mortality from coronary heart disease in people from the Indian subcontinent and the African commonwealth.[3,7] For the Chinese community, the distinct lack of basic epidemiological data has led to its exclusion from discussions concerning health and minority ethnic communities in the UK; there is an urgent need to address this.

Users of the London Chinese Health Resource Centre

In the past 5 years, the centre has had patients not only from London[4] but also from, for example, Surrey, Lincoln and Birmingham;[3] 63% of users are women, 54% of them describing themselves as housewives, retired or part-time workers. Catering workers and restaurant owners made up respectively 17% and 2% of the users, 3% were unemployed and 2% factory machinists. English was neither spoken nor understood by 70%, but even the 16% who spoke sufficient English to 'get by' with their English doctors still use the centre's services, showing that shared language alone is not sufficient for appropriate care. Official interpreters in the NHS are scarce, so patients often have to rely on their spouse, other relatives, friends and children. Before using the centre, one in six of the patients had consistently failed to attend hospital clinics or general practice because of difficulties in finding someone to communicate on their behalf.

The inability to use the health service meant that most patients had used private Chinese doctors, both those trained in Western medicine and Chinese herbalists. Each consultation costs £25–30 and the majority expressed concern about the cost. It was therefore a surprise to find a high level of faith in, and regard for the NHS, in spite of its failure to care for the majority of the community; 85% of the centre's patients were registered with a general practitioner and will attempt to see their doctor first when unwell, even though neither will understand what the other is saying. The difficulties experienced by the Chinese community in London are similar to those in Hull.[8]

Conclusion

The effects of politics on the health of minority ethnic communities, as indeed on any community, cannot be overemphasised. Voluntary organisations, such as the London Chinese Health Resource Centre, face constant financial uncertainty. The absence of secure funding means that a significant amount of energy is devoted to fundraising. This reduces the amount of work the centre can undertake and the instability affects staff turnover and morale. Political changes in the NHS affect relationships with state agencies. The implementation of the 1990 NHS and Community Care Act has formalised the role of the centre as a 'provider' of specialist health care and it has entered into several service contracts with health and local authorities. However, all too often, the consequence of major organisational change is that the health needs of minority ethnic communities will be the last on a long list of priorities.

In a recent annual report, the Chief Medical Officer highlighted the variation in morbidity, mortality and NHS usage of different communities.[9] The Patient's Charter makes explicit the rights of a patient to care in the NHS, and the range of national and local standards of service against which the performance of a health authority will be judged. The 1991 census, by collecting data on ethnic origin for the first time, has made possible the in-depth examination of the health profile of different minority ethnic communities.

The importance of primary care and the voluntary sector, and the need to target extra resources to pump-prime new developments in these two areas, were highlighted in the document *Making London better*.[10] For the majority of patients the primary care team is the first point of contact with the health care system. A study in east London which examined the range of problems presented by 17,000 patients to 21 general practitioners over a 3-month period has shown an under-representation of minority ethnic communities among the attenders.[11] Failure to make contact at this level precludes access to secondary care services, with greater likelihood of ill health presenting as crises. It is hoped that the contribution of initiatives such as the London Chinese Health Resource Centre towards bridging the gaps between mainstream primary and secondary health services and the community will be recognised. The model of care used should be made available to other minority ethnic communities.

The new national health strategy for England outlined by the government's Healthier Nation project offers the opportunity to set targets for improvement in health.[12] The specific health needs of minority ethnic groups should not be neglected in target setting, particularly in inner cities, where these communities are a significant population group. Otherwise targets cannot be achieved and, more important, the effort invested will not improve the health of the nation.

Recommendations

Training should be provided for NHS staff on health beliefs, employment patterns and demographic characteristics of the Chinese population:

- Mainstream NHS providers should develop good links with community and voluntary organisations to ensure improved access to health care.
- Commissioners and providers should ensure that sufficient numbers of trained health advocates and interpreters are available.
- Central resources are needed for further research on ethnically specific conditions.
- Initiatives such as the London Chinese Health Resource Centre should be incorporated into mainstream provision with adequate levels of funding for the services to continue to develop.

References

1 Balarajan R. *Ethnic diversity in England and Wales.* An analysis by health authorities based on the 1991 census. London: NIESH, 1997.
2 House of Commons Home Affairs Committee 1984–85. *The Chinese community in Britain.* London: HMSO, 1985.
3 Nazroo JY. Health and health services. In: Modood T *et al*, eds. *Ethnic minorities in Britain.* London: Policy Studies Institute, 1997.
4 London Chinese Health Resource Centre. *Annual report 1991–1992.* 43 Dean Street, London W1V 5AP.
5 World Health Organisation. *Constitution of the World Health Organisation.* Geneva: WHO, 1946.
6 Townsend P, Phillimore P, Beattie A. *Health and deprivation: inequalities and the North.* London: Croom Helm, 1988.
7 Balarajan R, Raleigh VS. *The health of the nation: ethnicity and health.* A guide for the NHS. London: Department of Health, 1993.
8 Watt IS, Howel D, Lo L. The health care experience and health behaviour of the Chinese: a survey based in Hull. *Journal of Public Health Medicine* 1993; **15**: 129–36.
9 Department of Health. Health and black and ethnic minorities. In: *On the state of the public health 1991.* Annual report of the Chief Medical Officer to the Secretary of State for Health. London: HMSO, 1992.
10 Department of Health. *Making London better.* London: Department of Health, 1993.
11 Li P-L, Jones I, Richards J. The collection of general practice data for psychiatric service contracts. *Journal of Public Health Medicine* (in print).
12 Department of Health. *Our healthier Nation.* London: Stationery Office, 1998.

25 | Assessing needs to improve health: an overview

Salman Rawaf
Director of Clinical Standards,
Merton Sutton and Wandsworth Health Authority;
Honorary Senior lecturer,
St George's Hospital Medical School, London

The twenty-four chapters in this book will probably lead the reader to many positive and negative conclusions on ethnicity and health. To me, at least three especially important points should be taken into account.

- A significant proportion of minority ethnic people are trapped in a disadvantage and inequality cycle despite opportunities for health and social systems to improve their living standards and health, so many suffer from excessive preventable morbidity and avoidable mortality.
- The issue most feared by many, if not all, minority ethnic groups is racism (in particular institutional racism) and discrimination, which increase inequality and injustice, contribute to social exclusion, impede access to health care, restrict ambition and equal opportunities, and increase anxiety, insecurity and ill health.
- A meaningful needs assessment based on ongoing profiling of the population, community or groups in terms of weight, value and priority rank (rather than merely counting and describing), undertaken by health authorities' public departments (in collaboration with primary care groups, hospitals, the voluntary sector and the communities), in any setting, will lead to improvement in health.

What is social exclusion about?

It is well recognised that minority ethnic groups are not homogeneous but diverse and particular religious and cultural groups that may be further defined in relation to social class and geographical location. In many chapters descriptions were given of some of these groups as trapped in a disadvantage and inequality cycle, as the gap between the rich and the poor, which is associated with a similar gap in health, has widened since the early 1980s.[1] In *Our healthier nation* it is recognised that today people's chance of a long and healthy life is basically influenced by how well off they are, where they live and their ethnic background.[1] Moreover, proportionately more people from ethnic minorities are socially excluded owing to illness, disability, poverty and racism. Social exclusion can be a cause as well as an effect of ill health (Fig 1). Social inequality and the problems faced by the socially excluded are targeted in many of the recent initiatives, for example the education White Paper, welfare to work for young people, the national child care strategy, the Crime and Disorder Bill and *The new NHS* White Paper.[2,3]

In promoting the health of minority ethnic people it is important to acknowledge the range of diversity and difference, and to develop methods and strategies that focus on the needs of specific groups and communities and in particular in inequality and social exclusion. Tackling inequality generally is the best measure of tackling health inequalities in particular. However, in order to address inequalities in health it is necessary to have a clear understanding of what the inequalities are and how they arise. Moreover, debating and tackling the issue of racism is important in dealing with social exclusion and giving equal opportunities in health care, employment and full social participation. It is quite worrying to note that a current of racist beliefs is clearly evident among more

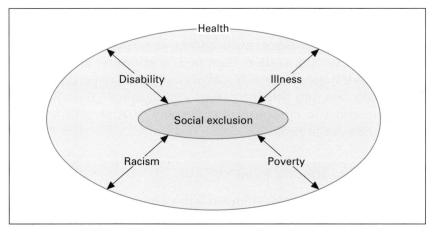

Fig 1. *Social exclusion: a cause and an effect of ill health.*

than one in five of the white population surveyed in the mid-
1990s.[4]

To assess (or not to assess) health needs

Some people may question the necessity for such exercises as
profiling the population on a continuous basis to assess their
needs, and weigh the expected benefit from the intervention(s)
for any given sets of priorities within acceptable social and professional values. Indeed, some health economists, during the health
service reforms of the early 1990s, dismissed the health needs
assessment approach for priority setting and advocated a purely
economic approach based on getting the greatest benefit for
each pound spent,[5] one of the by-products of the 'internal market'
philosophy of the 1990s which has led to widening of the inequality gap and many unmet needs. Since then, health needs
assessment has proved an important population approach to the
systematic tackling of inequality, responding to actual needs and
investing in effective interventions rather than haphazard uncoordinated reactive responses to demands. Other advantages of
needs assessment were given in Chapter 2, and all the chapters
have illustrated that comprehensive health needs assessment is a
prerequisite for any programme – national, local or practice
based – to improve the health of the targeted or general population. The experience of many authors demonstrated that many
minority ethnic groups were disadvantaged, their health status
was not profiled and their needs not prioritised to ensure that
mainstream services were culturally sensitive. Many health professionals, including those designing policy and setting priorities,
are ill informed on the health needs of minority communities,
and set priorities that may not reflect their needs. Systematic
approaches to assess the health needs of these groups were
reported in few places, mainly for the larger minority ethnic
groups. In a national survey into the health needs of minority
ethnic groups undertaken in 1993 in preparation for this book,
57% (117/207) of health authorities/boards in England, Scotland and Wales responded (Rawaf S, Ojwok O. Unpublished
data). Twenty-eight health authorities were involved in some kind
of health needs assessment (41 projects) for their ethnic
minorities; out of these only 15 engaged in or developed some
form of collaborative work. The minority ethnic groups whose
needs were assessed were Asians, African-Caribbeans, people
from the Middle East and some refugees. Approaches to needs

assessment were mainly epidemiological, restricted to the process of health service provision; few involved structured surveys based on questionnaires, networking and interviews, or group discussions. The above survey has shown that most, if not all, of these health needs assessment exercises were merely ways to *count* and *describe* needs but very few *assessed* such needs in terms of weight, value and priority rank. Furthermore, much of the research on ethnicity and health was rich in database and data driven analysis but poor in interactive social processes where a range of acceptable values is expressed to define needs. The use of mortality data for identification of individuals through their 'foreign' surnames was common to many of these analyses. Effective needs assessment can only be carried out against a background of careful analysis of the health status of ethnic minorities. It is of little use to assess health needs without careful consideration of how they will be met by current services and how future developments will take account of them.[6]

But how to improve health?

Clear illustrations were given in Chapters 2 and 3 of techniques for assessing health needs, in Chapter 4 on how to set priorities, and there are many examples in other chapters of initiatives to improve the health of local communities based on needs rather than demands. However, one question remains unanswered: Is there any systematic way(s) to respond to the identified needs, and how? At the heart of *The new NHS* proposals are 'health improvement programmes' (HIPs).[3] These programmes will be the new approach to tackling ill health and inequality and maximising the health gain through partnership among those serving the local health economy, ie health authorities, primary care groups (PCGs), NHS trusts, local authorities, the voluntary sector, local businesses, the pharmaceutical industry and communities. However, such HIPs cannot succeed without defining the 'shared population of interest' at whom they are directed, assessing their health and social needs properly and agreeing priorities for action at all levels of the clinical pathway (Figs 2 and 3). The district director of public health's independent annual report will be the starting point for the HIP. It will inform the decisions of both health authorities and its partners,[2,7] to enable them to improve the health of the population including minority groups under the new statutory duty placed on health authorities by the White Paper.[2]

Health improvement programmes for any condition, disease or

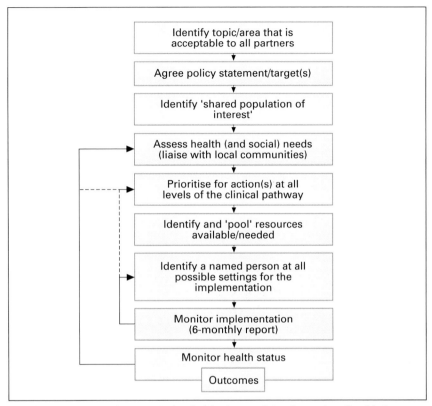

Fig 2. *A suggested framework for developing and implementing 'health improvement programmes'.*

care group could be addressed at health, health care, service and setting level, or any combination. Improving people's *health* further could be approached in terms of health choices and health promotion and maintenance. *Health care* HIPs are those that address access to appropriate and quality health care, effectiveness and equity. *Service and setting* relate to three elements – clinical safety, cost effectiveness, acceptability by patients and carers – based on evidence and best practices.[8–10] In planned ways, contributors to the HIP could enter the clinical pathway at any appropriate stage where their contribution would be maximised. For example, in a HIP for coronary heart disease, individuals, health promotion services (specialist and primary care), school health and local authorities will significantly influence health choices and healthy living to avoid major risk factors. Individuals, primary health care teams, schools, employers and health promotion services have major roles in reducing the harm associated with well known risk

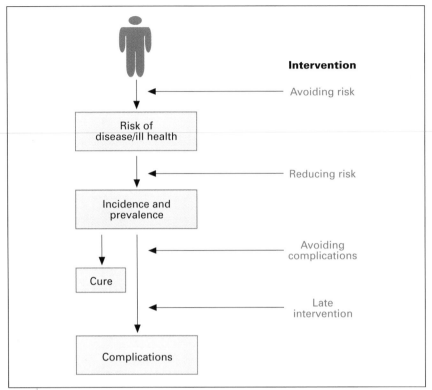

Fig 3. *Clinical pathway: levels of intervention and possible contribution to improving health.*

factors. Clinicians, both at primary care and specialist services, acting individually or with shared care responsibility, have more interest and influence in early intervention and the prevention of further attacks and complications. For any condition, it is therefore essential to analyse the possible clinical pathway, with possible effective interventions and contributors at each stage.

What needs to be done to improve health?

To improve the health of any population or subgroup of that population requires the co-ordinated efforts of many partners in health, ie health authorities, NHS trusts, PCGs, local authorities, the voluntary sector, local businesses, the pharmaceutical industry and organised groups of the society. Improving health is far more complex and long-term than the provision of health care, as some of the root causes of ill health (poverty, housing, lifestyle, employment, crime) are beyond the control of health services.

- The independent annual report of the district director of public health will be the starting point for identifying the health needs of the minority ethnic population in the district. It will inform individual and collective decisions of the health authority, the local authority, specialist NHS trusts, PCGs (primary care NHS trusts in the future) and other partners on ways to improve the health of the minority ethnic population. Such advice will be based on a full assessment of the health status and the experience and expectations of the population. The main approaches to health needs assessment are outlined in Chapters 2 and 3. The traditional reliance on service utilisation data is of less value in measuring minority ethnic populations' health needs as accessibility to services is often impeded by many barriers. A simple ten-step approach to needs assessment based on Chapter 2 is outlined in Fig 4.
- Local HIPs for major conditions and diseases should take into account the needs of minority ethnic groups. *The new NHS* acknowledges the variations in risk factors and mortality between different ethnic groups. Some of the approaches to improve health have been outlined in the preceding chapters. Health authorities with the new statutory duty to improve health will have a leading role in tackling health inequalities among their population including minority ethnic groups.
- Health and welfare services should be sensitive to the needs of all groups from diverse cultures and backgrounds. Staff should be trained in cultural diversity and kept updated on a regular basis. Clinicians should be aware of the different disease patterns among various ethnic groups. Information packs and clinical guidelines on priority disease areas should be available to all primary and secondary care clinicians. Through the new statutory duty to improve quality of care, providers of health care (PCGs, community services, mental health services, hospitals) should address the barriers to access experienced by many minority ethnic groups. Action plans should be published regularly. The book edited by Hopkins and Bahl is a good guide to dealing with the problems of access to health care for people from minority ethnic groups.[11]
- In health authorities with substantial minority ethnic groups, the 'health action zone' initiatives will help the disadvantaged, through partnership and innovation, to tackle health problems and inequality and reshape service to improve health.[2]
- Minority ethnic communities should be consulted and involved

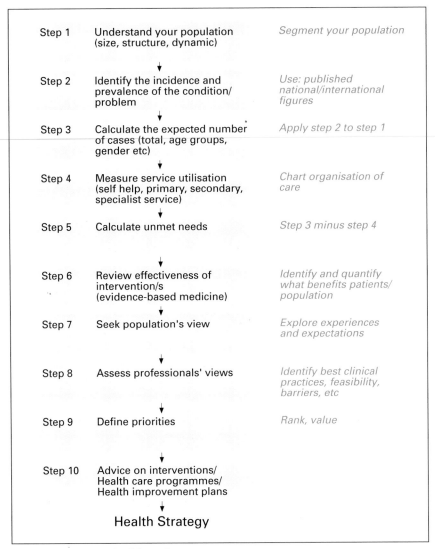

Fig 4. *Ten steps for health needs assessment.*

in their needs assessment, development of health improvement programmes, and monitoring of service delivery and measurement of health outcomes. *Our healthier nation* has stressed the importance of the perspective of local communities and the role of health authorities and PCGs and to reflect such perspectives in their health improvement programmes.[1]

- Health and welfare services should promote equal opportunities, debate and tackle racism and above all fight discrimination on all grounds.

Health services should be developed on the basis of 'need and need alone'. Assessment of a population's needs is essential if any health programme is to be effective in tackling the roots of inequality and address the variations in health.

References

1 Secretary of State for Health. *Our healthier nation: a contract for health.* London: Stationery Office, 1998.
2 Secretary of Stated for Health. *The new NHS: modern, dependable.* London: Stationery Office, 1997.
3 Griffiths S. From health care to health. *British Medical Journal* 1998; **316**: 300–1.
4. Modood T, Berthoud R, Lakey J, *et al. Ethnic minorities in Britain: diversity and disadvantage.* London: Policy Studies Institute, 1997.
5 Donaldson C, Mooney G. Needs assessment, priority setting, and contracts for health care: an economic view. *British Medical Journal* 1991; **303**: 1529–30.
6 Bhopal R. Is research into ethnicity and health racist, unsound, or important science? *British Medical Journal* 1997; **314**: 1751–6.
7 Department of Health *The Chief Medical Officer's project to strengthen the public health function in England.* London: Department of Health, 1998.
8 Gray JAM. *Evidence-based healthcare: how to make health policy and management decisions.* New York: Churchill Livingstone, 1997.
9 Sackett DL, Richardson WS, Rosenberg W, Haynes RB. *Evidence-based medicine.* New York: Churchill Livingstone, 1997.
10 Peckham M, Smith R, eds. *Scientific basis of health services.* London: BMJ Publishing, 1996.
11 Hopkins A, Bahl V, eds. *Access to health care for people from black and ethnic minorities.* London: RCP Publication, 1993.

Index